Communities of Faith in Africa and the African Diaspora

Communities of Faith in Africa and the African Diaspora

In Honor of Dr. Tite Tiénou

With Additional Essays on World Christianity

Edited by
CASELY B. ESSAMUAH
and **DAVID K. NGARUIYA**

☙PICKWICK *Publications* • Eugene, Oregon

COMMUNITIES OF FAITH IN AFRICA AND THE AFRICAN DIASPORA
In Honor of Dr. Tite Tiénou

Copyright © 2013 Wipf and Stock Publishers. All rights reserved. Except for brief quotations in critical publications or reviews, no part of this book may be reproduced in any manner without prior written permission from the publisher. Write: Permissions. Wipf and Stock Publishers, 199 W. 8th Ave., Suite 3, Eugene, OR 97401.

Pickwick Publications
An Imprint of Wipf and Stock Publishers
199 W. 8th Ave., Suite 3
Eugene, OR 97401

www.wipfandstock.com

ISBN 13: 978-1-62032-959-7

Cataloguing-in-Publication data:

Communities of faith in Africa and the African diaspora : in honor of Dr. Tite Tiénou / edited by Casely B. Essamuah and David K. Ngaruiya ; foreword by Joel Carpenter.

xx + 384 p. ; 23 cm. Includes bibliographical references.

Includes a bibliography of the works of Tite Tiénou (p. 381–384)

ISBN 13: 978-1-62032-959-7

1. Christianity—Africa. 2. Theology—Africa. 3. Theology—Africa, Sub-Saharan. 4. Tiénou, Tite. I. Essamuah, Casely B. II. Knaruiya, David K.

BR1360 C70 2014

Manufactured in the U.S.A.

Contents

Foreword by Joel Carpenter | ix
Preface | xiii
Acknowledgments | xvii
Contributors | xix

PART 1: Africa and the African Diaspora

1 The Journey of Tite Tiénou | 3
—Friends, Colleagues, and Former Students

2 "Enlarging Christian Coasts": Pentecostalism and Higher Education in Sub-Saharan Africa | 8
—J. Kwabena Asamoah-Gyadu

3 Wesleyan Camp Meeting History and the Revitalization of Ghanaian Methodism | 16
—Paul Kwabena Boafo

4 African Immigrant Religions in the Diaspora | 29
—Elias K. Bongmba

5 "Go Ye into All the West": Models of Mission among Ghanaian Methodists in the Diaspora | 47
—Casely B. Essamuah

6 New Angles on African Christianity | 70
—Paul Kollman

7 The Multifaceted Genesis of the 2007–2008 Postelection Violence in Kenya | 82
—David K. Ngaruiya

8 How Indigenous Traders Brought Christianity to Northern Nigeria | 90
—Caleb O. Oladipo

9 Sickness and Witches in Northwestern Tanzania:
Listening to Pentecostal Ministers | 99
—Steven D. H. Rasmussen

10 Gender Roles and Recruitment in Southern African Churches,
1996–2001 | 116
—Dana L. Robert

11 The Role of Personal Friendships in Effective Cross-Cultural
Christian Mission | 135
—Kenneth R. Ross

12 Ethiopian Orthodox Christology: Interacting with
an Ancient African Perspective | 149
—Stephen Strauss

13 Alone and Frightened in Uganda: Living
in the Shadow of HIV | 170
—Angela M. Wakhweya-Essamuah

14 African Evangelists: The Case of Apolo Kivebulaya | 181
—Emma Wild-Wood

PART 2: Other Selected Essays

15 The Medium and the Message | 201
—Miriam Adeney

16 Inculturation and the Church's Mission: Theological
and Trinitarian Foundations | 214
—Stephen B. Bevans

17 Pre-Christendom Faith in a Post-Christendom World | 234
—Jonathan J. Bonk

18 World Christianity and the New Ecumenical Frontier | 250
—William R. Burrows

19 Funerary Rites and Ancestral Roles in Japan:
Reassessing Their (Non-)Religious Character | 261
—How Chuang Chua

20 The 2008 Financial Crisis and the Great Commission | 283
—J. Nelson Jennings

21 Researching Contextualization in Churches Influenced
by Missionaries | 299
—Robert J. Priest

22 "Please Be Extra Vigilant": On Being Attentive to World Christianity | 319
—Cathy Ross

23 Global Evangelical Theology: "Luke Theology" and the Dialogue of the Deaf | 335
—Mark Shaw

24 The 1860 Liverpool Conference on Missions | 347
—Andrew F. Walls

25 Asia and Latin America: Taking the Gospel to the "Ends of the Earth" | 361
—Allen Yeh

A Bibliography of the Works of Tite Tiénou | 381

Foreword

A DECADE HAS PASSED since Tite Tiénou became the dean of Trinity Evangelical Divinity School, but I have not forgotten the first time I saw public evidence of his new role. His visage was gazing out from a Trinity advertisement in *Christianity Today* magazine. It made me smile, because I know Trinity, and I know Tite. Here was a major theological school, which grooms leaders for the predominantly white, not-too-charismatic, conservative evangelical networks of the *Christianity Today* variety, announcing its new leader. And there was Dr. Tiénou, exuding West African vigor and Francophone intellectual command, tres formidable. Immovable object meets irresistible force, I thought. God has a grand sense of humor.

God is also full of surprises. And one of the most heartening of these for me is that American evangelicals are learning to embrace Christianity's changing location and mission in today's world. New leaders and issues have arisen to point the way forward, and they have come from surprising places. Tiénou's early home was in Mali, Francophone West Africa, a region where Islam predominates, and where the main issues confronting Christians do not concern finding answers to atheists and skeptics but ministering to the poor, the sick, the hurt and vulnerable, and relating to neighbors who follow other faiths.

Andrew Walls, one of the contributors to this volume, has been prophesying for nearly forty years that these issues will come to the fore, because Africa is becoming the new Christian heartland. Africans, along with Asians and Latin Americans, he said, "will be the representative Christians; those who represent the Christian norm, the Christian mainstream of the twenty-first and twenty-second centuries . . . The most significant Christian developments in theology, . . . or ethical thinking, or the Christian impact on society, will be those that take place in the southern continents, not those that take place in the West. The development of theological and ethical thinking and action in Africa and Asia and Latin America will determine mainstream Christianity."[1]

From the redoubts of North American theological schools, however, this still reads like a prophecy, and a rather unlikely one at that. Our seminaries and divinity schools are preoccupied with the great and powerful Western intellectual and academic edifice, that great fortress of post-Enlightenment, post-Christian rationalism and empiricism. It has been laid siege by the postmodernist philosophers, but they too operate with naturalistic assumptions. Yet Walls insists that the Western academy does not represent a "world standard." In fact, it betrays "pre-Columbian maps of the intellectual universe."[2] Western Christian scholars have focused on the challenges of post-Enlightenment secularity, with strategies that are highly contextualized to the North Atlantic situation. But now the world is shrinking, and we interact regularly with other people and other worldviews. Indeed, the rest of the world is coming our way and settling in with us here. These new neighbors see the world differently and raise different questions about religious belief and practice. So our theological mission and strategies need to change.

Professor Tiénou knows these trends well; he has lived them. And he has not been shy in calling North American evangelical thinkers to account. At a major national conference of Christian scholars, convened just days after the September 11, 2001, attacks, he flatly declared that "the future of Christianity no longer depends on developments in the North."[3] It follows, he stated further, that the future of Christian scholarship does not depend on them either. In recent times a growing number of theological schools have decided to add "world Christianity" courses and they have begun to hire professors to teach them. But what Walls and Tiénou have in mind is something far more radical: the reorientation of the whole body of Christian scholarship, starting with theology. That is a tall order, they note, because theology has been more resistant to the de-centering of the West than many of the more secular fields.

So in making Tiénou their dean, Trinity's leaders did something more subversive than they might have realized. Professors in newly arrived fields of study often remain marginal to the main enterprise, but faculty members cannot ignore their dean. Anyone who has tried academic leadership

1. Andrew F. Walls, "Christian Scholarship," 173.

2. Walls, "Of Ivory Towers and Ashrams: Some Reflections on Theological Scholarship in Africa," *Journal of African Christian Thought* 3 (2000) 1–2.

3. Tite Tiénou, "Christian Scholarship and the Changing Center of World Christianity," in *Christian Scholarship . . . for What?*, ed. Susan M. Felch (Grand Rapids: Calvin College, 2003), 91.

quickly learns that it is about as easy as herding cats, but with strong and winsome leadership, colleagues—and institutions—can begin to change. This collection of essays gives ample evidence of the changes afoot at Trinity, in North American religion and theology fields more generally, and out in the international networks of evangelical theology and mission studies. It is heartening to think that what these essays and essayists all have in common is the broad influence and inspiration of a remarkable world Christian, Tite Tiénou.

Joel Carpenter
Nagel Institute for the Study of World Christianity
Calvin College

Preface

THE CHRISTIAN FAITH IS global. Dr. Tite Tiénou, the honoree of this Festschrift, along with both editors and the contributors, illustrate the faith's movement. It defies domestication as the exclusive faith of any one cultural context. It has rewritten the history of the world, deflecting its course as it may, becoming enshrined in economics, constitutions, and governance in many nations. It has affirmed diversity within a larger unity among those who embrace it. Tiénou has helped many of us embrace true unity in Christ, whatever our original moorings.

Theology has moved from being fashioned as monolithic and brittle to being contextual and malleable. The tunes of global Christianity now may be heard in the Amazon jungles, the Savannahs of Africa, the Mongolian mountains, the German Alps, the land of the Maoris, the Midwest of North America—and that's merely representative.

More and more we hear the many voices of global Christianity. That's clearly the case in this Festschrift. About a third of the contributors have studied under Tiénou. Other authors in this volume are admiring colleagues and friends. They join a growing number of scholars whose various perspectives reflect the globalization of the faith. Their efforts enrich Christian history in an increasingly globalizing world.

The growing phenomenon of short-term missions also attests the reality of global Christianity. Men, women, and not least, children traverse the globe to share the Good News through the vehicle of short-term missions. Modern technology and human philanthropy are motivating factors in short-term missions, but the greatest motivation may be the reality of Christianity as a global faith. Although representatives of other faiths also traverse the globe, Christianity is and continues to be the forerunner and frontrunner.

The Christian faith not only takes different forms in different contexts; it also shows how each of us is enriched by the other's contextual expression. In the words of Andrew Walls,

> When the Scriptures are read in some enclosed Zulu Zion, the hearers may catch the voice of God speaking out of a different Zion, and speaking to the whole world. When a comfortable bourgeois congregation meets in some Western suburbia, they, almost alone of all the comfortable bourgeois of the suburbs, are regularly exposed to the reading of a non-bourgeois book questioning fundamental assumptions of their society. But since none of us can read the Scriptures without cultural blinkers of some sort, the great advantage, the crowning excitement which our own era of church history has over all others, is the possibility that we may be able to read them together. Never before has the church looked so much like the great multitude whom no [person] can number out of every nation, and tribe, and people and tongue. Never before, therefore, has there been so much potentiality for mutual enrichment and self-criticism as God causes yet more light and truth to break forth from his word.[1]

A last story to bring the point home. Walter J. Hollenweger recalls his secretary's reflection on global Christianity:

> The history of the English language and the history of Jesus of Nazareth have many parallels. English, was, so to speak, invented in England. Today, more people speak English who are not English. But they also change it. The Americans, Irish, Indians, Germans, all speak English their own way. And what is English, proper English, can no longer be determined in a normative way by the English. Some of the non-English speakers, like the Irish, or the Indians, or the Americans, have become experts in their own way of using the English language. Some of the greatest English writers are not English but Irish or Indian or American. And so it is with Jesus of Nazareth.[2]

The essays in this volume reflect the realities of global Christianity, from East to West, with special attention to Africa and the African diaspora. They are offered in honor of Tite Tiénou, friend and mentor. In their reflection of the global reach of the Christian faith, may we all be enriched.

---

1. Andrew F. Walls, "Gospel as Prisoner and Liberator of Culture: Is There a 'Historic Christian Faith'?," in *Missionary Movement in Christian History: Studies in the Transmission of Faith* (Maryknoll, NY: Orbis, 1996) 15.

2. Walter J. Hollenweger, "Discipline of Thought and Action in Mission," *International Review of Mission* 80 (1991) 95.

Acknowledgments

EVERY BOOK IS A collaborative effort and this more so than many. Each of the contributors participated amid demanding schedules. They demonstrated extraordinary patience as we collected and edited this Festschrift. Their esteem for our honoree Tite Tiénou and their desire to advance scholarship is admirable.

The editors value every moment that they have spent with our brother. This is the least we can do to return thanks for his friendship.

David is grateful to his wife Annie, who has been such a great support throughout his career. Casely cherishes his wife Angela's commitment to him, the family, and the cause of Christ around the globe.

We owe special thanks to Mr. and Mrs. Milton Pierce, Christian and Missionary Alliance (C&MA) missionaries to West Africa in the 1960s, who knew Tiénou when he was still a youth, and who played a key role in securing a college education for the young Tiénou at the C&MA college in Nyack, New York. They also provided us a detailed account of Tiénou's family and his early years in West Africa. Charles Kraft of Fuller Theological Seminary, the late Douglas Carew, President and CEO of Africa International University, and a graduate of Trinity International University, Ronald Walborn, Dean of Alliance Theological Seminary, and other C&A graduates provided insight into Tiénou's cultural sensitivity and personalized teaching style.

There is a name that is missing from the cover. One person painstakingly copyedited all the manuscripts. He went beyond the call of duty to make each essay read as tellingly as possible. He ensured that the language was accessible to the widest possible readership. He pointed out blind spots on more than one occasion, and the contributors appreciated the fact that their essays read better after his editorial work. That person is Robert Coote. The editors insisted he be named a coeditor. He declined, but we cannot say enough how grateful we are for his diligence in bringing this work to a fitting conclusion.

Finally, we owe thanks to Mr. James Tedrick and other members of the staff of Wipf and Stock, who guided this volume through from its digitalized form to the press and into circulation.

Casely B. Essamuah
David K. Ngaruiya

Contributors

Miriam Adeney teaches anthropology at the School of Theology, Seattle Pacific University, and is a teaching fellow, Regent College, Vancouver, British Columbia. Her books include *Kingdom without Borders*; *Daughters of Islam*; *God's Foreign Policy: Practical Ways to Help the World's Poor*; and *A Time for Risking: Priorities for Women*. A past president of the American Society of Missiology, she lectures on five continents, serves on the Board of Christianity Today International, and is an associate of the World Evangelical Alliance Mission Commission.

J. Kwabena Asamoah-Gyadu is the Baeta-Grau Professor of African Christianity and Pentecostal Theology at Trinity Theological Seminary, and Director, Center for the Study of Christianity in Africa at Trinity Theological Seminary, Legon, Accra, Ghana. He has published widely on Christianity in Africa, including several essays on African Pentecostalism and media. Asamoah-Gyadu is the West Africa coordinator of the African Theological Fellowship.

Stephen B. Bevans, SVD, is Louis J. Luzbetak, SVD, Professor of Mission and Culture at Catholic Theological Union, Chicago. He is author of *Models of Contextual Theology* (2002), *An Introduction to Theology in Global Perspective* (2009), and co-author with Roger Schroeder of *Constants in Context* (2004) and *Prophetic Dialogue* (2012).

Paul Kwabena Boafo is an ordained minister of the Methodist Church Ghana, senior lecturer in church history and Wesleyan studies in the Department of Religious Studies, and Protestant chaplain of Kwame Nkrumah University of Science and Technology, Kumasi, Ghana.

Elias K. Bongmba is professor of religious studies at Rice University, Houston, Texas, where he holds the Harry and Hazel Chavanne Chair in Christian Theology. He is president of the African Association for the Study of

Religion. His book *The Dialectics of Transformation in Africa* won the Frantz Fanon Prize in 2007. He has published on HIV/AIDS.

Jonathan Bonk, recently retired director of the Overseas Ministries Study Center, was editor of the *International Bulletin of Missionary Research* and founding editor of the *Dictionary of African Christian Biography*.

William R. Burrows is managing editor emeritus of Orbis Books and research professor of missiology at New York Theological Seminary. He has recently finished a book on the ordeal of Jacques Dupuis, SJ, and is working with Scott Sunquist and Dale Irvin on volume 2 of Orbis's *History of the World Christian Movement, Vol. 2 (1454–1989)*.

Joel Carpenter, author of the foreword, directs the Nagel Institute for the Study of World Christianity at Calvin College, where he served ten years as provost. Earlier he directed the religion program at the Pew Charitable Trusts. His most recent book is *Walking Together: Christian Thinking and Public Life in South Africa* (2011).

How Chuang Chua is a missionary with OMF International and serves as academic dean, Hokkaido Bible Institute in Sapporo, Japan. He studied under Tiénou at Trinity Evangelical Divinity School, Deerfield, Illinois, where he received his PhD in 2007 for his research on Japanese theology.

Casely B. Essamuah is global missions pastor at Bay Area Community Church, Annapolis, Maryland; previously he served Park Street Church, Boston. An ordained minister of the Methodist Church Ghana, he also serves Ghanaian Methodist churches in the diaspora. He is a member of the board of directors of World Relief, Overseas Ministries Study Center, and the Harvard Divinity Alumni Council. His book *Genuinely Ghanaian: A History of the Methodist Church Ghana, 1961–2000* was published in 2010.

J. Nelson Jennings is executive director of the Overseas Ministries Study Center, New Haven, Connecticut. He was editor of *Missiology: An International Review* and taught world mission at Covenant Theological Seminary from 1999 to 2011. He served in Japan from 1986 to 1999 in church planting and theological education.

Paul Kollman teaches in the University of Notre Dame's Theology Department, focusing on African Christianity, mission history, and world Christianity. Author of *The Evangelization of Slaves and Catholic Origins in Eastern Africa* (Orbis), he is preparing a book on the Catholic missionary evangelization of eastern Africa.

David K. Ngaruiya is Associate Professor in Intercultural Studies and Deputy Vice Chancellor, Finance, Administration and Planning at the International Leadership University, Nairobi, Kenya. His research interests include the development of leaders for the church and academy in Africa.

Caleb O. Oladipo is the Duke McCall Professor of World Christianity at Baptist Theological Seminary, Richmond, Virginia. He is the author of *The Will to Arise: Theological and Political Themes in African Christianity and the Renewal of Faith and Identity* (2006). His writings explore some of the leading figures in African Christianity.

Robert J. Priest is professor of mission and anthropology at Trinity Evangelical Divinity School, Deerfield, Illinois. He holds a PhD in anthropology from the University of California, Berkeley. Among his publications are *This Side of Heaven: Race, Ethnicity, and Christian Faith* and *Effective Engagement in Short-Term Missions*.

Steven D. H. Rasmussen is lecturer in missions and intercultural studies at Africa International University, Nairobi, Kenya. After pastoring in the United States, he taught ministers at Lake Victoria Christian College in Mwanza, Tanzania, from 1995 to 2008. He holds a PhD in intercultural studies from Trinity International University, Deerfield, Illinois.

Dana L. Robert is the Truman Collins Professor of World Christianity and History of Mission at Boston University School of Theology. Her books include *American Women in Mission: A Social History of Their Thought and Practice* (1997) and *Christian Mission: How Christianity Became a World Religion* (2009).

Cathy Ross comes from Aotearoa, New Zealand, and has worked in Rwanda, Congo, and Uganda as a mission partner with the New Zealand Church Missionary Society. She teaches contextual theology at Ripon College, Cuddesdon, and is lecturer in mission at Regent's Park College, Oxford. Her current research explores hospitality as a metaphor for mission.

Kenneth R. Ross, Church of Scotland minister at Netherlorn in Argyll, served as professor of theology at University of Malawi and as general secretary of the Church of Scotland Board of World Mission. His recent books include *Edinburgh 2010: Springboard for Mission* and *Atlas of Global Christianity, 1910–2010*.

Mark Shaw is professor of historical studies and director of the Centre for World Christianity at Africa International University, Nairobi, Kenya.

Steven Strauss (1955–2013) lived and ministered for nineteen years in Ethiopia, primarily at Evangelical Theological College and Ethiopian Graduate School of Theology, after which he was the U.S. director for SIM (Serving in Mission) for eight years. His final service was with Dallas Theological Seminary as head of the World Missions Department and professor of mission and intercultural studies.

Angela M. Wakhweya-Essamuah graduated as a medical doctor from Makerere University, Kampala, Uganda, and received a master's degree in economics from the University of London. She worked for fifteen years in public health and international development in sub-Saharan Africa in the field of HIV prevention and support for orphans and other vulnerable children.

Andrew Walls served in Sierra Leone and Nigeria and taught at Aberdeen and Edinburgh Universities and Princeton Theological Seminary. He is currently honorary professor, University of Edinburgh, professor of the history of mission at Liverpool Hope University, professor at the Akrofi-Christaller Institute in Ghana, and research professor, Africa International University, Nairobi.

Emma Wild-Wood is director of the Henry Martyn Centre for the Study of Mission and World Christianity, Cambridge, having previously taught in Democratic Republic of the Congo and Uganda. She is author of *Migration of Christian Identity in Congo* (2008) and co-editor of *The East African Revival: History and Legacies* (2010).

Allen Yeh is associate professor of intercultural studies and missiology at Biola University's Cook School of Intercultural Studies, La Mirada, California. He has lived in New England and the United Kingdom and has preached and done missionary work across five continents. His special areas of interest are China and Latin America.

PART 1

Africa and the African Diaspora

1

The Journey of Tite Tiénou

BY FRIENDS, COLLEAGUES, AND FORMER STUDENTS

"Exactly where God wants you"

IT WAS MIDNIGHT OR later when the student left the library. He looked up and saw a light in his seminary professor's second-floor office. Going up and finding a welcome, he confessed to being at a loss as to what to do with his life. "All that I am sure of is that God loves me and he exists." Looking him in the eye, the professor responded, "That's exactly where God wants you."

Today the student, Scott Moats, finds himself chief academic officer of Crown College, a Christian and Missionary Alliance school outside Minneapolis, Minnesota.

On that midnight hour in 1986, it was Professor Tite Tiénou who assured Moats of the primary importance of his spiritual foundation. Tiénou taught theology and missiology at the Christian and Missionary Alliance (C&MA) seminary, in Nyack, New York. Being "exactly where God wants you" involves both spiritual foundation and year-by-year leading. Tiénou found his spiritual foundation in his pastor-father's home in Burkina Faso, West Africa; his career path was to involve eight major moves and three continents.

Tite Tiénou was born January 16, 1949, in Sanekuy, Mali, then a part of French West Africa. A Muslim-majority nation, Mali wasn't always welcoming. So in Tite's early years the family relocated to the other side of the border, in Burkina Faso (formerly Upper Volta). The American missionaries in Bobo-Dioulasso, a city of nearly a half million, used the English "Titus" while the locals preferred "Tite," the French version. Tite's pastor-father, Pierre—who was actually his step-father, his father having died of a snake bite when Tite was very young—made sure that his children had nothing to do with Bobo culture, beliefs, and practices. The family viewed the wider community as rooted in African idolatry.

The Christian grade school that the Tiénou children attended, founded by the C&MA, was back on the other side of the border, in Mali. A newly arrived missionary, Milton Pierce, who relied on Pierre Tiénou for language mentoring, remembers helping a group of youngsters get to school in the rainy season. On one occasion the missionary's car got only so far before the road turned to a waterway. Pierce reports, "We had no choice but to let the boys finish their journey by foot. They put their few belongings on their heads and, wending their way up to their waists in the water, disappeared into the distance." Tite was eleven years old.

Following grade school, Tite attended the Cours Normal Protestant school in Daloa, Côte d'Ivoire (Ivory Coast), and then the Lycée Ouzzin Coulibaly, in Bobo-Dioulasso, back in Burkina Fasso. His family lived some distance away, so missionary Pierce rented for Tite a one-room dwelling in the city. It was equipped with a kerosene lamp, a simple table and stool, and a bamboo bed with a hard mattress. Tite distinguished himself by winning prizes for academic excellence, all the while learning English from the Pierces.

At a time when missionary policy discouraged out-of-country education, the Pierces secured a work scholarship for Tite to attend the C&MA college in Nyack, New York, beginning fall term 1968. (The scholarship involved cleaning local IBM offices.) Paul Rentz, who was to be Tite's fellow student, met him at the airport. One of the first things he discovered about this young man from West Africa was that he had no coat. On the way back to Nyack they stopped at Korvettes department store and bought a coat for the coming winter. Rentz remembers that Tite got him through French class. In three years Tite earned a BS in theology, *cum laude*.

Returning home to Bobo-Dioulasso in 1971, for the next two years Tiénou pastored the French-speaking Central Church of the Christian Alliance and at the same time taught English and French in the local college. Many in the church had grown up in non-Christian homes. Tiénou soon discovered that "ridicule based upon ignorance could not help me address the concerns of my parishioners." The Catholic priest in town, Anselme Titanma Sanon, who had converted out of Bobo religion, was a great help. He showed Tiénou how Bobo religious vocabulary, symbolism, and ritual could be adapted to the ministry of the Gospel.

In 1973, again with C&MA initiative, Tiénou enrolled in the Faculté Libre de Théologie Évangélique de Vaux-sur-Seine, France. He graduated in 1976 with an MA in theology. This was strengthened by special studies at École Pratique des Hautes Études, Sorbonne, Paris.

Returning to Bobo-Dioulasso in 1976, Tiénou became the founding director of the Maranatha Institute. At the same time he served as professor of English at the local college and again pastored Central Church.

Four years later, Tiénou headed to the United States for studies at Fuller Theological Seminary, Pasadena, California. Within a year he was named teaching assistant to Professor Charles Kraft in the School of World Mission. In 1984 he graduated with an MA in missiology and a PhD in intercultural studies; he was also presented the Contextualization Award for 1984. Kraft affirms that "the promise we saw in him when he was in our classes has certainly been fulfilled in the career he has had. [He is] known for his keen mind and outstanding scholarship [and] his approachability and love for his students."

1976: Member, World Evangelical Fellowship Theological Commission

1977–1980: Executive secretary, Association of Evangelicals in Africa and Madagascar theological commission

1980s: Chairman, Accrediting Council for Theological Education in Africa

1985: Member of Mission Leadership Forum, OMSC, New Haven, CT

1986–89: Member of the International Advisory Council for Lausanne II, Manila

1989–92: Chairman, and Chairman Emeritus, International Council of Accrediting Agencies

1990, Jan–May: Senior Mission Scholar, OMSC, and Research Fellow, Yale University

1991: Member, African Studies Association

1994: Contributing Editor IBMR

2000–2009: Member, Board of Directors, OMSC, New Haven

2004, June 21–22: Participant in consultation honoring Paul Hiebert

2008: Chairman, Board of Directors, Christian International Scholarship Foundation

Current: Member, African Theological Fellowship

For the next nine years, Tiénou taught theology and missiology at Alliance Theological Seminary, Nyack, New York. Here it was that Scott Moats sought Tiénou's midnight counsel. Former students like Moats and Joseph Modica, chaplain at Eastern University (Philadelphia), remember being challenged by his emphasis on contextualization and courses like "Ministry in the Midst of Pluralism."

Once again, in 1993, Tiénou returned to Africa, where he was appointed president and dean of the Faculté de Théologie Evangélique de l'Alliance Chrétiene, in Abidjan, Côte d'Ivoire. This school was the first to provide advanced theological education in the former French West Africa—Côte d'Ivoire, Guinea, Mali, Gabon, and Burkina Faso. At the same time he served as director of the African Theological Initiative, which championed the need for applying the Gospel in a way that was captive neither to the Western church nor African indigenous religion. As Stephen Bevans recalls in this volume, Tiénou urged that the challenge for African theologians was to develop "a theology that seeks to permanently anchor the gospel deeply into current African cultures." Tiénou kept his ties with the C&MA in the United States by serving as adjunct professor of the seminary; he was also recognized as a C&MA missionary associate.

Today, Tiénou serves at Trinity Evangelical Divinity School (TEDS), Deerfield, Illinois, outside Chicago. He began in 1997 as professor of theology of mission and in 2001 was appointed chair of the department of Mission and Evangelism. Since 2002 he has been Senior Vice President of Education, Academic Dean, and Professor of Theology of Mission. He and his wife, Marie, live in Gurnee, Illinois, a neighboring community of the seminary. Their four children—Adonija, Eric, Claudis, and Lea—have spread out from the Midwest to the East Coast.

David K. Ngaruiya, a PhD graduate of Trinity International University, now Senior Lecturer and Acting Deputy Vice Chancellor, Planning and Development, Nairobi International School of Theology/International Leadership University, and co-editor of the present volume, salutes Tiénou's scholarship: "He integrates theology and anthropology in the cause of Christian mission, stressing the importance of constructing a global theology, confronting political and economic issues, and securing a liberated African identity."

Douglas A. Sweeney, TEDS Professor of Church History and History of Christian Thought, and director of the Carl F. H. Henry Center for Theological Understanding, who began at Trinity the same year as Tiénou, states that Tiénou's influence helped him "interpret traditional Western materials in light of what God has done in other parts of the world." The late Douglas Carew, President of Africa International University, Nairobi, agreed: "He and others are key African scholars who are bringing African perspective to the worldwide church." The Overseas Ministries Study Center, New Haven, Connecticut, welcomed him in 1990 and again in 2013 as Senior Mission Scholar. Recently retired executive director Jon Bonk notes that his annual one-week seminar on ethnicity has been a regular feature of OMSC's study program.

On August 28, 2008, Tiénou returned to Nyack College and Alliance Theological Seminary (ATS) to speak at the annual faculty retreat and to receive the honor of being named professor emeritus. The occasion marked, almost to the day, the fortieth anniversary of his arrival in Nyack to begin his college education.

For ATS staff and faculty, Tiénou's name is synonymous with the concept of contextualized theology and contextualized ministry. It was his course on Ministry in the Midst of Pluralism in 1986 that helped shape a student by the name of Ronald Walborn. Walborn, who today serves as ATS dean, states,

> Tite is most fondly remembered as a faithful friend, scholar, colleague, and instructor during nearly a decade of service at Alliance Theological Seminary. My own decision to pursue doctoral studies and a career in teaching was birthed in his classrooms. Without a doubt his fingerprints can be found in the curriculum and commitments of Alliance Theological Seminary and in my own leadership as its dean. No one could have foreseen the deep impact Tiénou would have on our school here in Nyack, Trinity Evangelical Divinity School in Chicago, and other institutions around the world.

Tite Tiénou's friends, colleagues, and students—not to mention Tiénou himself—could never have foreseen how divine providence would play out in his life. His career has featured three phases of advanced education, service twice as pastor in Bobo-Dioulasso, leadership of two schools of advanced education in West Africa, and teaching and leading in two graduate theological schools in the United States. His career has involved no less than three continents and eight major changes of venue. There's nothing like being "exactly where God wants you."

2

"Enlarging Christian Coasts"
Pentecostalism and Higher Education in Sub-Saharan Africa

J. Kwabena Asamoah-Gyadu

For an essay in honor of Tite Tiénou one could hardly choose a more appropriate topic than evangelical Christianity and higher education in Africa. First, Tiénou has had wide influence on Christian scholarship within the evangelical world. Second, as a professor of Christian mission, he has been involved in higher education both as a teacher and administrator. Third, in his capacity as an evangelical theological educator, Tiénou stands as an exemplar of what it means to be a global evangelical Christian academic; his services have been offered both within Africa and beyond the continent, and a number of Africans continue to work under his tutelage. Having worked both in non-Western and Western evangelical theological institutions, Tiénou clearly demonstrates that evangelical involvement in higher education constitutes a vital aspect of Christian globalization.

Today's new church-related universities in sub-Saharan Africa are not products of historic Western missions. Instead, it is the new mega-size pentecostal/charismatic churches that have moved to the forefront in higher education.

Given their already large ministries, that pentecostal churches would set up universities and other institutions of higher learning is itself an important development. Historically such revivalist movements focused on the Second Coming and judgment. The clarion call revolved around modest living, personal holiness, and saving souls for eternity. The choruses of choice included, "I have another world in view; my Savior is gone to prepare me a place; I have another world in view." The new pentecostal churches covered in this essay have moved away from the classical eschatological agenda for a new message centering on empowerment, success, promotion, and prosperity in this life.[1]

This could not be made clearer than by the establishment of new evangelical universities in Africa by pentecostal leaders. This should be understood as part of a deliberate mission agenda to address national corruption and failed economic policies. Higher education is seen as the key to extending evangelical influence in the public sphere. The primary case study for much of this essay is Central University College (CUC), established by the International Central Gospel Church of Accra, Ghana. CUC's slogan is "Raising Leaders, Shaping Vision and Influencing Society through Christ." Its story and the stories of similar schools that have been founded in recent years will appear later in this essay.

The lead element in the above title, "enlarging Christian coasts," reflects the prayer of Jabez found in 1 Chronicles 4:10. The mega-pentecostal churches highlighted below see a vital relationship between higher education and globalization, and their prayer is that God will "enlarge their coasts" as a result of their educational mission. Physical and spiritual dominion is seen as part of what God the Holy Spirit may be doing through today's movements of renewal. Higher education is one way by which the new Evangelicals express their theology of dominion. Education offers a way by which those who were previously marginalized will be able to "enlarge their coasts" in public life at both the local and international levels.

EVANGELICAL CHRISTIANITY IN SUB-SAHARAN AFRICA

Evangelicalism is that stream of Christianity emphasizing the "born-again" experience as the only way of salvation, the Bible as the authoritative Word of God, the pursuit of Scriptural holiness, and the need for evangelism. To these hallmarks, Pentecostals and Charismatics add personal encounter with the power of the Holy Spirit. In much of the West, evangelical Christianity

1. Asamoah-Gyadu, *Taking Territories*.

is typified by the Wesleyan holiness movement, which sometimes is identified as the "mother" of modern Pentecostalism. Pentecostalism itself is not monolithic. It manifests itself in classical pentecostal denominations, in renewal movements within historic Protestant denominations, and in autochthonous urban-based charismatic churches. The latter have great attraction for Africa's upwardly mobile youth. Each of these streams are placed together in this essay because of their emphasis on renewal in the Holy Spirit as the key to genuine faith.

In sub-Saharan Africa, Christianity generally tends to be of this evangelical type. This means even historic mission-founded churches such as the Methodist, Anglican, and Presbyterian churches (which in the West are more often known as "mainline" rather than "evangelical") also display such tendencies. Understandably, the strength of renewal is stronger in some churches than others, but on the whole contemporary Christianity in Africa tends to have a certain evangelical orientation.[2]

The general characteristics of the pentecostal/charismatic churches I have in mind in this essay include the following:

1. A charismatic and often well-educated, gifted, articulate, and professional leadership.

2. Mostly urban-centered mega-size congregations that appeal to an upwardly mobile youth; and, linked to this, fashion-conscious and relaxed dress codes for members.

3. Worship styles that are exuberant, affective, emotionally laden, expressive, and dynamic.

4. Innovative uses of modern media technologies such as interactive internet websites and power-point in preaching.

5. Extensive and evangelistic uses of media for advertising religious programs and mediating religious services and supernatural power.

6. An internationalism that is evident in the names, choice of religious symbolism, the worldwide missionary peregrinations of the leadership, and the establishment of transnational networks, including the formation of foreign branches.

7. The preaching of a Christian message that directly addresses contemporary concerns of upward mobility; seizing of social, political, and

---

2. This explains in part why Christians belonging to historic mission denominations and now living in the diaspora often choose not to join "mother" churches in the West. They prefer rather to come together as "Ghanaian Methodists" or "Nigerian Presbyterians" in order to worship in their own ways and stay connected to the types of evangelicalism with which they were familiar before relocating abroad.

economic opportunities; and the application of certain social and biblical principles for the realization of success in this life.

PENTECOSTALISM AND HIGHER EDUCATION

In an essay with a focus similar to this one, Joel Carpenter refers to higher education as "one of the most striking contemporary forms of globalization."[3] As he observes, new universities are arising out of movements for evangelization and spiritual renewal in many parts of the world. They respond to global economic and political conditions and "local dynamics as well."[4]

Accra's Central University College (CUC) and its sponsor, International Central Gospel Church, is an obvious case in point. Mensa Otabil, pastor of the church and chancellor of CUC, is a very gifted and entrepreneurial leader. He has endeared himself to the public as a sound teacher of the Word of God, both through his church and "Living Word," his media ministry. Otabil's vision for the school is suggested by his handling of Genesis 1:28: "People who fill the earth," he says, "are the ones who have influence."[5] CUC is committed to producing people of influence in Ghana.[6]

CUC is by no means alone. In Lagos, Nigeria, there is Covenant University, established by the Living Faith Church Worldwide, also known as "Winners' Chapel." Its founder, Bishop David O. Oyedepo, claims that God called him to make people materially wealthy. This school, one of the most well-resourced in Nigeria after only a decade of existence, proclaims on its website, "We are committed to raising a new generation of leaders who will positively impact their nation, the African continent and the world at large." Back again in Accra, there is Dominion University College, sponsored by Action Chapel International. "Dominion" reflects the self-understanding of the new pentecostal/charismatic leadership across sub-Saharan Africa. Christian influence in the public sphere, grounded in university-level education, is what the new pentecostal churches see as part of their evangelical mission agenda. Leadership and dominion are viewed as the keys to the influence they seek to exercise in society.

Christian higher education in Ghana started with the establishment of the Valley View University of the Seventh-day Adventist Church. Valley

---

3. Carpenter, "New Evangelical Universities," 151–86.
4. Ibid., 152, 153.
5. Otabil, *Four Laws of Productivity*, 73.
6. Much of the inspiration for the establishment of evangelical universities in Africa has come from the success stories of Oral Roberts University in Oklahoma and Pat Robertson's Regent University in Virginia Beach, Virginia.

View is one of a number of such universities that the Adventists operate around the world; in other words, it is part of the denomination's international educational mission. Government regulations in Ghana since the 1990s require all universities to comply with national regulations under the supervision of the National Accreditation Board. In addition to the already mentioned CUC and Dominion University, there are other church-related schools in Ghana offering higher education: Methodist University College, Catholic University College, Presbyterian University College, and All Nations University College, among others.

A number of the church-owned universities in Africa were originally founded as seminaries. St. Paul University in Limuru, Kenya, the Christian Service University College in Kumasi, Ghana, and CUC, our primary example in this essay, are major exhibits. The latter has developed to the point where the faculty of theology, the mother of the institution, is now a minor partner in the whole enterprise. Increasingly, the disciplines of choice in the new universities are management, economics, architecture, engineering, information technology, medicine, pharmacy, nursing, and education.

CENTRAL UNIVERSITY COLLEGE

In September 2007 Ghana's print and electronic media ran a series of sponsored promotions for Central University College (CUC). Chancellor Otabil has an office on its campus. In October 2007 CUC relocated a greater part of its campus from the heart of Accra to Miotso, a small community in the Greater Accra Region. As one of the first privately owned university colleges in Ghana, it is newsworthy for being sponsored by a pentecostal church, which represents a stream of Christianity not traditionally connected with higher education. It is also the case that Pastor Otabil has emerged as a leading advocate for authentic translation of spirituality into practical everyday action.

CUC began in 1988 as a short-term pastoral training institute for pastors. It became Christian University College in 1993 and has expanded its programs over the years to offer full-fledged academic study of Christian theology, business administration, economics, computer science, and a number of modern languages, including French. Most of its current programs are offered up to the graduate level. CUC currently has plans for the establishment of schools of architecture, planning and, pharmacy. The Ghana *Spectator* has described CUC as "a university college in a class of its own." CUC is the first private university to run a weekend school that affords workers the flexibility of combining work and university-level study.

"Enlarging Christian Coasts" 13

Prof. Victor P. Y. Gadzekpo, current president of CUC, declared in the *Spectator* that the church, under the leadership of Pastor Otabil, "has been able to fulfill its dream of giving holistic higher education to its students who will serve as agents of change as its contribution to address the needs of Ghana and Africa as a whole." The reference to "agents of change" can be understood in relation to the admonishment of Jesus Christ that his followers are to serve as salt and light in the world. Involvement in Christian higher education affords the church opportunity to bring its moral message to bear on the lives of the men and women who are training to become the leaders of industry and the political and economic policy makers in Africa. The emerging Christian universities in Ghana are open to people from diverse religious backgrounds and moral persuasions, but school policies will ensure a conscious effort to teach the importance of morality in public life.

CONCLUSION

In most sub-Saharan African countries like Ghana, formal education has always been an integral part of Christian mission. Wesley Girls High School, Mfantsipim School, Adisadel College, Mawuli, St. Roses, the Presbyterian Boys Secondary School in Ghana, to name only a few, were established by Christian missions. It is these educational institutions, combining academic work and Christian moral virtues, that helped form the core leadership of post-independent Ghana following the end of colonialism. Now that the leading pentecostal churches are venturing into higher education, they are building on a rich intellectual and religious heritage.

Heretofore as far as missions were concerned, advanced education was provided as seminary training. A particularly notable example is Trinity Theological Seminary, which celebrated its sixty-ninth anniversary in 2011. That marks it as the oldest tertiary educational institution in Ghana. While its alumni served mainly as church pastors, many also served as chaplains in secondary schools. This involved the church in the academic training and character formation of young people before they entered university life. Ghana's universities historically have had a Christian orientation, too. Every residence hall at the University of Ghana has a chapel attached to it.[7] Regret-

---

7. During my years as the pastor of the Interdenominational Church in Legon, where the university is located, our congregation met in the Legon Hall Chapel. I always wondered why the pews were built to face each other. A senior member of the university explained to me that they were built that way to protect the integrity of the chapel as a place of worship. The seating arrangement helped assure that despite the growth of the university in the future, the chapel would not be converted into a lecture hall.

tably, from the time of the government of Kwame Nkruma, the Christian orientation of the universities became less explicit. Under government pressure, the divinity school evolved into a department for the study of religions. Until the influx of neo-pentecostal churches in the 1990s, evangelical fellowship was largely provided by the local chapter of the International Fellowship of Evangelical Students.

The current flowering of Christian higher education through the leading pentecostal churches can help promote social responsibility in the community. Any form of education that promotes Christian morality and ensures the formation of credible leadership helps the church gain greater influence and voice in society. Covenant University's website purpose statement is illustrative of the tone and spirit:

> Covenant University is a growing, dynamic vision-birthed, vision-driven University, founded on a Christian mission ethos and committed to pioneering excellence at the cutting edge of learning. We are driven by the compelling vision of raising a new generation of Leaders for the African Continent on the platform of a Holistic, Human Development and integrated learning curriculum, in order to raise Total Men who will go out to develop their world. Our Core Values of Spirituality, Possibility Mentality, Capacity Building, Integrity, Responsibility, Diligence and Sacrifice define our commitment to excellence. . . . Our experiences over the last three years strongly indicate the great potential we have as a University in instituting a learning context that is rich in educational opportunities, research and scholarship. Our aim is to build a world-class university that will be a pride of Africa as well as take its place among the Ivory League Universities on the global platform.
>
> Our mandate as a University is to revolutionize the educational landscape of Africa. Ours is indeed a rescue mission in education, driven on the platform of Christian ethos and life-transforming values. The integration of the fundamental requirements stipulated by academic and professional quality assurance bodies, a global outlook and impact-driven learning emphasis, provides a powerful synergy for empowerment in enabling the inculcation of intellectual and creative abilities via a platform of a solid commitment to self-discovery.[8]

At the same time, there will be challenges along the way. One is the cost of higher education. Sometimes one wonders if the churches established their new universities for the children of the rich. Private universities

---

8. www.davidoyedepoministries.org.

are drawing on the existing faculty of government universities, paying higher salaries in the process. This can result in a shortage of faculty in the government institutions attended by the children of middle and lower class families.

In any case, education remains the key to the future development of Africa. Joel Carpenter notes that the new church initiatives in education "are creations of the new spirit of mission agency and agenda-setting that is animating non-Western Christianity."[9] Pentecostal/charismatic churches, by getting directly involved in education, have identified a key area of mission that will impact public life. Leadership with integrity is the key to Africa's future.

BIBLIOGRAPHY

Asamoah-Gyadu, J. Kwabena. "An African Pentecostal on Mission in Eastern Europe: The Church of the Embassy of God in the Ukraine." *Pneuma: The Journal of Pentecostal Studies* 27 (2005) 297–321.

———. *Taking Territories and Raising Champions: Contemporary Pentecostalism and the Changing Face of Christianity in Africa 1980–2010*. Inaugural lecture delivered at the Trinity Theological Seminary, Legon, Ghana, December 16, 2010.

Carpenter, Joel. "New Evangelical Universities: Cogs in a World System or Players in a New Game?" In *Interpreting Contemporary Christianity: Global Processes and Local Identities*, edited by Ogbu U. Kalu and Alaine Low, 151–86. Grand Rapids: Eerdmans, 2008.

Otabil, Mensa. *Four Laws of Productivity: God's Foundation for Living*. Tulsa: Vincom, 1991.

---

9. Carpenter, "New Evangelical Universities," 167.

3

Wesleyan Camp Meeting History and the Revitalization of Ghanaian Methodism

Paul Kwabena Boafo

In the history of Methodism open-air preaching and camp meetings extending over several days have served as major mission strategies. Indeed, the role of camp meetings in Ghana Methodism can hardly be exaggerated. However, in recent decades camp meetings have experienced steady decline. And, not only have the daily gatherings diminished, but the number of participants who elect to reside overnight at the camp has also declined. This situation is most pronounced in the metropolitan circuits, where a majority of the people choose to commute daily from their homes rather than stay overnight at the camp grounds. This essay reviews the history of open-air preaching and camp meetings in Ghana Methodism and emphasizes their continued relevance for the Methodist Church Ghana in the twenty-first century.

THE WESLEYAN HERITAGE

Wesley's "Conversion" to Open-Air Evangelism

Outdoor preaching began when John Wesley made a fundamental decision that launched his ministry into the history of spiritual awakenings. The leaders within the Anglican church deemed as dangerously radical any attempt to move religious activities outdoors; it struck many as a vile profanity, a desecration of the holy.

Wesley himself wrestled over open-air preaching when George Whitefield called upon him to preach at a revival meeting at Bristol. He wrote in his journal, on Saturday, March 31, 1739, "In the evening I reached Bristol, and met Mr. Whitefield there. I could scarce reconcile myself at first to this strange way of preaching in the fields, of which he set me an example on Sunday; having been all my life (till very lately) so tenacious of every point relating to decency and order, that I should have thought the saving of souls almost a sin, if it had not been done in a church."[1]

Two days later, Wesley, having been convinced by the biblical evidence that Jesus not only preached and taught in the temple and synagogues but also on hillsides, from boats near the shore, and in open fields, again wrote in his journal: "At four in the afternoon, I submitted to be more vile and proclaimed in the highways the glad tidings of salvation, speaking from a little eminence in a ground adjoining to the city to about three thousand people."

Wesley's acceptance of field preaching proved to be a seminal moment in Methodist history; its importance is difficult to overstate.[2] It is believed that from this period Wesley boldly moved preaching of the Word and faith formation into the open air. This was where marginalized people, who were reluctant to enter the chapels, gained new access and opportunity to hear and respond to the Gospel. Wesley typically preached in natural settings—under shade trees, in fields and forest clearings, in town commons, on top of boulders, amid downpours and snow showers, in natural amphitheatres, market places and even standing on his father's grave.[3] Driven out of the chapels and cathedrals of the Church of England, Wesley made the world his parish. If he was to follow the imperative of the Gospel—to save souls—he felt that he had no choice.[4]

Most people first encountered Methodism through field preaching. As the early Methodist preachers travelled the length and breadth of the

---

1. Jackson, *Works*, 1:185.
2. Jackson, "Collecting and Preserving," 54.
3. Jackson, *Works*, 4:23.
4. Curnock, *Journal*, 7:422.

land organizing open-air meetings, masses of new people responded to the Gospel. Profound changes in their lives gave undeniable evidence that the Spirit of God was moving among them. Wesley recorded from his preaching at Wapping:

> Some sunk down, and there remained no strength in them; others exceedingly trembled and quaked: Some were torn with a kind of convulsive motion in every part of their bodies, and that so violently, that often four or five persons could not hold one of them. I have seen many hysterical and many epileptic fits; but none of them were like these, . . . By talking closely with whom, I found reason to believe that some of them had gone home to their house justified. The rest seemed to be waiting patiently for it.[5]

Reflecting on the number of people that assembled to listen to him in the fields, Wesley recounted that field preaching offered the best way to preach to the multitude that could not be contained in any building. He acknowledged the importance of this phenomenon in his journal entry of September 23, 1759:

> A vast majority of the immense congregation in Moorfields were deeply serious. One such hour might convince any impartial man of the expediency of field preaching. What building except St. Paul's church would contain such a congregation? And if it would, what human voice could have reached them there? By repeated observations I find I can command thrice the number in the open air, than I can under a roof. And who can say the time for field preaching is over, while, 1. Greater numbers than ever attend: 2. The converting, as well as convincing power of God is eminently present with them.[6]

Wesley preached his last open-air sermon in the fields at Winchelsea in October 1790. It was still his concern for the souls of men and women that, in his eighty-eighth year, he would go out in the open fields to preach. He noted; "I went over to that poor skeleton of ancient Winchelsea. . . . I stood under a large tree, on the side of it, and called to most of the inhabitants of the town, the kingdom of God is at hand; repent, and believe the gospel."[7] One of the elements and characteristics which gave Methodism its special

---

5. Jackson, *Works*, 1:203.
6. Ibid., 2:515.
7. Curnock, *Journal*, 8:102.

place was precisely open-air preaching. Hence Methodism could be deemed to have been born not only in song (as often noted) but also in the open air.

AMERICAN CAMP MEETINGS

The incorporation of outdoor preaching can be traced to the American frontier in the early 1800s. From the outset, camp meetings were devoted to evangelism and spiritual renewal. The immigration of thousands of people to America in the early nineteenth century created a religious vacuum. There were relatively few authorized houses of worship and even fewer ordained ministers. This created a ready audience for outdoor preaching.

Most camp meetings extended over several days. They took place in a cleared area surrounded by trees with overhanging limbs that formed a shelter. In the absence of printed announcements, local communities heard of up-coming meetings by word of mouth. Due to the hazards and difficulty of transportation, those attending needed to leave their homes for the duration of the camp meeting. These gatherings often drew participants from a large area, some out of sincere interest and religious devotion, others out of curiosity and a desire for a break from the arduous frontier routine of daily life.

From America to England

Camp meetings spread to England through the preaching of Lorenzo Dow (1777–1834), an American evangelist. Reports had appeared in the Methodist magazine, but it was Dow who gave a graphic and full account when he visited England. His account and preaching influenced some Methodist evangelists, Hugh Bourne, William Clowes, and Daniel Shoebotham. They took his account as an answer to complaints from their members that their weeknight prayer meetings were too short. Bourne also saw the meetings as a potential antidote to the general debauchery that characterized the wakes in that part of the county. On May 31, 1807, the first English camp meeting was held at Mow Cop under the leadership of Hugh Bourne (1772–1852) and William Clowes (1780–1851).[8] It is possible they had participated in Wesley's outdoor meetings and witnessed the impact those meetings made on the evangelical movement. Their zeal prompted them to organize numerous camp meetings. But the leadership of the Wesleyan Connexion viewed them as sectarian, and they refused to admit the converts to their churches.

8. Davies, *Methodism*, 135.

When Bourne and Clowes refused to cease their activities, they were dismissed from the Wesleyan Connexion. In 1810, after two years waiting in vain for re-admittance, they founded the Society of the Primitive Methodists. "Primitive" indicated that they wanted to conduct themselves according to the practice and ethos of Wesley and the early Methodist preachers, particularly in regard to open-air revival meetings. Long before the reunification of the Methodist families in 1932, field preaching and camp meetings were affirmed as effective methods of doing evangelism.

OPEN-AIR STRATEGIES IN GHANA

In Ghana the use of the open-air preaching and camp meetings dates to 1835. That year marked the beginning of missionary work by the Wesleyan Methodist Missionary Society (WMMS). Open-air preaching led to the planting of many Methodist societies, from the coastline to the hinterlands. Local preachers and singing groups announced the Good News in village after village. The Reverend Thomas Birch Freeman held many revival meetings, including open-air camps, in the Anomabo and Mankessim area in 1873. People came by the hundreds to listen to the Gospel message. Huts were erected; singing, praying, preaching followed. Women cried in ecstasies and fell to the ground. The camps ended in love-feasts, with 1,500 to 2,000 participants.[9]

In September 1875 at Ekroful near Saltpond, the Reverend Joseph Hayford held special evening open-air meetings. He stressed the importance of each person knowing the need of personal salvation. He recorded in his correspondence to the mission home office,

> There was at first a pause, a momentary stillness, and then a rush, as by the force of some mighty influence—the place at the front does not suffice. . . . A shy woman prayed in the spirit solemn but vehement addresses heavenward, intermingled with sobs and cries of "Saviour have mercy upon me and forgive me my sins," followed by profound responses of "Amen." . . . Then a violent wrestling—all impatient and eager for the common object of the meeting—ran through the company. Now was there abundance of weeping and bitter cries of distress, with long struggles as in the pangs of death, and ending generally in apprehensions of emphatic trust in Christ, of conscious pardon

---

9. Debrunner, *History of Christianity in Ghana*, 177.

of praise and thanksgiving. Seventy members were admitted on trial, and the movement spread.[10]

Programs in the Harmattan Season

Camp meetings were typically organized during the dry season, when the harmattan winds meant that the meetings would not be disrupted by the seasonal rains.[11] Activities included counselling and healing sessions. Church members valued the annual camps for Christian fellowship and a means of grace. It also gave members a chance to engage in evangelism and to seek new members for their churches. As Methodists shaped by Armenian teaching, they were reminded that the Great Commission obligated them to win souls for the Lord. This motivated the members of the churches to fully participate in the camp meetings.

Winning Souls for the Kingdom

The winning of lost souls motivated Ghana's preachers to trek the length and breadth of their communities with the message of Christ. They believed with Wesley that one soul won for the Lord is worth all the merchandise in the world.[12] During the period of the camp, "dawn preaching" by local preachers was heard in the early morning hours through the streets of the village, urging the people to come to the camp grounds. The preachers, singers, and campers converged at the camp for morning devotions consisting of preaching, singing, and incessant praying.

Church members were encouraged to visit homes in the community to speak to the people about the love of Jesus Christ. They engaged in conversation and distributed tracts. Those who showed interest were invited to the camp ground for further counseling.

Open-air preaching and camp meetings focused on mass evangelism. The sermons always had the purpose of calling people to repent and make a decision for Christ. Backsliders were called upon to rededicate or renew their commitment to Christ. As in the early Wesleyan pattern, the goal of

---

10. Hayford to the mission home office, 29 September 1875. Archives of the Methodist Missionary Society, London. Documents concerning the mission to Ghana since 1835.

11. In Ghana the harmattan season runs from November to early March. It marks the rest period before the farming season begins, and therefore the farmers are free to participate in church programs.

12. Telford, *Letters of John Wesley*, 8:222.

field preaching and camp meeting sermons was to awaken people to the Gospel.

Biblical Singing at Camp Meetings

The singing of hymns has always played a significant part in Methodist outreach and evangelism in Ghana. As choirs passed through towns, they sang the hymns of Charles Wesley and others with the hope that the people would come to hear the preaching. There was also singing as the crowd waited for the preaching to begin.[13]

In addition to the familiar Wesleyan hymns, Ghana Methodism developed a type of singing common in rural areas known as *ebibindwom*. In place of the traditional words, the churches created new Bible lyrics. With a high illiteracy rate, converts could not sing from printed music. However, they soon learned the new words and sang from memory. A cantor would recount the biblical narratives and the people responded in harmony.[14] *Ebibindwom* singing was sometimes accompanied by drums and other musical instruments.

The singing group Christ Little Band, formed in 1886 under the leadership of Rev. Ato Ahumah, helped to popularize *ebibindwom* singing. In addition, church choirs and other singing groups participated in evangelistic singing, sometimes filling the streets with multiple groups, inviting people to the camp grounds.

It is estimated that in 1876 and 1877 some three thousand converts were added to the Methodist Church by way of the open-air preaching and camp meetings.[15] There are many accounts of fetish priests and whole communities converting to Christ and burning their gods after hearing the powerful messages delivered at camp meetings. When converts came from a community where previously there were no Methodists, they became the nucleus of new societies.

Counseling and Healing

During the camp meetings, ministers set aside time for pastoral counselling. The camp meetings also included sessions for faith healing, which was considered just as important as the evangelistic preaching. Many church

---

13. Jackson, "Collecting and Preserving," 54.
14. Asiedu, "Gaddiel R. Acquaah," 32.
15. Debrunner, *History of Christianity in Ghana*, 177.

members attended, and they also invited unchurched family members and friends facing spiritual challenges. Thus, the quest for healing became a motivation for attendance at the camp meetings.

The centrality of the cross in healing was represented by a large wooden cross erected at the center of the meeting grounds. Those who needed healing and spiritual breakthroughs gathered around the cross as the preacher invited the sick and the troubled to come forward. Quarterly, synod, and annual conference reports contain many testimonies of healings and spiritual breakthroughs. Many non-members who had been healed subsequently joined the church.

As Casely B. Essamuah asserts, healing ministry remains central in today's Ghana: "Healing is a major motif in the mission outreach of African churches, hence any missionary method that ignores that will be ineffective."[16]

Camp Meetings for Christian Nurture

Camp meetings nurture faith and bring members to a fuller understanding of the saving grace of God. In earlier days in Ghana, because getting to the camp site involved a bit of travelling, the journey seemed like a spiritual pilgrimage.[17] Being away from home gave participants the opportunity to enter a new daily rhythm. With the usual daily responsibilities left behind, campers were free to explore the physical, relational, mental, and spiritual dimensions of their Christian lives. The change of worship venue impacted people long after the events were over.

It is a fact that when people engage in something out of the ordinary their senses are stimulated and heightened. Participants focus on their relationship with God through personal and corporate prayers and in-depth searching of the Scriptures. New opportunities are created for individuals to focus and deepen their relationship with God. New disciples are made and new spiritual leaders developed. In addition, these gatherings become as much a social as a spiritual event, providing a meeting place for old Christian friends in an atmosphere of spiritual renewal.

---

16. Essamuah, "Heart Music," 15.

17. In the days when societies hired vehicles to transport people to the camp meetings, the vehicles carried announcements that a spiritual journey was taking place. The passengers sang enthusiastically as they passed through the towns.

CONTEMPORARY DEVELOPMENTS

Students in Church Evangelism

In the late 1980s Methodist students from Ghana's high schools and universities formed Students in Church Evangelism. During school holidays these students collaborate with local Methodist evangelism committees to promote district camp meetings. The camp meetings are designed to revive weak Methodist societies and open new societies in the hosting circuits. The students sing hymns and choruses, show Christian films, and share the Word of God. During the day they go house-to-house with their Gospel witness and invite people to the evening programs. In recent years Students in Church Evangelism has added a social dimension to its work. The students collect clothing, books, and household articles that they distribute to the communities they visit. The medical students among the campers promote health education and screen the population for common health problems. Serious problems are referred to the nearest hospitals. In some cases the students contribute to the cost of hospital care. The national church has given awards to the Students in Church Evangelism for its contribution to the geographical spread and numerical growth of Ghana Methodism.

Challenges to Camp Meetings

In 1944 a church commission investigated all aspects of church life and made recommendations for effective evangelism, membership growth, and the nurture of members. Camp meetings and the open-air preaching were highlighted as strategic tools.[18] Despite the commission's recommendations, participation in the camp meetings have continued to decline over the last half century. To some extent the decline is understandable. Many church members have become mobile and the national transportation system has improved considerably, so participants can travel from their homes daily. But at the same time, the high cost of traveling can discourage attendance. Some members are put off by the discomforts of camping, such as unsanitary facilities and sleeping on student mattresses in large rooms with other campers.

A major complaint is the shift in primary focus from soul winning, Christian conferencing, and renewal of faith, to fund-raising. The organizing circuit sometimes cites the amount of money raised at camp meetings as

---

18. "I Will Build My Church," the report of the commission appointed by the Synod of the Methodist Church, Gold Coast, to consider the life of the Church, Methodist Book Depot, 1944, 4.

the index of evaluation instead of the number of souls won for the kingdom of God. Another challenge to modern-day gatherings is the mobile phone phenomenon, leading to distractions in the middle of sermons, Bible studies, and quiet times.

Though these challenges might be justifiable, the significance and impact of open air and camp meetings to evangelism and church growth gives the opportunity to reposition the Church for its mission. The new urban setting must not be allowed to stifle the programs and activities that brought Methodist expansion in Ghana. The rural evangelism through open air revival meetings must be revisited with all urgency.

REPOSITIONING THE CHURCH FOR ITS MISSION

Social Welfare in *Missio Dei*

To many Christians it may seem that the *Missio Dei* and social welfare should be kept separate. It may be argued that while the Gospel has a social message for the welfare of the community, the primary purpose of the church is to bring into its fellowship those that are outside. The words of Wesley, "You have nothing to do but to save souls," might be interpreted as meaning that nothing more is needed than to convert the individual. However, there is a strong case to be made for seeing evangelism and social welfare as inseparably bound. They are two expressions of one principle: The Gospel is for the blessing of the individual and for the blessing of the community. In a sermon in 1786, "On Visiting the Sick," Wesley observed, "Having shown that you have regard for their bodies you may proceed to inquire concerning their souls."[19] For Wesley, authentic Gospel ministry entailed the employment of all gifts and graces that would enhance the physical and spiritual well-being of the poor.

As noted above, most camp meetings in Ghana are held in rural communities, which often lack basic social amenities. Camp meetings that are held for the purpose of renewing faith, gaining members, and establishing new societies must begin to produce economic as well as spiritual benefits. The planning committee of a Methodist camp meeting should have a short, medium and long-range plan to improve the life of the chosen community. As part of the short-term plans, there could be health education and medical screening for the community and distribution of food and clothing to the needy. As the hosting circuits build chapels for the new societies, they can also work with the community to provide potable water, build a clinic,

---

19. Outler, *Works of John Wesley*, 3:391.

or establish a school for the children. Camp programs can educate people about environmental concerns and address sanitation and poverty issues. The church, as a major stakeholder in achieving Ghana's Millennium Development Goals, can include plans for addressing the nation's goals in the camp-meeting programs.[20]

Camp Meetings and Technology

Modern information technology can provide a major boost to evangelism, especially in the organization of open air meetings and camp programs. MCG's ten-year strategic plan includes the use of information technology to meet the spiritual and material needs of its people and to expand and enhance evangelism and discipleship.[21] In the traditional setting, publicity for the camp meetings was limited to pulpit announcements and the services of the village gong beater. Electronic media can now be added to local newspapers, posters, hand bills, and flyers. Camp programs, and of course regular church programs, will increasingly make use of internet technology, public address systems, films, electric generators, and musical instruments, all of which can facilitate mass evangelism.

Nurturing New Converts

Contemporary Ghanaian Methodism has lost many new converts and societies because they were simply neglected. Wesley always charged his preachers to follow up new converts. The nurture of converts and societies must go well beyond the mere teaching of catechisms for baptism.[22] Whenever postconversion discipleship is neglected, new converts all too easily slip through the net and revert to their former states. David L. Watson highlights how the early Methodist classes sustained the responses that occurred in the fields.[23] Today's evangelism committees must put in place a monitoring and evaluation team to the follow-up of new converts. The nurture of new societies requires a shepherd and a suitable chapel. In northern Ghana, societies that

20. Ghana's national Millennium Development Goals are: (1) Eradicate extreme poverty and hunger; (2) Achieve Universal Primary Education; (3) Promote gender equality and empower women; (4) Reduce child mortality; (5) Improve maternal health; (6) Combat HIV and AIDS, malaria, and other diseases; (7) Ensure environmental sustainability; and (8) Create Global Partnership for development.
21. Aboagye-Mensah, "Strategic Plan."
22. Jackson, *Works*, 1:416.
23. Watson, *Early Methodist Class Meeting*, 149.

were left to worship under trees survived no longer than the first rainy season. Societies in the south who met in temporary quarters have faded as attendees left to join better established societies.

CONCLUSION

Camp meetings and open-air preaching will continue to be key factors for the healthy growth of the Methodist church in Ghana.[24] The MCG has set for itself a goal to build a vibrant spirit-led church, one that will be marked by holistic evangelism, on-going discipleship, and the transformation of society. This will require the church to rekindle the Wesleyan zeal for holiness, evangelism, and mission.[25] National statistics indicate that there are many unreached people and villages in Ghana. The Methodist Church Ghana should promote the open-air revival meeting as a quarterly event for all societies and insist on annual camp meetings organized by the circuits. The content of all field and camp meeting must be the Gospel of Christ and the corresponding call to follow him. To sustain the camp meeting tradition, dioceses should build modern retreat centers with suitable accommodations and the required ambience for spiritual nurture.

The relevance of camp meetings is evident in the fact that most Christians today, due to socio-economic factors, spend relatively little time focussing on God. At the same time, most church programs simply do not emphasize personal spiritual growth. The regular organization of camp meeting would represent an effective means for members to address and deepen their spirituality. Renewal of the camp meeting tradition will advance the mission of God and reaffirm the Ghana's priceless Wesleyan heritage.

BIBLIOGRAPHY

Aboagye-Mensah, Robert. "Strategic Plan of the Methodist Church Ghana 2007–2016," online: http://www.methodistchurch-gh.org/download.html.
Asiedu, Henry Ampaw. "Gaddiel R. Acquaah and the Hermeneutics of Vernacular Hymns." In *Christianity, Mission and Ecumenism in Ghana*. Edited by J. Kwabena Asamoah-Gyadu. Accra, Ghana: Asempa, 2009.

---

24. In recent years the Methodist Church Ghana has strategized to increase membership. As part of the 2005 celebration of the 170th anniversary, the church took the theme "Making disciples of all Nations" and challenged each member to win a soul and thereby double MCG membership.

25. Aboagye-Mensah, "Strategic Plan."

Curnock, Nehemiah, editor. *The Journal of the Rev. John Wesley*. London: Epworth, 1938.

Davies, Rupert E. *Methodism*. Middlesex, U.K.: Penguin, 1964.

Debrunner, Hans W. *History of Christianity in Ghana*. Accra, Ghana: Waterville, 1967.

Essamuah. Casely B., "Heart Music as Identity Marker: *Ebibindwom* and Ghanaian Methodism." In *Christianity, Mission and Ecumenism in Ghana*, edited by J. Kwabena Asamoah-Gyadu. Accra, 9–22. Ghana: Asempa, 2009.

Jackson, Jack. "Collecting and Preserving Disciples: Verbal Proclamation in Early Methodist Evangelism." *Wesley and Methodist Studies* 2 (2010) 45–66.

Jackson, Thomas, editor. *The Works of the Rev. John Wesley*. 7 vols. Oxford: John Mason, 1829.

Outler, Albert, editor. *The Works of John Wesley*. Bicentennial ed. Vols. 1–4. Nashville: Abingdon, 1984.

Watson, David L. *The Early Methodist Class Meeting: Its Origin and Significance*. Nashville: Discipleship Resources, 1992.

Wesley, John. *The Letters of the Rev. John Wesley, A.M.* Edited by John Telford. 8 vols. London: Epworth, 1931.

4

African Immigrant Religions in the Diaspora

ELIAS K. BONGMBA

AFRICAN PRESENCE IN THE West greatly intensified in the latter part of the twentieth century and even more so in the opening years of the twentieth century. This essay examines the impact of African immigration—specifically the religious impact—in the West, with priority on its scope and significance in the United States.

A NEW DEMOGRAPHIC CONTEXT

Increased immigration to the United States from Africa began with the 1965 U.S. Immigration and Nationality Act. This legislation opened the door to a more representative cross-section of the world. The 1990 Diversity Visa program (known as the Green Card Lottery), which targeted areas like Africa that historically accounted for a disproportionately low number of immigrants, produced greater immigration opportunity. As a result, African immigration, which was miniscule in the early decades of the twentieth century, reached more than 50,000 in 1995; in recent years the average annual immigration from Africa has exceeded 75,000.[1] The increasing

---

[1] For information and statistics on immigration to the United States, see U.S. Census Bureau, *Foreign-Born Population: 2000*; U.S. Department of Justice, *2000 Statistical*

numbers should be seen in light of the standard push-and-pull factors that drive immigration worldwide: political upheavals, economic hardships, and refugee crises. For many immigrants, the challenges of relocation prove to be daunting, requiring the deployment of all resources, especially spiritual resources.

The relationship between migration and religion is not new, especially in the United States, where religion featured prominently in the earliest movement from Europe to the Americas. Later, Catholicism played an important part in the lives of a new generation of immigrants. In the age of globalization, Africans are prominent among the new agents of religious transplantation.[2]

J. Kwabena Asamoah-Gyadu views African immigration from a religious standpoint. It represents, he believes, what God is doing, "not so much with individual African churches, but rather with African Christianity, especially in its independent nondenominational charismatic streams in the Diaspora." Asamoah-Gyadu points to the interracial composition of groups like God's Embassy, in Kiev, Ukraine, as indicating that "African initiatives in religion in the Northern continents may be more complex than previously thought."[3] Jacob Olupona adds that African immigrant religions are not merely part of black religions in the United States.[4]

THE RELIGIOUS LANDSCAPE

The African Diaspora in Europe and North America sees itself as contributing to a global spiritual quest. It presents that quest as a common human experience, its Africanness being a historical accident. Interdisciplinary studies portray immigrant African religious populations as aiming to become multinational communities.[5] The instinct for internationalism can be seen even in the home countries of Africa. One famous example is the *International* Central Gospel Church of Accra, Ghana, pastored by Mensa Otabil

---

Yearbook; and Terrazas, "African Immigrants in the United States."

2 Olupona and Gemignani, *African Immigrant Religions*; Haar, *Religious Communities in the Diaspora*; Adogame and Weisskӧppel, *Religion in the Context of African Migration*.

3 Asamoah-Gyadu, "African Pentecostal on Mission," 314–15.

4. Olupona and Gemignani, *African Immigrant Religions*, 27–46; in the same vol., Daniels, "African Immigrant Churches," 47–60. See also Adogame, "Betwixt Identity and Security," 24–41, and Gerloff, "Significance of the African Christian Diaspora," 115–20.

5. In his 1991 investigations, Olupona described some immigrant religions as "reverse missions." See Olupona and Gemignani, *African Immigrant Religions*, 45.

(emphasis added).⁶ The instinct to be international is intentional, indicating that the members of such churches do not see themselves as merely African.

The Aladura family of churches (the name comes from a Yoruba expression meaning "the praying people") has a long presence in Europe. Included are the Cherubim and Seraphim, Christ's Apostolic Church, Church of the Lord Aladura, Celestial Church of Christ, and the Evangelical Church of Yahweh. These churches began in the early 1920s in Lagos, Nigeria, and spread to other countries in Africa, and ultimately to Europe, North America, Asia, and South America. While they share a common distinction as Aladura churches, each has its own ethos, leadership roles, organizational structures, and attitudes towards African culture.

The Church of the Lord, Aladura made its appearance in England in 1964. The Cherubim and Seraphim Church followed the next year, and the Celestial Church of Christ began in 1967 (all three in London).⁷ These churches drew members from the community of Nigerian students and their families. In an atmosphere of discrimination and racism, many of the Nigerians became agents of change.⁸ Students who experienced difficulties with education, child care, housing, unemployment, immigration, and family life found in the Aladura churches people who could help them.⁹ The new churches followed the patterns of their churches back in Nigeria, holding regular prayer meetings, singing and praising God, witnessing the presence of the Spirit of God, sometimes falling into trances as they pronounced messages from God, with other members of the community interpreting. At its first anniversary the London Cherubim and Seraphim church reported a congregation of about 500 people, 200 of which were regular members.¹⁰ Additional Aladura churches were organized not only in Birmingham, Glasgow, Manchester, and Liverpool, but also in Austria, Belgium, France, Germany, Italy, Netherlands, and Switzerland. Rufus Ositelu has described the work of these churches as a re-missionization of the West.¹¹

In the Netherlands it was Ghanaians who first began immigrant congregations. These churches are unique in that they are not transplants from Africa but wholly new. They grew so rapidly that by 1997 there were 40

---

6. Asamoah-Gyadu, "African Penetecostal on Mission," 299; see also Gifford, *African Christianity*; and Gifford, *Ghana's New Christianity*.

7. Harris, *Yoruba in Diaspora*, 21.

8. Ibid., 39.

9. Ibid., 39–40.

10. Ibid., 45.

11. Adogame, "Engaging the Rhetoric," 498.

congregations spread across the country.[12] In the Ukrainian capital of Kiev, Pastor Sunday Adelaja established the Embassy of God church. At its tenth anniversary, in 2004, it had 20,000 members, mostly local Ukrainians.[13] Another immigrant church in Kiev is Victory Christian Church, led by Henry Madava of Zimbabwe.

After Adelaja completed his university studies in Russia, he relocated in the Ukraine. He testifies that God gave him a vision that he would use the people of the former Soviet Union to gather Christians before the coming of Jesus. "Though I am a foreigner, God has given me the ability to go and minister beyond race, culture, and denominational barriers."[14] In the beginning things did not go smoothly. He prayed and fasted until God told him to take care of the lowly and God would bring him those who were higher up in society. Adelaja and seven other people started to reach out to the outcasts of society—drug addicts, robbers, prostitutes, alcoholics, and others who were neglected. As changes took place in the lives of these people, the city began to notice the work of the African pastor.

On the church's eighth anniversary, Adelaja announced that God had given a new name: the Embassy of the Blessed Kingdom of God for all Nations. The church is viewed as an embassy with a mandate to establish the reign of God on earth, which is for all people regardless of race. As God's ambassador, every believer is "called to give the world peace, success, and the joy of God."[15] Adelaja encourages the Ukrainian members to "stand for Jesus," adding that if God can use him as a foreigner, they can do more.

AFRICAN RELIGIOUS COMMUNITIES

The Christian Home Away from Home

Researchers agree that African immigrant religions provide members with a sense of "home away from home."[16] Studies of Southeast Asian communities in the United States, for example, confirm that immigrants join religious communities because, in addition to salvific purposes, they are looking for

---

12. Haar, *Religious Communities in the Diaspora*, 156.

13. For information about the development of the church, see Asamoah-Gyadu, "African Pentecostal on Mission," 297–321. This essay was written before the legal issues that subsequently arose regarding the church, about which I have no information.

14. Asamoah-Gyadu, "African Pentecostal on Mission," 302.

15. Ibid., 305.

16. The expression "a place to feel at home" was initially applied to African Initiated Churches in Kenya. See Welbourn and Ogot, *Place to Feel at Home*.

ways of dealing with economic and other forms of marginalization.[17] The late Princeton anthropologist Clifford Geertz's stated, "The importance of religion lies in its capacity to serve . . . as a source of general, yet distinctive, conceptions of the world, the self and the relation between them."[18] The religious life of immigrants gives them a sense of home. It was because Olu Abiola and his African friends in London did not feel at home in Anglo mainline churches that they founded the Aladura International Church in 1979. This created a space for the mostly student workers in London to worship and provide support for one another.[19]

Immigrant religious communities deal with what has been called existential limbo.[20] In the U.S. context, immigration status, with its rules and paper work, is the paradigmatic limbo. Studies of Ghanaian immigrants indicate that many turn to religion to address immigration issues.[21] Opoku-Dapaah notes that Ghanaian immigrants have "existential anxiety" because of their immigration status. About 90 percent of the people he interviewed had been in the United States for over ten years and were holding visas that had expired. Church leaders reported that two-thirds of their members had immigration problems; many feared the raids of officials from the Department of Homeland Security.[22] Opoku-Dapaah reports, "Adherents who have immigration problems believe that ritual obligations, including offerings to the sect, constant meditation, fasting, anointment with holy water and abstinence, can assist them in resolving their post-immigration insecurities, hence their attraction to the sects."[23] Two-thirds of the people Opoku-Dapaah interviewed earned between $10,000 and $15,000 a year, well below the poverty line. Many of the immigrants were not adequately prepared to work in a postindustrial economy and lacked the skills needed to enter the job market. However, many members of the churches believe

---

17. Kurien, "Constructing 'Indianness'"; Fong, *Contemporary Asian American Experience*.

18. Geertz, *Interpretation of Cultures*, 123.

19. Adogame, "Engaging the Rhetoric," 498.

20. Stoller, *Money Has No Smell*, 6.

21. Opoku-Dapaah, "Ghanaian Sects in the United States," 231–53.

22. Ibid., 248.

23. Ibid. Opoku-Dapaah calls these religious groups "sects," defining them as "a subdivision of a larger religious group (e.g., Christian Church) whose members have, to some extent, diverged from the larger group by developing deviating beliefs and practices." I take exception to the term "sect," as it tends to perpetuate negative attitudes some people have about African immigrant religions. In addition, the author refers to members of these churches as "fanatics," and Ghanaian ritual experts as "fetish priests" (232ff.). I find both terms objectionable.

that their leaders can call on supernatural forces to intervene in their struggle to regularize their stay in the United States.

Sizable Ghanaian religious communities are found in Atlanta, Baltimore, Charlotte, Chicago, Dallas, Detroit, Jersey City, New York, Newark, and Washington, D.C. Ghanaians are also present in other parts of the country, though not in large numbers.[24] Religious communities such as Lighthouse Chapel in New York and Maranatha Power Mission in Atlanta draw more than 1,000 worshipers on Sunday mornings. "Prophets," typically charismatic figures serving as pastors, lead the churches. Members take their problems to them. The prophets work with councils of elders that manage the activities of the community. In many cases, however, the real authority remains with the prophet. He assures members that their problems—witchcraft, poverty, marriage issues, immigration—can be solved by supernatural intervention.[25]

For lonely immigrants, worshiping in a place where they feel at home is vital; they share their stories with other Africans and get spiritual encouragement. Their difficulties are often seen as part of a larger cosmic struggle between the forces of good and evil. In church, they receive assurance that victory has been secured by Jesus Christ.

In a global religious landscape, the repetition of familiar rituals and the adaptation of new ones provide a sense of home. But sometimes the immigrant's devotional life intrudes into the ability to navigate the system effectively. Take the case of Evelyn, who is a nurse. She has to balance her work schedule with family responsibilities, attend church on Sunday and mid-week services on Wednesday (and sometimes an all-night prayer vigil), and gatherings of her ethnic group. In some cases, an immigrant may be pursuing a diploma through a community college or university.[26] Such schedules are tough to keep. Many claim that it is their faith and their religious community that sustains them. When you ask Evelyn how she manages, she jokingly replies, "na dis America, if man no do so, how we go do?" There are many Evelyns among African immigrants who affirm, "We serve a mighty God who takes care of us."

I have talked with Christian and Muslim immigrants, often well educated, who find that adjusting to the structures, systems, services, and a new social world in America is not as easy as they had imagined. The uncertainty of getting a job comparable to what they had at home prompts some immigrants to leave their families in Africa, thereby creating the loneliness of

---

24. Ibid., 239.
25. Ibid., 244.
26. Personal conversation. Evelyn is not her real name.

"commuter marriages." Some worry about what is going on at home. One woman confessed that she worries that the money she sends to her husband at home is being spent on other women.

For the lonely immigrants, worshiping in a place where they feel at home enables them to share their stories with other Africans and get spiritual encouragement. Their difficulties are often seen as part of a larger cosmic struggle between the forces of good and evil. In church, they receive assurance that victory has been secured by the blood of Jesus Christ.

The Muslim Home Away from Home

For Muslims, transition into American society involves a struggle to make a living while remaining faithful to his or her devotional life.[27] Standard Muslim practices include worship at the mosque on Friday, an ongoing regimen of prayer, and observance of Muslim holidays such as *Id-al Fitr* and *Id-al Adha*.[28] At worship, Muslims listen to the message in Arabic, but they use their African language for prayers. The reproductions of familiar rituals and the adaptation of new ones are acts of insertion and rootedness that sustain the faithful in a global religious landscape. Their personal and public rituals, which are constantly negotiated in this new context, are a quintessential characteristic of African religions in the new diaspora.

Sierra Leonean Muslims use their religious identity to address issues resulting from their absence from home in Sierra Leone and as an anchoring tool to help them settle in the new home. Immigrants often decorate their homes with art and religious images that remind them of their religious tradition and national roots. Some Sierra Leonean Muslims hang pictures of the Ka'ba and verses from the Qu'ran in their homes.[29] Use of the Qu'ran signifies that they share the sacred text with the global Muslim community, but they also proudly identify themselves as Sierra Leoneans.[30] Our Muslim friend Zeinabu, who moved to Houston five years ago, often says that she is from the Gambia. "Muslim identity in the new diaspora is increasingly expressed via personal attire and the decoration of private and public

---

27. Stoller, *Money Has No Smell*, 5.

28. In New York, a group that identifies with Mouridiya, an Islamic Sufi movement, celebrates the birthday of Sheikh Amadou Bamba (1850–1927), the Senegalese founder of the movement.

29. D'Alisera, *Imagined Geography*, 30. Use of the Qu'ran signifies that they share the sacred text with the global Muslim community, but they also proudly identify themselves as Sierra Leonean.

30. Ibid., 37.

spaces—mosques and Islamic centers, domestic doorsteps and interiors, personal space in or at the work site, vehicles with religious markers."[31]

Muslims in the Washington, D.C., area worship at the local Islamic Center, which offers diverse religious and social activities such as lectures, banquets, weddings, and instruction classes. The texts used for instruction include English translations of the Qu'ran and the Hadith.[32] At study sessions held every Saturday, the imams explain difficult passages and give counsel to members of the community. Some find that their religious life involves fewer prohibitions than experienced back home in Sierra Leone.[33]

Immigrants from the West African nations of Niger, Mali, Senegal, and the Gambia, who settled on the U.S. East Coast, sometimes have worked as street vendors. Some of the items for sale may seem inconsistent with their Islamic faith, yet they need the money to support themselves and their families back home.[34] Among the immigrants are clerics; they communicate their faith in an effort to create a context where they will feel at home.[35]

The idea of feeling at home sometimes involves a moral critique of the new society. Researcher Paul Stoller introduces El Hadj Harouna Souley as representative of Muslim immigrants who find the lack of morals in American society appalling.[36] Religious activities for such people provide a base for dealing with what they consider the inconsistency of contemporary American behavior as compared with the nation's religious history.

Holistic Development

Many African immigrants in the United States are well-educated professionals, and their influence is felt in the development of holistic church programs. Congregations participate in regular Bible studies during the week and Sunday school classes on Sunday mornings. It is not unusual for a congregation to offer kindergarten programs, and bookstores where DVDs of worship services, books, and church supplies may be purchased.

But for an organization unequaled in church development and holistic ministries, one looks back to Africa and the Redeemed Christian Church of God (RCCG), 30 miles north of Lagos, Nigeria. The RCCG compound, known as "Redemption Camp," or "Redemption City," serves

31. Ibid., 9.
32. Ibid., 71.
33. Ibid., 65.
34. Stoller, *Money Has No Smell*, vii.
35. Ibid., xi.
36. Ibid., 166.

as the movement's international headquarters. There are about 2,000 RCCG parishes in Nigeria, and another 3,000 around the world in 100-plus countries, including Canada and the United States. The North American branch, headquartered on 400-plus acres near the town of Floyd in Hunt County (an hour northeast of Dallas, Texas), is in the early stages of development. Both the Nigerian original and the budding North American effort maintain impressive websites.[37]

The parent RCCG presents its vision on the Nigerian website:

> We have a vision for a better nation; a Nigeria of frank and candid academicians, dependable and honest artisans, God-fearing and faithful pastors, decent and law-abiding citizens, trustworthy and upright youths, caring and compassionate doctors, honorable and truthful politicians, open and sincere business community, courageous and reliable public servants.
>
> We have a vision for a country where judges are just and impartial, soldiers, policemen and women are compassionate and considerate, traditional rulers embody distinction, dignity and decorum, [and] bankers are honest and honorable. We have a vision for a future generation of creative, innovative and inventive entrepreneurs. We want to mould a generation of kind, thoughtful and gentle adolescents, who are motivated to build and sustain a better Nigeria where peace, justice, fairness and Godliness reign. We are looking forward with optimism and intense anticipation for a Nigeria we can all defend, protect and be proud of. We have a desire and an aspiration for a nation whose trust is in the Lord God Almighty. This is our vision at the Redeemer's University (RUN), where we want to build the future of Nigeria, today. Because you embody this vision, we are honoured and privileged to have you with us as our core partners, as we RUN with the vision for a better Nation.[38]

The RCCN vision for the world includes the following: "We will plant churches within five minutes walking distance in every city and town of developing countries; and within five minutes driving distance in every city and town of developed countries. We will pursue this objective until every nation in the world is reached for Jesus Christ our Lord."[39]

---

37. See http://www.rccg.org. The April 12, 2009, issue of the *New York Times* carries an 8,500-word article on the RCCG movement, including its development in the United States.

38. Http://run.edu.ng/About_us.html.

39. Http://www.rccg.org/.

Dr. Enoch Adeboye, the RCCG General Overseer since 1980, is a gifted academic and organizer. The RCCG believes in the power of the Holy Spirit, yet at the same time the emphasis on education and training may signal that the routinization of charisma has begun. Church leaders are expected to have specific training that meets general academic standards. The Nigerian compound is the site of the RCCG university, which features colleges of humanities, management sciences, and natural science. The college of humanities offers degrees in English, history, international relations, and theatre arts. Programs in the planning stage include philosophy, religious studies, French, Yoruba, and linguistics.

Redemption City hosts major festivals of the church, and healing and miracle services. Guesthouses cater to high-level civil servants; more affordable quarters are provided for general visitors. Also on the property are health facilities, an orphanage, bookstores, post office, gas stations, supermarket, bakery, canteen, three banks, secondary school, Bible school, and university.

Observers of movements such as the RCCG suggest that new African immigrant religions could be a catalyst for the revival of religious life in the West. Philip Jenkins explores this theme in *The Next Christendom: The Coming of Global Christianity*.[40] The growth in the global South has now spread to Northern countries that historically were the source of mission to African counties.

Conflicting Perspectives on African Traditions

African indigenous traditions are the source of contested beliefs among African religious communities in the United States. Some view ethnic traditions as distinct from religious beliefs and do not see them as a big issue. But other immigrants disagree strongly; their leaders see practices such as initiation rituals as "ancestral curses that should be abandoned." I have attended weddings in Houston that included a ceremony in which the presiding pastors prayed in Jesus's name for the couples standing before them to be released from ancestral curses. The pastors did not spell out what was meant, but it was clear that curses are thought to follow Africans wherever they go. At a funeral ceremony I heard a pastor indicate that ancestral curses hinder people from economic success. People who have been in the United States for a long time without buying a home of their own are judged to be under an ancestral curse. But I have also been in discussions among

---

40. Jenkins, *Next Christendom*.

Africans who contend that such negative views oversimplify a complex situation and are not fair to African traditions.

In 1994 the Muslim community in Washington, D.C., faced the issue of female genital circumcision. Two Sierra Leonean women sought asylum in the United States claiming that they would be subjected to female genital cutting if they returned to their country of origin. One court granted one of the women asylum, but another court rejected the other woman's claims.[41] Some Sierra Leonean women felt that the media presented the story in a stereotypical manner. Anthropologist JoAnn D'Alisera comments, "[The] two women played into negative perceptions . . . lending greater credence to a discourse that simplifies and seeks to criminalize a complex ritual process without discussing broader meanings."[42] One of D'Alisera's informants said that in her case it was her mother who made the decision. Her father had opposed it because he believed Islam did not support it. When she almost died after the initiation, people in her community blamed her, saying that her own powers conflicted with the powers of those who presided at the ceremony.

OMEGA MINISTRIES IN HOUSTON

I now turn to Omega Gospel Center, sometimes known as Omega Gospel Mission or simply Omega Church. Omega Church is an African immigrant congregation in Houston, Texas, whose members are mostly from Cameroon. Much of what follows is based on a survey I conducted among members of the church in 2008 and on interviews with Pastor Victor Mbah.[43] I have studied Omega Gospel Mission on and off since it opened its doors in 2001. It is a church-plant of Omega Gospel Ministries in Washington, D.C., a national organization begun in 1998 by Dr. Toby Awasum.[44] Omega Gospel Ministries is related to the Church of God of Prophecy, a U.S. pente-

41. D'Alisera, *Imagined Geography*, 95.

42. Ibid., 99.

43. Other Cameroon-led churches in Houston include a ministry by Brigit Fomunyam Israel and a Cameroon Catholic congregation under the auspices of the Catholic Archdiocese of Galveston and Houston.

44. Pastor Awasum studied Civil Engineering at the University of Wisconsin and earned graduate degrees from Howard University and University of Pennsylvania. He and his wife started a health care company in 1993 that now employs more than two hundred people. Awasum has traveled around the world as an evangelist for The Harvest Team, a ministry of the Church of God of Prophesy. He is author of *Ministering to Your Pastor*, the proceeds of which helped establish the Gospel Worker's Support Fund. The fund supports ministerial education, gives scholarships to children of pastors, builds parsonages, and gives support to pastoral ministries.

costal denomination. In addition to Houston, Omega Gospel Ministries has churches in Dallas, Texas, Cincinnati, Ohio, and Cleveland, Ohio. In Cameroon, the home country of the Awasums, there are churches in Douala, Tiko, Mamfe, and in South Africa.

Profile of Survey Respondents

Omega Gospel Center today has about 150 members, immigrant worshipers from Cameroon, with a few from other parts of Africa. Pastor Mbah recalls that concerns about marriage and business relationships were the catalysts that started the church. The weekly schedule includes Sunday service, Wednesday evening Bible study and choir practice, and youth meetings and intercessory prayer on Saturdays. Men's and women's meetings take place as needed. Omega Church supports an international medical mission work and sometimes sends teams of volunteers to Cameroon.

Of the forty-five survey respondents, thirty-seven are from Cameroon. A large majority of these are from the Anglophone sector, while a few represent the Francophone sector of Cameroon. Eight respondents are from other African countries. At the time of the survey the average age of the respondents was forty-two, and the average length of residency in Houston was 13.4 years. More than half of the respondents are married. Several members were admitted into the United States through the 1990 Diversity Visa program. Most came to Houston because relatives or friends from the same village in Cameroon had already settled in Houston.

Ten of the respondents indicate they have a bachelors degree, eight a masters degree, and nine an associate degree. More than half work full time, with the lowest income being $12,000, while the highest is about eighty thousand dollars. It may be that some of those who arrived in the United States in recent years are still adjusting, which would explain the disparity in financial resources. Several members work part-time jobs, some as security attendants. Omega Church provides newcomers with groceries, assists some with their rent, and offers legal advice. The church also works with couples who are having marital problems. Members who do not earn a lot are encouraged to believe that God will bless them. When Dr. Awasum visits Houston, he speaks about prosperity, and using himself as an example, assures his audiences that God is ready to bless all believers.

The survey indicates that a few members travel to Africa (an expensive proposition) on a regular basis. Three go back every year, nine about once every five years. Many of the church members with family roots in the Moghamo English-speaking region in northwest Cameroon belong to the

Houston chapter of the Moghamo Association. Members organize graduations, weddings, and funerals. At these events they wear the brightly colored "Bamenda Gown." (Bamenda is the capital city of the North West Region of Cameroon.) They also have a cultural dance troop, complete with masked figures. The troop performed at the wedding of Pastor Victor Mbah and his wife Muriel, and for His Royal Highness, the Hon. Fon Angwafor of Mankon, during a visit to Houston.

Perspectives on Social Issues

The survey asked about social issues: gay rights, the use of condoms to prevent sexually transmitted diseases, a woman's right to end a pregnancy, interracial marriage, a patient's right to die, same-sex marriage, and the ordination of gay ministers.[45] Most respondents said they do not support gay rights; a handful was undecided. Pastor Mbah indicated that the church's stand on the gay lifestyle is based on the Apostle Paul's letter to the Romans, chapter 1. (The national Omega website includes an essay on sodomy.[46]) The general attitude among Cameroon immigrants is that homosexuality is a Western practice.

Omega members were also asked about the use of condoms to prevent sexually transmitted diseases (STD), especially, HIV/AIDS. Almost half agreed that condoms should be used to prevent STD, while a third opposed the use of condoms. One respondent who opposed the use of condoms is in the upper income bracket and works in the health professions. Another indicated that only married couples should use condoms.

Regarding interracial marriage, nearly two out of three approved, while one third disapproved. (There are Cameroonian women in Houston who have married Caucasians, though none in Omega Church.) Respondents were also asked if they supported the right of a woman to end a pregnancy, and whether a patient on life support should have the right to die. More than two thirds objected to the deliberate ending of a pregnancy; just four respondents supported a woman's right to end a pregnancy. One in four supported a patient's right to end life rather than remain on life support indefinitely.

---

45. Mojubaola Olufunke Okome of New York City has studied some of these concerns. See Daniels, "African Immigrant Churches."

46. Http://www.omegaministry.org/OT_January_2008_2.asp.

Perspectives on Political Issues

More than three quarters of the members of Omega Church voted for Obama in the 2008 election, according to Pastor Mbah. Their hope was that Obama as president would have some leverage on African politics, and that he would work with African leaders and get them to observe term limits. (Cameroon's Paul Biya, now in his late seventies, has been in power since 1968.)

The members of Omega Church certainly have not forgotten Cameroon. Respondents named churches in Cameroon, in the Democratic Republic of Congo, in Malawi, and in Zambia that Omega Church relates to. Some noted that Pastor Victor has traveled to Africa to preach and that Omega provides support for pastors in Africa to do evangelism. They maintain a modest missionary activity in Africa, working through some of the churches with whom they have established relations.

Cameroonians are very polarized on political questions. Some people in the diaspora support the government of President Paul Biya and have organized branches of the ruling party in some U.S. cities. The other parties in Cameroon, including the Social Democratic Front (a vocal opponent of Biya), also have supporters in the United States, many of whom live in Houston. In 2004, Omega church organized a seminar and prayer time for Cameroon and invited several speakers. The event was well attended, and many commented that it was a wonderful gathering because participants stopped talking politics and lifted up the country and its leaders in prayer.

For a long time scholars have viewed African pentecostal churches with jaundiced eyes because of well-known connections with overseas televangelists.[47] Too often the focus is on material prosperity to the neglect of religious life. Earlier studies of religious movements in Africa pointed out that the new indigenous groups used their rituals to deal with material poverty and political marginalization.[48] Some scholars regret the shift from black theology, theologies of liberation, and inculturation. Omega Gospel Ministries (the national body) and Omega Gospel Center in Houston do not fit any of these categories.

Asked to identify what they believed should be the priorities of the church in Africa, more than half named church unity as most important. Three topics tied at fifty percent: political reform, HIV/AIDS, and unemployment. Just under half of the respondents named world evangelization

---

47. Gifford, *African Christianity*.

48. Fields, *Revival and Rebellion*; Rangers, "Religious Movements and Politics," 1–69.

and elimination of poverty. (For unknown reasons, a third of the respondents failed to express themselves on this part of the questionnaire.)

IMPACT OF AFRICAN IMMIGRANT RELIGIONS

Immigrant Churches: Ethnic or International?

Are immigrant churches to be seen as ethnic churches, implying little impact on the adopted countries? The proliferation of studies in recent years typically speak of Nigerian Churches, Ghanaian Pentecostals, or African immigrant religions, suggesting that immigrant religious communities represent little more than ethnic religions.[49] Nevertheless, I contest the academic consensus, insofar as one speaks of the self-perception of African immigrants themselves.

While the religious groups in Houston are proud of their African heritage, many of them go out of their way to indicate that ethnicity is not their priority. Their identity as Christians takes priority, because all believers belong to the family of God. Even with Ethiopian Churches, one would be hard pressed to find members who claim that their churches cater only to their ethnic group. While some African immigrant churches sing songs in Yoruba and other African languages, they take their context seriously and do not merely want to perpetuate their ethnicity. African Independent (or Initiated) Churches and indigenous pentecostal congregations call attention to the founding of their churches in Africa, but they also emphasize the universal dimension of the Christian tradition. They see themselves as carrying the message of the Gospel, and proclaiming the healing power of Jesus to everyone, not merely Africans. Therefore, they do not label themselves "Nigerian" or "Cameroonian." Quite the contrary: Omega Gospel Mission, Redeemed Christian Church of God, Embassy of the Blessed Kingdom of God for All Nations, Aladera International Church; one could name multiple examples many times over. The places of their origin, or the fact that most of the members come from a particular region in Africa, is considered a historical accident. For now, though most immigrant congregations may be peopled by one nationality, members believe that they are called to preach to all nations, and in God's time, others will join.[50]

---

49. Ebaugh and Chafetz, *Religion and the New Immigrants*, 80.

50. I have argued elsewhere that African immigrant congregations do not advertise themselves as ethnic congregations. See Bongmba, "Portable Faith."

CONCLUSION

It is not clear how the role of the Omega Gospel Mission might change in the future. Some Cameroonians in Houston fault Omega and other immigrant churches at home and abroad for not providing strong leadership in a time of crisis. Back in Cameroon, where most members of Omega come from, Archbishop Paul Verdzekov of the Bamenda Archdiocese sent out pastoral letters to all Christians in the archdiocese urging them to exercise their civic responsibility and vote. The archdiocese also trained election observers. Cardinal Tumi of the Douala Archdiocese published memoirs in which he gave an account of his differences and struggles with the regimes of President Ahidjo and his successor, Paul Biya.[51] Cameroonian philosopher Fabien Eboussi Boulaga, in his magisterial work *Démocratie de transit au Cameroun*, offers a critique of the so-called democratic transition in Cameroon.[52] Still, to this day little change can be detected in the lives of Cameroonians under the long rule of Biya, reelected in 2011 for another seven-year term.

In the meantime, African immigrant churches continue to grow in the African diaspora, setting their own terms, agenda, and prioritizing their understanding of religion. In the 1960s, following the work of Peter Berger and the long misinterpretation of the work of German theologian Dietrich Bonhoeffer, many people were quick to talk of an increasing secularization of society in the countries of the Northern hemisphere. It is safe to argue now that there is a religious resurgence afoot. In part, this can be traced to African immigrants in the North. For it is the case that for many new immigrants, and perhaps especially for Africans, religious experience is central to their being-in-the-world, and their instincts call for a new internationalism based on the gospel of Jesus Christ.

BIBLIOGRAPHY

Adogame, Afeosemime. "Betwixt Identity and Security: African New Religious Movements and the Politics of Religious Networking in Europe." *Nova Religio: The Journal of Alternative and Emergent Religions* 7 (2003) 24–41.

———. "Engaging the Rhetoric of Spiritual Warfare: The Public Face of Aladura in the Diaspora." *Journal of Religion in Africa* 34 (2004) 493–522.

Adogame, Afeosemime, and Cordula Weissköppel. *Religion in the Context of African Migration*. Bayreuth African Studies Series. Bayreuth, Germany: Eckhard Breitinger, 2005.

---

51. Tumi, *Political Regimes*.
52. Boulaga, *Démocratie de transit au Cameroun*.

Asamoah-Gyadu, J. Kwabena. "An African Pentecostal on Mission in Eastern Europe: The Church of the Embassy of God in the Ukraine." *Pneuma: The Journal of Pentecostal Studies* 27 (2005) 297–321. Originally published in *Life and Death in the Power of the Tongue*, by Sunday Adelaja. Kiev: Fares, 2003.

Bongmba, Elias K. "Portable Faith: The Global Mission of African Initiated Churches." In *African Immigrant Religions in America*. Edited by Jacob K. Olupona and Regina Gemignani. New York: New York University Press, 2007.

Boulaga, Fabien Eboussi. *Démocratie de transit au Cameroun*. Paris: L'Harmattan, 1997.

D'Alisera, JoAnn. *An Imagined Geography: Sierra Leonean Muslims in America*. Philadelphia: University of Pennsylvania Press, 2004.

Daniels, David. "African Immigrant Churches in the United States and the Study of Black Church History." In *African Immigrant Religions in America*, edited by Jacob K. Olupona and Regina Gemignani, 47–60. New York: New York University Press, 2007.

Ebaugh, H., and J. Chafetz, editors. *Religion and the New Immigrants: Continuities and Adaptations in Immigrant Congregations*. Walnut Creek, CA: Alta Mira, 2000.

Fields, Karen. *Revival and Rebellion in Colonial Central Africa*. Princeton: Princeton University Press, 1998.

Fong, Timothy P. *The Contemporary Asian American Experience: Beyond the Model Minority*. Upper Saddle River, NJ: Prentice Hall, 2004.

Geertz, Clifford. *The Interpretation of Cultures: Selected Essays*. New York: Basic Books, 1973.

Gerloff, Roswith. "The Significance of the African Christian Diaspora in Europe: A Report on Four Meetings in 1997–78." *Journal of Religion in Africa* 29 (1999) 115–20.

Gifford, Paul. *African Christianity: Its Public Role*. Bloomington: Indiana University Press, 1998.

———. *Ghana's New Christianity: Pentecostalism in a Globalizing African Economy*. Bloomington: Indiana University Press, 2004.

Haar, Gerrie ter, editor. *Religious Communities in the Diaspora*. Nairobi: Action, 2001.

———. *Imagining Evil: Witchcraft Accusations in Contemporary Africa*. Trenton, NJ: Africa World Press, 2007.

Harris, Hermione. *Yoruba in Diaspora: An African Church in London*. New York: Palgrave Macmillan, 2006.

Jenkins, Philip. *The Next Christendom: The Coming of Global Christianity*. New York: Oxford University Press, 2002.

Kurien, Prema. "Constructing 'Indianness' in Southern California: The Role of Hindu and Muslim Indian Immigrants." In *Asian and Latino Immigrants in a Restructuring Economy: The Metamorphosis of Southern California*, edited by Marta Lopez-Garza and David Diatz, 289–312. Stanford: Stanford University Press, 2001.

Olupona, Jacob K., and Regina Gemignani, editors. *African Immigrant Religions in America*. New York: New York University Press, 2007.

Opoku-Dapaah, Edward. "Ghanaian Sects in the United States of America and Their Adherents within the Framework of Migration Challenges Since the 1970s." *African and Asian Studies* 5 (2006) 231–53.

Rangers, Terence. "Religious Movements and Politics in Sub-Saharan Africa." *African Studies Review* 29 (1986) 1–69.

Stoller, Paul. *Money Has No Smell: The Africanization of New York City*. Chicago: University of Chicago Press, 2002.

Terrazas, Aaron. "African Immigrants in the United States." Migration Policy Institute, 2009. Online: http://www.migrationinformation.org/USfocus/display.cfm?id=719.

Tumi, Christian Wiyghan. *The Political Regimes of Ahmadou Ahidjo, and Paul Biya, and Christian Tumi, Priest*. Douala, Cameroon: MACACOS, 2006.

United States Census Bureau. *The Foreign-Born Population: 2000*. Census 2000 brief. December 2003.

United States Department of Justice. *2000 Statistical Yearbook of the Immigration and Naturalization Service*. September 2002.

Welbourn, B. A., and F. B. Ogot. *A Place to Feel at Home: A Study of Two Independent Churches in Western Kenya*. London: Oxford University Press, 1966.

5

"Go Ye into All the West"
Models of Mission among Ghanaian Methodists in the Diaspora

CASELY B. ESSAMUAH

My association with Tite Tiénou goes back to the days of my doctoral studies. My adviser recommended that I take a course taught by Tiénou on the topic of ethnicity.[1] I came away with fresh confidence that I need not allow myself to be given a mono-cultural identity.

Previously, I knew Tiénou from his writings about African Christianity. He struck me as one who embraced everything with a degree of critical self-awareness. If you were to hear only one of his addresses, you might come away thinking he was anti-Western, or anti-evangelical, or overly critical of African Christianity. But a closer examination reveals that his goal is for all followers of Jesus Christ to subsume all other loyalties—including ethnicity—under the most significant loyalty of all, loyalty to Jesus Christ in the global village.

For expanding the boundaries of my self-identity, for encouraging me to see the supremacy of my Christian identity as trumping all other identities, I offer this overview of the Ghanaian Methodist diaspora in honor of Tite Tiénou. As Mother Teresa defined herself—"born in Albania, a national of India, and a citizen of the global kingdom of Jesus Christ, by blood, the

---

1. Tiénou, "Ethnicity as Gift and Barrier."

blood of the Lamb"—I too identify myself: born in Ghana, a national of the United States, and a global citizen of the kingdom of God, by blood, the blood of the Lamb.

We begin with the phenomenon of Ghanaian migration from the motherland. So significant is the diaspora that it has been dubbed the eleventh region of the nation.[2] Then we examine the Methodist diaspora in particular, exploring the challenges Ghanaian Methodists navigate in their adopted countries. After treating the Ghanaian Methodists in the United Kingdom, we turn to three European Ghanaian Methodist communities. Finally, this essay examines Ghanaian Methodists in North America, where various loyalties rooted in the homeland communities are evident. Navigating these loyalties has produced differing models of mission.

GHANAIAN MIGRATION

Ghanaian Methodism was born in 1835 out of a desire of local Ghanaian Christians for Bibles. The Wesleyan Methodist Missionary Society responded, sending Rev. Joseph R. Dunwell as its first representative. Today, Methodist Church Ghana (MCG) is one of the largest Methodist churches in the world, numbering more than a million members. The MCG maintains a very strong relationship with the British Methodist Conference, including reciprocal fraternal representation to each other's conferences.[3]

Over the last 50 to 60 years, Ghanaian Methodists have been caught up in several waves of migration. Today, in addition to 25 million Ghanaians in the homeland, it is estimated that as many as four million live outside Ghana. Six years ago Papa Owusu Ankomah, Ghana's Minister of the Interior, and a very active Methodist, cited an International Monetary Fund (IMF) report and noted that 25 percent of Ghanaian professionals with tertiary education had emigrated to North America and Europe.[4] Statistics from IMF indicate that since 2004 the remittances that Ghanaians abroad send home have outstripped all overseas development assistance. The Central Bank of Ghana reports that the monetary inflow from Ghanaian migrants in 2009 amounted to $1.6 billion; in 2010 the amount jumped to $2.12 billion.[5] These days the Ghanaian diaspora is known as "brain circulation" or "brain gain," no longer "brain drain" or "brain waste."[6]

2. Manuh, *An 11th Region of Ghana?*
3. An estimated 10 percent of all Methodists in the greater London metropolitan area belong to the Ghanaian community. LaCamera, "Ghanaians Find Home," n.p.
4. Owusu-Ankomah, "Emigration from Ghana."
5. Dogbevi, "Remittances from Ghanaians Abroad."
6. Zeleza, *Barack Obama and African Diasporas*, 115.

The Ghanaian diaspora retains an on-going commitment to the motherland,[7] including financial support of the socio-political and developmental agenda of the country. Whether the remittances are motivated by "altruism, self-interest, the need to repay the family and social debts of their upbringing, for co-insurance purposes against future risks, or out of plain abandonment guilt which they seek to assuage by maintaining connections," such support represents a huge commitment to their country of birth.[8]

Between 1981 and 1995, 14,000 Ghanaian teachers left the homeland to teach elsewhere. Micah Bump of Georgetown University's Institute for the Study of International Migration, reports that between 1995 and 2002, 69 percent of Ghana's medical doctors worked outside the country; this included 1,200 in the United States, 300 in the United Kingdom, and 300 in Germany.[9] In the field of health care generally, 23 percent of Ghana's health care professionals, including dentists, pharmacists, and nurses, left to work elsewhere. Factors typically cited for leaving Ghana include low salaries, limited career prospects, and poor management of the nation's health system.[10]

THREE WAVES OF GHANAIAN MIGRATION

In the course of a generation there have been three waves of migration from Ghana.[11] These can be associated with colonialism, post-colonial upheaval, and economic policies mandated in the 1980s. The first wave, in the 1950s and '60s, mostly involved scholars sent overseas by the government to be trained for leadership in Ghana. However, quite a number did not return when the nation went through a spate of coups d'état and military interventions. The second wave was linked to the political instability that the military interventions engendered. But by far the most significant wave began in the mid-1980s with the introduction of the Structural Adjustment Policy, an economic program required by the World Bank, International Monetary Fund, and Western countries as a condition of aid. This involved removing subsidies on essential commodities, including food, which greatly increased poverty and hardship.

Initially, a majority of migrants settled in neighboring Cote d'Ivoire and Nigeria. At the time, Nigeria was benefitting from the second decade

---

7. Ghana is one of three African countries that grant dual citizenship status to its nationals living abroad. The other two are Egypt and South Africa.
8. Zeleza, *Barack Obama and African Diasporas*, 120.
9. Owusu-Ankomah, "Emigration from Ghana."
10. Bump, "Ghana: Searching." Bump has been a widely used source for this essay.
11. Tonah, "Ghanaians Abroad."

of its oil boom. But as the economic climate worsened in each country, the Ghanaian immigrant community was made a scapegoat and was forced to return to Ghana. Many of these returnees subsequently became part of the third wave to Europe and North America.

EUROPE AND NORTH AMERICA

The desire to acquire further education and be gainfully employed characterized the third wave. The fact that the educational institutions in Ghana train more than the workforce is able to employ makes foreign employment more than an option; it is potentially the only way out of poverty. It is said that every nuclear family has a sibling, parent, child, or close relative living outside Ghana. The third wave included many young people, women, and unskilled workers. It is particularly this third wave, which may have involved as many as two million people (when Ghana's population was no more than 15 million), that created a significant and visible Ghanaian community in some of the major cities of Western Europe and North America.

> **GMF Mission Statement**
> The Ghanaian Methodist Fellowship U.K. aims to heed the calling of the universal Christian Church to respond to the gospel of God's love in Jesus Christ and to live out its discipleship in worship and mission through the various Ghanaian languages; and will seek to help its members to grow and learn in harmony as Christians in the traditional Ghanaian hospitality by caring and supporting one another spiritually and materially, and also, evangelize more people and make them followers of Jesus Christ—irrespective of race, gender or age—and being good neighbors to all manner of people especially those in need. (gmf-uk.org)
>
> **Vision Statement**
> The Fellowship will encourage and ensure that all members are enabled and supported to discern and fulfill their calling by their continuity of witness and to take a spiritual journey to discover the relevance of the Bible in their personal lives and thus aspire to either train as Ministers, Local Preachers, Prayer Secretaries, Worship Leaders, Church Stewards, Choristers or Junior Church Teachers—as well as contributing in any other way to influence and transform the thinking and life of their local church and community. "We come as young and old from every church, bringing all our treasuries of prayer, to join the dynamic spirit's search to press beyond the truth we share. We bring our traditions' richest store our hymns and rites and cherished creeds in anticipation that strife and bigotry shall cease and faith be lost in praise and sight" (Richard G. Jones, Hymns & Praise, 765).

GHANAIAN METHODISTS IN THE UNITED KINGDOM

Due to colonial ties, for many decades the United Kingdom has been the destination of choice for Ghanaian emigrants. Ghanaians represent one of the U.K.'s longest and largest African migrant communities. Much growth throughout the 1990s and early 2000s resulted from the granting of student visas, work permits, and refugee status. In 1991 England and Wales welcomed 32,277. In 2001 the figure was 55,537. In 1998 the U.K. enacted the National Health Plan, which involved the recruitment of foreign healthcare workers. As of 2003, 2,468 Ghanaian nurses had applied for "verification," the step prior to obtaining visas.[12] It is fair to estimate that the numbers have at least doubled in the last decade.

GHANAIAN METHODIST FELLOWSHIP

One of the earliest Ghanaian Methodist communities in the United Kingdom is that of the Ghanaian Methodist Fellowship (GMF), recognized as an organization within the British Methodist Conference. This began in the mid-1970s as a fellowship of Ghanaian immigrants in London. GMF literature states categorically that the Fellowship is "not a Church and there is no intention of making it one."[13] Drawing from all the Methodist churches in and around London, the fellowship consists entirely of Ghanaian immigrants. Even as its members adjust to the cultural and social worldview of their adopted country, the GMF gatherings provide participants opportunity to express their faith in their own heart language and culture.[14] Today there are GMF groups in several other English cities and in Scotland.

The GMF aspires to be a symbol of "reverse missions," Christian immigrants from lands formerly the focus of Western missions, now serving as Christian witnesses in their adopted nations. Christians from Ghana now not only worship in their adopted countries with people of like faith but also with the intention of reaching out beyond their ethnic circles.

GMF groups formed in the 1980s in the Walworth Road Methodist Church (Clubland), Bermondsey Methodist Church, Brixton Hill Methodist Church, Upper Tooting Methodist Church, and in other neighborhoods in the London area. As the 1990s ended, a Ghanaian Methodist minister in the U.K., Rev. Dr. Hayford Adu-Darkwa, was appointed overseer of GMF,

---

12. Ibid.
13. Ghanaian Methodist Fellowship U.K., online: gmf-uk.org.
14. Ibid.

and thus a chaplaincy program was born. Beginning at Walworth, the chaplaincy program has steadily extended to other GMF groups.

One of the most active organizations of the Ghanaian Methodist fellowship of the U.K. is the Susanna Wesley Mission Auxiliary (SUWMA). Named after the mother of John and Charles Wesley, SUWMA seeks to gather all women in the GMF and "inculcate in them the spirit of holiness and godly living, both at home, in the Church and in society." The women of SUWMA help educate younger women and the illiterate, assist in the training of ministers, provide cleaning for the houses of worship, serve refreshments, visit the imprisoned, the aged, the destitute, conduct pre-marital, marital, and career counseling, address poverty and crime, and, as if these objectives were not enough, seek to win souls and build the body of Christ.[15]

Alongside efforts to integrate Ghanaian immigrants with their British brothers and sisters, fellowships of Ghanaians are also thriving. The lingering separation is surely explained by factors unique to Ghanaian Methodism: The love of *Ebibindwom* (Ghanaian Methodist sacred lyrics), the exuberance of worship, the participation of all involved, and preaching that prioritizes application over dogma.[16] Until a decade ago, Ghanaian Methodists used for their liturgy the 1933 Book of Service, long discarded by the original British publishers. The Ghanaian use of canticles as part of regular Sunday worship is also a sine qua non of their identity.

GHANAIAN METHODISTS IN EUROPE

The Netherlands

Analysts of elections in Ghana, in 2003, were amazed to find that almost 40,000 people of Ghanaian descent, who were living in the Netherlands, registered to vote in the Ghana elections of that year. Previously there was information on only 18,000 living in the Netherlands.[17]

In the early part of 1997, a few Ghanaian Methodists worshiped in a predominantly Caribbean Methodist church in Amsterdam, in the western part of the city. The British pastor, who had served as a missionary in Ghana, missed the exuberant worship of Ghanaian Methodism. Two Ghanaians, Samuel Amankwah and Nana Kwame Arhin, who were visiting the church,

---

15. A tongue-in-cheek review is provided by Prof. Mattia Fumanti of St. Andrews University: "A Light-Hearted Bunch of Ladies." Fumanti spotlights excessive materialism and showmanship as the women go about their church and social activities.

16. Essamuah, *Genuinely Ghanaian*.

17. Bump, "Ghana: Searching," 5.

were inspired by the pastor to reach out to their fellow Ghanaians. Soon a worship place was found in the Bijlmermeer area of Amsterdam, in the southeast of the city. A local Ghanaian radio station brought the church to the attention of a wider public, and the first service was held on September 21, 1997, conducted by one of the accredited lay preachers from Ghana.

Over time, three other Ghanaian Methodist churches were established: in The Hague in 1998, in Rotterdam in 2002, and in Antwerp, Belgium, in 2011. In June 2000, the Presiding Bishop of the MCG, the Most Reverend Samuel Asante-Antwi, on a visit to the Netherlands, inaugurated the Methodist societies of The Hague and Amsterdam. In the same year Rev. Isaac S. Amoah was appointed as the first full-time Superintendent Minister of the Holland Mission Circuit.[18] Unlike the Ghanaian Methodists in the U.K., who formally relate as members of the U.K. Methodist Conference, the Ghanaian Methodists in the Netherlands view themselves as being directly linked to the MCG.

Germany

Ghanaian Methodists in Germany serve under the United Methodist Church (UMC), USA. It is estimated that by the end of 2004, 20,000 Ghanaian passport holders resided in Germany; they were the third largest African immigrant community after Moroccans and Tunisians.[19] Again, after almost a decade, one can expect a significantly larger number of Ghanaians in Germany.

In 1988, the U.S. UMC conference approved a pilot project with the UMC conference in Germany to meet the needs of the non-German speaking immigrant community. Initial leaders were bishops Hermann Sticher and Walter Klaiber; they were succeeded by Bishop Rosemarie Wenner. Over time, this ministry has been enlarged to meet the needs of all immigrants, not only those from the U.S. and the U.K.. Several Ghanaian ministers have served these churches, including John Ekem (while a student in Germany), Isaac Amoah (already mentioned in regard to the Netherlands), Kwasi Owusu-Acheaw, Clarence Antwi-Bosiako, Bishop Albert Ofoe Wright, Jane Odoom, Conrad Roberts (Berlin and Hamburg),

---

18. Prior to this, Amoah, a graduate of Trinity Theological Seminary in Legon, Ghana, had served for five years as pastor of the Ghanaian United Methodist Church of Hamburg, Germany. Under his ministry, the Hamburg church grew to almost 500 Ghanaian adults and children. He also assisted in developing a UMC Ghanaian congregation in Düsseldorf.

19. Bump, "Ghana: Searching," 5.

and Frederick Gyamfi Mensah. The latter serves Ghanaian congregations in Frankfurt and Stuttgart. In their communications, these two churches inform visitors that the congregation worships in the Ghanaian languages, and "sometimes in English." Furthermore, "we blend the Wesleyan tradition (orderly and methodical way of worship), with drumming and dancing."

Although Ghanaian expatriates constitute large numbers in Germany, the language barrier has forced them to affiliate with other English-speaking expatriates; hence, their mission model entails serving under the UMC of the United States.

Italy

The Ghanaian population in Italy grew from 11,443 in 1990 to 32,754 in 2003.[20] While Ghanaian Methodists in the Netherlands and Germany formed their own communities of faith, the practice of Ghanaian Methodists in Italy has been to integrate into the Waldensian-Methodist family. The success of this mission model of integration is attested by the fact that the Methodist Church of Italy has Richard Kofi Ampofo as its vice president. Ampofo was a delegate at the August 2010 World Methodist Conference in Durban, South Africa. Four years ago, two 4-wheel-drive pick-up trucks were donated by the Italian Waldensian-Methodist Church to the MCG.

In March 1989, the Italian Methodist church in Milan decided that its mission priority was to offer hospitality to the stranger and "to be the church together." Beginning with a small core of people from Ghana, Côte d'Ivoire, the Philippines, Korea, the United States, Japan, and Italy, the group now has more than 200 members, representing 18 countries. The foreign and Italian communities form one congregation, offering both Italian and bilingual worship, Christian education, and other ministries and activities. The Reverends George Ennin and Dennis Buadu currently serve the larger Christian community, with particular responsibility for the oversight of the Ghanaian members.

A similar program was launched in the Methodist church in Parma Mezzano in 2000, under the initiative of Rev. Maximum Aquilante. Aquilante was followed in mid-2000 by Rev. Sergio Ribert. Ribert describes the church's purpose as "strengthening the relationships of integration, brotherhood, and cooperation with immigrant evangelicals." He believes the official database of the immigrant population is unreliable. Instead of 100,000, he puts the numbers between 250,000 and 300,000. He points out that the integration of evangelical immigrants will make the Italian Protestant church

20. Ibid.

more diverse and increase the number of active Protestants in Italy. He concludes, "An all-white church that excludes immigrants denies itself and is no longer a church but a cult." What is at stake is "the very nature of the church."[21]

In a predominantly Catholic Italy, Ghanaian Methodists have strategically integrated into the established Protestant church.

GHANAIAN METHODISTS IN NORTH AMERICA: CANADA

According to the Canadian census, 16,985 Ghanaians were living in Canada in 2001. In the decade ending in 2004, the annual increase was almost 1,000 per year, which suggests now, nine years later, the Ghanaian diaspora in Canada may be approaching 30,000.

The initiative for starting the first Ghanaian Methodist church in Canada came from Agnes Summers. In Ghana she had been an active member of her hometown Methodist church. In Toronto, Ontario, she became well known in the Ghanaian immigrant community as the proprietor of a chain of shops marketing Ghanaian groceries and other goods. Thus, she was well placed to become the catalyst for the establishment of an immigrant church. Her initiative brought together fourteen men and women and their children. The first service was held May 1, 1994. It was led by Rev. Dr. Charles K. Cofie, a Ghanaian Methodist pastor studying in Toronto.

The group's first gathering took place in the basement of the Summers home. It was quickly realized that greater space was needed. Inability to agree on a new location brought about division. The majority chose the name Ghana Calvary Methodist Church as their name. In 1996, a Ghanaian Methodist minister, Rev. Kwaku Abakah, on a visit to Canada, assisted the two groups as they grew. In 1997, The Most Reverend Prof. Emeritus Kwesi A. Dickson delegated a three-member committee to find a solution to the impasse between the two groups. A reconciliation service took place at Toronto's Westminster United Church, Sunday, May 25, 1997.[22]

---

21. Information from correspondence with Dennis Buadu, April 2012. I am indebted to Buadu for translating the papers from Italian into English. For a theological reflection on this mission model of integration in Italy and the role of Ghanaian Methodists, see Passarelli, "Between Past and Future," 100–119.

22. The original group, Ghana Methodist Church, Toronto, has had the following as ministers: Dr. Kwasi Kwakye-Nuako, Rev. Helena Opoku-Sarkodie, Rev. Emmanuel K. Ofori, Rev. Samuel O. Agyapong, Jacob French. The current minister is Dr. Emmanuel K. Asare-Kusi.

But it was not to last. The members of Ghana Calvary Methodist Church continued to meet separately. When the MCG leadership in Ghana was unable to effect reconciliation, the members of Calvary were advised to seek affiliation with the United Church of Canada, under the UCC's Ethnic Ministries Council. This was accomplished in January 1998.

Calvary's search for a permanent building was initiated by the Reverend Emmanuel K. Ofori between 2001 and 2004. In June 2010 the campus of the Beverly Hills United Church of Toronto was donated to the church.[23]

In 2004, on a visit to Canada, another reconciliation effort was undertaken by MCG's presiding bishop, Rev. Dr. Aboagye-Mensah and the lay president, Atto Essuman. As a result of this and other efforts, the Ghanaian Methodists in Canada have a more amicable relationship than their counterparts in the United States. For instance, those in Toronto hold joint services for the Easter season. There is frequent exchange of pulpits and a viable working relationship that cuts across their MCG and UCC denominational affiliation. Thus, Ghanaian Methodists in Canada operate under two mission models of affiliation, MCG and UCC.

GHANAIAN METHODISTS IN NORTH AMERICA: THE UNITED STATES

Economic and political factors in their homeland have helped propel Ghanaians to North America. But in the case of the United States, a change in immigration policy also played a major role. The government's 1965 Immigration and Nationality Act opened the door for people of non-European stock.[24]

In the United States the Ghanaian population is reported to have jumped from 20,889 in 1990 to 65,570 in 2000, an increase of 210 percent. Some observers believe that, today, the total Ghanaian population in the United States could be as high as 300,000.[25] Permanent residents are al-

---

23. Following Ofori, the Reverends Maclean Kumi, Peter Yaw Acheampong, and DeGraft S. Obiri have served as Calvary's ministers. The author is indebted to Rev. Obiri for information on the Canadian churches. Obiri has compiled the information in a yet-to-be-published manuscript, "Methodism in Ghana and Her Missions Abroad: Some Services and Contributions."

24. This law abolished quotas based on national origins, which had greatly limited the number of immigrants from Africa. The new law treats all countries alike, with no more than 20,000 individuals allowed from any one country. A series of preferences is followed: First, relatives of U.S. citizens and permanent resident aliens; then professionals, scientists, artists, and those needed where workers are in short supply.

25. Bump, "Ghana: Searching," 5.

lowed to sponsor spouses, dependent children and, in some instances, even parents. As impressive as these figures are, in both Canada and the United States one must also take into account the thousands of Ghanaians who visit as tourists or students but are unable to convert their visa status into permanent residency. Many remain as illegal immigrants.

What makes North America so attractive to Ghanaian emigrants? Two factors: the vast contiguous continent provides many options for settling down; and the possibilities for gainful employment are enormous compared to other destinations in the diaspora. The media and culture of the United States are more widely known in Africa than any other outside influence. As a former British colony, Ghana also shares linguistic affinity with Canada and the United States.

Why Not Affiliate with Methodists in the USA?

Given the close ties between the UMC of the United States and the British Methodist Conference (the parent church of MCG), one might assume that Ghanaian Methodists would have found in the UMC a cordial family environment. But about half of the Ghanaian churches in the United States have kept their association with the homeland denomination to the exclusion of relating to the UMC.

Quite apart from the Methodist diaspora, the UMC appears to be at risk of losing the next generation, a reality conceded in UMC publications. In 1968, the church had a membership of 10,754,973. In 2009, the figure was 7,679,850, a decrease of 29 percent. Furthermore, while the average American is thirty-five years of age, the average UMC member is 57.[26]

The potential for integration with the predominantly African-American churches of Methodist persuasion is also limited. Paul Tiyambe Zeleza argues forcefully,

> Antagonism is engendered by stereotypes and poor communication on both sides. Several studies have recorded the negative stereotypes the two groups hold about each other. African-American stereotypes evoke negative bodily images, whereas African stereotypes of African Americans evoke negative behavioral images. The bodies of African blacks are despised for their color and alleged ugliness, while African Americans are detested for their alleged propensity to violence and criminality. African Americans blame Africans for having sold them into

26. *UM Connection* 22, June 8, 2011. *UM Connection* is published by the Baltimore-Washington Conference of the United Methodist.

slavery and see them as embodiments of cultural and economic backwardness, while Africans accuse African Americans of laziness and not taking advantage of their country's enormous resources. And both sides sometimes see each other as arrogant.[27]

As a result, the North American Ghanaian Methodist diaspora has followed different models of mission.

GHANIAN CHURCH INITIATIVES

The Reverend Jacob Owusu Sarfo, a Ghanaian Methodist minister, while studying in the New York area, initiated the first MCG church in the United States in 1985: Ghana United Methodist Church, Bronx, New York. While visiting the various ethnic associations in New York, he collected 62 names of potential members.[28] The first meeting was held at the Salem Methodist Church in Harlem on January 4, 1986. The Reverend Dr. Samuel Akesson co-officiated with Sarfo. The objectives set out by this New York-based MCG were as follows: Worship in the language and style unique to Ghanaian Methodists; offer assistance to members in times of difficulty; and offer financial support to the mother church, i.e., MCG in Ghana. (All churches springing from MCG in the diaspora follow similar objectives.) The formal inauguration, held April 17, 1988, was led by the late Reverend Dr. Bassaw (deputizing for the late Reverend Dr. Jacob S. A. Stephens). Later on, the late Reverend Prof. Kwesi A. Dickson encouraged the church to seek affiliation with the UMC, which was accomplished in June 1993.[29] Soon after the formal inauguration of the Bronx church, a group of members formed another MCG branch, Ghana United Methodist Church, in Brooklyn. Like its mother church, it is also under the UMC. The Reverend Dr. Samuel Acquah-Arhin serves as its pastor.[30]

While these two New York Ghanaian-majority UMC churches operate under the U.S. UMC, the first congregations in the Washington, D.C.—Virginia area provide an alternative pattern of diaspora Ghanaian Methodist

---

27. Zeleza, *Barack Obama and African Diasporas*, 108.

28. Ghanaians in the diaspora have ethnic associations linked to particular ethnic groups. The most popular ones are the Asanteman, Okuapeman, Akan, and Okyeman.

29. In addition to founding pastor Jacob Sarfo (1986–98), the following have served as ministers: Issac K. Buamah (Dec. 1998–June 2000); Dr. Samuel Q. E. Ghartey (Jan. 2001–April 2002); Ebenezer K. Dadson (Aug. 2002–June 2006); Dr. Victor E. Acquaah-Harrison (July 2006–2010), and the current minister, Rev. Samuel Edubate Nketsia.

30. For more details on the founding of the Brooklyn church, see Essamuah, *Genuinely Ghanaian*, 50–54.

churches in North America. Ebenezer Methodist Church, Hyattsville, Maryland, is the mother-church of the Ghanaian Methodist congregations in the D.C. beltway. The church was launched May 17, 1992, the result of the vision of Rev. Dr. Joseph Kow Ghunney, who served as the first pastor (now in Ghana serving as bishop of the Winneba diocese), Mrs. Cecilia Ghunney, Dr. Kofi Abruquah, and the late Dr. Joseph Kofi Attah. These four expressed "unflinching determination" to strictly adhere to Ghanaian Methodist liturgy. Initially, the congregation met at the First United Methodist Church (1993–97) and subsequently in the annex building of the National Wesleyan Church, both being Hyattsville UMC churches. Kwesi Dickson, when serving as president of the Methodist Church Ghana, officially inaugurated the church on June 11, 1995. Over a period of almost two decades, the church has experienced several rifts as the Ghana homeland church posted or removed ten different pastors. The current pastor is Bishop Benjamin K. Asare, who is playing a key role in dealing with tensions among North American Ghanaian churches. (See "Conclusion.")

Within the church's first decade, Ebenezer members initiated three other Ghana Methodist congregations, two in the wider D.C. area—the Gaddiel R. Acquaah Memorial Ghana Methodist Church, Alexandria, Virginia, and Calvary Redeeming Ghana Methodist Church, Rockville, Maryland (meeting at the Millian Memorial UMC)—and the third, in Baltimore, Maryland, St. Paul's Ghana United Methodist Church.

The establishment of Calvary Redeeming Methodist Church came about after two, three-week periods of prayer and fasting by Rev. Dr. John Bonful, a member of Ebenezer. He felt a calling from God to start another church; it held its inaugural service on May 7, 1997.

St. Paul's, the third church with ties to Ebenezer, held its first service on September 16, 2001, a few days after the tragic events of 9/11. An unpublished history of the origins of the church states that the first members wanted a place to "worship in the way that we have been brought up." After meeting at the St. Andrews Episcopal Church for two years, the church now worships at the Loch Raven United Methodist Church of Baltimore. The team that established the church, Joseph and Christiana Blankson, and Kwame and Victoria Asafu-Adjei, has been joined recently by an elected seven-member leadership team. (The author serves this church in a part-time capacity.)

Ebenezer and its three daughter churches have made significant contributions in cash and kind to the newly established Methodist University College of Ghana, to the hometown churches from which the diaspora leaders have come, and to the home office of the MCG.

In September 1998, Rev. Kofi Bart-Martin, with the counsel of Kofi Abruquah, initiated the formation of the Association of Ghana Methodist Churches of North America. Another important advance that took place in 1998 was the formation of the Association of Ghana Methodist Church Choirs of North America. This was initiated by the church choir of Ebenezer in conjunction with Ghana United Methodist Church Choir of Bronx, New York, the Ghana Community Church Choir of Atlanta, Georgia, and Ghana Methodist Church Choir of Toronto, Ontario.

The MCG churches in the United States have pursued three different mission models, involving affiliation with MCG or UMC, or simply operating as independent churches. Regrettably, acrimonious situations have occurred.

DIVISION WITHIN THE DIASPORA

The early 1990s saw the formal adoption of a covenant designed to create healthy relationships between the MCG-related churches and the UMC-related churches. The preamble begins,

> We seek to engage in covenant with other Christian churches wherever more visible Christian unity can increase effective mission in the modern world. This covenant is a symbol of the search for deeper relationships with churches that are part of the whole Covenant people of God . . . It is aimed at encouraging a new sense of global common cause, mutual support, mutual spiritual growth, common study of scripture and culture, creative interaction as ministers in the mission of God's Church, cross-fertilization of ideas about ways to be in that mission, sharing of resources, and exploring new forms of service directed at old and emerging needs.

But the central issue persisted, at least from the side of the MCG-related churches. Should they be members of the UMC, or should they continue to identify only with MCG? And from the perspective of MCG in the homeland, from the very outset it viewed its diaspora churches as a form of mission outreach, with congregations responsible to the homeland church.

Today, congregational practice continues to vary. Some churches formally affiliate with the United Methodist Church in the United States or the United Church of Canada. But the majority choose to remain with the MCG. There are also congregations that choose to remain independent of any denominational connection, even though they maintain "Ghana Methodist" in their name.

Attempts to Overcome Division

In response to calls for direction from the Ghana Conference, in May 2004 the Most Reverend Dr. Robert Aboagye-Mensah, who had been appointed presiding bishop the year before, attended a meeting of Ghanaian Methodist church leaders in North America. As a response to conflicted input at that gathering, he charged the Right Reverend Ebenezer K. Dadson, Rev. Professor Emmanuel Lartey, and Rev. Dr. J. Kwabena Asamoah-Gyadu to assess the situation and suggest a way forward.[31] In its June 2004 report, the committee concluded that, if nurtured well, Ghanaian Methodist congregations, whatever their affiliation, could become significant extensions of MCG's mission. But they also noted that many Ghanaian Methodist congregations had been "fraught with problems ranging from conflicts regarding proper modes of Ghanaian Methodist worship, unstable pastoral leadership, difficulties with financial management, church discipline, power struggles, definitions and meanings of affiliations and related issues of governance and control."[32]

The committee noted two key questions: 1) Are Ghanaian Methodist churches extensions of MCG or should they affiliate with UMC? 2) Must pastors be ordained by MCG, or can they study abroad and be ordained elsewhere? The report concluded by highlighting the benefits of UMC affiliation: UMC facilitates the immigration process for ministers coming from Ghana; provides good salaries, housing, pension plans; helps in litigation issues; and aids the education of the children of pastors.

Dissension continued. In May 2007, at a general meeting of Ghanaian Methodist churches, Rev. Lartey emphasized the ecumenical spirit of John Wesley and world Methodism. He characterized Ghanaian Methodist churches in North America as in a critical state, poised between great opportunity and grave danger. He characterized the situation in familiar words: *To be or not to be?* Should Ghanaian churches identify or should they not identify with the church of their adopted land? As someone who benefitted from his own upbringing in an ecumenical setting, Lartey argued for

---

31. Dadson, committee chairman, was serving as minister of Ghana United Methodist Church, Bronx, New York (retired 2010); Lartey was Professor of Pastoral Theology, Care and Counseling, Candler School of Theology, Emory University, Atlanta, Georgia, a position he continues to hold; Asamoah-Gyadu, secretary-recorder of the committee, is professor of Contemporary African Christianity and Pentecostal Theology at Trinity Theological Seminary, Legon, Accra. In 2004 he was serving as senior research fellow at Harvard University Center for the Study of World Religions.

32. "Report of Committee Established to Advise on Ghanaian Methodist Congregations in North America and Canada," report submitted to General Purposes Council, Ghana. A copy is in author's possession.

a system that took into account all people of Christian faith.[33] He also called for a creative blending of Ghanaian Methodist worship, including both the inherited 1933 order of service and the praise and worship style that had come from Ghanaian Pentecostal churches. Finally he asked whether churches are planted "to meet the needs of . . . neighborhoods and locations without the services of a church, or to serve the interests of particular ministers and lay leaders? Too often churches split and new churches are formed to provide support and employment for persons rather than to spread the gospel of Christ. Whilst it is a thing of joy when the gospel is spread, it is a matter of sadness and shame when the motivation for the establishment of a church is selfish gain."[34]

Lartey's presentation reverberated as far as the Ghanaweb, Ghana's leading internet news source. In the ensuing response, many people took opposing sides, arguing for affiliation with UMC or solely with MCG.

At an expanded General Purposes Council of MCG in Ghana, in June 2007, it was resolved that all Ghanaian Methodist churches in North America should "function under the auspices of the Methodist Conferences in their host countries."[35] This policy directive didn't go down well with the congregations that had argued all along for Ghanaian churches in the United States to maintain exclusive affiliation with MCG.

Probably no Ghanaian congregation has devoted as much attention to the issue as Ghana Wesley United Methodist Church, Arlington, Virginia. Prof. Albert M. Wright, the church's longtime "caretaker,"[36] has written at length on the subject of affiliation.[37] As Wright notes, prior to the establishment of Ghanaian churches in North America, Ghanaians attended U.S. or Canadian churches or none at all. With the establishment of Ghanaian congregations, some worshipers maintained dual membership, worshiping in U.S. churches in the mornings and Ghanaian Methodist churches in the afternoons.[38] Wright, in documents prepared for the leadership meetings

33. Lartey grew up as a Methodist member of Ridge Church, Accra, Ghana's foremost ecumenical church, comprised of Methodists, Presbyterians, Anglicans, and others.

34. Emmanuel Lartey, "Conversation on the State of the Work of God in the Ghanaian Methodist churches in North America," April 14, 2007, 4. Circulation of this and other papers was limited to local Ghanaian churches.

35. Aboagye-Mensah, "Pastoral Letter."

36. The Methodist term for the interim lay leader of a congregation.

37. Albert M. Wright, "Ghana Methodist Churches in North America and Canada: Affiliation Issues," November 25, 2007; and "Some Questions and Answers about Affiliation with the UMC," January 19, 2008. Circulation of this and other papers was limited to local Ghanaian churches.

38. Wright, "Affiliation," 1–2.

of the Arlington church, bemoaned the fact that the matter of affiliation "continues to fester as a divisive issue, especially among the church leaders; and the first casualties of this divisiveness have been truth, Christ-like love, humility, and church-growth, all being elements of the fruit of the spirit."[39]

In his presentations Wright acknowledged the thinking of those who preferred to relate to the MCG only. Their reasons, he said, included the following:[40]

1. The need to safeguard Ghanaian Methodist church property so that in case of any legal wrangling they don't automatically become the property of UMC.
2. The need for Ghanaian immigrants to be able to benefit from a church burial when their bodies are flown home for burial.[41]
3. The concern that affiliation with UMC benefits only the Ghanaian ministers who would enjoy a reasonably better salary and benefits package than what the Ghanaian churches are presently able to afford.
4. That coming under the administrative and spiritual oversight of UMC rekindles colonial subjugation.
5. That UMC has a more favorable policy toward homosexuals, with which most Ghanaians disagree.

In response, Wright argued that the UMC, far from being overbearing, is of assistance to MCG churches in every way. For instance, in regard to burial in the homeland, all that is needed is a letter confirming one's membership in a UMC congregation. Finally, he reminded his audience that in the early 1990s UMC and MCG signed an Act of Covenant/Concordat Agreement, which limited the UMC to a supervisory role, leaving authentic Ghanaian congregations intact. Therefore, he concluded, most of the present issues were moot.

Finally, Wright argued for a "modified hybrid model," one in which Ghanaian Methodist churches would come under the Ethnic Ministries department of the UMC and be "administratively affiliated with the United

---

39. Ibid., 3.

40. It was at the request of Presiding Bishop Aboagye-Mensah that Wright drafted the five points representing the position of the MCG congregations. The five points do not represent the view of Wright himself.

41. The question of church burial is a very emotive one. During the missionary era, it was a policy that assisted in reducing the incidence of polygamy among Ghanaians. Anyone who was in a plural marriage forfeited the right to have their bodies sent to the church premise for pre-burial service. This punitive measure is still used, especially in rural areas, to ensure that members faithfully fulfill their financial obligations; otherwise they are threatened with non-church burials.

Methodist Conference . . . for day-to-day oversight; however, the Ghana Methodist Conference would maintain special relationship and responsibility with the churches in America"; in other words, there would be dual affiliation, UMC and MCG.[42]

SHIFTING POLICIES

When the Most Reverend Dr. Samuel Asante-Antwi was MCG presiding bishop, from 1997 to 2003, the policy toward the diaspora churches was to encourage sole affiliation with MCG, that is, with the mother church in Ghana. This was a reversal of policy positions taken by the two previous successive presiding bishops, Jacob Stephens and Kwesi Dickson. When the Most Reverend Dr. Robert Aboagye-Mensah held the office of presiding bishop, from 2004 to 2009, he reverted to the former model of encouraging affiliation with the Methodist conferences of the host countries.

Neither approach overcame the tensions. Clearly, within the Ghanaian diaspora in the West, Methodists have multilayered loyalties. There are some who value their national heritage above all else. Others, having successfully adjusted to their adopted societies, want little to do with the homeland. The vast majority are caught somewhere between the two identities. Though they could not achieve the life they wanted in their homeland, the immigrants left a rich cultural background that underlies their identity. The Western world indeed affords great opportunities for employment and desirable lifestyles, but at the core of their being, the immigrants feel an undeniable foreignness.

And so, Ghanaian Methodists navigate the tricky trail of tradition and globalization. Some, heavily steeped in traditional worldviews, contend with others who embrace Western values and worldviews. They struggle with multiple loyalties and bring these struggles to the Christian communities to which they belong.

CONCLUSION

Clearly, two decades after the 1990 Covenant had been signed, placing North American MCG churches within the UMC framework, the terms remained in contention. Many not only wanted their churches to be identified with the MCG North American Mission but also be recognized as one of the dioceses of the homeland church.

42. Wright, "Affiliation Issues," 20 (see n. 37 above).

Subsequent events in Ghana have had significant impact on the North American diaspora churches. The Most Reverend Prof. Emmanuel Kwaku Asante, who became presiding bishop in October 2009, succeeding Aboagye-Mensah,[43] charted a new path. He called for a conference in Aburi, Ghana, in May 2010, where he hosted leaders of the churches in the United States and Canada.[44] This conference produced two very significant directives. First, in the matter of affiliation, it established an all-inclusive approach, recognizing the following categories as under the umbrella of the North America Mission of Methodist Church, Ghana:

- Ghana Methodist churches in North America currently linked to MCG and viewed as units of the MCG North American Mission;
- Ghana Methodist churches in North America that are members of the UMC, USA;
- Ghana Methodist churches in North America that are members of the United Church of Canada;
- Ghanaian Methodist churches in North America that have chosen to be independent and unrelated to any of the above.

This outcome incorporates the policies of all the previous MCG administrations. By inviting Ghanaian Methodists in North America to Ghana for a roundtable conference, Bishop Asante ensured that the deliberations on the policy would have the widest participation. Launching it as a written document also maximized its potential longevity. But finally, probably the most significant aspect of the Aburi policy is the appointment of a Supervising Missions Coordinator, based in North America and tasked to implement the new policy. Among other things, he serves as the liaison between MCG and the churches in North America; fosters cordial fellowship among all Ghana Methodists and their churches in North America; receives and processes all applications from Methodist churches that wish to operate under MCG; facilitates communication between the MCG, the UMC, United

---

43. Asante graduated from the London Bible College (now London School of Theology) in 1979. Next, he studied philosophy and theology at the University of Saint Paul, Ottawa, Ontario, gaining two bachelors of theology, an MA in theology, and a PhD. Returning to Ghana in 1986, he served in a number of capacities before moving to Trinity Theological Seminary in Accra, where he served as lecturer, vice-principal, academic dean, and ultimately as president (1999–2006). He has served the Christian Council of Ghana, Ridge Church as Methodist chaplain, 1994–98, and Trinity United Church as senior minister, 1999–2006. Finally, in 2009, he was appointed presiding bishop of MCG, succeeding Robert Aboagye-Mensah.

44. The thirty-one church leaders at the Aburi meeting represented almost all of the North American Ghana Methodist churches. See list at conclusion of essay.

Church of Canada, and Ghanaian Methodists in other churches in North America; is responsible, in cooperation with MCG, for Methodist order and discipline within the MCG churches in North America; and exercises oversight of the character and fidelity of the ministers in the MCG, North America Mission.

Subsequent to the Aburi conference Bishop Benjamin Kwabena Asare was appointed and assumed responsibility for this task.[45] Arriving in North America in October of 2011, he lost little time in calling leaders together for a conference entitled "Unity and Reconciliation." It took place December 2–4, 2011, in Chevy Chase, Maryland. Participation included virtually every Ghanaian Methodist congregation in North America and cut across all divisions. The bishop's address, "Christ's Ambassadors of Reconciliation," was based on 2 Corinthians 5:18: "All things are of God who has reconciled us to himself through Jesus Christ and has given to us the ministry of reconciliation." He underlined the need for unity and reconciliation because of broken relationships, and reminded participants that the cross is a symbol of God's reconciliatory act, an act by which God abolished all racial and ethnic enmity. Thus, in Christ there is no Jew, Greek, man or woman, Asante or Fante, Ga or Ewe. He enumerated some of the causes of disunity, as follows:

- Poor leadership and deception. Some leaders manipulate members for their own personal advantage.

- Tribal sentiments. Laity from one ethnic area follow a minister from that area and band together against a new minister from another area, as when Fantes follow Fante ministers and Asantes follow Asante ministers.

- Lack of transparency in finances. Members are not told what their monies are used for. There are even cases of embezzlement.

- Personality conflicts. Disagreements between individuals spill over into the congregation and affect the ministry.

- Ignorance about MCG procedures. Some do not know Methodist principles and policies and try to impose different practices.

---

45. A graduate of Trinity College (now Trinity Theological Seminary) and ordained in 1977, Asare gained a World Council of Churches scholarship to study at Ecumenical Institute, Bossey, Geneva. In 1983, following other studies, he participated in the World Church in Britain program, earned an MA in 1989 at the University of Bradford, and completed other studies, including church administration at the Urban Theology Unit, Sheffield, England. After his return to Ghana, he served MCG in a number of capacities, from superintendent minister, Kwadaso Circuit, to synod secretary and superintendent minister in Kumasi District and Kumasi circuit. Several bishoprics appointments followed, preceding his current assignment in North America.

- Treating church as a social club, similar to an ethnic association rather than as a spiritual fellowship focused on worship, edification, and witness.
- Poor understanding of the Scriptures. Members have an inadequate understanding of who they are in Christ.
- Lack of relationship with Christ. Some members, living without a close relationship with Christ, conduct church business in a worldly manner.
- Mistrust of ministers. With ministers embroiled in divisions, members don't respect their ministries. Ministers have lost credibility.

In concluding the conference, Bishop Asare led participants in the prayer of St. Francis of Assisi:

> Lord, make me an instrument of your peace.
> Where there is hatred, let me sow love.
> Where there is injury, pardon.
> Where there is doubt, faith.
> Where there is despair, hope.
> Where there is darkness, light.
> Where there is sadness, joy.
> O Divine Master,
> grant that I may not so much seek to be consoled, as to console;
> to be understood, as to understand;
> to be loved, as to love.
> For it is in giving that we receive.
> It is in pardoning that we are pardoned,
> and it is in dying that we are born to Eternal Life.
> Amen.

Today, after a full generation of striving for unity and harmony, the Ghana Methodist churches of North America have a fresh opportunity to demonstrate the true love of God, and become witnesses to the Gospel given to the Church by the Lord of mission. MCG and UMC affiliated churches alike must remember that they are on mission. And "mission has its origin neither in official church nor in special groups within the church. It has its origin in God. God is a missionary God, a God who crosses frontiers towards the world. . . . Mission is God giving up himself, his becoming man, his laying aside of his divine prerogatives and taking up humanity, his moving into the world, in his Son and Spirit."[46]

---

46. Bosch, *Witness to the World*, 239.

And so, laudable as it is to have institutions recognized as Ghanaian Methodist churches, the predominant loyalty must be to what we are in Christ; that identity trumps all others. It is only in that recognition that the MCG diaspora can flourish, pass on its riches to the next generation, and expand and grow as an ecclesiastical organization.

Unity and Reconciliation Conference, Dec. 2–4, 2011
Participating churches

Bethel Methodist Church, Queens, NY	Ghana Methodist Church, Ottawa, Canada
Calvary Redeeming Methodist Church, Rockville, NY	Ghana Methodist Church, Ottawa, Canada
Covenant Methodist Church, Silver Spring, MD	Ghana Mission United Methodist Church, Charlotte, NC
Ebenezer Methodist Church, Hyattsville, MD	Ghana Resurrection Methodist Church, Alexandria, VA
Ebenezer United Methodist Church, Columbus, OH	Ghana United Methodist Church, Bronx, NY
Gaddiel R. Acquaah Memorial Methodist Church, Alexandria, VA	Ghana Wesley Methodist Church, Worcester, MA
Ghana Calvary Methodist Church, Irvington, NJ	Ghana Wesley Methodist Church, Newark, DE
Ghana Calvary Methodist Church, Grand Prairie, TX	Ghana Wesley United Methodist Church, Arlington, VA
Ghana Calvary Methodist United Church, Toronto, Canada	Ghana Wesley United Methodist Church, Brooklyn, NY
Ghana Ebenezer Methodist Church, Denver, CO	Good Shepherd Ghana Methodist Church, Worcester, MA
Ghana Ebenezer Methodist Church, Queens, NY	Mt. Olivet Methodist Church, Columbus, OH
Ghana Ebenezer Methodist Church, Tucker, GA	Mt. Zion Ghana Methodist Church, Atlanta, GA
Ghana Ebenezer Methodist Church, Charlotte, NC	New Covenant United Methodist Church, Cincinnati, OH
Ghana Emmanuel Methodist church, Newark, NJ	St. Paul's United Methodist Church, Baltimore, MD
Ghana Methodist Church, Toronto, Canada	Wesley Methodist Church of Ghana, Brooklyn, NY
Ghana Methodist Church, Montreal, Canada	Wesley United Methodist Church, Worcester, MA

BIBLIOGRAPHY

Aboagye-Mensah, Robert. "A Pastoral Letter, from the Office of the Presiding Bishop to Congregations of Ghanaian Methodists Abroad." June 2007.

Bosch, David. *Witness to the World: The Christian Mission in Theological Perspective.* London: Marshall, Morgan & Scott, 1980.

Bump, Micah. "Ghana: Searching for Opportunities at Home and Abroad." *Migration Information Source.* March 2006. Online: http://www.migrationinformation.org/USFocus/print.cfm?ID=381.

Dogbevi, Emmanuel K. "Remittances from Ghanaians Abroad Outstrip Overseas Development Assistance." *Ghana Business News.* Online: http://www.ghanabusinessnews.com/2011/09/13/remittances-from-ghanaians-abroad-outstrip-overseas-development-assistance/.

Essamuah, Casely B. *Genuinely Ghanaian: A History of the Methodist Church Ghana, 1961–2000.* Trenton, NJ: Africa World Press, 2010.

Fumanti, Mattia. "A Light-Hearted Bunch of Ladies: Irreverent Piety and Gendered Power in the London Ghanaian Diaspora." *Africa* 8 (2010) 200–223.

LaCamera, Kathleen. "Ghanaians Find Home through London Fellowship." UMC.org. December 18, 2007. Online: http://www.umc.org/site/apps/nlnet/content3.aspx?c=lwL4KnN1LtH&b=1752971&ct=4819205.

Manuh, Takyiwaa. *An 11th Region of Ghana? Ghanaians Abroad.* Ghana Academy of Arts and Sciences, inaugural lecture, 2006.

Owusu-Ankomah, Papa. "Emigration from Ghana: A Motor or Brake for Development." Keynote address, 39th session of the United Nations Commission on Population and Development, New York, April 4, 2006.

Passarelli, Alessia. "Between Past and Future: Reflection on How Migration Has Been Taken into Account by the Protestant Churches in Italy and How This Has Affected Their Ecclesiological Self-Understanding." *Vieraanvaraisuus ja muukalaisuus.* Conference publication. Suomalaisen Teologisen Kirjallisuusseuran julkaisuja series 269. Helsinki: Suomalainen Teologinen Kirjallisuusseura, 2011.

Tiénou, Tite. "Ethnicity as Gift and Barrier: Human Identity and Christian Mission." Annual Seminar offered at the Overseas Ministries Study Center, New Haven, Connecticut.

Tonah, Steve. "Ghanaians Abroad and Their Ties Home: Cultural and Religious Dimensions of Transnational Migration." Paper presented at a conference at the Center for Inter-disciplinary Research, Bielefeld, Germany, May 31–June 1, 2007.

Zeleza, Paul T. *Barack Obama and African Diasporas: Dialogues and Dissensions.* Athens: Ohio University Press, 2009.

6

New Angles on African Christianity

Paul Kollman

As Christianity in Africa grows and diversifies, those who study it also produce more and more information. Such study takes increasingly varied forms, not only the expected academic journal articles, books, and the proceedings of conferences, but also films and other artistic productions. It also occurs in ever more diverse educational institutions and affiliated research programs. Those who study African Christianity also engage and draw upon a variety of disciplinary perspectives, especially from within the humanities and social sciences, as they seek to understand an ever-expanding reality in all its complexity.

Tite Tiénou, who has worked in a variety of academic and church-related institutions inside and outside of Africa, has also long moved between and among disciplines in considering Christianity in Africa. In so doing he has gained familiarity with varying approaches in order to grasp correspondingly varying insights. He knows how academic disciplines both generate particular insights and obscure reality—that is, they both disclose and conceal. His versatility has helped make his analyses especially rich. He is mindful as well of the institutional frameworks that foster good scholarship and has worked to support the study of African Christianity in a broad sense with practical initiatives.

In an effort to honor Tiénou's achievements, this paper will seek to revisit some of the themes motivating his own writings in light of recent research. It will become clear that many of the questions that have long preoccupied him have not gone away. At the same time, along with obvious continuities, there are new perspectives on such questions that arise from novel circumstances as well as creative new scholarly approaches.

This discussion will be organized around three questions, each of which represents a longstanding concern of Tiénou. The first question, which prompted some of his earliest works quite directly and has never disappeared, is "How should Christian theology in Africa proceed?" Writing from an evangelical perspective and shaped by his own life story, Tiénou has offered prescient insights into this issue over the past several decades. The second—sometimes in the foreground, sometimes in the background of his writings—is "How should African culture shape African Christianity?" Avoiding both an uncritical acceptance of African culture and also a stern rejection of it sometimes associated with certain approaches to evangelical theology, Tiénou has probed its place in the theological endeavor. And the third question, also a regular underlying concern of Tiénou's and at times one that he has engaged directly, is "How should the Bible be appropriated in African Christianity?" As a committed Evangelical, Tiénou has long sought to bring to bear the life-giving vitality of Scripture to African Christians and their communities.

The purpose here lies not in summarizing or evaluating Tiénou's evolving approaches to these questions. Instead, it will consider contemporary writings that address prominent issues that he has engaged over the years. In so doing, it seeks to appreciate what he has achieved and also offer perspectives on how questions he has long asked are now being approached by others.

HOW SHOULD CHRISTIAN THEOLOGY IN AFRICA PROCEED?

Theological development in Africa has proceeded in two somewhat contradictory ways in recent years. First, there has clearly evolved a more professionalized, ecumenical, and transnational sense of shared undertaking among what one might call "professional" Christian theologians of Africa. This has happened in the face of great obstacles to such scholarship, many due to shortages of resources and absence of institutional support, often traceable to political and social instabilities in much of post-colonial Africa. Nonetheless, impressive work continues to be done. Numerous so-called "mainstream" Christian bodies have supported theological inquiry, and newer, more local Christian bodies have also created networks and resources for research and reflection. Second, there has been theological development through increasingly fragmented informal reflection on lived Christian experience, as the ways of being Christian in Africa diversify around the continent and in the diaspora, and as people reflect on their lives as believers.

On the one hand, the widely acknowledged "deep river" of African theological reflection has grown more and more robust, with accompanying institutional reinforcement, encouragement from Christian communities and their authorities, and other familiar signs of a settled sort of prestige. Conferences, degrees, and publications with an international reach belong to this part of Africa's theological growth. At the same time, however, there is also a bewildering array of lesser-known theological efforts, what might be called small tributaries and runlets that move away from the deeper river. This is witnessed sometimes through formal theological reflection that occurs in local settings apart from any ecclesial oversight, but more often in informal ways as individual Christians and Christian communities reflect on their experiences in light of Christ's life at work among them.

Tiénou has foreseen and encouraged both of these trends. In the first place, like many others, early on in his career he decried the state of theology, especially evangelical theology, in Africa.[1] In the face of such inadequacy he urged boldness: "Our call is to develop a theology in Africa which will be a truly African doxology to God: Father, Son and Holy Spirit."[2] Besides simply calling for such work, however, he was mindful of the need for institutional supports for theological education, and in several articles he listed a number of initiatives that Christian bodies ought to undertake to support serious theological writing and research.[3] Such suggestions have contributed to the fruitfulness of African academic theology today. In addition, while admitting that there were a variety of challenges to theology from various directions, he reflected on the internal obstacles to theology that he found within evangelical circles.[4] Looking back, it is easy to see that his calls for its development have both embodied the advances made and inspired new directions. He has worked ecumenically and with students in a variety of institutions to pursue theological reflection appropriate for Africa's Christians.

Yet Tiénou also acknowledges that theology is not simply an academic undertaking, and he has shown himself appreciative of its diverse forms

---

1. Tiénou, "Threats and Dangers," 40–47.
2. Tiénou, *Theological Task*, 8.
3. Ibid. See also Ngewa et al., *Issues*, 3–11.
4. Tiénou, "Threats and Dangers."

apart from formal academic settings. In fact, he has been dismissive of much that passes for theological work. He wrote in 1998: "If our academic theology results only in obtaining degrees and writing pompous books, then I for one want nothing to do with it. But if it encourages more missionary proclamation, more discipleship, and more faithfulness to our Lord, then assuredly this is the kind of theology that makes sense for Africa."[5] The needs for mission and proclamation must, Tiénou believes, direct theology to address the real lives of African Christians. Only a few years ago he wrote, "The most pressing challenge for evangelical theology in Africa is the requirement to serve fully the needs of Christians and churches in Africa." At the same time he saw the need to avoid both slavish imitation of Western theology and uncritical acquiescence to traditional African cultural practices. The theology he calls for must serve African Christians "without being an appendix of Western or other theologies and also without being an exotic mixture of Christianity and African cultures or religions."[6] With calls like this, Tiénou foresaw the myriad smaller examples of theological activity across the continent, nearly all of them occurring without fanfare.

African theologians today have taken heed of these calls by Tiénou and others. In the work of people like Kenya's Philomena Mwaura, Uganda's Emmanuel Katongole, and Nigeria's A. E. Orobator—and one could mention many others—one discerns formidable grounding in the church's traditions of theological reflection along with a keen awareness of the pastoral challenges facing contemporary African Christian communities. Mwaura's studies of women in African pentecostal churches, for instance, draw attention to the ways that the practices and spirituality of such churches appeal to African women, allowing Christ's healing and grace to meet them where their needs are most acute.[7] Orobator's *Theology in an African Pot* addresses a rather traditional list of theological topics long familiar in Catholic seminary education, but does so in a decidedly African way.[8]

Katongole's more recent *Sacrifice of Africa* represents a groundbreaking effort in African social ethics that seems to embody some of Tiénou's hopes for African Christian theology. Some years back, Andrew Walls suggested that negotiating relations with the nation-state would likely be the greatest theological challenge for African Christians[9], and Katongole's work

---

5. Tiénou, "Theological Task," 11.

6. Tiénou, "Evangelical Theology," 221.

7. Mwaura's works appear in many edited collections. See, e.g., "Gender and Power," 359–88.

8. Orobator, *Theology Brewed*.

9. Walls, "Africa in Christian History," 85–115.

represents the most significant attempt so far to address that challenge in a comprehensive way. Drawing on theological work associated with so-called narrative theologians like Stanley Hauerwas and those associated with the movement known as Radical Orthodoxy like John Milbank, Katongole is also keenly attentive to African social and political realities. He brings this theological grounding to such realities, and calls into question past theological responses to the African state proposed by theologians and churches.

Past efforts by Christians to address the nation-state and its problems in Africa, Katongole argues, have taken three forms. First, many have operated from what he labels a spiritual paradigm that pursued deeper evangelization, focusing on the inner life of individuals who, the assumption was, would act more responsibly in political roles if better evangelized. Second, more socially aware Christians have pursued a pastoral program focusing on development, urging intervention to better the lives of Africans who face suffering from inadequate education or health care, for example. Third, some theologians have also urged an embrace of direct political action through some combination of mediation between political rivals, advocacy for responsible governance, and even formal participation in efforts at reconciliation.[10]

In each of these three responses, however, Katongole discerns a failure to ask the prior question of why Africa suffers so regularly and so profoundly. African Christians, he believes need, on one hand, to overcome their learned reticence before political authorities, and, on the other hand, to avoid an activism that looks no different than that of the familiar political authorities. Instead, he urges, they need to rediscover the deeper call to living a new life in Christ, which derives first and foremost from a new way of imagining the world. Katongole writes, "[T]he most determinative contribution Christianity can offer" is "that of imagining the social frames of reference in new and fresh ways grounded in her unique story and calling."[11]

In order to flesh out his alternative to failed approaches of the past, Katongole describes remarkable work undertaken by African Christians. He draws on the examples of three heroic individuals in particular—a bishop in Sudan, a mother in northern Uganda, and a peacemaker in Burundi—who have let their own buoyant, Christ-inspired visions imagine conflict-ridden situations anew. Such people, far from seeing Christianity as a religion that is separate from politics, see the faith as itself a form of politics that ought to shape ethical behavior in every realm. The heroes Katongole describes carry out their work far from centers of power. He shows how their marginalized

10. Katongole, *Sacrifice of Africa*, 33–47.
11. Ibid., 47.

situations allow the prophetic discipleship that Africa needs and its Christians have been too slow to provide.

Katongole is not an Evangelical—like Mwaura and Orobator, he is a Roman Catholic—yet it is easy to see that the portraits he admiringly draws celebrate people who have been seized by the Gospel and bring it to their distinctly African experiences with faithfulness and creativity. Moreover, the ethical analysis he offers draws upon theologians from a variety of traditions as well as social scientific research from various disciplines—much like Tiénou's own work. In addition, he takes very seriously the regular ineffectuality of Christians at countering Africa's political and social problems. One thinks of how Christians have faced recent political crises in Zimbabwe, Kenya, Ivory Coast, and Nigeria—not to mention that breathtaking tragedy in Rwanda—and Katongole's alternatives seem important indeed. He does theology in a way that, I believe, Tiénou would approve.

HOW SHOULD AFRICAN CULTURE SHAPE AFRICAN CHRISTIANITY?

Missiologically informed approaches to African Christianity have long urged attention to African cultures in the development of theology responsive to African needs; Tiénou's voice has been part of that chorus for decades.[12] At the same time, however, Tiénou has shown a typically evangelical concern that African cultural features not be accepted uncritically. With Paul Hiebert and others, he has noted a certain anthropocentrism within African religion (or religions) that is hard to square with traditional Christianity.[13] Yet his refusal to reject African religion out of hand is also quite clear, and he does not want fear of syncretism to stand in the way of real understanding. He writes, "In itself, a call for Christians to seek a better understanding of African and other religions must not be viewed as a disguised plan to advance the cause of idolatry or paganism."[14]

There are two aspects of recent approaches to culture within the social sciences that bear upon the place of culture within African Christianity. In the first place, anthropologists and historians have convincingly shown the limits of structural-functionalist approaches to culture that were in the past assumed by many missiologists who sought to appropriate anthropological insights in their reflections on Christian mission. That older notion of

12. Tiénou, *Theological Task*, 22ff; Tiénou, "Which Way," 256–63; Tiénou, "Biblical Faith," 138–47; Tiénou, "Christian Response," 209–19.

13. Hiebert et al., *Understanding Folk Religion*. See also Tiénou, "Biblical Faith."

14. Tiénou, "Christian Response," 215.

culture sought to explain difference between peoples through postulating a more-or-less coherent shared set of socially learned features that identified a given people. The idea that a certain, clearly bounded people share a univocal "culture" in equal ways that differentiate them from others, and that they do so over time through common linguistic and other social practices—something that mission scholars have grasped onto in order to orient missionary strategy to just such a people sharing such a culture—has long been seen wanting by most anthropologists. Older notions of "adapting" theology to some essentialized culture, therefore, sound quite naïve. Invocations of culture in this sense even seem sometimes to be part of politicized strategies that deflect criticism of certain cultural norms deemed "authentic" to a culture, such as excision and other practices at times labeled "female genital mutilation."

That said, if the notion of plural cultures, mutually distinguishable and clearly bounded, is no longer defensible, there is ongoing appreciation for the ways that social and cultural experiences shape people in distinctive ways that merit close understanding. Those who care about African Christianity know how common values and shared practices reinforce each other, creating shared social expectations even when there is also widespread divergence in a social body.

The second important aspect of how culture is approached today relates to this last point. It is connected to the emerging subfield that goes by the name of the anthropology of Christianity. Starting about a decade ago, a number of anthropologists sought to bring together those of their number who studied Christianity to try to consider common problems and issues they faced. One of their goals was to think about how Christianity could be studied as a single object without losing sight of its many variations. Research associated with this growing subfield has studied Christianity in a number of times and places, generating a new seriousness and sense of shared undertaking about the social-scientific approach to Christianity.[15]

Two interrelated consequences of the findings coming from those associated with anthropology of Christianity have implications for how culture shapes African Christianity. In the first place, such research, in uncovering the diverse ways of being Christian in a place of Africa, has unsettled oft-held assumptions about what it means to be Christian. In so doing, they carry out the important descriptive work of showing just how differences once subsumed under the label "culture" profoundly shape Christianity as it is lived—even when something like the unitary notion of culture is absent. They thus complexify both our understanding of culture and of

---

15. For an overview of this field, see Lampe, "Anthropology of Christianity," 66–88.

Christianity. Such anthropological research plays an important corrective role in much missiological thinking. Unlike many other scholars of mission, anthropologists usually have little stake in reaffirming the supposed solidity and inspiring Christian qualities of believers. They are not concerned with reinforcing the prescriptive "oughts" that guide Christian leaders. Instead, shaped by a presumption of the unboundedness and lack of coherence in any supposed shared sense of "culture," they have become adept at finding the paradoxes and puzzles that arise in actual discourse and practices in which Christians are engaged.

For example, the anthropologist Frederick Klaits has studied Christians belonging to a pentecostal church in Botswana and discovered that central to their identity as Christians is neither a clear set of beliefs nor practices of a liturgical sort.[16] Instead, these Christians place in the foreground the moral passion that allows them to serve each other tenderly, especially amidst the suffering wrought by HIV/AIDS. Rarely speaking of sin, preachers urge instead practices expressive of *tumelo*, Setswana for "faith" or "belief," but most identified as a proper sentiment toward those suffering. It is also a sentiment that situates people in the context of their family networks as they have evolved over time. Klaits writes, "For Baitshepi [the church's name] members, *tumelo* in the context of death is an intersubjective memory work, consisting of efforts to orient one's own and other people's sentiments in particular directions, undertaken with recognition of the difficulties and possible failures of the enterprise."[17]

Besides simply describing the varieties of Christianities at work in a place like Africa, underscoring Christian variety and the contingent nature of much that is assumed essential to Christianity, anthropologists of Christianity have also brought forward certain concepts that lend themselves to productive comparisons and contrasts. Such concepts can become tools for missiologically inclined scholars to grasp more fully the ways Christian identity evolves. I have been particularly intrigued by the notion of semiotic ideology invoked by Webb Keane to name the operative approach to material objects at work among believers.[18] Once alerted to something like a semiotic ideology, it is easy to recognize that different Christians possess different semiotic ideologies. In addition, changes in an individual or group's semiotic ideology over time are one way to gauge changes in religious identity, for example deepening identification with transnational

---

16. Klaits, *Death in a Church of Life*.
17. Ibid., 81.
18. Keane, *Christian Moderns*.

Christian expectations. One realm in which to discern differing semiotic ideologies is in different approaches to Scripture.

HOW SHOULD THE BIBLE BE APPROPRIATED IN AFRICAN CHRISTIANITY?

As a committed Evangelical, Tiénou has unsurprisingly emphasized the centrality of the Bible for all Christian theological reflection, including in Africa. He defines an Evangelical as "one who conforms to the essential doctrines of the Gospel and to the basic facts and truths of Christianity."[19] That said, he is not naïve or simplistic in how he appropriates the Bible; he acknowledges the need for appropriation. Early on he asserted, "The Bible should be taken to lighten our path in our task of developing theologies in context,"[20] but he is never simplistic about how such a lightening occurs. In addition, more recent writing shows his own sophisticated approach to Scripture.[21]

Anthropologists and historians have long been alert to the diverse ways in which the Bible functions in Christian communities.[22] The earliest sub-Saharan African Christians, for example, were often attracted to literacy as a new potency, and over time mission-educated Africans used such skills to forge anti-colonial, proto-nationalist movements. In some places, it seems, the Bible served as a touchstone for emerging cultural and ethnic identities, biblical translation often creating a shared social identity through a constructed linguistic unity.[23]

More recent studies by those pursuing the anthropology of Christianity have disclosed new types of appropriation of the Scriptures in Africa and elsewhere. Matthew Engelke, for example, has analyzed a group of Pentecostals in Zimbabwe who dislike the Bible because it gets in the way of the living and direct contact with God that they esteem; to draw on the notion that Webb Keane developed, they present an unusual semiotic ideology for a Christian group, to be sure.[24] Thomas Kirsch, another anthropologist, studies a church in Zambia whose use of the Bible in worship is less unusual.[25]

19. Tiénou, *Theological Task*, 9.
20. Tiénou, "Biblical Foundations," 447.
21. Tiénou, "Samaritans," 211–22.
22. For a recent overview, see Bielo, *Social Life of Scriptures*.
23. One study that analyzes the emergence of an African ethnic identity, placing the translation of the Bible within a number of other factors, is Peel, *Religious Encounter*.
24. Engelke, *Problem of Presence*.
25. Kirsch, *Spirits and Letters*.

His theme is not so much how they use Scripture in worship, however, but how biblical expertise becomes a way to buttress the charismatic authority of church leaders. In so doing, he seeks to show the problematic nature of sociologist Max Weber's long influential distinction between charisma and institution. In Weber's formulation, charisma, usually embodied in an outstanding individual, gives rise to new social and religious movements. The resulting innovations, according to Weber, tend to undergo institutionalization or routinization, the process whereby newly founded organizations inevitably become bureaucratized in order to persist into the future through ordinary means of social reproduction. Kirsch shows how Weber's supposed dichotomy fails to apply in his case, where charismatic authority lies precisely in being able to control words through their institutionalization. Kirsch's point is that there are a variety of what he calls "literacy practices" operating in Christian bodies, and we should not assume that dichotomies operative in one place and time—for example between the charismatic spirit and the institutional letter, to borrow from his title—are at work everywhere. He wants to draw attention to the very specific and local forms of "literacy enablement," by which he means "those activities, qualities and devices which, in a particular socio-religious field, are seen as necessary for attempting to bridge between the divine-scriptural sphere and the worldly realm."[26]

Work like Engelke's and Kirsch's show how something like the place of Scripture in a Christian body can be profitably examined to grasp just how Christianity emerges in particular settings. And a notion like semiotic ideology can become one category by which to compare different Christian groups.

CONCLUSION

Research like that emerging from the anthropology of Christianity suggests that Evangelicals like Tiénou are right to be wary of how cultural realities shape manifestations of Christianity, including the appropriation of Scripture. They also show, however, the ways in which Christianity is "at large" more than ever before, taking protean forms that show the remarkable ingenuity of believers, as well as the fertility of the Word of God.

If early on in his career Tiénou might have been quick to call into question many such Christian manifestations as unbiblical, one wonders whether he might be more reluctant to move toward condemnation now. In a recent piece he celebrates early African sub-Saharan missionaries,

26. Ibid., 25, 169–79.

who toiled in the face of condemnations from those who had brought the message to them in the first place. The heroic figures he celebrates, recent African converts who took seriously the call to preach the Good News they had received, stood accused of unbiblical behavior by missionaries, the latter likely being unable to extricate themselves from a racist and colonial set of presumptions.[27] One wonders whether the diverse forms of African Christianity appearing today merit a reverence that such African Christian pioneers were too often denied.

BIBLIOGRAPHY

Bielo, James S., editor. *The Social Life of Scriptures: Cross-Cultural Perspectives on Biblicism*. New Brunswick, NJ: Rutgers University Press, 2009.

Engelke, Matthew. *The Problem of Presence: Beyond Scripture in an African Church*. Berkeley: University of California Press, 2007.

Hiebert, Paul G. R., et al., editors. *Understanding Folk Religion: A Christian Response to Popular Beliefs and Practices*. Grand Rapids: Baker Academic, 2000.

Kalu, Ogbu U., editor. *African Christianity: An African Story*. Trenton, NJ: Africa World Press, 2007.

Katongole, Emmanuel. *The Sacrifice of Africa: A Political Theology for Africa*. Grand Rapids: Eerdmans, 2010.

Keane, Webb. *Christian Moderns: Freedom and Fetish in the Mission Encounter*. Berkeley: University of California Press, 2007.

Kirsch, Thomas G. *Spirits and Letters: Reading, Writing and Charisma in African Christianity*. New York: Bergham, 2008.

Klaits, Frederick. *Death in a Church of Life: Moral Passion During Botswana's Time of AIDS*. Berkeley: University of California Press, 2010.

Lampe, F. P. "The Anthropology of Christianity: Context, Contestation, Rupture, and Continuity." *Reviews in Anthropology* 39 (2010) 66–89.

Mwaura, Philomena N. "Gender and Power." In *African Christianity: An African Story*, edited by Ogbu Kalu, 359–88. Trenton, NJ: Africa World Press, 2007.

Ngewa, Samuel, et al., editors. *Issues in African Christian Theology*. Nairobi: East African Educational Publishers, 1998.

Orobator, A. E. *Theology Brewed in an African Pot*. Maryknoll, NY: Orbis, 2008.

Peel, J. D. Y. *Religious Encounter in the Making of the Yoruba*. Bloomington: Indiana University Press, 2000.

Tiénou, Tite. "Biblical Faith and Traditional Folk Religion." In *Biblical Faith and Other Religions: An Evangelical Assessment*, edited by David W. Baker, 138–47. Grand Rapids: Kregel, 2004.

———. "Biblical Foundations for African Theology." *Missiology* 10 (1982) 435–48.

———. "The Christian Response to African Traditional Religion(s)." In *Christian Witness in Pluralistic Contexts in the Twenty-First Century*, edited by Enoch Wan, 209–17. Pasadena, CA: William Carey Library, 2004.

---

27. Tiénou, "Great Commission," 164–75.

———. "Evangelical Theology in African Contexts." In *The Cambridge Companion to Evangelical Theology*, edited by Timothy Larsen and Daniel J. Treier, 213–24. Cambridge: Cambridge University Press, 2007.

———. "The Great Commission in Africa." In *The Great Commission: Evangelicals and the History of World Missions*, edited by Martin I. Klauber and Scott M. Manetsch, 164–75. Nashville: B&H, 2008.

———. "The Samaritans: A Biblical-Theological Mirror for Understanding Racial, Ethnic, and Religious Identity?" In *This Side of Heaven: Race, Ethnicity, and Christian Faith*, edited by Robert J. Priest and Alvaro L. Nieves, 211–22. Oxford: Oxford University Press, 2007.

———. "The Theological Task of the Church in Africa." In *Issues in African Christian Theology*, edited by Samuel Ngewa et al., 3–11. Nairobi: East African Educational Publishers, 1998.

———. *The Theological Task of the Church in Africa*. 2nd ed. Achimota, Ghana: Africa Christian Press, 1990.

———. "Threats and Dangers in the Theological Task in Africa." *Evangelical Review of Theology* 5 (1981) 40–47.

———. "Which Way for African Christianity?" *Evangelical Missions Quarterly* 28 (1992) 256–63.

Walls, Andrew F. "Africa in Christian History." In *The Cross-Cultural Process in Christian History: Studies in the Transmission and Appropriation of Faith*, 85–115. Maryknoll, NY: Orbis, 2002.

7

The Multifaceted Genesis of the 2007–2008 Postelection Violence in Kenya

David K. Ngaruiya

Horrified by the post-election violence in Kenya, a Catholic bishop commented that, among Christians, "the blood of tribalism is thicker than the water of Baptism."[1] Between the end of December 2007 and February 2008, we heard and saw on TV the mayhem that followed Kenya's presidential election in December 2007. At first, the world called it tribal conflict, and some suggested that it was genocide. About 1,000 people died and 500,000 fled or were forced from their homes. In a country where eight out of ten are Christians, how could gruesome stories of pain, paralyzing fear, and disrupted living unfold? How could ethnic communities become so pitted against each other that national elections would produce such loss of human life and internal displacement? How could this happen in a land where all prayerfully sing,

> *O God of all creation*
> *Bless this our Land and nation*
> *Justice be our shield and defender*
> *May we dwell in unity*
> *Peace and liberty*

1. Nagele, "Election Chaos," 7.

Plenty be found within our borders.
Let one and all arise
With hearts both strong and true
Service be our earnest endeavour
And our home land of Kenya
Heritage of splendour
Firm may we stand to defend.
Let all with one accord
In common bond united
Build this our nation together
And the glory of Kenya
The fruit of our labour
Fill every heart with thanks giving.

In this essay I will explore the multiple factors that led to the violence. I will argue that it reflected colonial history, contemporary politics, and the dynamics of power in human relations and material realities, not merely tribal violence, as has been simplistically charged.

THE COLONIAL LEGACY

The colonial legacy in Kenya left a divide-and-rule strategy entrenched in multiple facets of national life, including church denominations, the national constitution, academic institutions, and businesses. To missionize effectively, a deep knowledge and use of local customs are necessary tools, but the colonists, many of whom were Christians, disregarded and actually sought to destroy local customs. Ngugi Wa Thiong'o, a renowned Kenyan author, writes that the dynamics of colonialism was geared toward "flattening or fossilization of its victims' culture." This meant the wholesale demonization of social institutions, naming systems, religions, history, and language. Coupled with this was the destruction of the works of artisans, which the missionaries interpreted as "symbols of witchcraft or graven images of the devil."[2]

The analysis by Ngugi Wathiong'o of post-colonial Kenyan culture as a reproduction of the colonial culture is pertinent to our discussion.[3] He argues not for the rejection of European customs but for a plurality of

---

2. Wathiong'o, *Moving the Centre*, 42–43.
3. Ibid., 91.

cultural centers, recognizing that colonial patterns distorted the multiplicity of indigenous cultures.[4]

Western anthropologists such as W. H. R. Rivers also have pointed this out. As early as the 1920s, in regard to the approach of Christian colonial evangelists, Rivers asserted that "in destroying the religion, or rather in destroying or undermining its ritual and beliefs, [they were] at the same time, and unwittingly, destroying all that gave coherence and meaning to the social fabric."[5] This demonization of culture by the colonists and missionaries continues to be reflected in the present time by ethnic groups that play the tribal card as they seek to eject other ethnic groups from particular regions.

There has also been a resurgence of ethnic religion such as practiced by the Mungiki cult in Kenya. This cult is currently under ban by the government. The battle between Mungiki and the present establishment has parallels in Kenyan colonial history. The cult has roots in Kikuyu traditional religion and espouses cultural patterns such as polygamy and circumcision of women, practices that are abhorred today in many churches, just as early missionaries abhorred them.

CONDEMNATION OF INDIGENOUS CULTURE

The view that indigenous culture in Kenya is evil has strong historical, missional, theological, and scientific roots. The mission movement in Kenya emanated primarily from England. Pagan lands with a two-tier view of the world, such as Kenya, were considered to be Satan's domain by both colonialists and missionaries, while the mission movement was viewed as representing God's kingdom.[6]

The British rulers expected the colonized to fully submit to civil authority, justifying their demands by the teaching of the Protestant Reformers, Luther and Calvin. Of the two, Luther favored religious tolerance, once remarking that "use of force can never prevent heresy." Calvin, on the other hand, advocated the use of secular authority to enforce Christian virtue and suppress dissent.[7] Understandably, Kenyans resisted colonial enforcement of Christianity.

When it came to Kenyan politics, it was not unusual for Christians to be told by their churches to avoid all involvement, even though they could

---

4. Ibid., 11.

5. Beideman, *Colonial Evangelism*, 133 (quoting Rivers, 1920).

6. This is not to deny that abominable practices such as witchcraft were a reality in Kenya.

7. Höpfl, *Luther and Calvin*, 30.

not escape the consequences of the policies set by politicians. However, God is concerned about injustice, greed, oppression of the poor and weak, corruption, and the choice of national leaders. Thankfully, today many Christians in Kenya exercise their rights and responsibilities in the political sphere, in keeping with sound theological judgment.

There was also a scientific aspect to the social and political dynamics in Kenya. Evolutionary theory placed African Traditional Religion(s) at the bottom of the evolutionary ladder. Christian missionaries in East Africa may not have embraced evolution, but sometimes they appear to have unconsciously followed its conclusions just the same.

RANGE OF RESPONSE TO THE GOSPEL

The belief that indigenous cultures were evil led to the notion that the heathen must first be civilized first before they could embrace the Gospel. Subduing a people's culture by might overlooks the importance of the incarnation. Through the Incarnation, the love of God permeated and won many of his enemies and continues to do so today.

The mighty force of colonization alongside the spread of Christianity is evident to this day in Kenya. The Agikuyu people, for example, divided into three groups in response to the missionaries' condemnation of their traditions: the Abolitionists, the Arathi, and the Karing'a.[8]

The Abolitionists complied with demands of the colonial government that certain cultural practices, including polygamy, be abandoned. This group negotiated with the colonial government on matters of taxation, forced labor, and land alienation.

The Arathi rejected modernism. They embraced the Old Testament teachings but ignored the New Testament. Militant and inward looking, they waited for the reign of God, when evil would be eradicated and a golden age would enable Kikuyu culture to flourish.

Unlike the Arathi, the Karing'a embraced modernism and demanded justice from the authorities. (The group also tolerated syncretism.) The Karing'a established their own schools and churches with local resources and grew so socially powerful that the colonial government closed its institutions in the 1950s.

In 2010 Kenya adopted a new constitution. There is now a term limit for the office of the head of state, a feature that is the source of much contention in the past. Following the disputed presidential election of 2007, the office of the Prime Minister was created to devolve some of the presidential

---

8. Ethe, "African Response," 41; Sandgreen, *Christianity and the Kikuyu*, 150.

powers. Under the promulgated constitution, Kenyans will now have a greater exercise of power at county, regional, and national levels as the new laws and structures are implemented.

Major challenges created by colonization include economic disparities in the allocation of land and economic resources. Governance structures designed to contain people within specific boundaries for the purpose of subjugating them and obtaining cheap labor, are slowly crumbling.

LAND CLASHES AND BIBLE TRANSLATION

The Ndungu report presents different perspectives on the cause of clashes over land. On one hand, ethnic groups that consider the Rift Valley to be their ancestral home argue that the unjust allocation of land to outsiders following Kenya's political independence is the underlying cause of ethnic clashes. On the other hand, it can be argued that Kenya is a multiethnic country and that many of the 42 ethnic groups of the nation are living peacefully side by side. Others maintain that the cause of ethnic clashes is multiparty democracy. These arguments fail to take account of the fluidity of ethnicity. It is not uncommon for Kenyans to change their ethnic identity through intermarriage or ritual, after which they gain all the rights and privileges of insiders.

Although societies may divide along racial lines, that does not legitimize the devaluation of one community by another. The American Anthropological Association emphasizes this point:

> How people have been accepted and treated within the context of a given society or culture has a direct impact on how they perform in that society. The "racial" worldview was invented to assign some groups to perpetual low status, while others were permitted access to privilege, power, and wealth. The tragedy in the United States has been that the policies and practices stemming from this worldview succeeded all too well in constructing unequal populations among Europeans, Native Americans, and peoples of African descent. Given what we know about the capacity of normal humans to achieve and function within any culture, we conclude that present-day inequalities between so-called "racial" groups are not consequences of their biological inheritance but products of historical and contemporary social, economic, educational, and political circumstances.[9]

---

9. "American Anthropological Association Statement on 'Race,'" adopted by the Executive Board of the American Anthropological Association, May 17, 1998, online: http://www.aaanet.org/stmts/racepp.htm.

Kenya is a young democracy. Many nations have endured civil war in the process of creating a united nation. The mid-nineteenth century Civil War in the United States is a case in point. Even though democracy is desirable for the entire world, conflict can be expected in the process.

"Democracy" has sometimes been used to justify violence. This was the case in the burning of a church in Eldoret, Kenya. A number of Christians, including women and children, had taken refuge in the church, but they were victimized on the basis of a "democratic" right to evict fellow citizens from the area. Those who intervened in the attempt to save lives were injured in the process. The late Reverend Michael Kamau, who used to pay children's school fees when he was a parish priest, was killed by an armed youth simply because he was a Mugikuyu.

Democracy comes with a cost, but it must not be used to justify loss of life, no matter what the ethnic group. Kenya needs to pursue an authentic democracy that unites her people.

In mission history, Bible translation has been an inadvertent factor reinforcing ethnic identity. Translators came with their denominational background, and the churches that were formed in the communities that received the translations tended to adopt the denominational identity of the translators. Is it surprising, then, that one finds whole communities in Kenya loyal to particular denominations, each reflecting a distinct ethnic group?

The alignment of ethnic groups with certain regions often reflects the historical practice of "comity," whereby missionaries of particular denominations were assigned to specific tribal areas and colonial boundaries. This history may contribute to the contemporary linking of specific groups to certain areas, producing "we" versus "they" conflicts. But it must be noted that this is not necessarily an indicator of ethnocentrism per se.

PREMEDITATED VIOLENCE

In the 2008 post-election upheaval it is believed that some of the violence was premeditated. It is alleged, for instance, that "the opposing party, led by . . . Odinga, a Luo, is responsible for organizing ethnic violence against Kikuyus; according to reports Kikuyus have also carried out attacks."[10] Government spokesman Alfred Mutua told BBC World News that "Odinga's supporters . . . are engaging in ethnic cleansing and they are not doing it in a haphazard manner, they are doing it in a very organized, calculated

---

10. Orso, "In Kenya, Religious Orders Model Peace," 11.

manner ... [with] military precision."[11] There are people who say that prior to the elections, Kikuyus received threats against their lives or their property if they did not vacate the places where they had settled. Men who swear by the Bible dominate the Kenyan parliament. Have the aggressors set aside their Christian identity in favor of their ethnic group?

The degree to which the violence was premeditated is under investigation. Drawing from the Kenya National Commission on Human Rights report among other sources, the Waki report indicated that evictions of some ethnic communities from areas such as Kipkelion in the Rift Valley were premeditated.[12] Some in the Kikuyu community buried their belongings in anticipation of being attacked. A culture of impunity in Kenya is a factor in premeditated ethnic violence.

The power of the media in informing the world about the post-election chaos cannot be underestimated. It was reported, for instance, that the opposition won in six out of the eight provinces, implying that the incumbent president could not have won the election. But the report fails to acknowledge that the incumbent had a substantial number of votes in those six provinces. When these votes were added to the very strong showing in the other two provinces, the total for the incumbent was greater than those for the opposition. The media report led to charges that the Kenyan electoral commission had admitted its "own ... incompetence."[13] So powerful is the press that, in my thinking, the first president of every nation is the press.

Another factor that contributes to the creation of violence is the weak economy. With a huge proportion of the country's population being under 35, Kenya has not been able to create enough jobs to absorb the youth in an economically productive culture. This leads to the rise of crime, particularly as Kenya urbanizes. Young people get involved with organized crime as a way to generate income. This leads to gangs and vigilante groups, some of which have been used by politicians to achieve political goals. Too often political power in Kenya functions without accountability.

CONCLUSION

Although Kenya's ethnic conflict was sparked by politics in the context of multiparty democracy, the roots of the conflict are multidimensional, with historical, missional, theological, and scientific aspects. To term the conflict "tribal" is simply inaccurate and is based on oversimplification. While not

11. BBC News, January 1, 2008.
12. "Waki Commission," 147.
13. Ouko, "Kenya: Why the Violence," 23–25.

denying the ethnicity factor, it is more valid to speak of "post-election violence" than "tribal violence."

The stewardship of power in Kenya is a daunting task for the church to address. The church itself must demonstrate good stewardship of power, which the nation can emulate. Let the church adopt effective structures of power that will preempt chaos rather than merely react when trouble occurs.

The Gospel offers a peace that unites Christians. Christians in Kenya's many ethnic groups need to embrace unity that flows from being members of one body and under one head, that is, Christ. Sometimes memorandums of understanding adopted by political factions have exacerbated divisiveness among Kenyans; only the peace of the Gospel will unite a diverse Kenya.

Christians also should guard against the "prosperity gospel" and promises of painless living. Christians are called to suffer for righteousness. The church should address injustice and oppression and be prepared to embrace suffering for the sake of Christ and his kingdom.

God's people are multiethnic. Christian teaching and preaching should be geared toward realities faced by multiethnic societies. With rising urbanization, multiethnic societies will continue to grow, challenging churches to minister effectively in diversity.

BIBLIOGRAPHY

Beideman, T. O. *Colonial Evangelism: A Social-Historical Study of an East African Mission at the Grassroots*. Bloomington: Indiana University Press, 1982.

Ethe, Kamuyu-Wa-Kang. "African Response to Christianity: A Case of the Agikuyu of Central Kenya." *Missiology: An International Review* 16 (1988) 23–44.

Höpfl, Harro. *Luther and Calvin on Secular Authority*. Cambridge: Cambridge University Press, 1991.

Nagele, Susan. "Election Chaos: A Report from Kenya." *Commonwealth,* Jauary 2008.

Orso, Joe. "In Kenya, Religious Orders Model Peace." *National Catholic Reporter*, February 28, 2008.

Ouko, Charles. "Kenya: Why the Violence Was so Virulent." *New African*, February 2008.

Sandgreen, David P. *Christianity and the Kikuyu: Religious Divisions and Social Conflict*. New York: Lang, 2000.

"Waki Commission." Judicial Commission of Inquiry, Kenya, October 15, 2008.

Wathiong'o, Ngugi. *Moving the Centre: The Struggle for Cultural Freedoms*. Oxford: Currey, 1993.

8

How Indigenous Traders Brought Christianity to Northern Nigeria

Caleb O. Oladipo

Who planted the Christian church in the Muslim stronghold of Northern Nigeria? In the days of colonial rule the British government denied Christian missions access to the Muslim north. This policy prevailed until the mid-twentieth century. As a result, it was not missionaries but Nigerians from the south, beginning half a century prior to the entry of missionaries, who put down roots and established the first Christian communities in Northern Nigeria.[1]

When at last missionaries gained entrance to the north in the 1940s and 1950s, their effectiveness was facilitated by the presence of indigenous believers, and their subsequent success can be attributed in part to the pioneering, indigenous Nigerian Christians.

An understanding of how and why Yoruba Christian laity from the south established Christianity in Northern Nigeria, and under what circumstances and limitations, will help us gain a better understanding of the diverse Christian manifestations in modern-day Nigeria. A question that historians have not addressed thoroughly is whether an already established Nigerian multiculturalism allowed for the creation of a Christian identity in Northern Nigeria, or whether it was Christian influence itself in the early

---

1. Bamigboye, *History of Baptist Work in Northern Nigeria*.

years of the twentieth century that helped develop a unique multicultural and multi-religious people in Northern Nigeria.

In any case, despite Islamic dominance in Northern Nigeria for over seven hundred years, Baptist laity played an important role in turning Northern Nigeria into a multi-religious society.[2] For the foreseeable future both Islam and Christianity will coexist as faiths of Northern Nigeria, despite continuing tensions.

This essay covers the historical background of the south-to-north movement; challenges met by Yoruba traders in the north, and how southern Christians related to Muslim neighbors. The conclusion celebrates today's multiethnic Christian communities in the north.

HISTORICAL BACKGROUND

The early decades of the twentieth century in Southern Nigeria can be characterized as a time of indigenous Christian identity formation. Local Christians began to use indigenous idioms to express their Christian faith. Prominent leaders who had taken Anglo names reverted to their original Yoruba names. Basic theological tenets were expressed in Yoruba idiom.

Although missionaries from the United States entered Southern Nigeria as early as the 1850s with the arrival Thomas Jefferson Bowen, the British colonial authorities did not permit them to enter Northern Nigeria, where the majority of the population was Muslim (and remains so today). The Hausa and Fulani ethnic groups under Islamic caliphates collaborated with the British colonial authorities in enforcing this policy.

In addition, the threat of deadly disease discouraged early missionary presence in Nigeria. When, in the early 1830s, the Presbyterian mission sent missionaries from America to Liberia, a near-neighbor of Nigeria, six of them died within a year. Their deaths made it difficult for the Southern Baptist Convention (SBC) in the United States to recruit volunteers for service in Nigeria.[3] The frequent deaths of missionaries due to malaria, typhoid fever, and other tropical diseases, led to labeling Africa the "white man's grave."[4]

---

2. Cook, *British Enterprise*, 149–88; see also Ayandele, *Nigerian Historical Studies*, 151–61.

3. The Southern Baptist Convention, incorporated in Georgia in 1845, continues to send and support missionaries to Nigeria.

4. Bamigboye, *History of Baptist Work*, 22.

For a time, it was the policy of the SBC to send American blacks to Nigeria. It was reasoned that black missionaries, who were African by nature, would be more effective in converting fellow Africans to the Christian faith.[5]

Baptist missionaries in Southern Nigeria were few in number, and the needs were overwhelming. As late as the 1940s SBC missionaries were concentrating on building schools and planting new congregations in the south. As a result, establishing a Christian presence in the north was left to ordinary church members from the south.

In the absence of missionary influence, one factor in southern migration to the north was the building of railways in Nigeria, beginning in 1914. The intention of the British authority was the political amalgamation of the north with the south. Christians in the south, however, saw it as an escape from the excessive taxes imposed by the British colonial government in the south.

During the building of the railways, many people worked as laborers for the British contractors. As the construction moved north, so did the laborers. Some settled down in the north after the railroad was completed. Others used their savings to purchase goods for trading in the south and eventually in the north.

There was also a completely unforeseen development that became a major impetus to indigenous leadership in the south and also the north. Since the late 1880s the Baptist mission had employed nationals as translators and pastoral assistants. A particular gifted young man was Moses Ladejo Stone, born about 1850. Earlier he had served the Baptist church in his hometown of Ogbomoso.

In 1888 the pastor at First Baptist Church, Lagos, was missionary W. J. David; Stone was his translator and pastoral assistant. One day, when Stone approached Rev. David with the idea of getting more education, the missionary denied his request. In an exchange of words that followed, Stone remarked that the Baptist work in Nigeria was primarily the responsibility of the Nigerian Christians not the white foreign missionaries. Stone offered his resignation a week later, and David accepted it without consulting the congregation. When leading members of First Baptist Church heard what happened, they saw it as a clear evidence of racial discrimination. Sixty-three members, including primary leaders, withdrew their membership and

---

5. The three-self formula of Henry Venn, that churches should be self-supporting, self-propagating, and self-governing, was used to justify this preference for black American missionaries. See Ajayi, "Henry Venn." See also Crampton, *Christianity in Northern Nigeria*, 16, 21.

formed a new congregation less than three miles away, calling it Ebenezer Baptist Church, with Stone as the pastor.

Following the establishing of Ebenezer Baptist, other new churches were started by Nigerians without missionary involvement. Indigenous identities were reclaimed with a return to Yoruba names. Ebenezer church leader David Vincent became Majola Agbebi. Some years later Agbebi became "Dr. Majola Agbebi," first president of the Yoruba Baptist Association.

Ogbomoso, about 200 miles northwest of Lagos and Stone's birth town, was a prominent trading center. First Baptist Church and the Yoruba Christian Association were noted for their vitality. In 1893 the church sent a delegation to First Baptist, Lagos, seeking candidates to pastor new churches.

In 1900 there were well over 100 members attending Sunday services at one of the new churches in Ogbomoso. This church later became the mother church for many other Baptist churches across the country. By the end of 1926 Ogbomoso and the surrounding district had 34 Baptist congregations and 29 outstations.[6] At least five of them were highly organized, with more than 100 members. Many of those who became leaders in building Christian communities in Northern Nigeria came from the Ogbomoso Baptist community.

CHALLENGES FACED BY YORUBA TRADERS

Key to the spread of Christianity in Northern Nigeria was a network of Yoruba traders. The presence of British colonial administrators, merchants, and missionaries in the south led to the demand for Western products. Umbrellas provided shade against the scorching equatorial sun. The traders also sold matches, flashlights ("torch lights"), chocolate products, and sporting goods. The agrarian society in the south soon included a flourishing commercial sector selling European products. Before long, young southern traders saw the opportunity to expand their routes into parts of the north.[7] These migrant traders became the vanguard of indigenous "missionary" workers, forming Christian communities in Northern Nigeria.

Another incentive drawing southern traders to the north had to do with agriculture. The south was fertile and supported agriculture, while the north was arid. Most southerners were farmers, which meant that there was hardly anyone to sell to during harvest time. Cola nut trees, which were abundant in the south, would not grow in the arid soil of the north, and the

---

6. See Collins, *Baptist Mission of Nigeria*.
7. Bamigboye, *History of Baptist Work*, 30.

people in the north enjoyed cola nuts more than the people in the south. Therefore, traders extended their routes to sell cola nuts and other farm products to northerners. They also offered brass, copper, swords, aluminum, knives, horse trappings, bowls, jugs, trays, wooden chairs, jewelry, rings, and hair pins.

Eventually the Yoruba traders discovered other economic opportunities such as tailoring and auto mechanics. Some engaged in embroidery, hat making, mat making, and leather working.

Another situation prompting moves to the north was the imposition of new taxes by the colonial administration in the late 1930s. Southern farmers were accustomed to paying taxes with farm products to the traditional rulers. When additional taxes were introduced, payable in cash, it was viewed as double taxation. This unexpected financial burden, coupled with the understanding that people in the north did not pay a colonial tax, drove many southerners to Northern Nigeria in the 1930s and 1940s.

Christians were the earliest to protest against unjust taxation. As early as 1922, the Olorunda Society at Ogbomoso emerged to defend the cause of the poor. When a number of people at Ogbomoso refused to pay the new tax, the colonial administrator imposed financial penalties. Ogbomoso residents saw such actions as arbitrary and pernicious, and in violation of Christian principles. Disorder reached a peak as young men and women were indiscriminately arrested and imprisoned. Young people who already had moved north urged their relatives in the south to join them. So it was that a large number of Christians in the south migrated to the north in the 1930s and 1940s. E. A. Ayandele called their migration "the Ogbomoso diaspora."[8]

This history of southern Christian Yorubas among the Muslim Hausa and Fulani peoples in Northern Nigeria has not always been peaceful. Traditionally, the Hausa and Fulani have regarded Northern Nigeria as a pure Islamic enclave. The migration of Christians from the south, enlarging settlements along the railway line, made it difficult to determine where Southern Nigeria ended and Northern Nigeria began. The presence of Christians enlarged the boundaries of the Christian community and turned Northern Nigeria into a multicultural and multi-religious society.

---

8. Ayandele, "Ogbomoso Rip Van Winkle." See also Bamigboye, *History of Baptist Work*, 53.

HOW CHRISTIANS RELATED TO MUSLIM NEIGHBORS

Christian traders from the south faced enormous obstacles in the north. At first, the Baptist traders felt quite at home. Those who settled in Jos spoke of it as their second "hometown." Some named their compounds after family compounds at home in the south.[9] The economic climate of the Christian diaspora created a network of people of similar origin, as well as membership in social organizations patterned after those in the south.

However, sooner or later the Christians faced aggressive behavior by the clannish northerners. The earliest persecution arose in Jos when Muslims mocked the Yoruba Christians as "infidels."[10] (To some extent this persists in the present time.) The Christians were not discouraged, however, but saw the mockery as an opportunity to tell Muslims about their faith. They began carrying their Bibles to the shops and market places. This helped to disarm the Muslim assumption that Islam was the only religion that emphasized piety and devotion. The common Muslim charge that Christianity created dependency upon foreign missionaries began to fade.

The Christian traders sometimes placed Christian literature on the articles for sale, indicating that they were just as devoted to their faith as the Muslims.[11] Muslim buyers sometimes asked questions about the Bible. In response, the traders shared the Gospel.[12]

The Yoruba people are known for their traditional warmth. Some traders not only spoke the Hausa language but also invited Muslim customers and neighbors to the colorful marriage ceremonies of their sons and daughters. The playing of gramophone records and radios attracted the Muslim youths to Christianity, although strict Muslim parents objected to the materialism and British education associated with Southern Nigeria.

In recent times U.S. missionary Ethel Harmon wrote, "Like the early Christians, the Yoruba Baptists established Churches and places of worship wherever they go. Most of our Northern Churches have been started by the Yoruba Baptist Christians who have gone north as traders, miners or even government workers." Harmon observed that since missionaries were not allowed to work directly in the Muslim dominated towns and cities, the Yoruba traders as citizens and private individuals were free to take their religion with them.[13]

9. Gobum, "Ogbomoso of Jos," 5.

10. Yoruba Christians consider an infidel to be one who professes no religion, whereas Muslims consider any non-Muslim to be an infidel.

11. Bamigboye, *History of Baptist Work*, 56.

12. Ibid.

13. Harmon, Foreword, 23.

In 1914 a group of Baptist women at Jebba started attending a non-Baptist church on Sunday evenings. This required them to cross the Niger River. Their husbands worried about canoe accidents that were common because of crocodiles. They eventually persuaded their wives to stay at home for the Sunday evening prayer meeting, which, in 1915, became First Baptist Church on the southern side of the river.

Later that year a small congregation at Jebba left for Zungeru, the next railway station, for trading, and eventually they formed the first Baptist congregation in Zungeru.

By 1916, motivated by the economic success of fellow traders, the majority of the Yoruba traders moved from Jebba to Zungeru. Initially Sir Frederick Lugard, the British colonial administrator, proposed making Zungeru the political capital of the north. But Zungeru was invested with mosquitoes, and so Kaduna, the next town to the north, was selected as the new political capital of Northern Nigeria.[14]

The attempted amalgamation of Nigeria by Lugard proved to be fraught with social obstacles. The creation of a northern capital further accentuated the cultural and religious differences between the Muslims and Christians. In Kaduna the southerners were treated as foreigners and were restricted to a ghetto known as Sabon Gari, which was notorious for harboring hooligans. But over time, Sabon Gari became transformed into the most developed part of Kaduna, with elegant shops and churches established by the Baptist traders from the south. Teachers from the south also settled there, and Sabon Gari gradually took a step ahead of the traditional Muslim cities in educating the children.[15]

One of the challenges faced by Yoruba Christians was securing plots of land from the British colonial government on which to build churches. In the predominantly Muslim north the building of Christian churches risked creating additional tensions with the Muslim neighbors. A colonial official in Kaduna advised the Baptists not to locate church buildings in the city.[16] The Christians were expected to build their church on the outskirt of Kaduna, some five miles away. In direct defiance, they began construction in the city. Summoned to explain their actions, they assured the administrator that building the church in the city would increase government revenue because

---

14. Bryant, *Guide to Kaduna*, 2.

15. "Sabon Gari became the most attractive center, where commercial activities such as shopping centers, banks and schools were established and flourished." Bamigboye, *History of Baptist Work*, 74.

16. Ibid., 77. This was consistent with strict regulations against religious activities in Islamic dominated cities.

many southerners would move into the city for trading. After further consideration, the administrator relented and the church was built.

In Kontagora, another developing town in the north, the First Baptist Church was founded between 1916 and 1917 by a group of Yoruba traders who left Zungeru in 1915. The Yoruba Baptist traders approached the Emir of Kontagora for a piece of land and were led out of the town far away into the bushes.

In 1920, a group of traders went to the chief at Ijagbo, a front door to the north (modern day Kwara State), and asked for a piece of land to build a church. The land was generously granted free of charge, and then permission was secured from the British colonial government to build a church on the site.

In Zaria, in 1926, a group of Christian traders approached the Emir of Zaria and requested a piece of land for their church building. Opposing their request, the Emir directed that the Christians be given land about four miles from the city gate, to build a house for "their god."[17] It was entirely different in Funtua, another northern town. At the Christians' request, the Emir of Funtua granted land near where they lived.[18]

The pastors in the north were often from the south. Rev. Adegoke, the pastor of First Baptist Church in Funtua, for example, was from Ogbomoso. He realized that Christianity would not be firmly grounded in the north without northern leadership. At the same time, Muslim leaders saw the economic advantage of allowing Yoruba Christian traders in town, the source of material benefits, even though they feared Christianity would dilute the purity of the Muslim north. In this delicate situation, Rev. Adegoke determined to create positions of leadership in the church for native northerners. Ultimately a dynamic church was established with a predominantly Hausa membership.

When a new church had been established at Kwanki, Muslim leaders arrested five Hausa converts for erecting an illegal structure. On the sixth day of confinement, they appeared before the area court and were formally charged for building a church illegally. They told the court that they had not built the church but their leader, Rev. Adegoke, a southerner, built it. The men were discharged and acquitted. The following day the court summoned Adegoke. Knowing that the legal code of the time allowed a mosque to be built anywhere in Nigeria, on the night before his appearance Adegoke went

---

17. Ibid., 83.
18. Ibid., 84.

to the church and replaced the church sign with one that read: "Nasarawa Christian Mosque."[19]

The next morning Adegoke invited the court to see that he had built a mosque, not a church. When the judge reached the place, he saw the sign: "Christian Mosque." At a later hearing the case was dismissed on a technicality.

CONCLUSION

Christianity remains a religion of the minority in Northern Nigeria. Yet the witness of the Yoruba Christians has been unquestionably positive. By 1975 Christians in Northern Nigeria included all ethnic groups. Hausa and Fulani believers serve as leaders, interpreters, and pastors. It is fair to say that Christians in Northern Nigeria are often more committed to the new path than Christians in the south. Christianity has become a cementing factor among different ethnic groups.

Much has been achieved through the Christian lives of indigenous traders for over a century or more, from dedicated ministry of Baptist missionaries since mid-century, and the steady commitment of local Christians from multiple ethnic groups in Northern Nigeria.

BIBLIOGRAPHY

Ajayi, J. F. Ade. "Henry Venn and the Policy of Development." In *Tradition and Change in Africa: The Essays of J. F. Ade Ajayi*, edited by Toyin Falola, 57–67. Trenton, NJ: Africa World Press, 1999.

Ayandele, E. A. *Nigerian Historical Studies*. London: Cass, 1979.

———. "Ogbomoso Rip Van Winkle." In *The History of Baptist Work in Northern Nigeria, 1901–1975*, by Ezekiel A. Bamigboye, 53–54. Ibadan, Nigeria: Powerhouse, 2000.

Bamigboye, Ezekiel A. *The History of Baptist Work in Northern Nigeria 1901–1975*. Ibadan, Nigeria: Powerhouse, 2000.

Bryant, K. J. *A Guide to Kaduna*. London: Macmillan, n.d.

Collins, Travis. *The Baptist Mission of Nigeria, 1850–1993: A History of the Southern Baptist Convention Mission Work in Nigeria*. Ibadan: Oduseye, 1993.

Crampton, E. P. T. *Christianity in Northern Nigeria*. London: Chapman, 1979.

Gobum, Katdapba Y. "The Ogbomoso of Jos." *Nigerian Standard*, January 8, 1994.

Harmon, Ethel. Foreword to *Nigeria Foreign Mission Abroad*. SBC annual report, 1974.

---

19. Ibid., 120–21.

9

Sickness and Witches in Northwestern Tanzania

Listening to Pentecostal Ministers

Steven D. H. Rasmussen

Four-year-old Grace was very sick. For several days the hospital had difficulty discovering what was wrong. Most locals were saying she was bewitched, and at least four different people were accused of bewitching her. Since the hospital had failed, many urged Grace's parents to take her to a local healer. Her Christian parents were so anxious they were tempted to try anything.

Grace's grandfather, Benester Misana, a Tanzanian pentecostal pastor, deals with sickness and death regularly.[1] Pastor Misana acknowledges

---

1. Much of a Tanzanian pastor's work is praying for healing and comforting the grieving. This is true in their families as well as their congregations. Like almost all of the pastors I know in Tanzania, one of his children had died. On another occasion, when he was some 160 miles away from home at the Bible school, he received word that a second daughter had died. But upon his return home he was greeted with the news that she had been resurrected. His wife recounted how the daughter had been taken to the hospital suffering with malaria, and after a week she had died. The mother prayed over her but at last realized she was dead; the doctors tried to help but could only confirm that she had passed away. About three hours later she began to breathe. The doctor and a nurse witnessed the girl's revival themselves and joined in praise to God.

the existence of witches, but he resists accusations of witchcraft.² When his 80-year-old mother died, he called a family meeting to stop rumors that a relative had killed his mother.

Misana ministers in an Abakwaya village outside Musoma, Tanzania. Several people have been killed here because they were suspected of being witches. In his area 80 percent of the people go to the diviner before they ever go to the doctor.³ At the time of his granddaughter's illness, the nearest clinic was a two-hour walk away and had no resident medical personnel. But "every third house" in his village had a neo-traditional, local healer.⁴ As a pastor, Misana represents the third alternative. He turns to God for answers to his neighbors' health needs and their accusations.

Tite Tiénou, the honoree of this Festschrift, has urged theologians and missiologists to "reflect seriously on suffering in the African experience. . . . Africa, more than any other continent on earth, is in need of healing in all of its dimensions."⁵ Africa struggles with much more sickness and early death than the rest of the world. Health workers in Africa are confronted with

- 1% of the world's health care resources
- 3% of the global health workforce
- 11% of the world's population
- 25% of the global disease burden⁶

---

2. In Northwestern Tanzania a witch (*mchawi* in Swahili) is generally understood to be a person who intentionally causes illness or death by invisible or spiritual means.

3. Nyaga, "Impact of Witchcraft," 247–68.

4. I am using the term "local healer" as a direct translation of the Swahili *mganga wa kinyeji*. Local healers are also known as diviners, because they consult with ancestors or other spiritual beings for diagnosis and treatment. With rare exception, they use mystical powers, including *dawa*, which can mean medicine or herbs or poison or charms (a physical entity), or any combination of these, all of which usually involve spiritual powers. A *mganga* distinguishes him/herself as a helper and healer and defender, unlike a *mchawi* (witch) who has evil motives and only harms. Although Pentecostal ministers in Tanzania understand both the mganga and the mchawi to be empowered by demons and accuse many waganga (plural of healer) of doing *uchawi* (witchcraft), they keep the two categories distinct (unlike many English speakers).

Researchers Wijsen and Tanner describe many Sukuma beliefs and practices in northwestern Tanzania as "neo-traditional" because they use traditional terms and concepts but often in demonstrably new ways. Waganga claim to use traditional methods/knowledge but their methods are continually changing. In urban settings they often blame spirits rather than ancestors as they did in villages in the past. See Wijsen and Tanner, "*I Am Just a Sukuma*," 35.

5. Tiénou, "Training of Missiologists," 98–99.

6. World Health Organization, "Global Shortage of Health Workers and Its Impact."

In Tanzania churches and other faith-based organizations provide nearly half of health care services.[7] Churches with a Western missionary heritage have usually denied local understandings of the role of witches in causing disease and providing cures. Neo-traditional healers, on the other hand, offer social and spirit-world explanations and prescriptions for sickness. In this environment the practice of independent and pentecostal churches praying for healing through Jesus often fits more closely the local people's understanding of sickness than the strictly medical explanations offered by missionary-heritage churches. In other words, Pentecostals are more likely to identify with traditional beliefs and practices since they work with a similar worldview. This addresses people's deep questions about why they have become sick and who may have caused it.[8]

How should Christians in Africa respond to sickness and suffering? When looking for causes and cures should Christians ignore, fight, or accept neo-traditional understandings? Should they limit their understandings to biomedical factors alone? How do we know what is true? How can we use the Bible to understand and respond theologically and practically?

According to Tiénou, "Listening before speaking is the first act of sound missiology. Listening enhances the possibility of reflection . . . [to] prevent the practice of mission from being mere activism."[9] Together with Paul Hiebert, Tiénou has advocated a "missional theologizing," or "critical contextualization," process to take place in specific contexts about specific issues.[10] This process leads a group of Christians to listen to people, then listen to God, and finally minister out of what has been learned. Ultimately they should look for the interaction of the spiritual, cultural, social, personal, and bio-physical systems.[11] This essay presents the results of listening and missional theologizing with northwestern Tanzanian pentecostal ministers regarding sickness and death.

Online: http://www.who.int/mediacentre/factsheets/fs302/en/index.html6.

7. Craig Hafner, "Strengthening the Role of Faith-Based Organizations in Human Resources for Health Initiavies," *CapacityProject.org*, Legacy series 8, September 2009, online: http://www.capacityproject.org/images/stories/files/legacyseries_8.pdf.

8. But at the same time, members of these churches may affirm local cultural beliefs that do not fully fit the Bible.

9. Tiénou, "Training of Missiologists," 95–96.

10. Tiénou and Hiebert, "Missional Theology." In this essay I use "missional theology" and "critical contextualization" as synonyms.

11. Hiebert et al., *Understanding Folk Religion*, 33–35.

LISTENING PROCESS

After eight years of learning and teaching in Swahili at Lake Victoria Christian College, a pentecostal Bible college in northwestern Tanzania, I spent two years learning from experts like Tite Tiénou, Paul Hiebert, and Robert Priest at Trinity International University, Deerfield, Illinois. These teachers emphasized the need for careful listening and theologizing in specific contexts. I returned home to Mwanza, Tanzania, with a listening plan and a research proposal.

For three years, I listened to ministers in northwestern Tanzania. I collected information on what people say and do during episodes involving illness and death in northwestern Tanzania, with particular attention to the beliefs and practices involved and to the social outcomes of these beliefs and practices. The ministers audio-taped or wrote more than 150 stories of illness or death reported by friends or drawn from their own experience. I interviewed individually or in focus groups more than 100 pentecostal ministers for more than 130 hours; later these interviews were transcribed. I spent uncountable hours doing participant observation and typing 100,000 words of field notes. Nearly all of this was in Swahili. Finally the data was analyzed for themes and developed into case studies.

I used this material as the basis for a critical contextualization and educational program in Tanzania. The participants (mostly ministers who contributed to the research) grappled with the theological and pastoral issues the cases presented. I led this process in six different locations with various ethnic groups. I also had discussions with the deans of Lake Victoria Christian College, and particularly with the principal, Rev. John Mwanzalima.

RESEARCH RESULTS

When someone is seriously ill or dies in northwestern Tanzania, most often people say that "the hand of a person" caused it. They seek through divination, discussion, and other means to discover who caused it (most often an older woman thought to be a witch) and then how to deal with the disease and the person who caused it. Such is the challenge faced by pentecostal ministers who declare "Jesus is more powerful so we should trust him and not fear."

Beliefs about Causes and Cures

The worldview of the people of northwestern Tanzania is that the key to life is interpersonal relationships with others, whether living, dead, or spirits. My informants identified three possible systems of explanation for sickness: local/neo-traditional, pentecostal Christian, and biomedical. The neo-traditional system dominates local worldviews.

Both local healers and pentecostal pastors deal with interpersonal and spiritual causes of illness with rituals, prayers, words (and sometimes objects) of power. They also emphasize persevering in trust and following the rules stipulated by an ancestor or, in the case of the pentecostal ministers, by Jesus. Both the local healers and the pastors relate to spirits. But there are significant differences. For example, while local healers see spirits as possibly good or bad and conduct rituals to appease them, pentecostal ministers say all spirits are demonic. Therefore Pentecostals cast them out in the name of Jesus and refuse to negotiate with them.

People often argue about how a death or healing should be evaluated. Biomedicine points to physical and natural causes. Local healers point to witches and ancestors or spirits. Pentecostals point to demons as causes, the power of Jesus to cure, and the will of God to explain. The representatives of each system attempt to explain away or minimize the power of the other systems. Sometimes people convert from one belief to another or incorporate a few of the other system's beliefs into their system. Sometimes people desperate for healing try every system.

Most people in northwestern Tanzania believe that witches cause almost all illness and death. Witches are people who usually have significant relationships to the ill person, who use invisible means in causing the sickness. A person may also cause another to be ill through bad luck, curses, or *dawa* (medicine/herbs/poison/charms; see note 4). Spirits such as ancestors, *majini* (genies), or demons, who are present but invisible beings, may also cause illness or death or remove their protection. They do this because the afflicted person has broken their taboo, or they want to motivate the person toward a particular action. All of this involves an interpersonal causal ontology.

Northwestern Tanzanians usually understand moral and biomedical causal ontologies as secondary to the interpersonal.[12] Moral: "Your failure

---

12. I am using the categories of Richard Shweder. He says people seek causes in order to establish what is "normal," control future events, and assign blame. He focuses on three frequent causal ontologies: "1) Interpersonal . . . the ill will of others; 2) moral . . . you reap what you sow; 3) biomedical . . . events that take place outside the realms of human action, responsibility, or control . . . a material event . . . morally neutral."

allowed her to make you sick." That is, the ill person sinned, broke a taboo, or offended someone, and as a result an ancestor, spirit, or God caused his/her illness or removed his/her spiritual protection so that a witch or spirit could cause the illness. Bio-medical: Germs and other physical causes of illness may be used by a witch to attack a person. "She/he (the witch) used it" (i.e., the germ, mosquito, etc.).[13]

Each system looks for specific causes and cures. The neo-traditional explanation and treatment system focuses on relationships with relatives or neighbors (identified as witches) and sometimes with ancestors or spirits. The pentecostal Christian system says that the Creator through Jesus and the Holy Spirit is powerfully present to heal and protect Jesus's followers from witches, demons, Satan, and sickness. Some Pentecostals broaden the worldview to say that not all deaths are caused by witchcraft. God's will, sin, and biomedical causes also play a significant role. The biomedical system focuses on objects: parasites, bacteria, and viruses as causes of disease, and medicines for cure.

Cures and protection come primarily from ancestors (local system), Jesus (Christian system), and chemicals and procedures (biomedical system). Each of these systems assumes obedience to their respective experts: local healer, pastor, doctor. In the chart on the following page, the capitalized words are the primary focus of diagnosis and treatment in each system. Items in other boxes are secondary and supportive to the primary area of focus whether interpersonal, moral, or biomedical.

Relationship of Beliefs to Values and Feelings

Northwestern Tanzanians believe witches cause illness and death, and therefore they live in considerable fear and suspicion of witches. The failure or sin of the ill person may open them up to this evil but the sin is not the primary cause of the illness: it is witchcraft that is the primary cause. In a somewhat similar way, pentecostal Christians see Satan, aided by demons, as the primary cause of illness and death. (In the Bible and in preaching sin is primary, but Christians seldom attribute misfortune to the sin of the sufferer in the specific cases of those they know.)

Shweder, *Why Do Men Barbecue?*, 80–87. However these categories are not entirely satisfactory. For example, God and ancestors can in some sense be seen as interpersonal as well as potentially moral.

13. At the funeral of his daughter, a Tanzanian friend asked me a typical question: "Maybe a mosquito bit my child, but many children are bitten by mosquitoes and don't get sick, or if they do, they take some medicine and get better. Who sent the mosquito?" The implication: a witch, an enemy, an ancestor.

Blessings and wealth also have a spiritual source (ancestors for neo-traditionalists and Jesus for Pentecostals). Rituals such as sacrifices, being prophesied over, and prayed for can release wealth, provided that the proper rules continue to be followed. Witchcraft suspicions often arise with disputes over property, inheritance, and envy.

In sharp contrast, Westerners see wealth and illness as having mechanical and visible sources. Biomedical causes and treatments of illness have little moral content (except that Westerners feel a moral imperative for everyone to receive medical attention).

Change in Beliefs and Experiences of Suffering

Most Tanzanian Pentecostals convert in connection with seeking healing or protection from witches. People also convert to Islam after being afflicted by *majini*. They go to a Muslim healer who instructs them in Muslim practices and rituals designed to appease the *majini*. The majority of Tanzanians, however, follow neo-traditional practices to appease or seek protection from ancestors.

Cause of sickness	Local, neo-traditional System	Pentecostal System	Biomedical System
Interpersonal: "She/he made you sick"	WITCHES, ancestors	powers of darkness: SATAN/ DEMONS (may be disguised as ancestors or *majini*); witches God	
Moral: "You made yourself sick"	Offense against an ancestor; sometimes normal persons may get "justifiable" help from an expert to curse you	Sin angers God or allows powers of darkness	Lifestyle choices: not using mosquito net or pure water; smoking, etc.
Biomedical: "It made you sick"	*Dawa*: Medicine, poison, herbs, or a charm used by a witch or other person	Biomedical: acknowledged and treated, but less important	"GERMS": parasites, bacteria, viruses, cancer cells, etc.

Pentecostal Christians say that they experience suffering somewhat differently than others. They claim freedom from fear through trusting in the present and greater power of Jesus who heals now and gives eternal life after death. However, most grow to trust Jesus and fear God alone through a process that includes many experiences and much teaching. Naturally, those who experience the power of Jesus in a personal way persevere more than those who do not.

Social Outcomes of Beliefs, Words, and Actions

How do people respond to sickness and to those they suspect may have caused sickness? Neighbors, churches, and extended families spend considerable time and expense to help those who are sick and, especially, to properly bury the dead and comfort the relatives. This can be motivated by love or by fear of harm: the ancestor might be displeased; the community might not help someone who does not help others; anyone who does not mourn with others can be suspected of causing the death.

People accuse, shun, banish, beat, and sometimes kill those who are suspected of witchcraft. Those beaten or killed are most often postmenopausal women. Those without close male relatives to defend them, such as sons or husbands, live in the greatest danger.[14]

People believe that family members are most able and likely to bewitch them. Neighbors or others with whom one has close relationship are the next most likely to bewitch them. Therefore, suspecting, avoiding, accusing, or shunning suspected witches cuts off relationships within extended families and between neighbors who would normally help each other.

When a person is sick or dies, most people consult one of the many local healers/diviners. Healers give treatment and protection and answer the peoples' question, "Who caused this?"

Sometimes, fearless trust in Jesus allows Pentecostals to restore relationships broken by suspicion of witchcraft. At other times fear causes them to passively follow the community in suspecting and shunning a relative or neighbor. When a woman who is suspected of being a witch, joins the church, she is never fully trusted even by some fellow Christians, so their relationships remain ambivalent. Most northwestern Tanzanians are more likely to believe that a witch can turn into a hyena or an owl than to become a new creature in Christ.

---

14. "Between 1970 and 1988, 3,073 people were killed in the area of Sukumaland after being identified as witches." Mesaki, "Witchcraft," 189.

THE PROCESS OF CRITICAL CONTEXTUALIZATION

The listening process I experienced greatly enhanced my understanding, teaching, and preaching. I asked my friend John Mwanzalima, a pastor I had worked with for over a decade, why I had not realized that witches were blamed for every serious sickness or death. He replied, "You never asked." In addition to what I discovered through listening, I also learned about the limitations and lasting benefits of a critical contextualization, or missional theologizing, program.

The critical contextualization and education process related to illness and death stimulated intense, insightful discussion and open sharing. Mwanzalima and I had responsibility for teaching and facilitating the meetings, but the students, who were almost entirely pastors, talked more than we did. It was a powerful adult education process. Discussion of what people said and did when sick took more time than evaluating or planning a biblical response.

When we began evaluating, areas of agreement and disagreement emerged: We all agreed that physical entities like parasites and bacteria as well as spiritual entities like demons cause illness and death. We all agreed that Jesus is more powerful and does heal. Participants did not always agree about whether witchcraft or something else caused particular cases; or whether pastors should use local medicines; or whether local healers accurately divine illnesses and provide effective treatments.

The ministers outlined some characteristics of a Christian response to witches and demons. For pentecostal Christians the powers of darkness, like Satan, demons, and witches, do cause illness and death. They have heard about many witches, and most have experienced attacks by witches. But their relationship with a powerful, present Jesus brings them protection, healing and hope after death. In nearly every church service, they sing "There is no God like you," affirming that in the midst of many powers, Jesus has unparalleled power.

Pentecostal ministers accept some local assumptions but also challenge the local worldview. They have difficulty convincing people that they only need to go to Jesus for protection and healing and that Jesus can even convert people they consider to be witches. The pastors say local healers are either tricksters or empowered by demons. Biomedical treatment is acceptable. They believe all spirits are demons, whether called ancestors, *majini*, or something else. They cast them out with the authority of Jesus. They know that witchcraft does not cause all deaths and that biomedical reasons can fully account for some illnesses. Rather than search for "the hand of a person" in a death, they appeal to the will of God: "this is the plan of God."

They find it difficult when Jesus does not heal everyone they pray for. The ministers came to a greater appreciation during the class of the need to show that faith in Jesus brings perseverance and victory even when sickness and death remain.

Participants cited what "everyone knows" for their viewpoints, along with stories from others and their own direct experience to support their viewpoint. They pointed to the use of the Swahili word for "witch" in Scripture to support the reality of witches in their communities. I countered by asking for evidence in Scripture of a witch killing somebody or making someone ill.

Ministers testified to some personal changes as a result of the critical contextualization process. They said they understood better the challenge that illness, death, and witchcraft pose to their people. They said they learned the importance of researching and doing critical contextualization. A few led discussions about witchcraft with others in their home areas. A few reported becoming more firm in trusting Jesus and biomedicine and more suspicious of those suspecting witchcraft when faced with a serious illness.

Participants really enjoyed and hoped for more of the teaching method and this topic. They did wish that more conclusions had been drawn about what was truly real and how to help people. In my own evaluation, better preparation on everyone's part and a somewhat extended period of teaching would be helpful. I also recognized the need for more resources representing broader perspectives. More focus on the ontological realities and missiological responses could help participants come to more conclusions and possibly to make deeper shifts.

IMPLICATIONS FOR MISSIONAL THEOLOGY

Listening to stories, as I did in the research phase and as participants did in their meetings, is critical for entering another's experience. People display their beliefs, feelings, and values as they relate their personal stories. I used disciplined listening and observing through focus groups, interviews, and participant observation. Then I reviewed the recordings, transcriptions, and field notes. This was followed by more interviews with key informants.

Scripture encourages listening to others. (See, e.g., Prov 17:27–28; 18:2, 13, 15; 19:2.) Listening is central to loving our neighbor and God, to learning and ministry. But then we must move beyond listening. With the help of the Spirit, fellow saints and the Scriptures, we must listen to what God is saying in our lives. We must discern what is really of God. Then we must obey in ways that transform our lives.

One conversation in particular emphasized to me the need for this process in northwestern Tanzania. Grace's grandfather Misana and I had this exchange:

Me: "Faith comes by hearing." What do people hear here? Do they hear stories about witchcraft every week?

Misana: In our village they hear them every day.

How much do they hear the stories of the Bible, even in our churches? Not much, I fear.

Kunhiyop confirmed this: "As long as Christians have more stories of witchcraft, they will always feel that witchcraft has power over the child of God."[15]

A major part of God's revelation in Scripture is acting out and telling stories. Parents and pastors need to be telling those stories and connecting them with current stories of God's work. The best preachers I have heard in Tanzania tell stories well. They make the Bible story come alive and connect it with appropriate local stories and local needs. The very best preachers additionally use good hermeneutics to listen well to the biblical authors. Many pentecostal services also contain testimonies and multiple songs that tell or apply Bible stories in memorable ways.

The critical contextualization classes I conducted with the ministers produced good listening skills as they went to interview Christians and non-Christians in their community for stories of sickness and death. Then they listened to each other as they shared these stories in our meetings. The process also forced Mwanzalima and me to listen and learn as we were teaching and facilitating the classes. The critical contextualization process produced a focus group and led to action research. Although I laid out the parameters and added some theories and Scriptures, the ministers did most of the talking and controlled the conclusions. Based on this experience, I think using this process has great potential to produce contextualized theologies for multiple contexts in Africa and elsewhere.[16] It can also be used as a pattern for an individual to theologize, but produces the most change when the community theologizes together.

For most of the participants, the critical contextualization program did not change worldview. Since worldview is what a group thinks with, it is very hard to get outside of the worldview. Thus I have not had discussions with people that changed their minds about whether witches could harm the health of others. People continue to think and analyze within their

---

15. See Kunhiyop, "Witchcraft," 139.

16. There are similarities to the "pastoral circle" used by Catholic theologians. See Wijsen et al., *Pastoral Circle*.

worldview (ourselves included!). Multi-worldview discussions on causality between participants who do and do not believe in the reality of witches could help us notice and change our worldview. Most often they produce only a "dialogue of the deaf."[17] Believers in the efficacy of witches and those who don't believe in witches talk to a point and then usually dismiss the other as ignorant. Both sides argue from their experience: "You haven't lived in the village long enough." Both assume that what "everyone knows" is the truth for everyone everywhere.

Listening deeply to someone with a different worldview takes extra humility and insight, but it holds promise of expanding and transforming our view of reality and our theology. Christians who do and do not believe in the efficacy of witches nevertheless can agree that many widows, orphans, and other marginalized people suffer needlessly because of accusations of witchcraft. As Christians, we must respond more lovingly.

Deep epistemological questions remain. What counts as evidence? Americans say "seeing is believing" and try to analyze evidence "scientifically." Tanzanians are likely to tell another story. Kunhiyop writes from Nigeria,

> Africans believe that witchcraft is real because they have heard scores of stories about it. They have heard the confessions of perpetrators and the testimonies of victims. There are thousands and thousands of such stories.
>
> African Christians who are trying to be relevant to their culture must begin [by] accepting that there is something such as witchcraft, by which we mean the general power of Satan and his evil cohorts to bring suffering and misery to humanity. It is not unbiblical to accept this.
>
> How do we know whether a story is true? It is generally assumed that if someone has confessed to being a witch, he or she is to be believed. However, such confession may be false. Moreover, even if the person did perform some actions intended as witchcraft, all that the confession proves is a belief in the effectiveness of witchcraft as well as a belief that witchcraft harnesses evil forces. To underline this point: stories and confessions about witchcraft do not prove the reality and certainty of witchcraft. They simply affirm the belief in the existence of witchcraft.[18]

Therefore for those who trust God's revelation in Scripture, the Bible reveals what is invisible and explains God's purposes for illness and death.

---

17. Tiénou, "Christian Theology," 48–50.
18. Kunhiyop, *African Christian Ethics*, 378–80.

The primary message of Scripture is that God gives life and even sickness or death. For Tanzanians, since the Swahili and English have translated some words with *mchawi* (witch), their understandings of witches seem validated by Scripture.

However, the actions and social roles described by the Hebrew and Greek terms in Scripture appear to be different from what *mchawi* means in northwestern Tanzania.[19] If a Tanzanian pastor accepts that the Bible does not really contain a description of a witch causing harm to others through invisible means, the next response is "the Bible doesn't explain everything"; that is, "What I know about witches is still true even if it is never mentioned in the Bible." Yet the silence of Scripture contrasts sharply with the understanding held by most northwestern Tanzanians. At the same time, Scripture also contrasts with the assumptions of most Americans that all sickness is caused by germs, cancer cells, genetic deficiency, and so forth, and that this explanation is sufficient.

Clearly, more research is needed that listens deeply about suffering in specific contexts, bringing the Scripture and human contexts together. Especially necessary is such research across Africa. As Tiénou has often emphasized, Africa is very diverse across cultures, classes, settings, and history, making generalizations dangerous. In the multicultural Africa International University (AIU), my classes always have Africans with a mix of beliefs on this subject; some firmly believe in the efficacy of witches and others just as firmly do not. Some of my students in Africa International University maintain that "all Africans believe in witches and denying witches is denying the essence of an African." Yet Westerlund documents that while the Sukuma, Kongo, and Yoruba believe strongly that witches cause illness, their Maasai and San Bushmen neighbors do not. Also, beliefs change within societies. Over the past century among these groups, there has been an increase in the belief that living humans cause illness.[20]

Very few have taken up Tiénou's call to theologize about suffering in Africa, including sickness and witches. Pastors theologize orally and in action almost daily, but they need help from more skilled researchers. Isaiah Majok Dau's *Suffering and God: A Theological Analysis of the War in Sudan* is an excellent exception, as is Samuel Kunhiyop's *African Christian Ethics*,

---

19. "*Nowhere in Scripture do we find anyone attributing affliction or death to a human third party acting through evil occult means.* [emphasis in original] . . . Missionaries historically were not only handicapped by biblical silence on the subject of interpersonal causal ontologies, and by a revered history of mistranslations which seemingly ratified such ontologies, but they encountered translational challenges they failed to understand." Priest, "Missiology and the Witch."

20. Westerlund, *African Indigenous Religions.*

the last chapter of which deals with witchcraft.[21] Why has more research not been done? Tiénou has noted issues like limited resources, non-contextualized theological education, English dominance, the hegemony postulate of the West, and shame in suffering.[22] Some possibilities I have heard or observed: 1) Fear: Some fear breaking community taboos by talking openly about it. Some fear being suspected themselves when they seek information or interview suspects. Some fear witches harming them. For example, one of my AIU students complained that the witches were attacking her for exposing them in her paper. She and her children had gotten sick and one child had been bitten by a snake while she was writing the paper. 2) Witches are assumed to be real. Therefore spiritual warfare against witches is needed, not research. 3) Because of the mysterious nature of spiritual warfare, researching in this area is demanding and risky, and the academic and theological methods of investigation are not obvious. 4) Writing about witches risks shame or alienating someone. If a professor writes as if he believes in witches, he risks being mocked by the Western academy. If he writes that he does not, he risks being seen as ignorant in many African communities.

Tiénou calls us to engage in "sustained international and interdisciplinary scholarship on matters affecting all of us."[23] Missiological, biblical, theological, anthropological, psychological, economic, and medical researchers need to do more research on African understandings of sickness and causality, including the social, spiritual, and biological outcomes of these understandings. Witches and witch accusations in Africa and elsewhere are a crucial aspect that has barely begun to be understood in an interdisciplinary way.

At my dissertation defense, Tiénou highlighted the following paragraph, saying that I should make it even stronger:

> I am very thankful for the billions now being spent to combat AIDS and other diseases in Africa, but I wonder how effective this will be without serious engagement with local knowledge, feelings, values, and practices. If people believe biomedicine to be ineffective, can it be effective? If it doesn't address felt needs and deep questions, people will probably continue to go elsewhere for answers. Northwestern Tanzanians need a critically contextualized healing approach that understands local beliefs and practices and responds . . . with an integrated spiritual, social, psychological, and medical approach to illness.

---

21. Dau, *Suffering and God*; Kunhiyop, *African Christian Ethics*.
22. Tiénou, "Christian Theology," 45–51.
23. Ibid., 50.

Tiénou himself has watched millions of dollars wasted when activists did not listen to the locals. Local pastors could be excellent partners for those trying to improve health. Unlike local healers, they are not competing with biomedicine or focusing on discovering witches. They see themselves as more in partnership with biomedicine, although, like other locals, they see biomedicine as incomplete. Many rural Tanzanians find their pastors more available, inexpensive, and trusted than medical personnel. Improved healing theology and public health practice could emerge from such a dialogue.

THE REST OF THE STORY

I asked Pastor Misana how he evaluated the outcome of a 13-hour critical contextualization course I led in Musoma. He reported that the class helped not only the thinking of various students, but also in the crisis with his granddaughter with which I began this essay. Most locals said she was bewitched, and at least four people were accused. Misana recounted his story:

> Paul, Grace's father, and his family said someone from our side bewitched Grace.... My sister-in-law, who they said this about, is in our church. But my brother's sisters and other relatives said, "We told her [Flora] not to be married there, because they are witches."
>
> When my son-in-law, Paul, was still small, his father pushed out Paul's mother for killing one of their children with witchcraft. His father's three remaining wives raised Paul. When he was older, he was converted. He continued in the church and married my daughter. After three months he went to his mother's area and brought her back to live in his house. When Grace become ill, some of my relatives blamed Paul's mother: "She killed her child, now she is doing it again to her grandchild."
>
> When they talked about this, my daughter Flora started to be afraid and forgot her Christian faith. My wife and I encouraged her, but she was very disturbed. So we tried to encourage Paul and Flora: "Leave this and trust Jesus. Let the hospital do its work." Paul and his family wanted to take Grace out of the hospital and bring her to a local healer. They even brought local [neo-traditional] medicine into the hospital to give her. When my wife visited, she saw this medicine and asked Flora about it. Then she threw it in the toilet. Because her mother and I were the only ones among all the relatives who contributed to the cost of the hospital treatment, Paul and Flora listened to us and did not take her out of the hospital.

Grace was scheduled to have an operation. Her stomach was swollen, hard, full of blood. (But delays and mismanagement resulted in the operation never happening.)

Finally, Grace recovered and everyone changed their tune. "Truly, God is able," they said.

When I told this to the students in your class, they said, "This is something that we haven't just heard about but it is happening right here. If the family had not followed through and this child had died, there would have been a fight between these families."

The class also helped me because it made me doubt what people say. In the class discussions I noticed that everyone had heard many things, but no one had seen them. But, because they had heard many times, they said, "It is possible." So when people began saying Grace was bewitched by this person or that, I said, "If no one has seen it, let's forget it and just trust Jesus." What helped this situation was my wife's and my stand. One student who saw Grace before and after said, "If someone is healed from a miracle, it is this one." So they saw it. They saw that God is great.

So the class was important because it helps you know where to stand when there is trouble. The problem is if you start to stagger, there are many who will take you away. If they had taken Grace out of the hospital, she would have died because she had not eaten for two weeks. The IV helped her so much. . . . So I think we should keep teaching this class to each round of students. I think we can teach it now that we have seen it.

So the critical contextualization/missional theology process can change belief and behavior. It can even save lives. In fact it is incomplete until it changes behavior and produces new experiences and stories, as in Pastor Misana's case. Village pastors can use it to theologize with their congregations and teach others to do the same. At the same time, it can form the basis for PhD dissertations and scholarly works like *Understanding Folk Religions*. It needs to be taught and used at every training level. Village pastors and university professors must cooperate as they do missional theology in specific contexts. This humble listening and cooperation must span continents, cultures, and research disciplines. Missional theology about suffering, sickness, and death is only one important area. Christians (especially pastors) need to be trained as healers who understand and respond more lovingly in the local spiritual, social, cultural, personal, physical, and biological systems. Expert researchers need to help them understand each system and how it interacts with the others. These understandings must be used for in-depth biblical research.

Jesus began with thirty years of listening. He then challenged beliefs and behaviors that were against his Father's will. Jesus brought healing, life, and hope especially to those rejected by society. We need to follow him—together.

BIBLIOGRAPHY

Dau, Isaiah Majok. *Suffering and God: A Theological Reflection on the War in Sudan.* Nairobi: Paulines Publications Africa, 2002.

Hiebert, Paul G. R., et al., eds. *Understanding Folk Religion: A Christian Response to Popular Beliefs and Practices.* Grand Rapids: Baker Academic, 2000.

Kunhiyop, Samuel Waje. *African Christian Ethics.* Nairobi: Hippo, 2008.

———. "Witchcraft: A Philosophical and Theological Analysis." *Africa Journal of Evangelical Theology* 21 (2002) 127–45.

Mesaki, Simeon. "Witchcraft and Witch Killings in Tanzania: Paradox and Dilemma." PhD diss., University of Minnesota, 1993.

Nyaga, Stephen Nyoka. "The Impact of Witchcraft Beliefs and Practices on the Socio-Economic Development of the Abakwaya in Musoma-Rural District, Tanzania." In *Imagining Evil: Witchcraft Accusations in Contemporary Africa*, edited by Gerrie ter Haar, 247–68. Trenton, NJ: Africa World Press, 2007.

Priest, Robert J. "Missiology and the Witch." Presentation at the American Society of Missiology, June 19, 2010.

Shweder, Richard A. *Why Do Men Barbecue? Recipes for Cultural Psychology.* Harvard University Press, 2003.

Tiénou, Tite. "Christian Theology in an Era of World Christianity." In *Globalizing Theology: Belief and Practice in an Era of World Christianity*, edited by Craig Ott and Harold A. Netland, 37–51. Grand Rapids: Baker Academic, 2006.

———. "The Training of Missiologists for an African Context." In *Missiological Education for the Twenty-First Century: The Book, the Circle, and the Sandals; Essays in Honor of Paul E. Pierson*, edited by J. Dudley Woodbury et al., 93–100. Maryknoll, NY: Orbis, 1996.

Tiénou, Tite, and Paul G. Hiebert. "Missional Theology." *Missiology* 34 (2006) 219–38.

Westerlund, David. *African Indigenous Religions and Disease Causation: From Spiritual Beings to Living Humans.* Leiden: Brill, 2006.

Wijsen, Frans J. S., Peter J. Henriot, and Rodrigo Mejia, editors. *The Pastoral Circle Revisited: A Critical Quest for Truth and Transformation.* Maryknoll, NY: Orbis, 2005.

Wijsen, Frans J. S., and Ralph Tanner, editors. *"I Am Just a Sukuma": Globalization and Identity Construction in Northwestern Tanzania.* Church and Theology in Context 40. Amsterdam: Rudopi, 2002.

10

Gender Roles and Recruitment in Southern African Churches, 1996–2001

Dana L. Robert

THE MAJORITY OF CHRISTIANS in Africa are women. Given this reality, African Christian theologies and church histories must take seriously the lives of ordinary women. Future generations will look back on the unprecedented expansion of African Christianity during the late twentieth and early twenty-first centuries and wonder how it came to be. Without research on the roles of women in the growing churches of Africa today, the story of Christian growth will be woefully inadequate.

Study of the dialectic among African theology, cultures, and biblical Christianity characterizes the exceptional work of Professor Tite Tiénou. In addition, his personal support for women's leadership in church and academy make both the method and the subject of this paper a fitting contribution to his Festschrift.[1]

Research on why African women participate in Christian churches faces formidable barriers. Especially in rural areas, gender separatism precludes male researchers from closely studying women's lives. The mostly female, rural populations must be accessed orally, in their own languages.

1. I was honored to serve for a decade with Tiénou on the board of the Overseas Ministry Study Center in New Haven, Connecticut. An earlier version of this paper was delivered as a plenary-level address at the 16th World Congress of Sociology, Durban, South Africa, July 28, 2006.

Ordinary African Christian women lack opportunities for theological education that would help them articulate their perspectives. In postcolonial terms, rural African women are "subalterns" who remain voiceless and invisible in the construction of formal African theologies and church histories. And as Gayatry Spivak has famously asked, Can the subaltern speak, or is her voice automatically overridden by that of the outside researcher who seeks to "represent" her?

The above limitations notwithstanding, this paper offers a modest contribution to the meaning of church participation among African women. It is based upon interviews with Shona-speaking women in rural Masvingo Province, Zimbabwe. It also draws upon several other studies of Southern African women that suggest gender-linked factors in church recruitment.

Churches are the chief form of social organization for Southern African women and women are considered the backbone of the church. My research on Christian women in Zimbabwe found that women join churches because in them they find female solidarity and support for their roles in family and community life. Women are attracted to Christian movements because they offer the means for healing, improved well-being, and reconciliation with others in their communities. Church-based community support for women, and for healing and wholeness, can also provide avenues for women's leadership in patriarchal societies.

STRUCTURE AND LIMITATIONS OF THE STUDY

Since 1995, I have made annual visits to Masvingo Province, Zimbabwe, and worshiped among Shona-speaking Christians of various denominations. As the wife of Prof. M. L. Daneel, Ndaza Zionist bishop whose forty-five years of research among indigenous churches is unparalleled in the study of African Christianity, I received permission to conduct interviews among women in a wide range of rural churches.[2] The questions I brought to the research were generated by my interest in comparing church women across cultures: Do patterns emerge that might explain why Christianity in Southern Africa

---

2. In 1996, under the leadership of M. L. Daneel and funded by the Pew Charitable Trusts, a dozen scholars and indigenous church leaders from South Africa, Zimbabwe, Malawi, and Boston University launched the five-year project "African Initiatives in Christian Mission." The larger goal of the project was to document through qualitative research the emergence of African-founded Christian movements in southern Africa. Although the research upon which this paper is based was not directly part of the Pew Project, I undertook it with help from the DeFreitas Foundation alongside my participation in the larger project. Female team members, including Isabel Phiri and Lilian Dube, focused their investigations on women in rural Christian movements.

appeals to women today? Why do women join churches and remain active members? Are there similarities among women's concerns across different African cultures and with the findings of researchers on emerging churches in other parts of the world? Finally, what does church participation mean to women in the current context of rampant HIV-AIDS and the destruction of family life caused by disease?

My research included a formal period of structured interviews during the late 1990s and continued with informal observations into the 2000s. Interviews were conducted initially in Shona, with selected follow-up interviews by me of English-speaking informants. We interviewed forty-two women, spread across six indigenous, two mainline, and one pentecostal denomination.[3] Female, Shona-speaking researchers attended women's conferences, visited healing colonies, recorded women's sermons, and recorded interviews shaped by a standardized questionnaire.[4] The women interviewed were well-respected church members from their late thirties through sixties, a population confident enough to analyze clearly the meaning of church membership as well as to have experienced changes over time. They were not a random sample but were identified by male leaders in their churches as appropriate for the study, and thus included a large number of pastors' wives. The unprecedented access we gained to rural, Shona-speaking women, many of them in African-initiated churches, was the result of a network of relationships cultivated by my husband since the 1960s. That the initial interviews were conducted at the homesteads by Shona researchers, all of them women, allowed for an unusual level of trust between informants and researchers. In accordance with traditional gender roles, the older women we interviewed saw themselves as helping, through the interviews, to teach younger Shona women researchers about family and church life.

---

3. Denominations included: (1) Reformed Church in Zimbabwe (5 women); (2) Roman Catholic Church (5 women); (3) Ethiopian Chibarirwe (African Congregationalist) (2 women); (4) First and Second Ethiopian (5 women); (5) Zion Apostolic Church (Ndaza) (6 women); (6) Zion Christian Church (5 women); (7) African Apostolic Church of Johane Maranke (5 women); (8) Other Apostles (5 women); (9) Apostolic Faith Mission (Pentecostal) (4 women). Total: 42 women.

4. The major limitation of this research was my own lack of fluency in Shona. All interviews were transcribed and translated into English. I discussed the ongoing research with the primary field worker, Ms. Farai Mfanyana, shaped the questions, analyzed written transcripts of the interviews and sermons, and conducted follow-up interviews with selected English-speaking informants. The advantage of using female Shona interviewers was that the women relaxed and talked about intimate matters, including sexuality and marital relations. In the most sectarian churches, some women were nervous about being interviewed, even though permission had been gained from their bishops. Other researchers who assisted with transcription were Patience Marume, Memory Makoko, and Edson Chigweda.

Masvingo is the most heavily populated, largely rural province in the center of Zimbabwe. The period of time in which we conducted interviews was immediately prior to the 2001 land invasions and subsequent collapse of the Zimbabwean economy. In addition, the effects of the AIDS epidemic were beginning to put a severe strain on the extended family system. By the early 2000s, it became impossible for researchers to enter the volatile rural areas, and the formal phase of the project ended.

MAJOR THEMES IN THE RESEARCH

The interviews contained questions about the women's theologies. But except for women who had received formal theological training as mainline pastors' wives, questions about theology largely elicited discussions of women's daily lives in relationship to church as living community. Three major gender-based themes that motivated sustained church participation on the part of women emerged: (1) shaping domestic relations, including guiding norms of female behavior; (2) providing healing and well-being; (3) cultivating women's leadership.[5] These gender-linked areas embody holistic worldviews for rural Southern African women, who tend not to compartmentalize the spiritual from the physical. For women, church membership is meaningful because it provides divine validation and guidance for female behavior, and it provides supportive communities in which women's daily struggles for healing and well-being can take place.[6]

---

5. In a longer study I would break out the conclusions into more than three themes. It is significant that these three themes intersect the organizational concerns of the historic woman's missionary movement, even though they are contextualized in African cultural forms. (1) Female missionaries justified their participation in missions by pointing to the gender separatism of most non-Western societies and indicating that only women could reach women and children. They took with them a commitment to founding Christian homes in which women would be treated with respect, boy and girl children would be educated and kept clean, and Christian marriage customs such as monogamy and fidelity would become the norm. (2) Healing was also a major emphasis of gender-based missions. The first female missionary doctor went out in 1869, and by 1910, 10 percent of all American women missionaries were medical doctors. (3) The third area, women's leadership, was promoted by founding schools for girls and by training female teachers, doctors, and leaders for church and society. The founding of women's organizations in churches promoted women's leadership by encouraging grassroots women to lead meetings, pray in public, raise money through handicrafts, and act as evangelists. See Robert, *American Women in Mission*.

6. For a review of research on women's roles in emerging churches, see Robert, "World Christianity as a Women's Movement," 180–88.

Domestic Relationships and Gendered Behaviors

For both historic and indigenous denominations, Christian women's identity is connected to maintaining norms of female conduct and domestic relations. Whether she is a member of the Reformed Church of Zimbabwe, characterized by a network of secondary schools, nurses and teachers' training colleges, schools for the blind and deaf, hospitals and clinics, and vernacular literature; or the Roman Catholic Church, with its priests and system of mission stations; or the Apostles of Johane Maranke, a polygamous indigenous church with largely uneducated members, church members identify a Christian woman by how she keeps her home and raises her family. For rural women, obtaining and retaining a husband and family remain the foundation of their survival and the source of their respect within the community.

Women in all denominations use the church as a network of support for family life and for constructing female behavior. According to Mrs. Bakuri, who joined the Roman Catholic Church as a girl, "Much of Christianity is in women. We assist each other with our husbands as we bring up our family. We counsel each other on anything that is bad as far as our behavior is concerned."[7] Mrs. Gwamure of the Reformed Church of Zimbabwe notes that a Christian woman can be identified by her "righteousness," and that the truth of her religion is validated by her doing good. Righteousness involves praying with others, helping the sick, honoring one's parents, and keeping the Sabbath.[8] A nonbeliever can be identified by her lifestyle of sitting around doing nothing and neglecting her children. "As soon as the sun rises she goes for beer. [She is] sleeping in the beer halls while her children are starving."

Reflecting the realities of female peasant farming and male migration to urban areas, Mrs. Gwamure comments, "These days the head of the family is a mother. Fathers sleep at the beer halls, he goes for work, so I am the one who will be at home cultivating and looking after our cattle." Mrs. Chiwara, a member of the Maranke Apostles and the second wife in a polygamous marriage, says that the church teachings strengthen the family by counseling obedience to parents and proper care for husbands. Women in the church are healthy, work hard and do not steal, care for the sick, and encourage their husbands to attend church and pray. "If we don't

---

7. Interview with Mrs. Bakuri, April 7, 1996, 5. Page numbers, when cited, refer to the handwritten English translations of Shona transcriptions, or to English-language interviews. The original taped interviews and the Shona transcriptions are currently stored in Polokwane, South Africa.

8. Interview with Mrs. Gwamure, Chivi, June 5, 1996.

have devoted women, our husbands will be like animals of the forest." Mrs. Chiwara explains that Christian women obey their husbands according to biblical injunctions, cook for them, and keep them neat and clean.[9]

A discussion held with three of the wives of Bishop Rueben Mutendi, leader of the Zion Christian Church in Bikita, showed that women believe their collaborative work as church women improves their homes. Church women teach each other to give their husbands and in-laws warm water in the morning, to clean their yards, to wash the outside of pots as well as the inside, and to teach children to obey their parents. Even if one's husband is a drunkard, a woman gets support and good teachings by going to church and meeting with other women, including practical tips such as holding water in her mouth to keep herself from talking back to a drunken husband and provoking a beating.[10] Mrs. Rutsvara, of the ZCC, notes that women's teachings strengthen each other when they have marital problems by helping them turn to the Bible. Even a drunk husband must be cared for "so that he can allow you to go to church of God. If you are a widow, then the church itself becomes your husband."[11] Women help each other to receive Jesus as Savior by showing love and answering each other politely and with dignity. Many women comment that one could immediately distinguish a Christian from a non-Christian woman by her modesty and by whether her children were well-fed, attended school, and wore neat clothing. (Given that in Zimbabwe the payment of school fees is required for attendance, school attendance reflects the industriousness of the mother.)

One of the key areas of women's behavior addressed in interviews and in women's conferences was the need for Christian women not to gossip about each other—a pressing problem in subsistence societies with little privacy, in which women are competing for scarce resources and for attention from a husband who might have multiple wives. According to Mrs. Chabata, senior wife of an Ethiopian bishop, women are taught to respect the senior wife by bringing her bath water, and she in turn will feed the children of the junior wife.[12] Kind treatment of co-wives and their offspring is a vital area of Christian witness in polygamous churches.

Most but not all of the denominations in Southern Africa have a uniformed women's organization known as *manyanos* (South Africa) or *ruwadzanos* (Zimbabwe), namely "prayer movements." As early as 1962,

9. Interview with Mrs. Gudza Chiwara, Gutu, July 10, 1996.

10. Interview with Bishop Rueben Mutendi wives, Bikita, April 5, 1996.

11. Interview Mrs. Rutsvara, August 22, 1995. The prominent role of postmenopausal widows as well-respected church workers "married" to Jesus is a theme in other parts of Africa as well. See Hoehler-Fatton, *Women of Fire*, 99.

12. Interview Mrs. Chabata, March 1998, 22.

female prayer unions were being described as the oldest and most enduring "African organizations in South Africa."[13]

Methodist *manyanos* intersected with an Anglican organization, the Mothers' Union, introduced a century ago into South Africa by missionary deaconesses from Great Britain. Mothers' prayer organizations quickly took on African form, spread to other denominations, and outgrew their parent founders. By allowing space for female "praying and preaching," the attraction of these groups to women, in the words of historian Deborah Gaitskell, "underline how the spread and appropriation of Christianity has been gender-specific" in male-dominated churches and societies.[14] The weekly meetings of *manyanos* are characterized by prayer, singing, reflection on Bible passages, and testimonies of God's grace. Mother's Union members wear distinctive denominational uniforms to denote their solidarity, purity, and spiritual power.[15] They are the main fundraisers for women's needs and for church projects. They visit the sick and encourage the formation and maintenance of Christian families. One of their most important functions is that of mutual counseling and support for each other.

In Zimbabwe in the late 1990s, *ruwadzanos* sent their best preachers to other groups for weekend revivals and women's meetings. States Mrs. Gwamure, "If the church does not have a women's organization, it is like a person who goes to seek some firewood. The person gathers the firewood but fails to find a rope to tie the pile. You cannot carry them while they are just scattered. You cannot carry them if they are divided. Then the *ruwadzano* ties together with God and our church." The mainline Reformed, Methodist, and Roman Catholic Churches uphold monogamy and exert pressure on men to consent to church weddings. Informal liaisons or traditional weddings with second or third wives are frowned upon by Mothers' Union members in the historic mission churches, though the traditional practice of *lobola*, or "bride price," continues to play an important part even in Christian families.

VaShandira, a prominent faith healer among the Ndaza Zionists, notes that without a women's organization, there would be "consistent suppression of women." But the men see that the women's meetings encourage better home life, and so permit them to occur. Without the women's movement, according to VaShandira, women would neglect their families, sleep

---

13. Mia Brandel-Syrier, quoted by Gaitskell, "Hot Meetings," 73.

14. Gaitskell, "Praying and Preaching," 212.

15. On South African Anglican women's struggle against colonialist church authorities to wear their uniforms and maintain their own traditions, see Haddad, "Mothers' Union," 101–17.

in beer halls, and engage in prostitution.[16] The mothers instruct girls on how to work hard and marry their first boyfriend without premarital sex. The presence of Mothers' Unions also encourages men to counsel their sons not to date "ten girls"; and once married, to be righteous men who do not beat their wives.

When asked about the theological meaning of salvation or liberation, the theme of freedom from wife-beating was a common response among the interviewees. Mrs. Chabata, of the First Ethiopian Church, notes that the meaning of "liberation" for women is being married to a man affiliated with the church, because the church forbids the beating of women. "If the husband stops beating me I say God has liberated me."[17] According to Chabata, liberation from being beaten goes along with liberation from sins and taking on righteous behavior, so that life will proceed smoothly. Liberation both from sins and from being beaten creates "joy."

Outside the historic mission churches, the older indigenous churches allow polygamy. Nevertheless, interviews with plural wives in the Zion Christian Church, all of them active in the women's organization, showed the same concern for strong marriages and well-ordered households as did the Reformed and Roman Catholic women. The largest indigenous church in Zimbabwe, the Apostles of Johane Maranke, differs from the mission-founded churches in that it promotes polygamy. Maranke members are typically less educated and closer to norms of rural traditional culture than are members of mainline churches. The Apostles command strict obedience of wives to husbands and do not permit women to speak in church. Maranke women meet in household groups to pray, sing, prophesy, and teach each other, but the men do not allow them formal organizational structures like the *ruwadzanos*. Unlike most churches, women's organizations are not paths to leadership in the Apostles, although exceptional women of mature age receive callings as healers or prophets to assist other women.

One theme of women's responsibility in Southern African churches that particularly interested me was women's active role in guarding the virginity of their daughters. Mission-founded churches with strong *ruwadzanos* sponsored affiliated girls' organizations for teenagers from puberty until marriage. The women's organization held regular conferences to teach girls about the necessity of guarding their purity and preventing pregnancy and disease before marriage. This difficult traditional task has become even more urgent in the days of rampant AIDS. Women in mainline and pentecostal churches rely on prayer and instructions about obedience to protect

16. Interview with VaShandira, March 20, 1996, 33.
17. Interview with Mrs. Chabata, 96.

their daughters. They remind them that the body is the temple of God and must be kept pure, or else humiliation and disappointment will fall upon the girl and also upon her mother.

In the Reformed Church of Zimbabwe during the late 1990s, entrance into an informal liaison resulted in public disapproval and loss of special communion privileges for a year and the right to wear the girls' organization uniform. After repenting and obtaining a regular church wedding, the young woman was then allowed to join the *ruwadzano*.[18] According to Mrs. Chidhindi of the RCZ Bethel Assembly in Gutu, "Virginity holds significance since Mary was blessed by God when she was still a virgin. I do not think that if she had lost her virginity she would have been chosen to give birth to Jesus." Marriage preparation involves teaching the young woman how to care for her family. Mrs. Chidhindi finds biblical warrant for woman's role as nurturer because God sent the Israelites to Canaan, the land of milk and honey, and "milk came out of the breast of the mother while honey comes out of the mother bee."

To guard girls' purity, the polygamous and more rural Maranke Apostles members still rely on physical virginity examinations (*zemeni*) conducted at regular intervals by female prophets, also known as "policemen." This traditional practice was incorporated into the Apostles but was rejected as a double standard by mission churches and many Ndaza Zionist women.[19] If a girl fails the examination, her mother is given a piece of cloth with a hole punched in it. The girl is then considered spoiled and becomes a lower wife in a polygamous household, and thus loses any choice over selecting a husband. In the First Ethiopian Church, Mrs. Chabata reports that elderly women conduct the virginity exams. Girls who pass are given an acacia leaf, but those who fail are given a leaf with a piece bitten out. The parents are informed and the girl is disciplined and counseled to see the error of her ways. In the Zion Apostolic Church of VaShandira, the virginity exam traditionally occurs before a wedding. Women ululate when the pure bride is certified with a white cloth, but the failed one receives a punctured cloth.[20]

---

18. In the RCZ, the word *sungano* (covenant) is used instead of *ruwadzano*. All informants considered the terms to mean the same thing.

19. While there is great variation in women's attitudes within the Zionist movements, Ndaza Zionists tend to have a strong pro-monogamy and women's rights faction.

20. VaShandira interview, 58. Virginity exams were cancelled during the Chimurenga liberation struggle of 1965–1980, because so many girls were "called out" by freedom fighters, the implication being that they were raped and the church chose not to humiliate the girls further by conducting zemeni.

Over the past decade the traditional virginity examination has become both more widespread and more controversial with the spread of HIV-AIDS. In Southern Africa many women and girls are infected with HIV, largely because of a cultural climate that denies women control over their bodies and condones male sexual license even in marriage. Married women suffer from high rates of HIV because their husbands are unfaithful. In a context that lacks modern medicine, condoms, or birth control, and in which rape is shockingly common, strict control of girls' behavior is one of the few tools for preventing AIDS that is under the authority of women themselves. The fervency with which women preach self control to their daughters, and support monogamy, reflects their justifiable fears of premature suffering and death.

Professor Isabel Phiri of the University of Kwa Zulu Natal, one of the original research team members of our "African Initiatives Project," investigated a former Roman Catholic by the name of Nomagugu Patience Ngobese. Ngobese, who declared herself a traditional Zulu *sangoma*, reintroduced large-scale, monthly virginity testing in Pietermaritzburg, South Africa. As virginity testing was a traditional practice that had all but died out in mainline churches, its reintroduction as part of a rediscovery of African traditional practice is no surprise. Girls who fail the test are interviewed to see if they have been victims of rape or incest. Many of the thousand girls tested each month are Christians. Controversy follows this practice, which is born of desperation from the AIDS crisis, as mainline churches and government officials argue that it discriminates against girls, confirms widespread prejudices that assume women cause AIDS, does not protect married women whose husbands are unfaithful, and exposes virgin girls to rape by men who think it will cure their own AIDS.[21]

For women in churches throughout Masvingo Province in the 1990s, religious participation was intimately bound up with protection of girls, preservation of marriages—whether polygamous or monogamous—and responsibility for husbands, children, and households. The unfolding HIV-AIDS crisis lent special urgency to providing teaching on proper behavior to girls. Not only did church membership and the community of church women help to preserve relationships, but many women interviewed commented that the church itself was a family. For women, especially through their women's organizations, the relational model for the church was the family, and the family was strengthened by the church. The family thus provided a gender-based ecclesiology that corresponded to the daily realities of women's lives.

21. Phiri, "Virginity Testing," 63–78.

Healing and Well-Being

One of the main reasons women in Southern Africa join indigenous and pentecostal churches is because they seek healing.[22] Authorities in mainline churches are often suspicious of charismatic healers.[23] With the challenges of poverty, childbirth, inadequate medical care, and now the spread of HIV-AIDS, indigenous and pentecostal churches can be seen as healing movements, much as Pentecostalism in Latin America and house churches in China are healing movements. According to prominent Zionist healer VaShandira, healing and salvation mean the same thing, though only God has ultimate control of spiritual salvation at the final judgment day.[24]

In societies where spiritual and physical are closely knit, the need for healing reflects the social isolation suffered by women with health problems. Women are especially attracted to healing ministries for several reasons: First, barrenness is an almost unendurable curse for African women, as their worth is traditionally measured by their fertility. The ancient practice of *lobola*, or bride-price, is partly seen as payment for a woman's fertility, and her inability to conceive or deliver successfully requires desperate measures. Many healing ministries focus on barrenness, on women's gynecological problems such as painful menstrual periods, or on infant deaths due to premature birth. Second, the increase in HIV-AIDS is often blamed on women, just as witchcraft has traditionally been blamed largely on them. Because women as daughters-in-law in patriarchal systems typically move into the husband's village, their position as outsiders means they can be accused of witchcraft when problems emerge. Healing and deliverance are needed to restore women to relationships with extended families and communities. Third, indigenous churches that typically restrict women's leadership roles, or that forbid the formation of women's organizations, still allow exceptional women to become healers. Thus becoming a healer or prophet

---

22. In a major study of Zionism in the Cape Flats, African Initiatives project member Hennie Pretorius found that 42 percent of those who joined Zionist churches did so because they were healed, including from barrenness. Pretorius, *Drumbeats*, 55.

23. The most high-profile suppression of a healing ministry involved Catholic Archbishop of Zambia Emanuel Milingo, who lost his episcopal see in 1982 because of his exorcisms. In the 1990s Zimbabwean Anglican priest Lazarus Muyambi drew thousands with his healing ministry, but he was forbidden from working in the Harare diocese. Mainline discomfort with healing prophets is partly because their emphasis on healing and deliverance from witchcraft draws people away from mission churches. Sixty percent of converts to Zionism in the Cape Flats were previously members of mainline churches. Pretorius, *Drumbeats*, 54; Bate, "Inculturation in Process," and Shoko, "Mainline Church Healing in Zimbabwe," 177–235. See also Dube et al., *African Initiatives in Healing Ministry*.

24. VaShandira, Extended Case Study, 16. Based on field notes.

is a way to exercise leadership in rural tradition-oriented settings and may even provide a foundation for full-time ministry. Healing has become a major means of recruitment for indigenous churches. Inus Daneel states, "Healing is the main pivot around which African women's proclamation and understanding of the gospel message revolves."[25]

The founder/leader of the Zion Christian Church in mid-twentieth-century Zimbabwe was Bishop Samuel Mutendi. One of his specialties was *chibereko*, his ability to end barrenness. Testimonies of miracles of childbirth at Mutendi's hand were an important reason for the growth of Zionism into one of the largest indigenous churches in Zimbabwe.[26] This legacy of healing continues to the present, as a wife of his son Bishop Rueben Mutendi noted in 1996: "In our church, those who are barren are being prayed for and they bear children. Those who came with mental illnesses went back to their normal state. Those who came with any kind of disease were healed. Those who have sexually transmitted disease were helped in our church." Zionist church headquarters function as healing centers in which the barren, ill, and troubled can live for periods of time while church prophets pray over them. The biblical theme of "coming to Zion" thus has physical as well as spiritual meaning for barren women.

Another indigenous array of denominations, for which healing remains central, features various kinds of Apostles. Though lacking separate women's organizations, they allow women to become prophetic healers for other women.[27] Members of the Apostles do not permit the use of beer, medicine, marijuana, or cigarettes, and they worship in white garments to denote purity. Their refusal of Western medicine—and often its inaccessibility—is directly related to their reliance on faith healing. According to a female healer named Mrs. Borerwe of Kushinga Apostolic Church in Masvingo, people were converted to the church by prophets who healed them, and new assemblies sprang up in locations where Apostles visited the sick. To Mrs. Borerwe, the "major mission" of the church is to heal the sick. Prophets pray for them and inject them with holy water, but they also stress good health by teaching people hygiene such as keeping clean, brushing their teeth, constructing toilets, and washing their white garments. According to Mrs. Borerwe, good hygiene occurs because God loves good behavior.[28] Mrs. Gudza Chiwara, a lifelong member of the Maranke Apostles,

25. Daneel, "AIC Women," 257.
26. Daneel, "Women as Bearers of the Gospel," 321–22.
27. For a pioneer study of the work of a female Apostolic healer, the blind woman Febi, who specialized in "barren women, pre-natal care, childbirth and the treatment of young children" beginning in the 1950s, see Daneel, *Old and New*, 209–12.
28. Interview Mrs. Borerwe March 10, 1997, Masvingo.

said in an interview that she had serious problems with child delivery, but prophets assisted her with prayers and preserved her through eleven difficult childbirths. For this reason Mrs. Chiwara testifies that she will always be loyal to the Maranke Church.

In addition to recruiting women with childbirth problems, ministries that promised deliverance from evil spirits and from witchcraft draw female followers. These ministries remain controversial among theologians, mainline leaders, and educated secularists, but are very important to women at a grassroots level. (Most persons accused of witchcraft in traditional societies are women.) Prior to colonial laws, witchcraft accusations resulted in the execution of the presumed witches, or at a minimum their ostracism from ordinary society. A church that can purify accused witches and restore them to their rightful places in society will therefore attract women.

Some of the most important material on witchcraft-eradication churches has been collected over a 40-year period in the Chingombe chiefdom in central Zimbabwe by M. L. Daneel. One of the ministries studied was that of prophet Bishop Kiyai Zawa, who founded the Proverbs of the Apostles Church in the early 1990s. Zawa claimed to kill witchcraft-causing demons in the name of God in powerful rituals held deep in bat-filled mountain caves. Extensive counseling sessions at the church headquarters preceded the exorcism rituals. Bishop Kiyai integrated cleansed witches into his church, where they witnessed to their own healing and then assisted in the liberation of others.[29]

The witchcraft-eradication churches started with traditional beliefs in witchcraft, but then used the power of the Holy Spirit to effect liberation and reconciliation for women within the village community.[30] Testimonies of the cleansed witches contain sad stories of evil ways believed inherited from female ancestors who were also witches, including the killing of one's relatives and the eating of human flesh. The redeemed witches not only become leaders in Bishop Zawa's church but they resume their places in their families as honored mothers and grandmothers. Testified one redeemed witch, Mrs. Enia Mukanyange, in December of 2004, "My husband and I were living alone. My children took all their children away with them, fearful that I would bewitch and eat them . . . [After healing] my life was changed completely. Formerly the villagers ignored me and resented me. Now people greet me and treat me with respect . . . As a church member my

---

29. Daneel, "Coping with Wizardry," 51–70.

30. Unfortunately with the spread of HIV-AIDS in southern Africa, women have become scapegoats and are blamed for its spread. The role for indigenous and pentecostal churches that specialize in exorcism and healing has increased because of the AIDS pandemic.

life has changed beyond imagination. I no longer attend beer drinks or seek out the company of practicing witches. The Holy Spirit now fills me and I pray regularly to *Mwari* [God] . . . I am allowed to preach in the church. When a Bible is placed in my hands and the Holy Spirit fills me, I witness about my deliverance from *uroyi* [witchcraft] . . . But now we have hope for the future. Love surrounds us, here at the church and in our home. We pray and God blesses us. Even though we have nothing in our hands we are rich because of Mwari's blessings."[31]

Women's Leadership

The testimony of healed witch Enia Mukanyange leads me to the third theme of women's participation in the emerging churches of Southern Africa, namely that of leadership formation. After being healed by Bishop Zawa, Mrs. Mukanyange converted her kraalhead and his entire family. She was then appointed his security officer and eventually chairperson of the national political party delegates of her area. Her new life in the church, therefore, not only led to restored relations with her family and to honor in the church, but to a public position of authority in her village. As the story of Mrs. Mukanyange illustrates, as new churches spread in Southern Africa, their focus on healing and restoration to community life has empowered women to be leaders both in church and in the public realm. Sometimes being healed leads to a ministry as healer or midwife; at other times, women are able to transform their own personal tragedies into widely-recognized spiritual resources for the benefit of others.

Women's leadership emerges differently according to denominational tradition. In the older mission churches, with their powerful women's prayer unions, women's leadership emerges through well-established networks. Since mainline mission churches have strong traditions of supporting women's education, the wives of leading pastors have sometimes received theological training as preparation for their work among women. Catholic women who desire theological education are encouraged to become vowed Sisters. Mother's groups encourage the education of their daughters. In South and Central Africa, some Reformed, Presbyterian, Methodist, and Anglican churches now ordain women, but the number of ordained women remains small and their path to pastoral ministry fraught with difficulties. In 1995, for example, Malawian women church workers

---

31. Daneel, "Coping with Wizardry," 13, 21. This is an unpublished paper presented at conference in Amsterdam, 2005. The version I cite elsewhere, published 3 years later, does not contain all of the original material.

and theology students marched on the Blantyre Synod of the Presbyterian Church of Central Africa, asking for women's rights in the church.[32] The synod responded by suspending all the women who worked full-time in the synod. In 2001, however, growing support for the women's cause led to the ordination of the first female minister in the synod. In each mainline denomination, the struggle for ordination of women has been protracted and painful but has nevertheless made progress. Newer pentecostal churches often support women's ministries, but most of the acknowledged leaders tend to be pastors' wives who are tasked to work with women and children.

The most common ministry pattern in mainline, pentecostal, and indigenous churches remains work among women. Women learn to pray, teach, and preach through separate women's meetings, and evangelistic exchanges from church to church. Various offices such as deaconess, secretary, stewardess, and treasurer provide opportunities to gain administrative skills. Regional conferences of women's organizations showcase women's skills as organizers and spiritual and intellectual leaders.

In September of 1999, the Apostolic Faith Mission held its "Sisters' Union Conference" in Mucheke, the oldest high-density settlement in Masvingo. The Apostolic Faith Mission is a pentecostal denomination that spread to South Africa in the early twentieth century, and from there to Zimbabwe. Pentecostalism has been spreading in urban areas since the 1980s and tends to attract a more highly educated group of women than do the more rural, indigenous churches. Delegations from across the province, including both Shona and Ndebele speakers, arrived for two days of singing, preaching, and fellowship. Not only did women prepare the food and make the arrangements, but prominent women chaired the sessions by greeting everyone and introducing the preachers.

Over the two days, a series of women especially selected for the occasion preached sermons on biblical texts relating to women. Biblical women such as the Shunamite woman who fed the prophet Elisha, the prostitute Rahab who sheltered Joshua's spies and assisted in the overthrow of Jericho, and the woman who killed Abimelech with a millstone all became subjects of sermons that encouraged women to be firm against men's opposition and their own self doubt about their ability to make decisions and to lead others. Mrs. Chikava, for example, took Judges 9:53 for her text. She encouraged women to hold fast to the stone that was Jesus Christ. "[Do] not despise women. Look at the woman who stood up with the stone in her hand. She destroyed all the powers of the devil." Just as people despised David for being small against Goliath, so people despise women. Yet, "If a woman holds

---

32. Kapuma, "'Troubled,'" 348–69.

the stone that is called Jesus, it doesn't matter that you are a child, a girl, a boy, married or not—once you hold the stone . . . the one who is faithful will stand by your side." After praising the intelligence of the woman who crushed the head of Abimelech with the millstone, Mrs. Chikava exhorted the women at the convention to be confident in their God-given intelligence, wisdom, and ability to accomplish things. "We have some work to do in the house of God. God did not call us for nothing. He did not make us female for no reason. We were made not just to bear children while doing nothing. You have something to do before God. Work for God while you have the chance. The presence of your husband does not matter. . . . What impresses me most is that when we are going to heaven everyone will go according to his/her works."[33]

For church women in Southern Africa, the support they receive in women's groups helps them navigate their daily lives in situations of economic scarcity, disease, and male domination. It also empowers some of them to move beyond the social limitations of woman's sphere to start their own churches. Women in historic churches have supported female evangelists, sustained women's organizations, and eventually moved toward ordination. Women in older, indigenous churches functioned as healers. By the mid-1980s women in some of the newer pentecostal churches were beginning their own churches.[34] In Malawi, former Seventh Day Adventist deaconess Mayi Chipondeni founded the Namatapa Healing Church in 1992 after receiving a call from God and the baptism of the Holy Spirit. Because the Adventist Church did not recognize her call and gift of healing, she began her own ministry that emphasized the elimination of evil spirits through a communal process of confession of sins, ritual vomiting, and her own prophetic leadership. By 1999 Mayi Chipondeni and her followers had founded 75 branches of her church in Malawi and Mozambique.[35] Her churches represented a powerful evangelistic movement that combined a focus on traditionalist miracles of healing with a theology of being "born again" in Jesus Christ.

Another of the new Malawian women church founders is Bishop Mercy Yami. Born into an indigenous church, Yami had a powerful spiritual experience during a revival in 1978 and believed God was calling her to become an evangelist. Discerning that God had given her the gift of healing, she founded an independent Baptist church in 1982. Her unusual

---

33. Chikava, Address at the Sisters' Union Conference, Mucheke Stadium, Masvingo, Zimbabwe, September 1999.

34. Phiri, "African Women in Mission," 267.

35. Ibid., 275.

leadership abilities ultimately forced her to choose between her husband and her evangelistic work. As a divorced woman, led by dreams and visions from God, she began a *Zodabwitsa* (miracles) ministry in 1994. The ministry specializes in work among rural women whose husbands work in urban areas; the ministry also includes work among the blind and among prisoners. Yami's financial advisor stated, "The church has a very important vision. It deals with neglected people of the society that no other church is interested in. These are people with no money."[36] Bishop Yami faced gender discrimination because of her unusual supervisory position over a number of affiliated congregations. But her continuing experiences of the Holy Spirit reaffirmed her leadership, despite her female gender. Presumably her decision to work with the unwanted defuses some of the opposition she might face if she competed with men for a more desirable constituency.

Women's concern for family life, for healing and communal well-being, and for leadership, are interrelated themes in the churches of Southern Africa. Together they demonstrate women's holistic understanding of the Christian message. Their interconnection was illustrated in a speech made at a project conference in 1997 by South African Lydia August, a rare second-generation female leader of an African indigenous church, daughter of the famous Mother Christina Nku, who founded the St. John Apostolic Faith Mission Church in 1938:

> [In] the past three to four decades women in South Africa rose up from slavery. They refused to be restricted to the kitchen. Realising how important it is to be real women, they went out into the field to serve their communities. AIC women are the fountain of life, responsible for human growth through childbirth . . . In South Africa the AIC women's associations represent the majority of Christians. They have not only spread the Good News but are fully involved in the problems of their communities. As healers and intercessors they have drawn the masses. Though poor, with little support from abroad, they have built churches and schools . . . So, we have to be women of prayer . . . Make South Africa a liveable place for the Rainbow Nation![37]

---

36. Ibid., 286.
37. Robert, *African Christian Outreach*, 255.

CONCLUSION

Research among Shona-speaking women in rural Masvingo Province over the past 15 years has revealed powerful gender-based reasons for church affiliation. The varieties of Christianity in Southern Africa reflect different combinations of what on the surface appear to be contradictory elements—for example, submission to husbands plus relative empowerment through women's groups. The ongoing negotiations between submission and empowerment provided by church communities have helped women survive and even thrive in a rural subsistence economy characterized by the unfolding crisis of political instability and the HIV-AIDS pandemic. For women of all denominations, carefully negotiated combinations of traditional and modern values cohere in church communities to support women's roles in family life, healing and well-being, and leadership. For rural African church women, the concrete aspects of their daily lives provide the substance of the "enacted theology" or "lived religion" they express.

BIBLIOGRAPHY

Bate, Stuart. "Inculturation in Process: Influence of the Coping-Healing Churches on the Attitudes and Praxis of Mainline Churches." In *African Christian Outreach*, vol. 2, *Mission Churches*, edited by Dana L. Robert, 177–207. Pretoria: South African Missiological Society, 2003.

Daneel, M. L. *African Christian Outreach*. Vol. 1, *African Initiated Churches*. Pretoria: South African Missiological Society, 2001.

———. "AIC Women as Bearers of the Gospel Good News." In *African Christian Outreach*, vol. 1, *African Initiated Churches*, 312–27. Pretoria: South African Missiological Society, 2001.

———. "AIC Women in Mission." In *African Christian Outreach*, vol. 1, *African Initiated Churches*, 254–66. Pretoria: South African Missiological Society, 2001.

———. "Coping with Wizardry in Zimbabwe in African Initiated Churches (AICs)." In *Coping with Evil in Religion and Culture*, edited by Nelly van Doorn Harder and Laurens Minnema, 51–70. Amsterdam: Rodopi, 2008.

———. *Old and New in Southern Shona Independent Churches*. Vol. 2, *Church Growth, Causative Factors and Recruitment Techniques*. The Hague: Mouton, 1974.

Dube, Lilian, et al. *African Initiatives in Healing Ministry*. Pretoria: Unisa, 2011.

Gaitskell, Deborah. "'Praying and Preaching': The Distinctive Spirituality of African Women's Church Organization." In *Missions and Christianity in South African History*, edited by H. Bredekamp and R. Ross, 211–32. Johannesburg: Witwatersrand University Press, 1995.

Haddad, Beverley Gail. "The Mothers' Union in South Africa: Untold Stories of Faith, Survival and Resistance." In *Her-Stories: Hidden Histories of Women of Faith in Africa*, edited by Isabel Apawo Phiri et al., 101–16. Pietermaritzburg: Cluster, 2002.

Hoehler-Fatton, Cynthia. *Women of Fire and Spirit: History, Faith, and Gender in Roho Religion in Western Kenya*. New York: Oxford University Press, 1996.

Kapuma, Gertrude Aopesyaga. "'Troubled but Not Destroyed': Women of Faith Reclaim Their Rights." In *Her-Stories: Hidden Histories of Women of Faith in Africa*, edited by Isabel Apawo Phiri et al., 348–69. Pietermaritzburg: Cluster, 2002.

Phiri, Isabel Apawo. "African Women in Mission: Two Case Studies from Malawi." In *African Christian Outreach*, vol. 1, *African Initiated Churches*, edited by M. L. Daneel, 267–93. Pretoria: South African Missiological Society, 2001.

———. "Virginity Testing? African Women Seeking Resources to Combat HIV/AIDS." *Journal of Constructive Theology* 9 (2003) 63–78.

Pretorius, Hennie. *Drumbeats: Sounds of Zion in the Cape Flats*. Pretoria: Unisa, 2004.

Robert, Dana L., editor. *African Christian Outreach*. Vol. 2, *Mission Churches*. Pretoria: South African Missiological Society, 2003.

———. *American Women in Mission: A Social History of Their Thought and Practice*. Macon, GA: Mercer University Press, 1997.

———. "World Christianity as a Women's Movement." *International Bulletin of Missionary Research* 30 (2006) 180–88.

Shoko, Tabona. "Mainline Church Healing in Zimbabwe. Two Case Studies." In *African Christian Outreach*, vol. 2, *Mission Churches*, edited by Dana L. Robert, 208–35. Pretoria: South African Missiological Society, 2003.

11

The Role of Personal Friendships in Effective Cross-Cultural Christian Mission

Kenneth R. Ross

THE THEOLOGY OF TITE Tiénou has been distinguished by its integration of theology and anthropology. This chapter will argue that such integration has taken effect, through the missionary movement, in the form of profound, life-changing personal relationships.

Some might consider this to be a statement of the obvious. How is the Good News of Jesus Christ passed on if not from one friend to another across time and space? Yet studies of the missionary movement have often been so occupied with social, political, and cultural dynamics—all well worthy of study—that they have overlooked the fundamental reality: Amidst the playing out of these broader dynamics, there were individual human beings forming friendships. Indeed, it will be argued that the personal friendships formed in the context of missionary encounters often proved to be extraordinary both in their depth and in their transformative effect.

Retrieving this dimension of the missionary experience, moreover, is of much more than merely historical interest. The world in which mission takes effect today is one which is tired of ideology, suspicious of power, and wary of rhetoric. It may be that authentic personal friendship, more than ever, is the channel through which the Good News of Jesus Christ will cross boundaries and break new ground.

Primary reference will be made to Africa since African experience of Christian faith did much to help it to recover its relational aspect. The Enlightenment and the industrial revolution in the West had rendered an understanding of Christian faith that was more individual and cerebral. The strength of community life in Africa brought a perspective which retrieved the biblical emphasis on the relational. Whereas Descartes had convinced his European contemporaries that "I think, therefore I am," Africans countered with a view of life that has been characterized as "We are, therefore I am."

Western missionaries in Africa were drawn into this relational understanding of life, and one thing it offered to them was remarkable friendships. Not in every case did this occur. There were missionaries who remained aloof and condescending in their attitude to African colleagues. The heyday of the missionary movement coincided with the high noon of social Darwinism. By no means was every missionary immune to its influence. What is remarkable, however, is that so many were—breaking through the social, political, and philosophical consensus to form deep friendships in the African community. So much so that they sometimes became strangers in their original homeland. Such developments are not easily accommodated by orthodox post-colonial critique and, as a result, are often overlooked in scholarly analysis of missionary encounters.

This essay seeks to redress the balance. It will put the focus on the personal friendships that were formed in the context of missionary engagement and explore how this dimension might take effect in worldwide cross-cultural mission today and tomorrow. In pursuit of this question, it will range widely across the global scope of the missionary movement. However, the author makes no apology for a certain bias toward Malawi. For it was Malawians who first taught him about the possibility of crossing cultural boundaries to build mutually transformative friendships. Discovering this possibility through personal experience as a Scot in Malawi proved to be a key to understanding how it has taken effect in many other contexts also.

FRIENDSHIP AT THE HEART OF THE MISSIONARY MOVEMENT

If there was one meeting at which the modern missionary movement found its most concentrated summation it was the "Edinburgh 1910" World Missionary Conference. If there was one moment in that great conference which

Role of Personal Friendships in Effective Cross-Cultural Christian Mission 137

is remembered more than any other, it is the speech of the young Indian delegate V. S. Azariah. He addressed the question of race relationships within the missionary enterprise. Taking the bull by the horns, he complained of "a certain aloofness, a lack of mutual understanding and openness, a great lack of frank intercourse and friendliness" between European missionaries and national Christians.[1] Though not included in the official record, one participant recalled Azariah making another memorable comment: "Too often you promise us thrones in heaven, but will not offer us chairs in your drawing rooms."[2] In his concluding peroration he expressed both appreciation and exasperation: "Through all the ages to come the Indian church will rise up in gratitude to attest the heroism and self-denying labours of the missionary body. You have given your goods to feed the poor. You have given your bodies to be burned. We also ask for love. Give us FRIENDS!"[3] This indictment of the missionary movement, in a context where it was largely complacent about its supposedly self-evident virtue, struck the conference "like a bomb," according to one observer.[4] In subsequent years the bomb has continued to detonate as the speech has challenged churches to realize the ideals of oneness, catholicity, mutual respect, and friendship.

Dana Robert has recently pointed out an often-overlooked aspect of Azariah's speech: He was pleading for something he had already experienced.[5] It was because he had experienced this quality of friendship that he was able to appeal for it. Through his work in the Young Men's Christian Association (YMCA), Azariah had enjoyed some very close friendships across social, cultural, and national barriers. This gave him the vision that such a rich quality of friendship might characterize the missionary movement as a whole. It was by discerning what had lain at the heart of the missionary movement at its best that Azariah was able to point out where it had fallen short and urge it to fulfill its deepest instinct and highest calling.

The archetypal missionary experience was to begin with a patronizing attitude that assumed the missionary carried all the wisdom necessary to enlighten the "benighted" people to whom he or she went, but then gradually to come to love the people, their language, culture, and society to such an extent as to become more identified with them than with their own original compatriots in the homeland. If this was not true of all missionaries, it

---

1. World Missionary Conference, 1910, *Carrying the Gospel*, 411–12.
2. Houlder, "Edinburgh 1910," 3.
3. World Missionary Conference, 1910, *History*, 315.
4. Mrs. Isobel Whitehead, wife of the Bishop of Tirunelveli; cited in Stanley, *World Missionary Conference*, 126.
5. Robert, "Cross-Cultural Friendship," 100–101.

was certainly true of the best of them. E. Stanley Jones, for example, wrote, "I find that my love for India has a quality in it now that it did not have in the early days. I went to India through pity, I stay through respect. I love India because she is lovable, I respect her because she is respectable; she has become dear to me because she is endearing."[6] Similarly, James Legge, the Scottish missionary who became the greatest sinologist of his generation, confessed, "I thought of [the Chinese people] better, both morally and socially, when I left them, than when I first went among them, more than 30 years before."[7] There is more than a little truth in the cryptic saying that the untold secret of the missionary movement is that it was the missionaries who were converted!

In this process friendship was a decisive instrument. Reflecting on his experience as a missionary at Ahmednagar in Northwest India, Robert Hume observed, "The first word of the Gospel is the word Brother, never the word Sinner, nor even the word Christ, as is sometimes imagined."[8] Identification and solidarity were the hallmarks of effective missionary engagement. Of the many examples of missionaries who discovered an extraordinary quality of friendship among the people with whom they worked, consideration might be given to Edwin Smith, whose *Golden Stool* was one of the first books to offer a positive appreciation of African culture. This assessment had been informed in no small degree by his friendship with Mungalo. As he professed in the conclusion of his book, "If two men ever loved each other, it was Mungalo and I."[9] This, it should be noted, was written at the height of the colonial era when racism was at its most pervasive and institutionalized. Yet friendships made in the context of the missionary movement could break through all social and political pressures to achieve a quality of inter-personal relationship which was inspiring and productive to a remarkable degree.

A CASE STUDY: SCOTS AND MALAWIANS

This can be well-illustrated by the experience of Scots and Malawians who met through the Scottish missions in Malawi. The beginning of a remarkable series of friendships can be traced back to the arrival of the first missionary to reach Malawi, David Livingstone, who entered the area now known

---

6. Jones, *Christ of the Indian Road*, 252.

7. Legge, "Christianity and Confucianism," 34. Also see Pfister, "Striving," 233.

8. Hume, "Missionary Message," cited in Cracknell, *Justice, Courtesy and Love*, 202, and quoted by Robert, "Cross-Cultural Friendship," 101.

9. Smith, *Golden Stool*, quoted by Robert, "Cross-Cultural Friendship," 102.

Role of Personal Friendships in Effective Cross-Cultural Christian Mission 139

as Malawi in 1859. Livingstone's hostility to racism comes out in remarks which he made in the course of the Zambezi Expedition which took him to Malawi. He comments, for example, "Most writers believe the blacks to be savages, nearly all blacks believe the whites to be cannibals. The nursery hobgoblin of the one is black, of the other white. Without going further into these unwise comparisons, we must smile at the heaps of nonsense which have been written about the Negro intellect."[10]

This scornful attitude toward racism arose from the simple reality of having lived close to African communities, to the extent of becoming more comfortable among Africans than among Europeans. It is striking that Livingstone's relationships with fellow-Europeans were often stormy while his friendships with Africans were marked by a remarkable degree of affection and loyalty. Both in the trans-African trek which took him and his Makololo companions to Luanda on the west coast and in his final journeys searching for the source of the Nile in Tanzania and Zambia, Livingstone spent many months entirely in African company. This gave him a closeness to African community life, and an appreciation of its qualities (which would become rarer in the later colonial era in Africa) and reinforced the anti-racism he had developed in his early days in South Africa. Tellingly, he was able to say, "I have never met an African who did not know whose side I am on."

The generations of Scottish missionaries who followed Livingstone to Malawi were inspired by this vision. Time and again they resisted the advance of the racist regimes in South Africa and Southern Rhodesia in order to protect the (e)quality of human relationships which they enjoyed in Malawi.[11] Though not always living up to their highest ideals, the Scottish missions were characterized over generations by the profound and inspiring nature of the relationships formed between Scots and Malawians. The quality of such friendship can be gauged from the assessment offered by David Rubadiri, former Vice-Chancellor of the University of Malawi: "Malawi is very much a Scottish country because of the early presence of the Scots Mission here... Malawi is a Scotsman's country. The friends we knew and lived with are people who, though they've retired back to Scotland, are people who are in spirit with us here. I know it doesn't make sense to put it that way, [but] what I'm saying is that when you have lived and experienced at a spiritual and human level, human issues and problems being asked and answered, those you've experienced all those questions and answers with never leave! So though I know they are in Scotland, each time I move around Malawi, I feel them around . . . because they are part and parcel of

---

10. Livingstone, *Narrative*, 67.
11. See Ross, *Blantyre Mission*.

a great experience."[12] It is this extraordinary quality of friendship that has inspired the re-invigoration of Scotland-Malawi relations in recent times.[13]

To take but one example, consideration can be given to the close friendship formed between the leading Livingstonia missionary Donald Fraser and Jonathan Chirwa, whom he described, in the language of the time, as "my beloved native helper"[14] The friendship was tested in 1918 when Chirwa, one of the first African ministers within the Livingstonia Mission, confessed to adultery and resigned from the ministry. In line with the strict standards of the Mission, he was suspended from church membership. A year later the suspension was lifted but senior missionaries like Robert Laws and A. G. MacAlpine were adamant that he could never be restored to the ministry. Year after year petitions came to the Presbytery from the Ngoni community, which was convinced of the sincerity of Chirwa's repentance. Year after year these petitions were resisted by missionary leaders concerned to set high standards for the fledgling Christian ministry.

In these debates Fraser was unwavering in his insistence that Chirwa should be restored. The two were working closely together and Fraser had no doubt that his friend would prove worthy of restoration. Finally, in 1924, he was successful and Chirwa was restored.[15] To take this position involved Fraser in a head-on confrontation with his senior colleagues, but such was his confidence in Chirwa that he did not hesitate. The strength of their friendship was demonstrated after Fraser's death when his widow Agnes brought his ashes to be buried at Embangweni alongside the remains of Jonathan Chirwa.[16] The two friends share the same gravestone, with the simple inscription: "In Memory of Donald Fraser and Jonathan Chirwa." As Jack Thompson remarks: "Here, under a mixture of Scots pines and African indigenous trees, Fraser and Chirwa lie side by side—symbolizing both their friendship, and the mixed nature of the church (both African and Scottish) which they, and many others like them, helped to create amongst the Ngoni."[17]

Such memories might be expected to be of interest only to a diminishing band of scholars dedicated to the study of the missionary movement. In Scotland and Malawi, however, they have taken a very different direction.

12. Kay, *Scottish World*.

13. Ross, "No One Can Shave Your Head," 25–30.

14. United Free Church of Scotland Monthly Record, June 1924, 264, cited in Thompson, *Christianity in Northern Malawi*, 206.

15. Livingstonia Presbytery Minutes, 11 September 1924, cited in Thompson, *Christianity in Northern Malawi*, 207.

16. Thompson, *Christianity in Northern Malawi*, 274.

17. Thompson, "Remembering the Past," 30.

They have inspired the launch of an initiative in international development which is rooted in an ethic of mutual respect and friendship. A broad-based civil society alliance from 2004 took the form of the Scotland-Malawi Partnership which states its approach in these terms:

> The Scotland Malawi Partnership promotes a people-to-people model of development, rooted in the shared history between our two countries. It focuses on active relationships between people to foster a shared understanding of the development challenges facing Malawi and to support the development of practical, sustainable solutions. It is through this deeper understanding and shared human experience that the people of Scotland and Malawi will be able to effect real and lasting change, both through their own activity and by influencing the policies and actions of governments and institutions.[18]

Under the terms of the devolution settlement which gave Scotland its own Parliament and Government in 1999, there was no requirement or expectation that Scotland would have any independent engagement in foreign affairs. However, the sense of a special relationship with Malawi was such that there has been widespread support for the 2005 inter-governmental Scotland Malawi Cooperation Agreement, which states that it is "a reciprocal partnership based upon sharing experiences and skills . . . an opportunity to learn from each other."[19] Underlying the initiative at government level is a popular movement of individuals and communities who have forged relationships from which they draw inspiration. The scale of this effort can be gauged from a 2010 University of Edinburgh report that estimates at least 148,000 Malawians and 85,000 Scots are involved in the development activities currently underway between Scotland and Malawi. The value of their inputs over a 12-month period is at least U.S. $48 million, and the benefits are being experienced by at least 1.3 million Malawians and 280,000 Scots.[20] The experience and ethic of friendship between the two nations that originated with the missionary movement has now become the cornerstone of a new model of international development. A 2011 Chatham House report indicates, "Senior U.K. diplomatic officials have pointed to the focus on relationship-building as a factor which makes Scotland's involvement with Malawi stand out from that of other donors."[21] The main reason

---

18. "Scotland Malawi Partnership 2011–14," 5.
19. Ibid., 5–6.
20. Dritsas, "Valuing Scotland's Links," 5.
21. Anyimadu, *Scotland and Wales in Africa*, 16.

why it stands out is that it is rooted in an ethic of mutual respect and friendship, the legacy of the missionary movement.

A WORLD CRYING OUT FOR FRIENDSHIP

Cultural analysts have identified a significant shift that took place toward the end of the twentieth century. Thomas Friedman, for example, comments, "When the world starts to move from a primarily vertical (command and control) value-creation model to an increasingly horizontal (connect and collaborate) creation model, it doesn't just affect how business gets done. It affects everything—how communities and companies define themselves, where companies and communities stop and start, how individuals balance their different identities as consumers, employees, shareholders and citizens, and what role government has to play."[22] In this new context a decentralized way of working has quickly gained ground in commerce and culture. In the imagery of Ori Brafman and Rod Beckstrom, it is a change from the spider to the starfish. A spider is organized from the center—there is a brain which tells the legs what to do. Not so with a starfish. It is a network of cells each with its own autonomy and it functions in a completely decentralized way.[23] This is the direction being taken by business. Where once a corporation with a strong headquarters would put goods on the market, now E-bay allows buyers and sellers to interact in a totally decentralized way. Where once music was produced by a few large companies and put on the market for sale, now music can be exchanged on the internet through completely decentralized networks. Church and mission in the twenty-first century are not immune to this great change.

The realm of the relational now attains a prominence which comes as a surprise to those reared in the values of the industrial age. Kevin Roberts, CEO of Saatchi and Saatchi, has remarked,

> Today the stakes have reached a new high. The social fabric is spread more thinly than ever. People are looking for new emotional connections. They are looking for what they can love. . . . When I first suggested that love was the way to transform business, grown CEOs blushed and slid down behind their annual accounts. But I kept at them. I knew it was love that was missing. I knew that love was the only way to ante up the emotional temperature and create the new kinds of relationships brands needed. I knew that love was the only way business could

---

22. Friedman, *World Is Flat*, 201.
23. Brafman, *Starfish and the Spider*, 34–35.

respond to the rapid shift in control to consumers.... The idealism of love is the new realism of business. By building respect and inspiring love, business can move the world."[24]

If business people are talking the language of love, it suggests we are in a world where a call to "give us friends" is sure to have resonance.

At the same time, the art of friendship has become a scarce commodity. To find people who know and trust one another, who share at depth their thoughts and experiences, is increasingly rare. In the assessment of Jonathan Sacks, "Conversation, the heartbeat of democratic politics, is dying and with it our chances of civic, let alone global, peace."[25] Sacks goes on to argue, "The question is real and urgent: how do we live with moral difference and yet sustain an overarching community? The answer... is conversation—not mere debate but the disciplined act of communicating (making my views intelligible to someone who does not share them) and listening (entering into the inner world of someone whose views are opposed to my own)."[26] Sadly, one of the key findings of the *Atlas of Global Christianity* is that as many as 86% of all Muslims, Hindus, and Buddhists do not personally know a Christian.[27] It bodes ill for the future of the human community that there is such a lack of personal knowledge between members of different religious communities. From the perspective of Christian mission, it can only be a matter of profound regret that the quality of friendship through which God works is so largely absent. When the world is crying out for friendship, who is better placed to respond than those who profess to follow Jesus?

"I HAVE CALLED YOU FRIENDS" MISSION IN THE WAY OF JESUS

In the world of the early twenty-first century, religion has frequently had a bad press—often deservedly so. People have been dismayed to see religion being used ideologically to undergird political injustice, inter-communal enmity, or military aggression. They have noted that adherence to differing faiths is often, apparently, at the root of the most intractable and destructive conflicts in the modern world. They have also witnessed faith being reduced to a commodity, losing its transcendent reference, and being treated as a marketable product to serve the interests of those who "own" it. The abusive

24. McIntosh, *Hell and High Water*, 232.
25. Sacks, *Dignity of Difference*, 3.
26. Ibid., 83.
27. Johnson, *Atlas*, 312–17.

and exploitative use of religion has, understandably, caused extensive disillusionment—to the extent that it has become difficult in some quarters even to get a hearing for the Gospel of Christ. What is required is not a new form of words or a louder megaphone but rather a translation of the Gospel into a lived reality that vouches for its authenticity. As Ken Gnanakan has written, "While there is need to renew our allegiance to proclaim the word faithfully, there is greater need to flesh the message out in acts that express this kingdom. Proclamation is urgent, but demonstration is the priority. The world must hear the message of the Kingdom, but it will also want to see some concrete demonstration of this message."[28]

In a lecture given as part of the "Towards 2010" process in Edinburgh, Korean theologian Kyo-Seong Ahn proposed that, in contrast to the orthodoxy and orthopraxis which have characterized earlier periods of missionary engagement, today what is required is "orthopathy." This involves proclaiming the genuine truth "not from the head, not from the hand, but from the heart." Its keynotes are relationship, emotional intelligence, symbiosis, community, interdependence, empathy, and respect. This empathy-oriented missiology does not try to dictate or manipulate, but tries to respect others. What is indispensable in doing mission, is respect for the other human being, because with respect, a human being can keep his or her dignity in any situation. On this understanding of the task of mission, the love that makes for community is at the same time the action of evangelism.[29] Self-emptying, humility, and sacrifice are sorely needed to liberate the Gospel from captivity to projects of self-aggrandizement. It may be at the level of empathy that the Gospel will be seen in its true colors and show its converting power. In that case, the cultivation of friendship lies at the heart of the matter.

Perhaps it was a prophetic grasp of this emerging reality which led Lesslie Newbigin to the conclusion that "the only possible hermeneutic of the gospel is a congregation which believes it" and that therefore "the clue to evangelism in a secular society must be the local congregation."[30] In *Ancient-Future Faith*, Robert Webber writes that the most significant apologetic Christians will be able to offer in this century is the quality of life and welcome within the church. A community that embodies the experience of the kingdom will draw people to itself. He continues, "In this sense the church and its life in the world will become the new apologetic. People come to faith not because they see the logic of the argument, but because they have experienced a welcoming God in a hospitable and loving

---

28. Gnanakan, "To Proclaim," 9.
29. Ahn, "From Mission to Church," 74–84.
30. Newbigin, *Gospel in a Pluralist Society*, 232, and *Word in Season*, 155–56.

community."³¹ It is the quality of relationships it exhibits that will be decisive for the effectiveness of the witness of the church.

To be true to its calling, the church needs to function in the mode of hospitality. As Christine Pohl has written, "Hospitality should be understood as a way of life rather than a task or strategy. It is easy to slip into viewing hospitality as a strategy for reaching migrants and refugees, or for that matter, for reaching postmodern youth or homeless people. But such an approach misunderstands the basic orientation of hospitality. Hospitality is not a means to an end; it is a way of life infused by the gospel."³² To talk the language of hospitality is to move toward the kind of mutuality which is required by friendship. Anthony Gittins has suggested, "Unless the person who sometimes extends hospitality is also able sometimes to be a gracious recipient, and unless the one who receives the other as stranger is also able to become the stranger received by another, then, far from 'relationships,' we are merely creating unidirectional lines of power flow, however unintended this may be. And that is quite antithetical to mission in the spirit of Jesus."³³ Friendship might seem to be the most natural thing in the world, but to achieve it, especially across barriers of division, suspicion, or hostility, is not achieved without swimming against the tide. "Hospitality will not occur in any significant way in our lives or churches," argues Pohl, "unless we give it deliberate attention. But the practice has been mostly forgotten, and because it conflicts with a number of contemporary values, we must intentionally nurture a commitment to hospitality."³⁴

Through his deep experience and profound knowledge of the Christian missionary movement, John Taylor observed, "The word *allelous*—one another—rings through the pages of the New Testament like a peal of bells."³⁵ It is intriguing that the movement now underway in North America to enable the church to regain its missionary character in the context of secular Western society, has chosen the title "Allelon" to describe the "network of missional leaders, schools and para-church organizations that envisions, inspires, engages, resources, trains, and educates leaders for the church and its mission in our culture."³⁶ Relationships, in the experience of the Allelon network, are the key to effectiveness in Christian mission. The approach championed by the network is one where, "The group of people who are

---

31. Webber, *Ancient-Future Faith*, 72; cited in Pohl, "Biblical Issues," 12.
32. Pohl, "Biblical Issues," 11.
33. Gittens, "Beyond Hospitality?" 13.
34. Pohl, *Making Room*, 171; cited in Drane, *After McDonaldization*, 54.
35. Wood, *Poet, Priest and Prophet*, 204.
36. Roxburgh, *Introducing the Missional Church*, 7.

empowered by the [church] board to do a *getting to know* experiment must realize that they are simply to get to know people and listen to them. They are not to go out with their Bible up their sleeve, waiting for an opportunity to proselytize. Engaging neighbors with this experiment means that people simply become present in their neighbourhoods and begin to engage people in natural ways of friendship."[37]

To account for this theologically, it became a commonplace of the missionary movement that mission, in order to be authentic and effective, had to be incarnational in character. Jesus Christ, the Son of God, fulfilled his mission by identifying completely with the human community in which he lived. This has set out the path that all authentic Christian mission must follow. Friendship, therefore, is at the heart of it. A lifetime in the missionary movement allowed John Taylor to conclude, "Every opening of one's whole self towards another, every taking upon oneself the burden and the gift of another, contributes a little to that quiet tide which is flowing back and forth, carrying us with it into the very being of God, sweeping us back with God into the life of the world."[38] It is through such interpersonal relationships that God's mission comes to expression. The kind of friendship enjoyed between Azariah and his YMCA colleagues or between Smith and Mungalo or between Livingstone and his Makololo companions or between Fraser and Chirwa, does not sit easily with the standard post-colonial critique, yet it represents the inner dynamic which accounts for its effectiveness.

This quality of friendship, moreover, may emerge in the twenty-first century as the core of the missionary strategy through which the West will be re-evangelized. It may, in fact, hold the key to effective Christian witness in every part of the world. The evidence of the missionary movement suggests that an extraordinary depth of personal friendship has been experienced at the point where people engage one another within the movement that takes the Good News of Jesus Christ across cultural boundaries. Such friendships have been the hinge on which the movement of the Gospel into new situations has turned. As fresh cultural frontiers present themselves in the world of today and tomorrow, there will be need for evangelistic initiative at many levels. Not to be underestimated, however, are personal friendships forming the bridge that takes the Good News of Jesus Christ from one context to another, enriching both in the process.

---

37. Ibid., 187.
38. Wood, *Poet, Priest and Prophet*, 210.

BIBLIOGRAPHY

Ahn, Kyo-Seong. "From Mission to Church and Beyond: The Metamorphosis of Post-Edinburgh Christianity." In *Edinburgh 2010: Mission Then and Now*, edited by David A. Kerr and Kenneth R. Ross, 74–84. Oxford: Regnum, 2009.

Anyimadu, Adjoa. "Scotland and Wales in Africa: Opportunities for a Coordinated U.K. Approach to Development." Afrika Programme Paper: AFP PP 2011-12. London, Chatham House, 2011.

Brafman, Ori, and Rod A. Beckstrom. *The Starfish and the Spider: The Unstoppable Power of Leaderless Organizations*. New York: Penguin, 2006.

Cracknell, Kenneth. *Justice, Courtesy and Love: Theologians and Missionaries Encountering World Religions, 1846–1914*. London: Epworth, 1995.

Dritsas, Lawrence. "Valuing Scotland's Links with Malawi: Inputs from Scotland Malawi Partnership Members." Study by the University of Edinburgh School of Social and Political Science and Global Development Academy, October 2010.

Friedman, Thomas L. *The World Is Flat: A Brief History of the Twenty-First Century*. New York: Farrar, Straus & Giroux, 2005.

Gittens, Anthony. "Beyond Hospitality? The Missionary Status and Role Revisited." *International Review of Mission* 83 (1994) 397–416.

Gnanakan, Ken. "To Proclaim the Good News of the Kingdom." In *Mission in the 21st Century*, edited by Andrew F. Walls and Cathy Ross, 3–10. London: Darton, Longman & Todd, 2008.

Hume, Robert A. "The Missionary Message in Relation to Non-Christian Religions." Submission to the World Missionary Conference 1910, Commission 4.

Johnson, Todd M., and Kenneth R. Ross, editors. *Atlas of Global Christianity 1910–2010*. Edinburgh: Edinburgh University Press, 2009.

Jones, E. Stanley. *The Christ of the Indian Road*. London: Hodder & Stoughton, 1925.

Kay, Billy. *The Scottish World: A Journey into the Scottish Diaspora*. Edinburgh: Mainstream, 2006.

Legge, James. "Christianity and Confucianism Compared in Their Teaching of the Whole Duty of Man." Essay no. 2 in *Non-Christian Religions of the World*, edited by William Muir. New York: Fleming & Revell, 1884.

Livingstone, David, and Charles Livingstone. *Narrative of an Expedition to the Zambesi and Its Tributaries: And of the Discovery of the Lakes Shirwa and Nyassa*. London: Murray, 1865.

McIntosh, Alastair. *Hell and High Water: Climate Change, Hope and the Human Condition*. Edinburgh: Birlinn, 2008.

Newbigin, Lesslie. *A Word in Season: Perspectives on Christian World Mission*. Grand Rapids: Eerdmans, 1994.

———. *The Gospel in a Pluralist Society*. London: SPCK, 1989.

Pfister, Lauren F. *Striving for the "Whole Duty of Man": James Legge and the Scottish Protestant Encounter with China*. Vol. 2. Frankfurt: Lang, 2004.

Pohl, Christine D. "Biblical Issues in Mission and Migration." *Missiology: An International Review* 31 (2003) 3–15.

———. *Making Room: Recovering Hospitality as a Christian Tradition*. Grand Rapids: Eerdmans, 1999.

Robert, Dana L. "Cross-Cultural Friendship in the Creation of Twentieth-Century World Christianity." *International Bulletin of Missionary Research* 35 (2011) 100–107.

Ross, Andrew C. *Blantyre Mission and the Making of Modern Malawi*. Blantyre: Christian Literature Association in Malawi, 1996.

Ross, Kenneth R. "'No One Can Shave Your Head in Your Absence': Scotland and Malawi Today." *Edinburgh Review* 118 (2006) 25–30.

Roxburgh, Alan J., and M. Scott Boren. *Introducing the Missional Church: What It Is, Why It Matters, How to Become One*. Grand Rapids: Baker, 2009.

Sacks, Jonathan. *The Dignity of Difference: How to Avoid the Clash of Civilizations*. London: Continuum, 2002.

Scotland Malawi Partnership. "Scotland Malawi Partnership 2011–14." Edinburgh: Scotland Malawi Partnership, 2011.

Smith, Edwin W. *The Golden Stool: Some Aspects of the Conflict of Cultures in Africa*. London: Holborn, 1926.

Stanley, Brian. *The World Missionary Conference, Edinburgh 1910*. Grand Rapids: Eerdmans, 2009.

Thompson, T. Jack. *Christianity in Northern Malawi: Donald Fraser's Missionary Methods and Ngoni Culture*. Leiden: Brill, 1995.

———. "Remembering the Past, Celebrating the Present: The Centenary of Loudon Mission, November 2002." *Society of Malawi Journal* 56 (2003) 24–32.

Webber, Robert. *Ancient-Future Faith*. Grand Rapids: Baker, 1999.

Wood, David. *Poet, Priest and Prophet: The Life and Thought of Bishop John V. Taylor*. London: CTBI, 2002.

World Missionary Conference, 1910. *Carrying the Gospel to All the Non-Christian World*. Report of Commission I. Edinburgh: Oliphant, Anderson & Ferrier, 1910.

———. *The History and Records of the Conference*. Edinburgh: Oliphant, Anderson & Ferrier, 1910.

12

Ethiopian Orthodox Christology
Interacting with an Ancient African Perspective

STEPHEN STRAUSS

MOST WESTERN CHRISTIANS ARE unfamiliar with the Oriental Orthodox Churches, a family of churches in Armenia, Syria, India, Egypt, and Ethiopia. The Ethiopian Orthodox Church (EOC) is the largest of these ancient churches. Not only is it one of the oldest churches in the world; it is also an authentically African church, long isolated from the West, and so has developed many beliefs and practices that address its unique context.[1]

At the center of the EOC's identity is its understanding of the nature and person of Christ. The Christology of the Ethiopian Orthodox Church is representative of the other Oriental Orthodox Churches, but is also an authentic and ancient African contribution to the theology of the universal church. As Tite Tiénou has demonstrated, in an era of world Christianity, theologizing must be a world endeavor.[2] With the majority of the world Christians now in Africa, Asia, and Latin America, theological provincialism must be abandoned and Western theologians must engage with theologies that take center stage in other parts of the world. Though theologians

---

1. For a wider survey of the unique, indigenous features of the Ethiopian Orthodox Church, see Shenk, "Ethiopian Orthodox," 259–78.
2. Tiénou, "Christian Theology."

from other theological traditions may not accept the EOC's model of the union of Jesus's deity and humanity, they can learn much by interacting with the perspectives and concerns of Christological reflection in Ethiopia.

HISTORICAL BACKGROUND

Contending for non-Chalcedonian Christology has been at the center of the pivotal moments of the history of the Ethiopian Orthodox Church. First, from its founding in the fourth century, the church has had a close connection to non-Chalcedonian churches in Syria and Egypt, particularly the church in Alexandria, which was the center for opposition to two-nature Christology and Chalcedon.[3] The earliest translation of the Scriptures into the Ethiopian vernacular and the first widespread propagation of the faith throughout Ethiopia were the work of the Nine Saints, Syrian missionary monks who were fleeing persecution for their Christological beliefs, but who were also part of a program "of careful recruitment and selection by the (Monophysite) patriarchate of Alexandria" to spread non-Chalcedonian Christian faith.[4]

Second, in the seventh century, Portuguese Jesuits embarked on an aggressive campaign to bring Ethiopia into the Roman Catholic fold. At the center of their activity was an attempt to persuade the Ethiopian church and government to accept the Chalcedonian formula. Their efforts seemed to have achieved success when the reigning Ethiopian emperor, Susenyos, embraced Roman Catholicism and Chalcedon. But further Jesuit demands—that all Ethiopian Christians be rebaptized, all churches be reconsecrated, all Ethiopian priests be reordained, and that Latin be used in the Ethiopian liturgy—sparked a bitter civil war. The carnage brought by the war destroyed Susenyos' confidence, and he abdicated. When his son, Fasilades, took the throne, he expelled the Jesuits with the taunt, "The flock of Ethiopia has escaped from the hyenas of the West."[5] Despite their rejection of Chalcedon, the EOC believed that "the Lord Christ is perfect God and perfect Man. His

---

3. The Council of Chalcedon concluded that Christ had "two natures, inconfusedly, unchangedably, indivisibly, inseparably ... preserved, and concurring in one Person (prosôpon) and one Subsistence (hypostasis)" (Schaff, *Creeds of Christendom*, 62). This was given the status of "a binding document and a definition of faith which was not susceptible to negotiation." But it was never accepted in many parts of the East, and that led to an entirely separate ecclesiastical hierarchy. See Frend, *Rise of Monophysite Movement*, 49, 296–315.

4. Tamrat, *Church and State*, 23, 29.

5. Brake, "Historical Investigation of Monophysitism," 153.

natures are not separated nor divided, for neither of them subsist of itself."[6] The EOC's seventeenth-century confrontation with the Jesuits left them bitterly opposed to Chalcedon, convinced that only a one-nature Christology could be authentically Ethiopian.

Third, following the departure of the Jesuits, the EOC entered into a period of fierce internal theological debate over the anointing of Christ (Luke 4:18, Acts 4:27 and 10:38). For 200 years synods were held, battles were fought, and excommunications pronounced between the Union, Unction, and Three Birth positions. The details of the debate seem obscure to most Western theologians,[7] but the importance of the debate underscores the significance of the EOC's non-Chalcedonian Christology. "The purpose of the subtle argument on unction in Ethiopian Christology is to demonstrate whether one accepts a duality of natures in Christ or not," with each side seeking to outdo the others in warding off "the ever present danger of the Catholic doctrine of the two natures of Christ."[8] The effect of this period of internal conflict on the EOC was an even tighter weaving of one-nature, non-Chalcedonian Christology into the fabric of Ethiopian theology.

The history of development of EOC Christology has solidified the EOC's commitment to a one-nature Christology as a key component in a Christian faith that is authentically their own. What, then, does the EOC teach about the nature of Christ?

THE INCARNATION: THE DIVINE SON CONCEIVED BY THE VIRGIN

The EOC believes that at the moment of the incarnation, through the work of the Holy Spirit, the eternal Son of God took flesh and soul from the Virgin Mary to become a man. At the moment of conception, two natures—the divine nature of the Son of God and perfect manhood taken from Mary—united into one person and one nature.

---

6. Ludolphus, *New History*, 363–64.

7. This essay does not explore the history of the debate between the Tewahedo ("union"), Qebat ("anointing"), and Sost Ledet ("three births") groups within the EOC. Tewahedo was confirmed as the official position of the EOC at the Council of Boru Meda in 1878. Both the debate itself and its resolution, however, demonstrate the EOCs commitment to a one-nature Christology that avoids Eutychianism (after Eutychius, 380–456, patriarch of Constantinople). To better understand the debate itself, see Jones and Monroe, *History of Ethiopia*, 110ff; Crummey, *Priests and Politicians*, 20–27; Aren, *Evangelical Pioneers*, 75 ff; Hyatt, *Church of Abyssinia*, 102–4; Jowett, *Christian Researches*, 181–94; Strauss, "Perspectives," 78–85.

8. Hyatt, *Church of Abyssinia*, 102.

In the Incarnation God the Son united to Himself real and perfect manhood. Conceived in her womb by Mary the Virgin through the work of the Holy Spirit, He was born in the world as a real man. At the very moment of His conception, through the operation of the Holy Spirit, a personal manhood was formed in the Virgin's womb in union with God the Son. Thus God the Son united to Himself the manhood taken from the human mother and was born as perfect God and perfect man in the real sense.[9]

Therefore, from the moment of conception, the baby in the Virgin Mary's womb was fully the Second Person of the Trinity. The EOC and other Oriental Orthodox Churches emphasize that Mary was the *theotokos*—God-bearer—precisely because they are affirming the full deity of the whole person of Jesus from the moment of conception. Mary did not conceive or give birth only to the human nature or human twin of God the Son; she both conceived and gave birth to the Second Person of the Trinity.[10] This is absolutely crucial to the EOC's understanding of Jesus, for to say that Mary conceived or gave birth only to Jesus's humanity is to say that the eternal Logos did not himself become fully human, but that he was only joined together with a human twin.

In order to preserve the full deity of Christ from the moment of conception, the EOC insists that this union of deity and humanity was *not* the fertilization of a human egg in Mary's womb by the Holy Spirit. "The heretics . . . say, 'the Son is created sharing seed from the Holy Spirit and blood from Mary.' The above is a denial of the truth because it implies that the Holy Spirit is a creature and the Son is only man."[11] Therefore, the mystery of the incarnation is that "Christ is the Word of the Father and of the Holy Spirit, thus the Virgin Mary is the true Mother of God; the Mother of the Word."[12]

UNION INTO ONE NATURE

At the center of the EOC's Christology is the understanding of the Incarnation as the perfect union—*tewahedo*[13]—of the divine and human natures

---

9. Samuel, "Faith of the Church," 48.
10. Ibid., 18.
11. Belihu, "Understanding," 20.
12. Mekarios et al., *Ethiopian Orthodox*, 28.

13. Because Amharic and Geez are written in the Ethiopic script, and because transliteration into the English alphabet varies, Amharic spellings in the body of this essay may vary. All quoted Amharic or Geez words will be spelled as they appear in the

of Christ into *one nature*. After this union of the two natures, "Christ is not two persons or two natures, but one Person, one incarnate Nature of God the Son, with one will, but being at once divine and human."[14] Ethiopian Orthodox theologians emphasize that "without being separated in substance from the right hand of the Father" the eternal Word "took in His separate Person from the womb of the Virgin Mary flesh from her flesh, soul from her soul, and Godhead was united with Manhood. . . . 'Christ' is the name of union."[15] Christ has the same substance as God the Father and the same flesh and soul as Mary; he is fully God and fully man. However, the term "Christ" ("anointed") does not refer to his humanity alone, but to his unified person. The two natures were perfectly united into one.

The key term used by the EOC to describe the incarnation is *tewahedo* ("union"). "Things united by *tewahedo* are neither separated nor confused. It is like the food we eat is united with our body so that we cannot separate it after digestion."[16] "'Tewahido' is the Ethiopian term (meaning 'made one') which is the best expression conveying the faith of the Church since it emphasizes the inseparable unity of the Godhead and manhood in the Person of Christ. The Church's official title is 'The Ethiopian Orthodox Tewahido Bete Christian.'"[17] At the center of the EOC's understanding of Jesus is that he was the absolutely complete and perfect *union* of divinity and humanity in *one* nature and *one* person.

COMPOSITE UNITY: UNION WITHOUT CONFUSION

The EOC clearly affirms that this union of Christ's two natures into one nature at the moment of the incarnation was accomplished without the confusion of the attributes of the two natures. Christ's deity was still a perfect deity, not in some way diminished by his humanity, and Christ's humanity was still a perfect humanity, not in some way altered by his deity. Christ's deity and humanity each maintain their "absolute integrity and perfection with its respective properties, without change or division. Each of them continues in its dynamic reality."[18]

Even though they believe that the human and divine combined into one nature in Christ from the moment of conception, the EOC and other

---

original source.

14. Aymro and Motovu, *Ethiopian Orthodox*, 97–98.
15. Matthew, *Teaching of the Abyssinian Church*, 12.
16. Belihu, "Understanding," 45.
17. Aymro and Motovu, *Ethiopian Orthodox*, 98.
18. Samuel, "Faith of the Church," 51.

Oriental Orthodox Churches strongly reject the label "monophysite" (one nature) for several reasons. First, they affirm that Christ was two natures united into one nature, not simply one nature. They affirm that it was a full human nature that was united with Christ's divine nature, assuring that his human attributes would remain intact and unmixed with divine attributes after the union. Second, the term "monophysite" historically and linguistically may imply that one of Christ's two natures was absorbed by the other. The EOC strongly affirms the full deity and humanity of Christ after the union of his two natures into one nature, and so distances itself from the belief, as in Eutychianism, that Christ's humanity fundamentally changed into divine, incorruptible flesh by its union with deity.[19] "Non-Chalcedonian" is the preferred description of their Christology, but they will often also use the expression *miaphysis*, defined as "composite unity," to emphasize that Christ's deity and humanity preserved their essential attributes in the union of the two natures: "The properties of each nature are preserved without change after the union. Therefore, we believe that Christ is one Person and one Nature, and thus is both divine and human. We speak of one because of the union. We hold "mia physis," composite nature, one united nature. Again the Lord Jesus Christ is perfect man and perfect God. The word "perfect" closes the door to all quibble and prevarication. We accept both unity and duality in Christ who in acting performed as one."[20]

The Ethiopian Orthodox often emphasizes that there was ecclesiastical unity after the first three ancient ecumenical councils, councils which "proclaimed Christ as one true God and true man, but united, without confusion and without division" but that the two-nature theology of Chalcedon "was contrary to the teachings of the first three ecumenical councils." Following Chalcedon, Eutychianism was wrongly attributed to the EOC and its sister churches. "Without investigation and hence in ignorance, the word *monophysitism* was unjustly attributed to the Ethiopian and the oriental churches in general that have nothing to do with such a phrase, which should be exclusively attributed to Eutyches himself." Yeshaq goes on to strongly reject Eutyches's assertion that "Christ's body was absorbed by the divinity and became immaterial."[21]

---

19. For a brief survey of Eutychianism, see Frend, *Rise of the Monophysite Movement*, 30; Erickson, *Word Became Flesh*, 68.

20. Aymro and Motovu, *Ethiopian Orthodox*, 96.

21. Yeshaq, *Ethiopian Tewahedo Church*, 120; 103.

PERFECT MAN

The Oriental Orthodox Churches are frequently and simplistically accused of teaching that Christ's humanity was absorbed by his deity. However, the EOC emphatically affirms that the "the manhood of Christ was absolutely real and perfect."[22] "The Logos revealed Himself in our flesh and became man like us. He did all things that man does with the exception of sin (John 8:46). And at the same time he was truly God."[23] The result of *tewahedo* (union) and *miaphysis* (composite unity) is that the Lord Jesus Christ was both perfect God and perfect man in one person and one nature. "Jesus Christ, the incarnate God the Son, is one Person, continuous with Godhead and continuous with manhood. In Him Godhead and manhood continue, each in its integrity and perfection, in a state of indivisible and unconfused union."[24]

In order to emphasize Christ's complete humanity, Yeshaq expounds on the seven elements of a human being according to traditional Ethiopian philosophy: four elements of the flesh (wind, fire, water, earth) and three elements of the soul (rational thought, the power of speech, the property of life). Jesus, he affirms, had all seven, and, hence, was perfect man.[25] Samuel verifies that Jesus took both flesh *and* soul from the Virgin Mary, grew up, matured, hungered and thirsted as all people do, and explicitly denies Apollinarianism, the view that Jesus's deity overshadowed his humanity, making his humanity qualitatively different from other people.[26] Mekarios adds, "After birth He grew like men, doing all human works except sin."[27] Habte affirms that Christ's two natures are combined into one nature, but anathematizes "those who say that Christ's humanity was absorbed or swallowed up in His Divinity."[28]

Belihu relates a number of examples frequently given by Ethiopian theologians to distinguish the EOC position from Eutychianism: iron and fire, the eye and light, and the sewing together of purple and gold thread into a single fabric.[29] Each of these illustrates two elements that come to-

---

22. Samuel, "Faith of the Church," 51.
23. Aymro and Motovu, *Ethiopian Orthodox*, 95.
24. Samuel, "Faith of the Church," 48.
25. Yeshaq, *Ethiopian Tewahedo Church*, 124.
26. Samuel, "Faith of the Church," 49.
27. Mekarios, *Ethiopian Orthodox*, 47.
28. Habte, *YeIteyopeya Ortodoks*, 158.
29. Belihu, "Understanding," 104. In ethnographic interviews conducted by the present author, a young deacon explained the tewahedo union of Christ's deity and humanity into one nature without the confusion of attributes by comparing it to the

gether as one in an inseparable, composite unity in which each retains its distinct attributes. Christ's divinity and humanity were not absorbed into one another, nor did one destroy the other. The EOC thus officially rejects Eutychian or Apollinarian ideas that the union of the two natures made Christ something other than fully human, confessing that his natures were united "without confusion, without change" and that "the properties of each nature are preserved without change after the union."[30] While the clear emphasis of the Ethiopian Orthodox Church is on the unity of Christ into one person and one nature, the Church's official teaching is equally emphatic that, except for sin, he was a human being just like other human beings.[31]

Ethnographic interviews in one Addis Ababa parish in 1995 and 1996 confirmed that many common clergy and lay people in the EOC understand that Jesus Christ's humanity was like that of other people, except without sin. Some of the more educated subjects attempted to describe a union that preserved Christ's true divinity and true humanity. One *debtara* said that Christ was "true man" (*eunetenya sew*).[32] An older layman said that Christ was fully God and "exactly human" (*tekekelenya sew*) but without sin. A middle-aged man with a reputation for knowing Orthodoxy well said that Christ "was fully like a man at every state of humanity." Another layman said that Christ's death was necessary, not only to save, but also to prove he was human. Using a precise Amharic expression, one woman said "holding

---

heating of metal in fire: "The fire makes it red hot, and there is a union of heat and metal into one." A debtara (a lay teacher in the Ethiopian Orthodox Church; see fn. 32) explained tewahedo by contrasting it with the belief of a Eutychian-like sect within the EOC known as Qebat ("anointed"): "The union of Christ's divinity and humanity was the union of spirit and flesh, the spirit from God and the flesh from Mary, joined in the womb of the virgin Mary. The Tewahedo believe there was this union of spirit and flesh but the Qebat say that there was not a union but an anointing. But when you anoint something, there's not real union. For example, when a person anoints himself with butter he is simply covering himself. There is no real union between himself and the butter." Tewahedo, he said, describes a true, organic union of human flesh and divine spirit, not simply an outward covering of Christ's divinity with humanity. See Strauss, "Perspectives," 130–31.

30. Aymro and Motovu, *Ethiopian Orthodox*, 95–96.

31. Ethiopian Catholic theologians such as Tesfazghi, *Current Christological Positions*, 1973, Ayala, *Ethiopian Church and Its Christological Doctrine*, and Musay Tesfa Giorgis, interview by author (Holy Savior Catholic Church, Addis Ababa, January 8, 1997) point to the EOC's strong formal affirmation of Christ's full deity and full humanity—especially their use of Chalcedonian terminology such as "without confusion" and "without change"—and conclude that the EOC is Chalcedonian in actual belief, and non-Chalcedonian only in terminology; see especially Ayala, *Ethiopian Church*, 69–70.

32. The debtara are non-ordained "cantor-teachers of the Ethiopian Orthodox Church who gain their status through their knowledge of holy books and traditions" (Strauss, "Perspectives," 240).

onto divinity, he became a man (*amlakenet yezo, sew ho-ne*)."[33] Many subjects expressed Christ's humanity by explaining that he had every human experience except sin.[34] A woman said, "Every circumstance that came to people came to him. . . . He felt the same suffering we do." A deacon[35] said that Christ, "had a weak human flesh that hungered, thirsted, and got tired." Another deacon mentioned John 4, where it is stated that Jesus was thirsty. He exclaimed, "Here he was, the creator of water, yet he thirsted and asked for water. He had a weak flesh, a flesh that hungered and thirsted and got tired." When asked if Christ had ever hungered and gotten tired, one man answered, "He hungered powerfully! He got tired like any other man." A priest called Christ a "man of the earth (*miderawey*)" to describe his humanity.[36] The official teaching of the EOC and the popular belief of many of the Church's more educated members is that Jesus was a true human being, in every way like us, but without sin.

ALL CHRIST'S WORKS PERFORMED BY HIS UNITED PERSON

The EOC not only stresses the unity of Christ's single nature; it also stresses the unity of all of his actions. EOC theologians express particular concern at the Chalcedonian tendency to attribute some of Christ's actions to his divine nature and others to his human nature. Everything Christ did, including dying on the cross, he did as a single, unified person. Poladian criticizes Pope Leo for assigning Jesus's hunger, thirst, weariness, and sleep to his human nature but his feeding of the 5,000 and offering of living water to his divine nature. "At Chalcedon no real union was obtained. The human and divine natures were each left as separate entities, not really united."[37] He continues, "A being in whom now the God acts, now the man is equally repellent to faith and theory. . . . All that concerns Christ should be applied not to the *one* or the *other* but to *His entire Person in its unity*. . . . Miracles

---

33. The researcher did not hear this expression in any other interview or encounter it in any written source. It seems to have been this woman's own understanding of the relationship between Christ's divinity and humanity.

34. About two-thirds of all subjects agreed that Christ became hungry, thirsty, and tired just as other human beings do.

35. Deacons in the EOC are usually young men between age 20 and 30 who are preparing for the priesthood.

36. Strauss, "Perspectives," 134–41.

37. Poladian, "Doctrinal Position," 259.

were performed not by the Logos but by the Incarnate Son of God."[38] One of the central tenets of the Ethiopian Orthodox Church is that "all the tasks of Christ while He was on the earth are the tasks of the 'Tewahido' (composite unity) of the divine and human."[39]

EOC theologians believe that, in attributing Christ's actions to either his deity or humanity, Chalcedonians have fallen into the heresy of Nestorianism, which is particularly dangerous because it implies that Christ's suffering and death were only in his humanity.[40] They maintain that if Christ only suffered and died in his humanity, his death did not accomplish the world's salvation. Christ "could not save the world" if he were not "united in one person and one nature" when he was crucified.[41] If only Christ's human nature suffered, "God is still not after all living a human life." He is "still holding himself at a distance from its experiences and conditions."[42] It cannot be simply the human nature of Christ that was crucified and died; the divine had to die, as well. "If we say Christ performed divine acts in his divinity and human acts in his humanity, then salvation is only in his humanity, and the price God paid is useless; a human salvation is insufficient. Perfect union of humanity and deity without destroying either is necessary" for salvation.[43]

Since God cannot die, and since death in his humanity alone could not provide salvation for the world, the EOC emphasizes Christ's divinity was so unified with his humanity that his divinity died within his humanity. "The Divine Word without being united with the flesh cannot be crucified, because as God He is beyond suffering. But through the union with the flesh He was crucified and subjected to death. If, on the other hand, only the human body was crucified, He could not save the world."[44] Even more forcefully, Yeshaq emphasizes that "all concerning Christ should be applied to His entire person as one Lord . . . God suffered, God was crucified, God shed blood, God died, and God was risen up for the salvation of all men . . . If God the Word had not suffered on the Cross, the Christian hope for eternal

---

38. Ibid., 261.
39. Belihu, "Understanding," 78.
40. Berhanu, *Amde Haimanot*, 48; Habte, *YeIteyopeya Ortodoks*, 160.
41. Habte, *YeIteyopeya Ortodoks*, 158.
42. Poladian, "Doctrinal Position," 258–59.
43. Asrat, *Temhert Melekot*, 152–53.
44. Aymro and Motovu, *Ethiopian Orthodox*, 96.

salvation is vanity."⁴⁵ Jesus had to be one person, one nature, and one will, particularly in his death, in order to provide salvation.⁴⁶

"NATURE" AND "PERSON" IN ETHIOPIAN LANGUAGES

The EOC's suspicion that Chalcedonian theology is really veiled Nestorianism is exacerbated by the implicit meaning of the various words for "nature" in Amharic and Geez.⁴⁷ The word usually used in Amharic publications of the Ethiopian Orthodox Church to speak of the "nature" of Christ is *baheriy*. However, Tesfazghi gives a lengthy discussion of three words which have been used to speak of the "nature/s" of Christ in the writings of Ethiopian Orthodox theologians. All three words—*hellalwie* ("being, existence"), *baheriy* ("nature, character, essence, personality, trait, attribute, temperament"), and *tebay* ("nature, character, disposition, conduct, temperament,")⁴⁸—are also used to speak of the "person" (Amharic: *akal*) of Christ. Translations from ancient Greek documents use these four terms—*akal* plus the other three—interchangeably to translate ʹυποστσις, ουσια and φυσις.⁴⁹ Tesfazghi concludes his detailed study of the terms used:

> If we add to "hellawie" and "bahrey" (and sometimes also to "tabayee") the number "two" (kel-ettu), it would signify to the Ethiopian Orthodox theologians "two persons" or "two hypostasis" or two "prosopa" or "two natures" but separately existing or subsisting in themselves . . . "Tabayee" besides "bahrey" (nature) also signifies "aka," whether in Christology or in the Holy Trinity.⁵⁰

---

45. Yeshaq, *Ethiopian Tewahedo Church*, 103.

46. Concern that Christ not be divided into two persons extends even to the terminology the EOC uses to describe the incarnate Son of God. The terms "Jesus," "Christ" or even "Jesus Christ," are felt to imply that his humanity is being separated from his deity. The incarnate Son of God should be referred to as "our Lord and Savior Jesus Christ." See Belihu, "Understanding," 115–16; Tesfazghi, *Current Christological Positions*, 144.

47. Amharic is the most widely spoken language of most Ethiopian Orthodox, and Geez is the traditional liturgical language of the EOC. For a discussion of the importance of understanding implicit as well as explicit meaning in translation and theologizing, see Hiebert, *Anthropological Insights*, 144–58.

48. Definitions taken from Leslau, *Concise Amharic Dictionary*, 1, 85, 231. Leslau treats Baheriy and tebay as virtual synonyms; likewise Asrat, *Temhert Melekot*, 152, and Tesfazghi, *Current Christological Positions*, 23–46.

49. Tesfazghi, *Current Christological Positions*, 23–46.

50. Ibid., 45.

All of the words which can be used to describe the "nature" of Christ imply a separate, distinct person of their own. Therefore, it is very difficult to simply say in Amharic or Geez "Christ is two natures in one person." Rather, to Ethiopian Orthodox Church theologians, describing Christ as having two natures sounds like two-person Nestorianism.

In a careful examination of Amharic and Geez words used to translate ουσια/φυσις as "nature" and ὑποστσις/*prosopon* "person," Ayala points out,

> By "nature," the Orthodox Ethiopians also mean the spiritual and material components of man, taken separately, and for "person," what results from these components, in other words, the complete man . . . The word "nature" is used in so concrete, so realistic a sense, that to admit two in Christ repels them and seems something monstrous, such as might be felt in saying that a person has four legs, or four eyes, and so on . . . In the minds of the Orthodox Ethiopians, the term "baherey" (= nature), stands for a complete reality that has existence by itself, either in an hypostasis or in a person.[51]

Because "nature" is a concrete idea that always results in a "person," to speak of two natures in Christ infers two persons. As a Catholic Ethiopian, Ayala concludes that the terms for "nature" and "person" must be abandoned, and that Christ should be described as "one being, one individual, one single substance, one single subject of attribution; Jesus Christ is a true and perfect man, a true and perfect God."[52]

Tesfazghi's and Ayala's studies are supported by Alemayehu and Berhanu. Alemayehu feels that there is not an appropriate translation of φυσις ("nature") in Amharic. Two natures imply "that Christ has two behaviors." To the average Amharic speaker, speaking of two natures implies "two contradictory ways of thinking, two contradictory frames-of-mind, as if Christ could quarrel with himself." The idea of Christ having two natures is offensive to most people; they simply can't understand it.[53] Berhanu agrees, saying that "a person (*akal*) without a nature (*baheriy*) or a nature without a person doesn't make sense. If there are two natures, there *must* be two persons."[54] "'Bahrey' (nature) cannot exist without 'Akal' (person)."[55]

Kidan's Geez-Amharic dictionary further confirms these conclusions. Kidan defines *baheriy* as "the intrinsic elements not fully formed into a

---

51. Ayala, *Ethiopian Church*, 67, 72.
52. Ibid., 73.
53. Alemayehu Moges, interview by author, July 25, 1995.
54. Berhanu, *Amde Haimanot*, 48.
55. Belihu, "Understanding," 94; cf. 105.

nature; the elements by which nature forms its shape."⁵⁶ Though *baheriy* is not the same as *akal*, it always acts through *akal*; they cannot be separated. As an example, Kidan says one doesn't speak of a sickle cutting grain, but of a person cutting grain, because the sickle is only the instrument; the person is doing the cutting. In the same way that a person expresses himself through the sickle, so the *baheriy* expresses itself through the *akal*. One can never attribute an action to *baheriy*. The ramifications of Kidan's discussion for Christological understanding are clear. One cannot speak of two natures (*baheriy*) and one person (*akal*) because a *baheriy* always has to express itself through an *akal*.

Tesfazghi's summary is that "the problem of terminology in our Ethiopian theology . . . will remain as long as the ancient (i.e., pre-Chalcedonian) idioms are still used."⁵⁷ It is very difficult to speak of Christ's "two natures" in either Ethiopia's national language or her church language without also implying that Christ himself was divided into two persons.

SHARING OF ATTRIBUTES

The EOC's stress on a perfect union of Christ's deity and humanity leads to the characteristic of Ethiopian Orthodox Christology that has caused Chalcedonians to accuse them of Eutychiansim. Though the EOC's theologians affirm the union of Christ's deity and humanity in one nature without the confusion of his divine and human attributes, they also make statements that seem to indicate that Christ's humanity and deity absorbed one another, particularly that his deity so absorbed his humanity that his humanity was distinctly different from that of other people. This raises the question as to whether or not the EOC really believes that Christ was something other than truly human.

For example, immediately after saying, "Neither of the natures was assimilated by the other," Aymro and Motovu go on to say that "the properties of the Divine Word were attributed to the flesh and those of the flesh to the Divine Word . . . In the same way we can say that also the flesh was made divine. The attributes of the flesh can be given to the Divine Word and vice versa."⁵⁸ Chalcedonians might respond, "How is Christ's humanity not different from ours if 'the flesh was made divine' and 'the attributes of the flesh can be given to the Divine Word and vice versa'?" Samuel insists

---

56. Translation by author and Musay Tesfa Giorgis, January 8, 1997.
57. Tesfazghi, *Current Christological Positions*, 27.
58. Aymro and Motovu, *Ethiopian Orthodox*, 95–96.

that Christ "put on mortal flesh and made it immortal."[59] A *debtara* in Addis Ababa insisted that Christ's divinity and humanity were united into one nature such that "his flesh itself was divine."[60] If Christ's flesh became immortal and his humanity became divine it would seem that it was unlike the humanity of other people. "God became man and *man became God*" is a common expression used by EOC theologians and laypeople alike to describe the incarnation.[61] This expression seems to imply that Christ's humanity was transformed by his deity; his humanity was a divine humanity. At first glance, especially to Western theologians, statements such as these seem to reflect Apollinarian and Eutychian ideas that Christ's humanity was so changed by his deity that he was not truly human.[62]

EOC theologians insist that these expressions do not imply Eutychianism. "The human nature was not dissolved in the divine as Eutyches's conception taught."[63] Rather, they are attempts to emphasize that every part of the person of Christ was divine and, consequently, every part of Christ died for the sin of the world and every part of Christ can be the object of worship. EOC theologians point to Acts 20:28 as teaching that the blood of Christ is the blood of God. So it can be said that Christ's "flesh became divine of nature" in such a way that it did not subsequently lose its essential human properties. "Worshipping Christ is worshipping his whole person, including his flesh."[64]

The EOC believes that only by means of a thorough unity that made every part of Christ divine could his death be adequately salvific. In order for the Eternal Son of God to provide salvation to humankind, Christ's deity had to be united with his humanity so that "God died by means of flesh."[65] Only through a perfect union with humanity could deity die and so bring divine salvation to humanity.

---

59. Samuel, "Faith of the Church," 49.

60. Strauss, "Perspectives," 138.

61. Ibid., 88, 138.

62. Ayala quotes EOC sources which teach that Christ's divine and human attributes did not mingle and that Christ's suffering was "in his flesh" as evidence that the EOC really believes in two natures of Christ (Ayala, *Ethiopian Church*, 88). However, he overlooks other formal statements from the EOC that imply a mingling of divine and human attributes, as well as the EOC's strong emphasis that Christ never acted strictly as a human or strictly as God. The apparent contradictions in formal EOC statements of faith reflect a tension between the church's desire to preserve its non-Chalcedonian heritage and to teach the full deity and humanity of Christ.

63. Yeshaq, *Ethiopian Tewahedo Church*, 103.

64. Belihu, "Understanding," 64.

65. Berhanu, *Amde Haimanot*, 47.

Furthermore, only through a perfect union with deity could humanity be "deified," raised from its level of sinful poverty and redeemed by its union with the divine.[66] Christ honored humanity by taking it "into His divine substance." A Chalcedonian theology that simply unites two natures in a single person does not lead to a deified humanity in Christ, and so it is inadequate to overcome the poverty of fallen, sinful flesh and bring humankind to salvation."[67] Instead, the Ethiopian Orthodox believe, deity and humanity were so perfectly united that all that was God participated in Christ's humanity and all that was human participated in his deity in order to provide salvation to the world. What to Western theologians looks like incipient Eutychianism is, to the Oriental Orthodox, essential to preserve the salvific effectiveness of Christ's death.

Though EOC theologians insist that this understanding of the sharing of attributes does not jeopardize Christ's genuine humanity, questions remain as to whether the average Ethiopian Orthodox person understands that a Jesus who possessed "divine flesh" was genuinely human. Ethnographic interviews conducted in one Addis Ababa parish in 1995 and 1996 indicated that a significant number of laymen, laywomen, and at least one parish priest seemed to feel that he was not fully human, and at least some laypeople felt that he was only God, and not in any sense human.[68] When asked if Jesus was God or man when on earth, one man responded, "God the creator," followed by silence. When asked if he was also a man, the subject responded that Christ lived *like* a man and died *like* a man but, he also knew what was in the hearts of men. He had the knowledge of God on the inside, but he acted like a man on the outside. Another older man said that "Christ seemed to come as a man, but we believe he was God clothed in flesh to die. God is God. God is spirit." His idea seems to have been that Christ was spiritual God on the inside but human flesh on the outside. When asked if Christ was God, man, or both, a woman responded that he "taught as if he was God." When pressed with whether or not he was also man, the woman responded, "That is a 'thing of the mouth' [*afenya neger*; something which is rumored]. He was born of the Virgin Mary, and because of his birth of Mary, it was *said* that he was man. When those who were poor or in distress or suffering came to Mary, she was very sympathetic and would respond to their need." This woman could not bring herself to say that Jesus was truly human; she found greater comfort in the genuine humanity of Mary.

66. "Deified" is in reference to the Orthodox concept of theosis.

67. Poladian, "Doctrinal Position," 262; Mekarios et al., *Ethiopian Orthodox*, 27–28.

68. Cf. Strauss, "Perspectives," 100–71, for full description of research methodology and findings.

Two women said that in Christ God took on a human *se'el*, a word used to describe a painted picture. At least one priest doubted that Christ was fully human. He said that Christ "took the image of man to teach us and show us how to live. But he was true God, *not* true man (*eunetenya sew*)." This same priest was shocked at the suggestion that Christ could ever have become hungry or tired like an ordinary person.[69]

The tendency to doubt Christ's true humanity was graphically expressed by a 60-year-old man who had studied Orthodoxy most of his life. He said that Christ became a man to teach human beings, but that "he didn't come to dig. He didn't come to build a house. He didn't have our human nature (*tebay*). He was our king, above us." It seems that his idea was that Christ was human-like, but that he didn't come to do the common work that humans do.[70]

The feeling that Christ was not fully human was underscored by subjects who felt that he did not truly become hungry, thirsty, or tired when he was on earth.[71] When asked if Christ ever got hungry, thirsty, or tired, one woman responded, "How could he? He had all authority. He had no pain, he had no hunger. He feeds us, so how could he become hungry? There was one time during the 'time of pain,' the 40 days of fasting before Easter, when he fasted.[72] But he was not hungry like us, though he was passing through the time of hunger. But he only fasted like this to teach us to fast, not because he really was hungry." The older man who said that Christ had not "come to earth to dig," incredulously responded, "Christ hungry, tired?! No! Remember how he used five loaves and two fishes to make food for many thousands of people," implying that anyone with divine power would never suffer hunger. Another man said that Christ lived "without getting worn out" (*alselechem*).[73]

Several subjects affirmed quite strongly that Christ was only God and was not a man in any sense when he was on earth.[74] One woman asked,

---

69. Ibid., 134–35.

70. Ibid., 135–36.

71. Eight women, three laymen, and one clergy said that Christ did not truly become hungry, thirsty, or tired in the same way that other people do, and two women said they were too uncertain to answer the question. Seven subjects said that the purpose of Christ's apparent weaknesses was to teach his followers; three said his apparent weaknesses were only to test him.

72. The EOC teaches that Jesus fasted during the forty days before Easter as an example to his followers. Hence, his disciples should fast during the forty days of Lent.

73. Strauss, "Perspectives," 136–38.

74. Five women and one layman specifically stated that Christ was only God, and was in no sense a man, when he was on earth.

"How could he be a man? He is God. Is not God deity (*Igziabeher amlak aydelem*)?" Another woman insisted that he could not have had a human nature. He only had the nature of God. Still another woman affirmed, "He was God, the creator. How could he be a man? He was only God."[75]

In addition, almost all the laymen and laywomen and about half of the clergy interviewed indicated that, after his ascension, Jesus ceased being man in any sense; now he is only divine. Several drew a close connection between Jesus's not possessing a human nature and their need to approach God through "middle people" (*amalajoch*).[76]

The official position of the Ethiopian Orthodox Church is a one-nature Christology that claims that Christ had both "divine flesh" and a humanity that did not lose "its essential properties" as human. However, the results of this ethnographic survey indicate that at least some popular perspectives on Christ have slipped into Eutychianism.

CONTINUED REJECTION OF CHALCEDON: MORE THAN SEMANTICS

More recent publications of the Ethiopian Orthodox Church make it clear that the Church regards its differences with Chalcedonians as substantive, serious, and continuing. EOC theologians participated in a series of talks held between Chalcedonian and non-Chalcedonian Eastern Orthodox Churches between 1964 and 1993. During the talks the EOC representatives emphasized that they could not be expected to accept the Chalcedonian formula.[77] Nevertheless, at the conclusion of the consultations it was agreed that there was no basic difference in the Christology of the two groups. Both groups condemned Nestorius and Eutyches and "those who speak in terms of 'two' do not thereby divide or separate and those who speak in terms of 'one' do not thereby commingle, (mingle) or confuse."[78] Repre-

---

75. Strauss, "Perspectives," 141.

76. Amalaj (plural: amalajoch) is a notoriously difficult word to translate into English. The amaljoch are the angels or saints who stand between God and human beings, who intercede or mediate to God for human beings, and who are consequently the recipients of prayer and honor by most members of the EOC. "Intercessor" and "mediator" have been suggested as possible translations, but some native Amharic speakers insist that these words are too strong, preferring simply to translate them as "those who stand between" (cf. Strauss, "Perspectives," 11, 12, 240).

77. "Third and Fourth Consultations between Eastern Orthodox and Oriental Orthodox Theologians: Geneva and the Addis Ababa Consultations," *Greek Orthodox Theological Review* 16 (1971) 30.

78. Mekarios et al., *Ethiopian Orthodox*, 144; see also Papandreou, *Joint Commission*.

sentatives from both the Chalcedonian and non-Chalcedonian Orthodox Churches agreed that "both families have loyally maintained the authentic Orthodox Christological doctrine" and that each should lift the anathemas pronounced against the other.[79]

In spite of this agreement by the consultation participants, the EOC's official response to the talks was that "two natures, two wills, two energies hypostatically united in the One Lord Jesus Christ, was not felt to be the same as that of the Oriental Orthodox Churches' Christological formula of one nature, one will and one energy in the one and the same Christ." Thus, the EOC refused to lift the anathemas on the Chalcedonian fathers, continued to emphasize that it accepts no ecumenical council after Ephesus (AD 431), and called on the Chalcedonian churches to accept a Christological formula of the unity of the two natures of Christ into one nature.[80] Even though some EOC leaders occasionally refer to the difference between their theology and Chalcedonian theology as "terminological,"[81] Chalcedon continues to be an unacceptable Christological formula for the official hierarchy of the Ethiopian Orthodox Church.

LEARNING FROM THE ETHIOPIAN ORTHODOX CHURCH

The Christology of the Ethiopian Orthodox Church strongly illustrates the influence context has on theology. History, culture, and language have deeply shaped the EOC's commitment to a one-nature Christology, and convinced the leadership that this formula best expresses Christ's perfect deity and humanity and best preserves his ability to provide salvation to the world.

No church has a complete monopoly on understanding scriptural truth. The theology of the church in every part of the world has been at least partially shaped by its culture, history, and theological traditions. Because the church in any time and place looks at truth through the presuppositions of its own context, "Christians from other cultures can enrich our faith or help us correct our mistakes."[82] Every church can enhance its own understanding of the Scripture and correct its blind spots by interacting with the theology of churches from other contexts, or engaging in intercultural

---

79. Ibid., 17.
80. Mekarios et al., *Ethiopian Orthodox*, 128, 145–46.
81. Eadie, "Chalcedon," 142.
82. Tiénou, "Forming Indigenous," 248.

theologizing. "Every church must learn to be both learner and teacher in theologizing."[83]

What can Western Chalcedonians learn from the Ethiopian Orthodox Church? What can its one-nature Christology contribute to the universal church's understanding of the person of Jesus Christ?

First, Chalcedonians must not simplistically dismiss one-nature Christologies as necessarily denying the full deity or humanity of Christ. In certain contexts, linguistic, historical, and cultural considerations may make the language of "two natures in one person" confusing, or even understood in a sense contradictory to Scripture. There may be cultures outside of Ethiopia where "two natures" implies Nestorian ideas that Christ was sometimes God and sometimes man, or he was internally divided against himself. While the language of Chalcedon is a true reflection of biblical truth in most contexts, in some contexts it implies ideas that are not biblical. Even the most precious, accurate creeds and confessions of the church are contextual; there will be times and places where alternative language must be used to reflect biblical truth.[84]

Second, Chalcedonians must ask themselves whether or not suggesting that Christ acted at times "in his humanity" and at other times "in his deity" implies a Nestorian division of Christ. Did not the God-man act at all times as one person who was both perfect God and perfect man? Specifically, can Chalcedonians say that Christ died only in his humanity and preserve the full salvific effect of his death? Might it be more accurate to say that Christ—the perfectly unified God-man—died? The EOC informs the theology of the worldwide church by reminding her that the union of Christ's deity and humanity in one person was so perfect that all of Christ's actions—particularly his death and resurrection—were actions performed by the one God-man.

Finally, the EOC's theologians can also profit from intercultural theologizing. Given ethnographic findings that many laypeople understand the union of natures and sharing of attributes in Christ's one nature as giving him a humanity that was distinctively different from that of other people, EOC theologians and church leaders should ask whether or not their own Christological statements adequately preserve Christ's genuine humanity. In their zeal to protect Christ's deity and the full salvific effect of his death, have they endangered the equally important truth that, except for sin, Jesus Christ was and is fully human?

83. Conn, *Eternal Word*, 252.

84. See Strauss, "Creeds." This volume provides an expanded discussion of the role of creed and confessions in an era of global theologizing, illustrated by the Christology of the EOC.

Understanding the Christology of the Ethiopian Orthodox Church provides a helpful contribution to the worldwide church's understanding of who Jesus was and is. Jesus Christ lived and died as the perfectly united, perfectly human, and perfectly divine God-man. A careful study of the EOC's Christology also reminds us that Christian theology must become "a worldwide conversation . . . in which Christians from everywhere participate fully."[85] Theologians from Ethiopian Orthodox and Chalcedonian traditions can learn much from each other as to the best way to express this truth of Christ's perfect deity and perfect humanity in their own particular contexts.

BIBLIOGRAPHY

Abuna Mekarios et al., editors. *The Ethiopian Orthodox Tewahedo Church Faith, Order of Worship and Ecumenical Relations*. Addis Ababa: Tensae, 1996.

Aren, Gustav. *Evangelical Pioneers in Ethiopia: Origins of the Evangelical Church Mekane Yesus*. Stockholm: EFS Forlaget, 1978.

Asrat Gebre Mariam. *Temhert Melekot* [Spiritual Education]. Addis Ababa: Artistic Printers, 1991.

Ayala Takla Haymanot. *The Ethiopian Church and Its Christological Doctrine*. Addis Ababa: Graphic Printers, 1981.

Aymro Wondmagegnehu and Joachim Motovu. *The Ethiopian Orthodox Church*. Addis Ababa: Ethiopian Orthodox Mission, 1970.

Belihu Delelange. "Understanding the Current 'Official' Christological Positions of the Ethiopian Orthodox Church: A Search for an Indigenous Christology." Masters thesis, Ethiopian Graduate School of Theology, 2001.

Berhanu Gobena. *Amde Haimanot* [Pillar of faith]. Addis Ababa: by the author, 1993.

Brake, Donald L. "A Historical Investigation of Monophysitism in the Ethiopian Orthodox Church." ThD diss., Dallas Theological Seminary, 1977.

Conn, Harvie M. *Eternal Word and Changing World*. Phillipsburg, NJ: Presbyterian & Reformed, 1984.

Crummey, Donald. *Priests and Politicians: Protestant and Catholic Missions in Orthodox Ethiopia 1830–1868*. Oxford: Clarendon, 1972.

Eadie, Douglas G. "Chalcedon Revisited." *Journal of Ecumenical Studies* 10 (1973) 140–45.

Erickson, Millard. *The Word Became Flesh*. Grand Rapids: Baker, 1991.

Frend, W. H. C. *The Rise of the Monophysite Movement: Chapters in the History of the Church in the Fifth and Sixth Centuries*. Cambridge: Cambridge University Press, 1972.

Habte Mariam Worquineh. *Yelteyopeya Ortodoks Tewahedo Bete Krestiyan Emenetena Temhert* [The Faith and Teaching of the Ethiopian Orthodox Tewahedo Church]. Addis Ababa: Berhanina Selam, n.d.

---

85. Tiénou, "Christian Theology," 51.

Hiebert, Paul G. *Anthropological Insights for Missionaries*. Grand Rapids: Baker Academic, 1985.
Hyatt, Harry Middleton. *The Church of Abyssinia*. London: Luzac, 1928.
Jones, A. H. M., and Elizabeth Monroe. *A History of Ethiopia*. Oxford: Clarendon, 1935.
Jowett, William. *Christian Researches in the Mediterranean from 1815 to 1820: In Furtherance of the Objects of the Church Missionary Society*. London, 1824.
Leslau, Wolf. *Concise Amharic Dictionary*. Wiesbaden: Harrassowitz, 1976.
Ludolphus, Job. *A New History of Ethiopia*. Translated by J. P. Gent. London, 1682.
Matthew, A. F., editor. *The Teaching of the Abyssinian Church as Set Forth by the Doctors of the Same*. London: Faith, 1936.
Papandreou, Damaskinos. *Joint Commission of the Theological Dialogue between the Orthodox Church and the Oriental Orthodox Churches*. Geneva: Orthodox Centre of the Ecumenical Patriarchate, 1993.
Poladian, Terenig. "The Doctrinal Position of the Monophysite Churches." *Ethiopian Observer* 7 (1964) 257–64.
Samuel, V. C. "The Faith of the Church." In *The Church of Ethiopia: A Panorama of History and Spiritual Life*. Edited by Sergew Hable Selassie. Addis Ababa: Haile Selassie I University Press, 1970.
Schaff, Philip. *The Creeds of Christendom with a History and Critical Notes*. Vol. 2, *The Greek and Latin Creeds with Translations*. Grand Rapids: Baker, 1877.
Shenk, Calvin E. "The Ethiopian Orthodox Church: A Study in Indigenization." *Missiology* 16 (1988) 259–78.
Strauss, Steve. "Creeds, Confessions, and Global Theologizing." In *Globalizing Theology: Belief and Practice in an Era of World Christianity*, edited by Craig Ott and Harold A. Netland, 140–56. Grand Rapids: Baker, 2006.
———. "Perspectives on the Nature of Christ in the Ethiopian Orthodox Church: A Case Study in Contextual Theology." PhD diss., Trinity Evangelical Divinity School, 1997.
Tamrat. *Church and State in Ethiopia, 1270–1527*. Oxford: Clarendon, 1972.
Tesfazghi Uqbit. *Current Christological Positions of Ethiopian Orthodox Theologians*. Rome: Pontifical Institutum Studiorum Orientalium, 1973.
Tiénou, Tite. "Christian Theology in an Era of World Christianity." In *Globalizing Theology: Belief and Practice in an Era of World Christianity*, edited by Craig Ott and Harold A. Netland, 37–51. Grand Rapids: Baker Academic, 2006.
———. "Forming Indigenous Theologies." In *Toward the Twenty-First Century in Christian Mission*, edited by James M. Phillips and Robert T. Coote. Grand Rapids: Eerdmans, 1993.
Yeshaq. *The Ethiopian Tewahedo Church: An Integrally African Church*. New York: Vantage, 1989.

13

Alone and Frightened in Uganda
Living in the Shadow of HIV

ANGELA M. WAKHWEYA-ESSAMUAH

> Alone
> *Out there somewhere*
> *Alone and frightened*
> *Oh the darkness*
> *The days are long*
> *Life in hiding*
> *No more making new contacts*
> *No more loving arms*
> *Thrown around my neck*[1]

EVERY DAY OF THE year, 7,400 additional people are infected with the HIV virus, and every day more than 5,000 die of AIDS. These numbers reflect the United Nations World Health Organization HIV/AIDS figures for 2008: 2.7 million new infections and 1.8 million deaths. In addition, 16.6 million children were orphaned by AIDS.[2] In 2002 in Uganda alone, AIDS orphans were estimated to number 2 million.[3] The U.S. Centers

---

1. Lutaaya, "Alone and Frightened," first verse of AIDS anthem.
2. UNAIDS, *AIDS Epidemic Update*.
3. Wakhweya et al., "Situation Analysis."

for Disease Control and Prevention estimates that in 2008 there were 1.2 million people living with HIV in the United States, with one out of five unaware of their condition.[4]

The number of people around the globe living with HIV has risen from around 8 million in 1990 to more than 33 million in 2008. Since the beginning of the epidemic, nearly 30 million people have died from AIDS-related causes. The number of persons living with HIV has stabilized in recent years, though increases continue to occur in specific populations and geographic regions. The number of persons receiving anti-retroviral therapy for the management of HIV has increased steadily, particularly in low-income countries, reflecting the fact that bilateral and multilateral funding for HIV treatment poured in during the 1990s and early 2000s. With increased access to anti-retroviral therapy in the global North and South, the number of AIDS-related deaths has also declined.[5]

In the early 1990s I was a medical doctor working on the pediatric and obstetric wards of St. Francis Hospital—or Nsambya Hospital, as it is generally known—a Catholic mission hospital in Kampala, Uganda. My job during the daily ward rounds was to confirm the diagnosis of HIV infection in 60 to 70 percent of the patients. This meant breaking the news to a shocked mother, or telling an expectant mother she was infected and there was a strong chance her unborn child would become infected as well. The skin of my patients was parched and sagging, often mottled with Kaposi sarcoma, and of a pale gray color, the color of death. They were so thin you could make out their whole skeleton. I was overwhelmed by the enormity of the AIDS crisis. I would often go back to my small, two-bedroom flat, fall on my knees, and weep.

What was I to do? Some doctors and nurses would pass the beds of stricken patients with a nod and move on quickly. Nurses would look at me with a scowl when I delayed the pace of the ward rounds to sit on the beds of stricken patients. I held them by the palm of their hands, looked them in the eye, and said we needed to talk heart to heart about their affliction, and then, with their permission, talk with family members or caregivers they loved and trusted.

> *Take my hand now*
> *I'm tired and lonely*
> *Give me love*

---

4. CDC, "HIV in the United States: At a Glance," n.p., online: http://www.cdc.gov/hiv/resources/factsheets/us.htm/.

5. UNAIDS, *AIDS at 30*. The decline is measured by comparison with a decade ago. See Rivers and Rivers, "Fight for the Living."

Give me hope
Don't desert me
Don't reject me
All I need is love
And understanding

The early 1990s were mind-numbing: deaths upon deaths upon deaths, orphans upon orphans upon orphans, and no end in sight. Today, as a result of anti-retroviral therapy, the situation is light years from what I saw then. For many there are near miraculous returns from the brink of death. Patients who were bedridden and afflicted by opportunistic infections gain weight, fight off the infections, and rise from their beds like modern day Lazaruses.

In the New Testament we learn that Jesus reached out to lepers, prostitutes, the blind, the sick, and the broken, and in love he touched them. In the case of HIV/AIDS, beyond the physical, emotional, mental, and spiritual battles, there is the stigma and discrimination faced by victims once their status becomes known. In some church congregations there are those who say that HIV/AIDS is a curse from God and that it is only vested upon sinners, as though we all aren't sinners, with or without HIV/AIDS.

It has been over a decade since my brother was diagnosed with HIV. He is married to my new sister-in-law, who was brought to us by HIV/AIDS, for it was AIDS that claimed his first wife. Her death was followed shortly by that of my quiet niece, my brother's eight-year old daughter, who had become infected through mother-to-child transmission.

My sweet, smiling second cousin became another victim. She refused to accept her condition through to the bitter end. I believe it was because of the discrimination she feared. At her request we drove over eight hours home to what was certain death. I remember those penetrating eyes that silently asked, as I left her bedside, whether I still loved her. I prayed with her, kissed her, and gave her a firm hug for the last time in February of 1994, as I left for the United States. I had done what I could, for anti-retroviral therapy was not yet available. She succumbed to AIDS in a matter of days.

Sometimes, of course, blessing follows tragedy. As my brother struggled to come to terms with his HIV and the double loss of wife and child, he joined a Christian support group, where he met his present wife, my graceful and loving sister-in-law. Despite the risk of cross-infecting one another and any potential child they might have together, they took the risk of becoming pregnant. Today, through God's divine mercies and careful prenatal and obstetric care, they have a healthy, bright, spunky HIV-negative daughter, my niece.

In times of joy
In times of sorrow
Let's take a stand
And fight until the end
With open arms
Let's stand up
And speak out to the world
We'll save some lives
Save the children of the world

Of all persons living with HIV, close to 70 percent—the lion's share—live in sub-Saharan Africa. This has been an almost constant proportion for over a decade. The epidemic in Asia has remained relatively stable and largely concentrated in high-risk groups. On the other hand, the number of people living with HIV in Eastern Europe and Central Asia has almost tripled over the last decade. In the United States the HIV epidemic has stabilized but continues to increase in certain populations. In Central America and South America, it has remained at low ebb, much like the Middle East.[6]

Women are particularly vulnerable to HIV due to a variety of factors: biological, social, economic, cultural, religious, political, and environmental. At the end of 2008, women accounted for just over half of the 33.4 million adults living with HIV globally. Generally, women are at a greater risk of heterosexual transmission of HIV. Biologically, women are more than twice as likely as men to become infected with HIV through unprotected heterosexual intercourse. In many countries women are less likely to be able to negotiate for safer sex and are more likely to be subjected to nonconsensual sex.[7]

Women's childbearing role means that the risk of mother-to-child transmission of HIV remains a constant threat to the unborn child, and for generations of children to come. In addition, the responsibility of caring for orphans and for persons living with AIDS, typically falls on women.

Over the past three decades, out of a total of about 60 first cousins, I have lost at least 15 to the virus. At that point I stopped counting. I also lost a brother to AIDS. We could have celebrated his 42nd birthday. Instead, on a wintry March morning, he succumbed to AIDS. As with most families impacted by HIV/AIDS in Africa, you first reel from the shock of your loved one's death. Then you pull up your bootstraps—along with those of your mother, surviving siblings, and scores of nephews and nieces—and march on.

6. UNAIDS, *Report on the Global HIV/AIDS Epidemic.*
7. Dube and Kanvoro, *Grant Me Justice*, 25–59.

HIV continues to tear at the very fabric of families the world over, but especially families in Africa, rendering them desolate, fractured, and in constant pain.[8] What can you do when you experience this pain, heartache, and loss of hope firsthand? What part can you play in bringing families devastated by HIV/AIDS back together again? Can the global church play some role—any role—in helping families weather the storm?[9] Can the church prepare those in the end stages, helping them meet the transition with quiet dignity and strength?[10] Have we done enough? Is there more the church can do to reach out to those affected and infected? Can the church be more deliberate in helping the youth of Africa, especially the girls, change the tide of this epidemic?[11]

> *Let's be open*
> *Advise the young ones*
> *A new generation*
> *To protect and love*
> *Hear them singing*
> *Playing nothing*
> *Let's give them everything*
> *In truth and love*

The magnitude of the devastation of HIV can make you question your own faith. But though your faith may prove unshakeable even after witnessing the devastation firsthand, the battle is not won until you step out of your comfort zone and reach out to those afflicted and affected by this plague, most especially the orphans, the widows, the chronically ill, and the elderly left behind. You must do something other than stand by. You can help heal and nurture the bodies of those afflicted if you are in the medical profession. Those who are carpenters can mend broken houses and construct sturdy furniture. Seamstresses can clothe the naked; farmers can feed the hungry; teachers can instruct the younger generation. Perhaps most importantly, we can reach out with a visit, a touch, a prayer, and compassionate love, as we are commanded.

Many living with HIV suffer with the stigma of their disease. They remain hidden away from cameras, lonely and frightened, in an isolated hut, without a brother, a sister, a friend, or a pastor to hold their hand. Whereas

---

8. Toya, *La Sida*.
9. Morgan, "Has the Church Become Too Busy," 37–44.
10. Kuhn, "Religious, Political Leaders."
11. Warren, *Dangerous Surrender*.

a mother, sister, wife, or aunt may be with them to the bitter end, it is the women—after caring for others—who often die alone. Can we turn away without compunction, caught up in the busyness of our lives?

On a recent trip to Uganda, my husband and I found one such precious soul. She lay on a tattered mattress, surrounded by her daughters and young children in rags. She was withering away on the floor, unable to sit up, having been paralyzed for months. No one from the leadership of her church had been by to visit. We did what we could to make her end-stage more comfortable, but she died two weeks later, joining the estimated 8,000 in Uganda who died that year.

HIV/AIDS may one day be conquered by the discovery of a vaccine or medicine more powerful than the present anti-retroviral therapy, and universally accessible. Until then, HIV/AIDS must be "conquered" by a spirit of compassionate care and support. We must strengthen the safety net of families via churches, social organizations, local communities, and governments. Let us get the message to our young people that they are not invincible, and that they can control their fate and their future by making wise behavioral choices.

Philly Bongoley Lutaaya's message is simple and poignant: HIV can be a lonely disease; but if we work together toward preventing new infections, if we care for the sick and dying, if we never give up the fight to eradicate the disease, though we lose some battles and loved ones, ultimately we will win the war and save generations to come.

> *Take the message*
> *Cross the frontier*
> *Break the barrier*
> *We'll fight together*
> *The doors are open*
> *We'll lead the struggle*
> *We won't bow down*
> *In defeat we'll fight on*

There have been some major successes in the fight against HIV. In 2001 UN Secretary General Kofi Annan and others called for creation of a global fund to fight HIV/AIDS and other infectious diseases. It became known as the Global Fund for AIDS, Malaria and Tuberculosis. On the homepage we read:

> The Global Fund is a unique, public-private partnership and international financing institution dedicated to attracting and

disbursing additional resources to prevent and treat HIV and AIDS, TB and malaria. This partnership between governments, civil society, the private sector and affected communities represents an innovative approach to international health financing. The Global Fund's model is based on the concepts of country ownership and performance-based funding, which means that people in countries implement their own programs based on their priorities and the Global Fund provides financing on the condition that verifiable results are achieved.

Since its creation in 2002, the Global Fund has become the main financier of programs to fight AIDS, TB and malaria, with approved funding of U.S. $22.4 billion for more than 1,000 programs in 150 countries (as of 30 June 2011). To date, programs supported by the Global Fund have saved 7.7 million lives by providing AIDS treatment for 3.2 million people, anti-tuberculosis treatment for 8.2 million people and 190 million insecticide-treated nets for the prevention of malaria. The Global Fund works in close collaboration with other bilateral and multilateral organizations to supplement existing efforts in dealing with the three diseases.

The other major global success has been the U.S. President's Emergency Plan for HIV/AIDS, otherwise known as PEPFAR. In 2009, the *Washington Post* reported:

> One of the more positive legacies of the Bush administration is the President's Emergency Plan for AIDS Relief (PEPFAR). It is an unprecedented multiyear and multibillion-dollar commitment by the United States to combat the epidemic's deadly march across Africa. And, according to a just-released study, the program is working. PEPFAR, the brainchild of President George W. Bush in 2003, has targeted Vietnam, Haiti, Guyana and twelve sub-Saharan nations for HIV testing, counselling and treatment. Statistics through Sept. 30, 2008, show that more than two million men, women and children have received antiretroviral treatment because of the program. This would include almost 1.2 million pregnant HIV-positive women. As a result, 240,000 infants were born free of HIV infection. The upshot, according to the Annals of Internal Medicine: a 10.5 percent reduction in the AIDS death rate in twelve PEPFAR countries in Africa compared with neighbouring nations.
>
> The authors of the study concluded that "about 1.2 million deaths were averted because of PEPFAR's activities." The program spent $18.8 billion between fiscal 2003 and 2008 in all

PEPFAR countries. In 2008 Mr. Bush and Congress approved another $48 billion over the next five years to fight HIV/AIDS, tuberculosis and malaria.

The [study] also delivered a piece of sobering news: PEPFAR's success in lowering the AIDS death rate hasn't translated to a similar success in lowering the rate of people becoming HIV-infected. . . . Ultimately, the key to ending the epidemic is reducing the number of people who become HIV-positive.

The convergence of these two major funding streams in 2002 and 2003—the Global Fund and PEPFAR—increased access to HIV prevention, care, and treatment on an unprecedented scale. These funding streams coalesced with earlier herculean efforts against tremendous odds by grassroots community-based organizations such as The Aids Support Organization (TASO), founded in Uganda in 1987, national government awareness efforts in Uganda, Thailand and Senegal, mission hospitals such as Nsambya Hospital, Kampala, youth-focused biology classes led by forward thinking teachers such as Sr. Felicia Matola, and activists such as Philly Bongoley Lutaaya, Noeline Kaleeba, and Lydia Mungherera. This combination of efforts has resulted in an unparalleled increase in awareness of the epidemic and greater access to HIV testing, care, and treatment. Millions of lives have been saved.

In summary, what do we know and what should we be doing in order to come out of the shadow of HIV?[12]

1. **Keep surviving parents alive and families intact.** Many orphan-care programs focus on child sponsorship and child support, and often they encourage fostering and adoption. Yet many children plead for help to keep their parents alive. HIV testing needs to be supported, psychosocial and spiritual counseling services need to be offered, and anti-retroviral therapy and food access need to be improved dramatically. More parents can remain alive to see their children graduate and marry.[13]

2. **Focus on girls and women.** Globally, the majority of those living with HIV are women. The unequal power relationships between men and women and between older men and younger girls, especially in the "majority world," is at the root of this imbalance. We need to equip girls and women with the skills, knowledge, and tools to protect

---

12. Wakhweya et al., *Going to Scale*.
13. UNAIDS, *Home Truths*.

themselves. We also need to provide the skills, knowledge, and tools to help boys and men protect girls and women.[14]

3. **Change risky sexual behavior.** We must gain the skill and confidence to speak to our families, communities, schools, workplaces, and worship centers about risky sexual behavior. Our youth must learn about sexuality and ways in which they can protect themselves from HIV within the context of their family values.

4. **Strengthen family communication.** We need to strengthen the family and community networks to which our children belong. These networks should have a culture of openness to communicate about everything and anything, leaving little room for exploration or exploitation. Let's partner with our youth so that they do not need to find out by themselves the risk of infection.

5. **Improve local community and social service agencies.** Many churches and community organizations are working at the frontlines with little support. Let us connect them to the global church; let us walk alongside them and listen to their needs rather than dictate to them. We can contribute materials, personnel, and financial support.

6. **Educate all ages about sexuality.** A well-educated and informed child is the economic security of any family and any nation. Open communication, prevention education that is age-appropriate across the entire life span, from toddlers to great-grandparents, are critical to ensure that our youth have sufficient information, values, and tools to protect themselves.

7. **Family life counseling is critical.** Christian counseling programs can encourage individuals to ask fundamental questions about morality, mortality, behavior, beliefs, virginity, and values. The church—pastors and congregations—needs to be able to walk alongside youth, young adults, couples, and families, without stigmatizing brothers and sisters who may already be living with HIV.

8. **Resources are essential.** Resources from the rich North and West are helping to provide everything from basic material needs to life-saving medications. These resources need to be brought to bear proportionately to the areas and among the populations that need it the most. Twenty percent of the world's population, living in Europe and North

---

14. Wakhweya et al., "Children Thrive," 266–86.

America, controls 80 percent of the world's wealth. Let us do our part to devote these resources to where they can do the most good.[15]

9. **Partnerships exponentially increase effectiveness.** Partnerships between church and state, men and women, and North and the South are essential. No single organization, country, or individual has the resources and knowledge needed to combat this global pandemic. The tag line of the President's Emergency Plan for HIV/AIDS was apt: Partnerships for Prevention, Partnerships for Care, and Partnerships for Treatment. We cannot do it alone. Furthermore, no one approach will succeed. Many approaches synergistically working together will.

10. **Families first.**[16] Orphanages, fostering, and adoption should not disrupt families further. For orphaned and other vulnerable children, orphanages should be the solution of last resort. Children do far better when they are in a loving, nurturing family under adult care. Even with millions of children being orphaned, keeping them living with a surviving parent or with a surviving relative is the best option.[17]

> *Today it's me*
> *Tomorrow someone else*
> *It's me and you*
> *We've got to stand up and fight*
> *We share a light*
> *In the fight against AIDS*
> *Let's come on out*
> *Let's stand together*
> *And fight AIDS*

BIBLIOGRAPHY

Bourke, Dale Hanson. *The Skeptic's Guide to Global Poverty*. Colorado Springs: Biblica, 2007.
DeMarco, Renee. *Conducting a Participatory Situation Analysis of Orphans and Vulnerable Children Affected by HIV/AIDS: Guidelines and Tools*. Arlington, VA: Family Health International, 2005.
Dube, Musa W., and Musimbi Kanvoro, editors. *Grant Me Justice! HIV/AIDS and Gender Readings of the Bible*. Maryknoll, NY: Orbis, 2005.

15. Bourke, *Skeptic's Guide*. Also see UNAIDS, *Home Truths*.
16. Wakhweya et al., "Children Thrive."
17. DeMarco, "Conducting."

Kuhn, Josef. "Religious, Political Leaders Call for AIDS-free Generation." *Christian Century*, December 1, 2011.

Morgan, Timothy C. "Has the Church Become Too Busy with Death?" *Christianity Today*, February 7, 2000.

Rivers, Eugene F., III, and Jacqueline C. Rivers. "The Fight for the Living: AIDS, Orphans, and the Future of Africa." *Sojourners*, July–August 2000.

Toya, Jean-Samuel Hendje. *La Sida: perspective africaine*. Bafoousam Yaoundé: CIPCRE, 2003.

UNAIDS. *AIDS at 30: Nations at the Crossroads*. United Nations, 2011.

UNAIDS. *AIDS Epidemic Update*. Joint United Nations Programme on HIV/AIDS (UNAIDS) and World Health Organization (WHO), November 2009. Online: http://www.unaids.org/en/media/unaids/contentassets/dataimport/pub/report/2009/jc1700_epi_update_2009_en.pdf.

UNAIDS. *Home Truths: Facing the Facts on Children, AIDS, and Poverty*. United Nations, 2009.

UNAIDS. *Report on the Global HIV/AIDS Epidemic*. United Nations, 2010.

Wakhweya, Angela M., et al., editors. "Children Thrive in Families: Family Centered Models of Care and Support for Orphans and Other Vulnerable Children Affected by HIV/AIDS." In *The Challenges of Women's Activism and Human Rights in Africa*, edited by Diana Fox and Naima Hasci, 266–86. New York: Mellen, 2010.

———. *Going to Scale: Lessons Learned by the IMPACT Project on Meeting the Needs of Orphans and Other Vulnerable Children*. Arlington, VA: Family Health International, 2008.

———. "Situation Analysis of Orphans in Uganda. Orphans and Their Households: Caring for Their Future Today." Uganda Ministry of Gender, Labour and Social Development and the Uganda AIDS Commission. Kampala, Uganda, November 2002.

Warren, Kay. *Dangerous Surrender: What Happens When You Say Yes to God?* Grand Rapids: Zondervan, 2007.

14

African Evangelists
The Case of Apolo Kivebulaya

EMMA WILD-WOOD

CHRISTIANITY IN SUB-SAHARAN AFRICA has always been distinguished by its vitality and indigeneity. In the last 150 years it has spread throughout the region. Evangelists of all sorts—women and men, the recently converted, the trained and ordained, those appointed by a mission, and those responding to a direct calling from God—have shared their Christian faith with others. Some returned to their villages with the Good News, others set out for areas unknown to them, gathered young people around them, or influenced large crowds as they preached Jesus Christ. Many formed Christian communities; some spent little time in one place. Some encouraged literacy and bio-medicine, others healed and cast out evil spirits.

Many we do not know, but others are remembered or have been rediscovered beyond their locality.[1] This essay, which offers Apolo Kivebulaya as a case study, asks what insights do early evangelists give us into processes

---

1. For example, the online *Dictionary of African Christian Biography* (www.dacb.org) has promoted the gathering of information on local figures significant in the development of the church, recognizing such information as is often unavailable in standard scholarly reference works. From detailed, formal entries to short, familiar sketches, the website is a treasure trove of testimony to the lives of the African saints.

of conversion and Christianization, and how may we understand their influence?

HISTORICAL INQUIRY AND SELF-GOVERNANCE

Interest in African evangelists began with the first Western missionaries, who recognized their own inability to be effective evangelists in a strange culture—or indeed to survive a tropical climate[2]—and therefore expected early converts to spread the Gospel. The words of François Coillard of the Paris Evangelical Missionary Society about its mission to the Zambezi serve as an example: "If ever Africa is to be evangelized, it must be done by its own children."[3] Historical interest in indigenous evangelization emerged in the form of critique of a missionary movement that was perceived to have overstayed its welcome. The case of Samuel Adjai Crowther has often been used to illustrate this point. An evangelist who became the Anglican Bishop of the Niger Delta when the Church Missionary Society was actively pursuing a policy of self-propagation, self-finance and self-governance, Crowther later fell afoul of a new generation of missionaries and a shift in CMS policy.[4] Throughout the continent, in different ways and at different times, some European missionaries undermined the vision of the forebears and were reluctant to promote the initiative or leadership of Africans. Crowther's humiliation is recognized as an impetus for independence in West Africa, and independence became a focus of historical research into African Christianity, including African Instituted Churches (AICs) and their founders.[5] Although most African Christians remained members of missionary instituted churches, interest in the indigenous evangelists produced by these churches has generally received less attention.[6]

---

2. Africans were not always more able to survive changes in climate than Europeans. See Thompson, *Ngoni, Xhosa and Scot.*

3. Quoted in Zorn, *Transforming Gospel.*

4. Williams, *Ideal of Self-Governing*, 146–48; Sanneh, *West African Christianity*, 19–172. Also, in the *Dictionary of African Christian Biography* (www.dacb.org), see Elijah Olu Akinwumi's treatment of Samuel Crowther.

5. Sanneh, *West African Christianity*, 173ff. AICs and their founders fascinated scholars who were attempting to identify authentically African Christianity as well as scholars who were wary of apparent syncretism. See Sundkler, *Bantu Prophets*; Oosthuizen, *Post-Christianity in Africa.* For a recent study, see 93–244.

6. There are some exceptions to this. Sometimes the contributions of African evangelists are noted in cultural shifts such as the spread of literacy and Bible translation. See Sanneh, *Translating the Message*, 164–74.

Recently, scholars beyond the field of mission studies have taken an interest in African evangelists as catalysts in cultural and intellectual change and as examples of the lives of subaltern groups in empire.[7] They portray evangelists as creators of history, brokers in cultural exchange, and developers of new identities during times of societal upheaval. In doing so they have confirmed what mission historians have recognized for years, namely that "involvement of indigenous agents in the process of change is essential, indicating it is difficult to impose change on communities from outside. Change can only occur with support from within the community." Thus religious change in the colonial era can be "a creative dynamic, rather than a passive acceptance of new ideas."[8] This marks a welcome shift from a simple equation of the aims of the evangelists with those of the colonial authorities and missionaries. It challenges the assumption that missionary religion imposed a hegemonic structure on indigenous peoples, enforced by the use of literacy and ecclesiastical structures, with the latter replacing traditional charismatic activity and mysticism with modern bureaucratic rationalism.[9]

The work of African evangelists reminds church historians that the growth of the church often possessed a social and political significance beyond ecclesiastical communities. It also enables an interpretation of evangelists as people at the nexus of power relations during periods of cultural change. Evangelists are people who seek social, spiritual, and political empowerment. In the shifting influences of emerging colonial control, they are people literally and figuratively on the move to secure relations with divine power while in constant negotiation with political and social powers around them. Such a reading of African evangelists will be demonstrated by studying Apolo Kivebulaya.

INTRODUCING APOLO KIVEBULAYA

Apolo Kivebulaya was an evangelist, then a deacon, priest, archdeacon, and canon in the Native Anglican Church in Uganda. Born about 1865 in the central kingdom of Buganda, he attended reading classes in 1894, was baptized in 1895, and confirmed in 1896, the same year he began work as a Church Missionary Society (CMS) church teacher in the western kingdom of Toro. One of his attractions as a case study is that he left a substantial paper trail. He kept a diary for much of his life that charts his activities in

---

7. Brock, *Indigenous Peoples*; Peterson and Macola, *Recasting the Past*.
8. Brock, *Indigenous Peoples*, 7, 11.
9. The work of Jean and John Comaroff, *Of Revelation and Revolution*, is often cited to represent these views.

Toro and in the Boga area of what is now the Democratic Republic of Congo (DRC), until his death in 1933.[10] Many of the entries are simple notes of the events of the day, although there are a few longer and more reflective passages. He was well-known to CMS missionaries, who mention him in their writings, and some of the correspondence between Apolo and missionaries and Ganda Christians survives. Another attraction is that his ministry was a long one: Apolo was active during the early years of the Ugandan Protectorate into the high colonial era, from a time when the Christian movement was little more than 15 years old in Buganda until it had influenced large parts of the region beyond the Buganda kingdom. His life permits an enquiry into the changing relations between Christianity and colonial power and the unequal influence of the Ganda in both. His ministry became so highly regarded that he was the subject of several biographies in English and in a number of vernacular languages before and after his death. In these works he is most closely associated with the conversion of Mbuti pygmy groups in the Ituri forest.[11] He is revered as a saint by the Anglican Church of Uganda and also by the Anglican Church of Congo, whose members honor him as the founder of their church, a person of power and also of humility. Thus Apolo Kivebulaya leaves a legacy that can be explored.

The risk of focusing upon a single example is that Apolo might be understood as template for all evangelists. This clearly cannot be the case; socio-political context, cultural influences, church structures, personality, and events ensure that the patterns of individual involvement and outcomes vary greatly. Apolo was a product of a unique set of circumstances. In the process of great social upheaval during the 1880s and 1890s, Christianity rapidly became interwoven in the drive for political change in the Kingdom of Buganda and its neighbors. Christianity came to be understood by Ganda elites as progressive and was widely accepted by the Ganda and those under their influence. Louise Pirouet, in *Ganda Evangelists*, demonstrates the mixed motives of the early evangelists: their desire to spread the Gospel beyond Buganda was also a desire to spread Ganda influence, and those to whom they went understood this to be the case and reflected this understanding in their responses.[12]

---

10. Most Kivebulaya's diaries are in Makerere University archives, Kampala. They are written in Luganda. An unpublished translation into English is stored with them.

11. Lloyd, *Apolo of the Pygmy Forest*; Roome, *Apolo, the Apostle to the Pygmies*; Yates, *Apolo in Pygmyland*; Sinker, *Into the Great Forest*; Luck, *African Saint*. Vernacular biographies include Katongole, *Apolo Kivebulaya*; and *Kwa Imani Apolo* [author unknown].

12. Pirouet, *Black Evangelists*, 195.

Other evangelists on the continent necessarily worked in very different circumstances. In southern Africa, for example, William Koyi[13] and Bernard Mizeki,[14] working among the Ngoni and the Shona respectively, found less initial interest in Christianity. The Shona were suspicious of its connection with colonialism and mining interests.

Another danger of taking Apolo as a case study is that precisely because his sources are good he might be perceived as unique or as someone who acted alone. Fascination with heroes and pioneers is something in which the missionary movement frequently indulged, and Apolo's biographies can be read in the same vein. Apolo Kivebulaya, however, was part of a large movement of evangelists that developed two thriving and competing churches in Uganda, the Anglican church and the Catholic church.[15] He worked alongside other Ganda evangelists, CMS missionaries, and ultimately young men and women who had converted as a result of his ministry. Apolo cannot be made into a model for evangelists in any straightforward sense. Not all evangelists leave such a historical record, have such a lengthy ministry, or work in such relatively propitious circumstances. He can, however, aid the development of themes that can be pursued comparatively. The example of Apolo Kivebulaya will allow us to ask: What is an evangelist? What changes did they introduce? What impact did changes or continuities have on wider society? What relationship did early evangelists have with the Bible and with the Christian theology to which they were introduced? What did they preach and teach and to whom? What significant relationships did they have? What sort of Christian communities did they form and what legacies did they leave?

EVANGELIST

A study of Apolo Kivebulaya's life and mission first helps with an exploration of the complexities of the term "evangelist." Among missionary churches, the term "native evangelist" was often applied to those who were appointed to certain church activities by the mission or the church but who were not ordained. They might also be called "church teacher" or "catechist." The expectation in Uganda was that these individuals would spread the Gospel through itineration and by teaching people to read. Increasingly, however, the term became used for those in charge of a congregation or sub-parish.

---

13. Thompson, *Touching the Heart*.
14. Farrant, *Mashonaland Martyr*.
15. Pirouet, *Black Evangelists*, analyzes the impact of both Catholic and Protestant evangelists.

Some who preached the Gospel did not have the title of "evangelist" conferred upon them. Simon Kimbangu, in the west of Congo, for example, was turned down by Baptist missionaries for the position of evangelist before he embarked on his brief but powerful independent preaching and healing ministry.[16]

Apolo's own education was limited, and missionaries were initially unsure whether he would be a successful teacher. Other missions may not have accepted him as evangelist and would not have ordained him.[17] Apolo continued to itinerate once he was ordained, returning to places he had visited before and visiting other places for the first time. Thus the term "evangelist" is appropriate for him throughout his lifetime. His peregrinations took him first to Toro, a kingdom neighboring his own and with close relations to it. Then he moved further west, to the Konjo/Nande and Bwamba/Talinga before crossing the Semeliki River, to the Hema people (related to the Nyoro and Toro) and then the Ngiti and the peoples of the Ituri forest.[18]

If "missionary" is used to denote those who cross cultures to spread the Gospel, then those who, like Apolo, worked among peoples who spoke different languages and possessed different customs and social organizations, fulfilled the job description. Furthermore, if "missionary" is used to indicate acts beyond the verbal proclamation of the Gospel, Apolo was missionary because his preaching was accompanied by other activities. As was expected of CMS evangelists, he taught people to read, established a school, distributed medicine supplied by missionaries, and he introduced new forms of construction and agriculture and alterations to social behavior. He assumed that preaching the Gospel included working for transformation of society. The terms "evangelist" and "missionary" were usually applied according to origins rather than job description: Europeans and North Americans were "missionaries," Africans were "evangelists." We shall continue to use this shorthand because it indicates the imbalances of power between Westerners and Africans.

The word "evangelist" may also suggest a person working at a local, grassroots level, in touch with ordinary people, a straightforward person, unencumbered with worldly pretensions. Apolo is often portrayed like this. There is evidence to suggest, however, that he was seen as influential

---

16. Ustorf, "Kimbangu," n.p.

17. Bishop Tucker's policy for "native agents" allowed for greater variety in educational achievement than did that of many of his contemporaries. See Byaruhanga, "Alfred Robert Tucker"; Ward, "Alfred Robert Tucker," 682. For a detailed discussion, see Williams, *Ideal of the Self-Governing Church*, 243–57.

18. The Konjo/Nande and Bwamba/Talinga ethnic groups are known by different names on either side of the Uganda/Congo border.

because of his British and Ganda connections. By the end of his life he had become a prominent clergyman and many of his fellow Ganda evangelists were members of the ruling elite. Their roles as evangelists generally came to an end when they inherited a chieftaincy or assumed political office. Apolo wore a Ganda *kanzu* and a European jacket strikingly different to the bark cloth attire of those to whom he preached. He assumed names associated with political and cultural forms of power; "Kivebulaya" means "the one from Europe" and "Apolo" references not only the biblical character but the Ganda Prime Minister, Apolo Kagwa.[19] Apolo was willing to use his connections to his advantage. In 1896 he asks CMS missionary A. B. Lloyd to exert pressure upon the Boga chief to start a reading class.[20]

Yet his sense of authority is not predicated solely on such influences. He voluntarily returned to Boga after 1910 when the area was under Belgian control and British and Ganda connections became disadvantageous. During the 1920s he negotiated with Belgian officials who were particularly nervous of African evangelists after the stir caused by Kimbangu and who viewed his connections with the British protectorate with suspicion. The perceptions of evangelists' status and relation to political power varied not only from evangelist to evangelist but from location to location. As Apolo shows, they can shift through the lifetime of an individual.

CONTINUITY AND CHANGE

For some years scholars of African Christianity have been interested in continuities between the traditional beliefs and practices of Africans and their present Christian faith. While African theologians sometimes lament the lack of inculturation that they propose for African churches, historians have often noticed ways in which elements of the past are continued and adapted in the present expressions of Christianity. Ogbu Kalu, for example, has emphasized continuity between past and present in religious practice, identifying within a primal African religiosity a centuries-old legacy of revival from which contemporary churches take their charismatic energy and orientation.[21] The disciplines of both history and theology have been enriched by anthropology, which often focuses on traditional cultures and contemporary continuities with them.

African evangelists within mission churches have sometimes been understood as harbingers of cultural change, and as such they appear to

19. Wild-Wood "Saint Apolo," 105, 112–15.
20. Ibid. Based on Apolo's diary, January 8, 1897.
21. Kalu, *African Pentecostalism*, 23–40.

fit uneasily with an interest in continuities. Recently some anthropologists have suggested that expectations of continuity in the lives of their subjects causes them to be suspicious about Christian claims of transformation.[22] Now discourses of *dis*continuity, of conversion, and societal rupture are being re-examined, and an analysis of Christian beliefs and practices can convey more nuanced approaches to continuity and change among adherents. One might ask of evangelists not whether they favor continuity over change, but rather how their choices influence the complex web of dynamics associated with power and with negotiations with the powerful.

It is likely that Apolo and the peoples around him did not possess a significant distinction between temporal and spiritual power. Societal leaders often played interconnected religious and political roles, and their authority was frequently linked with their successful supplication of ancestors and other spiritual beings. Anglican novelties of literacy, bio-medicine, and access to the Creator through new beliefs and practices attracted Apolo and his converts. Furthermore they appear to have recognized a parallelism between Anglican polity and traditional socio-religious order. Apolo introduced to those receptive to his teaching the Book of Common Prayer, as well as the Bible, Anglican vestments and structures, prayer meetings, and church buildings. Anglicanism offered order, well-being, and contact with ultimate power. Apolo's story demonstrates an interest in Christianity because it offered access to socio-spiritual power in ways that both embraced changes and maintained some continuities.

Anglicanism offered a specific connection with the wider political and colonial situation in East Africa. In 1893 Uganda became a British Protectorate that included the Ganda and surrounding kingdoms. There is evidence from prominent Ganda writers that the Ganda saw themselves as partners and allies with the British;[23] both possessed kingdoms with wide areas of influence and both were desirous of progress and change. Apolo's work of evangelism took place at an intersection of a number of different African interests with European influence at time of societal change.[24] Apolo also used the strategies of CMS missionaries to target influential colonial leaders of centralized power structures, akin to the Ganda system, before encountering those groups with whom they had client relations. In using this approach, traditional power structures were often maintained and even reinforced. Apolo's actions, while relatively indifferent to wider politics, demonstrate a fascination with approaches that would help achieve empow-

---

22. For a prominent example, see Robbins, "Continuity Thinking," 5–38.
23. Kagwa, *Customs of the Baganda*; Mukasa, *Sir Apolo Kagwa*.
24. Wild-Wood, "Saint Apolo," 120.

erment for socio-spiritual well-being. The introduction of such Christian initiatives began a process that would distinguish socio-spiritual power from socio-political power.[25] Yet the adoption of Christianity in its Anglican form appeared to some to support the conservative social structure, while other converts were attracted by the changes introduced by Apolo because they empowered them to make the most of the colonial situation.[26]

TEACHING, THE BIBLE, AND CHRISTIAN BELIEF

Tracing the activities of African evangelists provides insight into engagement with literacy, early African theologies, and biblical interpretation. For many evangelists, literacy was a means of greater empowerment; familiarizing themselves with a text might acquaint them with the Almighty in a way unmediated by Western missionaries.

Apolo's diaries testify to his belief that behind the political and social powers of his day the power of God was at work. Like Christians down the ages, he witnessed to God's power at times of difficulty:

> When I was thus worried the Lord gave me strength and in His Power I overcame in that place. It was there that I saw that God the Father, the Son and the Holy Spirit remain with me and are with me. . . . Whenever I needed anything he gave it to me because my need was this, that I might have power to bring people to Jesus Christ and to enter them into that life. He gave me that power, and I had no fear at all.[27]

The assurance of empowerment by the Almighty was gained about four years after Apolo began work as an evangelist and appears to have given him greater fortitude and determination. He preached wherever he went and attracted to Christianity people who had little previous contact with it—although he did not draw crowds like contemporary evangelists associated with AICs, such as William Wade Harris in West Africa and Yoswa Kate Mugema in Uganda.[28] The number of listeners that he diligently recorded in his diaries never reached triple figures. The diaries give us some of the themes on which he preached: "We preached about how our Lord loves those who go to him." "We preached to them about the glory that

---

25. Ibid., 121–22.
26. For further discussion on this point see chapter 1 of Wild-Wood, *Migration*.
27. Wild-Wood "Saint Apolo." Apollo's diary, August 1, 1899.
28. Wild-Wood, "Saint Apolo," quoting Apolo's diary for December 11, 1895. Also see Wild-Wood, "Powerful Words."

would be theirs in the world to come." "I told them that God the Holy Spirit caused the Gospels to be written as they were written in the Bible, 'that you should read it and find out for yourselves.'"[29] He encouraged his listeners to tell others about Jesus.

Despite his limited education, Apolo was keen to improve his knowledge and to pass on what he knew to others. He saw literacy as an invaluable tool that gave access to information, and he avidly read the emerging Luganda literature generated by Ganda elites and European missionaries. He itinerated to establish an interest in the Gospel and then returned to the villages in order to teach people to read and to learn the catechism for baptism. Later he itinerated in order to support those evangelists who, inspired by his example, were teaching in the churches he had begun.

He was also involved in teaching children to read and write. It is likely that Apolo considered the ability to read and write as one of spiritual importance. An intimate relationship between reading and attending a worship service is reflected by the use, in many East African languages, of the same word for the two activities. Literacy allowed access to the Word of God, and it was the gateway to membership in the Christian movement. Apolo's early personal commitment to a reading class marked the beginning in his own path to conversion, and he expected to see the same commitment in others. He and his converts saw potential in literacy not only for accessing Scripture but for engaging in a wage-economy, developing trade, and for making representation before colonial authorities.

Evangelists grappled with the biblical texts in order to preach and teach but also to present them in new languages. Many evangelists were involved in formal or informal translations of the Bible. At a time when the Ganda Bible was nearing completion, Apolo was at work on the Runyoro/Rutoro translation of the Gospels with CMS missionary H. E. Maddox, which they completed in 1899. His own tongue, Luganda, had a linguistic affinity with Runyoro/Rutoro, and one can imagine that he was an invaluable participant in the project. Evangelists were at the forefront of the first processes of inculturation inherent in the work of translation, in which the Bible meets local thought forms.[30] Yet the acquisition of literacy did not evenly distribute the power it was perceived to imbue. Some languages like Luganda, and to a lesser extent Runyoro/Rutoro, gained prominence, while other languages were not reduced to writing until much later. Although Apolo translated a primer and St. Mark's Gospel into Lumbuti, or Efe, the

---

29. Wild-Wood "Saint Apolo." Apolo's diary, 1901 (no specific dates) and August 13, 1915.

30. Walls, *Missionary Movement*, 28; Sanneh, *Whose Religion*, 99, 107, 111, 115–18.

language of the Mbuti pygmies,[31] the work did not progress any further, and other languages likewise remained neglected as time and resources were applied to those considered more strategic.

J. D. Y. Peel, in his analysis of the writings of Yoruba evangelists, talks of a "trans-historical memory" in which a biblical lens is used to interpret daily life.[32] A similar process is apparent in Apolo's diary. The cadences of his writing often sound like biblical passages: "They put me in prison in chains . . . but when they took counsel they found that there was no fault in me,"[33] evokes St. Paul and John's first epistle. Particularly at times of trouble Apolo wrote out a Bible verse that helped him. After imprisonment he was given a number of gifts and notes. He concluded, "And this all came from the Lord and I remember the Scripture which says, 'Seek ye first the Kingdom of God and all these things will be added unto you,' Mt. 6.33."[34] When Jesus came to him in a dream, saying, "I am with you, fear not," Apolo took this as confirmation of God's promise never to leave him that he had read in the book of Joshua. The Bible gave to Apolo a resource for living life. He used it as script by which to live and to interpret his life.

Apolo's belief in God appears to be an orthodox Christocentric Trinitarian one. (He frequently names Father, "Child" and Holy Spirit). Apolo expected God to show his power and protection by intervening in daily concerns. He adopted a priestly role, praying on behalf of the people, as illustrated in his prayers for rain and his prayers for the demise of an unpopular chief, both of which he recorded as bring answered. In these prayers Apolo engaged with both political powers and elemental powers. He invoked the power of the Creator in a way that would resonate with the religious expectations of the peoples of the Semeliki escarpment. He appeared to share with his fellow Ganda the fascination and suspicion of European missionaries, and he noted the "bad customs" of some;[35] yet he was understanding of the ways of others.

---

31. Edwin Smith, as editorial superintendent of the Bible Society, greeted with great enthusiasm the two exercise books sent to him because they provided insight into the language and culture of the peoples of the Ituri forest. See Smith, "Language of the Pygmies," 464–70.

32. Peel, *Religious Change*, 9.

33. Wild-Wood, "Saint Apolo." Apolo's diary December 11, 1895. Also see Wild-Wood, "Powerful Words."

34. Wild-Wood, "Saint Apolo," quoting Apolo's diary for December 11, 1895.

35. Wild-Wood "Saint Apolo." Apolo's diary January 1, 1917. Here Apolo records a conversation he had with Lloyd about his presentation to the Kabaka of Ganda regarding the peoples he worked with in Congo.

Of one encounter with the peoples of the forest he writes, "I reached the people who worshipped God but they did not know Jesus. These call themselves Babuja. I preached Jesus as he came to save people, and they believed."[36] This suggests that he believed at least some of the people to whom he preached were already prepared for the Gospel through their traditional religious practices and their belief in a Creator. Apolo demonstrated a cultural affinity with people among whom he worked. It did not prevent him from criticizing some of their practices, but he did recognize the innate spirituality of the people among whom he worked—and he did so at a time when Western missionaries were still likely to dismiss African religions as mere superstition.[37]

The overarching impression that Apolo's diary leaves with the reader is one of movement and action rather than stasis and reflection, and it is here that Apolo has left hints as to his missionary sense of vocation. There is little about his life as a priest in Fort Portal;[38] rather he lists movement from one place to another, noting where he went, with whom and what he did in each location. Abari Balia, who as a young man itinerated with Apolo, mentions Apolo's close study of Paul's missionary journeys and his commitment of them to memory.[39] Not only did he find St. Paul an inspiration, his diary entries serve as a record of his own missionary journeys. He may not supply the detail or the narrative structure of Luke, but he recorded many "acts"—preaching, teaching, and building churches—and noted the spread of the Gospel and the development of the church. Modeling himself on St. Paul, he understood himself to be establishing Christian communities through his itineration. It is here that we have a glimpse into the trans-historical identity that Apolo created for himself.

RELATIONSHIPS, COMMUNITIES, AND LEGACIES

African evangelists were expected to develop new Christian communities by teaching, preaching, and translating the Gospel message. The quality of the relationships they developed was crucial to the success of their mission, and it is here that their ability to empower others can be assessed. The development of good relationships also sustained the church beyond the lifetime of the evangelists, and thus their relationships can hardly be understood

---

36. Ibid. Apolo's diary September 18, 1924.
37. Stanley, *World Missionary Conference*, 235–41.
38. It is possible that diaries of this period have been lost. Nevertheless in the extant diaries it is striking to note the emphasis on his journeys.
39. Luck, *African Saint*.

without an appreciation of the legacies such relationships engendered. Apolo was held in high esteem by his Ugandan and CMS missionary colleagues. They wrote letters of encouragement to him and expressed their admiration for him in their reports, in eulogies after his death, and in subsequent memoirs. Although we can only guess at the character of his early relations with the evangelists he accompanied to Toro, or with Sedulaka Zabunamakwata with whom he went to Boga, or with the villagers on either side of the Semeliki River, those who left written or oral testimony speak of a natural friendliness and a lack of pretension.

During the 1920s, Apolo itinerated with the young people of Boga, who had converted to Christianity. Both girls and boys were trained by him to be evangelists among their own people and five other local ethnic groups.[40] By 1933, the year Apolo died, there were 80 recognized church teachers in the area, some of whom worked in the church all their lives; some were ordained after Apolo's passing.[41] Some spent a short time as church teachers before they used their literacy skills to gain employment as traders or as clerks in the mining companies or colonial offices. Their memories of Apolo were passed to their children, and the love and admiration they felt was preserved in the legends of his life.

The genealogies of African evangelists are a source of illumination: In many AICs the sons of the founders take on the mantle of leadership from their fathers and succession appears to be hereditary; other evangelists have children who follow them into ministry or who bring their Christian conviction into other spheres of influence.[42] Apolo was unusual in that he did not marry and had no children. Yet Apolo's "boys" and "girls," who had itinerated with him in the forest, were given special respect in the Anglican Church of Congo. Until the 1990s, on May 30, the anniversary of Apolo's death, the surviving evangelists processed into the cathedral in Boga. Called upon long after his death both to maintain tradition and to advocate specific changes, Apolo has continued to play an active part in the churches he founded.[43]

---

40. Women were recognized evangelists in the Native Anglican Church of Uganda in its early years. Pirouet lists forty-six women from the Toro and Boga areas who were licensed as catechists in the church between 1902 and 1909. The women on this list received further training beyond the elementary stage that Apolo gave in Moa. There was a decline in women receiving training after 1914. Pirouet, *Black Evangelists*, 73–75.

41. Wild-Wood, *Migration*, 26.

42. For example, the children of prominent East African Revivalists of the 1930s are influential in the Museveni government in Uganda. See Ward, "East African Revival."

43. Wild-Wood, *Migration*, 47–48, 203–5.

When he was in Uganda, Apolo had close working relationships with CMS missionaries. In some literature an impression is given that the further away African Christians were from European missionaries, the more independent was their Christianity and the more authentically African. Yet cross-cultural friendship within the missionary movement had the potency to build bridges and develop deep appreciation of the other's way of life.[44] The relationship between Charles Pamla, Xhosa evangelist, and William Taylor, the American Methodist bishop for whom he translated, is a southern African example of close collaboration that resulted in revival in 1866.[45] The insistence on interracial friendship in the East African Revival from the 1930s onward is another example that demonstrates both the possibilities of such relationships and the need to be deliberate in cultivating them, due to the inequalities of power and influence that so often mitigated against them.[46] Albert Lloyd's admiration for Apolo is apparent in the three biographies he wrote in the 1920s and 1930s. Without paying too much attention to chronological or historical accuracy, Lloyd makes of Apolo a missionary hero.[47] He does so to advance the missionary cause, calling on Britons to respond to the call to help the many unknown "Apolos." Yet he also writes because he wishes to express his respect for a man who had become his friend. He describes Apolo as "an African gentleman whose life, wholly yielded to God, has been an inspiration to me during the whole of my missionary career . . . a tender-hearted, loving evangelist . . . a miracle of God's grace, a living power, an inspiration to the service of Christ."[48] We have less documentation from Apolo's side, yet in three letters to Lloyd he addresses the CMS Missionary as "my dear friend" and calls him "brother."[49] He also indicates a notion of seniority in the relationship by referring to Lloyd twice as "father" and once as "chief." The letters are warm and familiar; they indicate a long acquaintance and shared aspirations for the furtherance of the Gospel, accompanied by an attitude of respect that suggests Apolo maintained a sense of hierarchy in their relationship.

The often close relationships between African evangelists and Western missionaries, and the cultural affinity evangelists possessed with people among whom they worked, gave them the role of bridge between different

44. Robert, "Cross-Cultural Friendship, 100–107."

45. In Anderson, *Biographical Dictionary*; see entries by David Bundy on William Taylor, 660, and by Daryl Balia on Charles Pamla, 513.

46. Ward, "East African Revival."

47. For more information, see Wild-Wood, "Making of an African Missionary Hero."

48. Roome, *Apolo, the Apostle*, 87.

49. Lloyd, *Apolo*, letters of April 16, June 4 and 14, 1928.

societies. As Jack Thompson demonstrates for the Xhosa evangelists among the Ngoni, they spanned two worlds, allowing missionaries and Africans to pass across to each other.[50] The relationships Apolo established demonstrate his position as cultural broker operating as a translator of worlds. His own power was as mediator between CMS missionaries and Toro Christians, between a newly literate society and the Mbuti pygmies. He translated novelties introduced by the colonial rulers so that their potential could be understood within the cultural expectations of those among whom he traveled. He moved between peoples, connecting and introducing them. While his own cultural outlook undoubtedly changed during his lifetime as he engaged with different peoples, he inevitably promoted a Gospel that was suffused with the cultural forms and social connections that made him who he was. While he empowered others, he did so unevenly. The form of evangelism inherited from CMS work with the Ganda, as well as existing local power structures, caused him to prioritize the Hema above others. He may be universally admired, but his work reinforced some of the inequalities of client relationships and use of language that have influenced the church until today.

Lloyd's biographies of the 1920s and 1930s and Anne Luck's biography of the 1960s created a legacy for Apolo as "Apostle" and "African Saint" in order to inspire British Christians to mission work and to understand the commitment of an African Christian and the development of the church in central east Africa. Yet today these books are largely unknown. There are those in the African diaspora, however, who continue to remember him as an ancestor of the faith. For example, consider Yeremiya Gyagenda, who was converted through Apolo's work. Gyagenda's son also knew Apolo and passed on his admiration to his children. Today three of these children are church leaders: in Kampala, in the United States, and—in the person of John Sentamu, Archbishop of York—in the United Kingdom.[51]

CONCLUSION

Postcolonial thought and development in central east Africa reflect mixed identities that are the product of migratory processes. Indeed, contemporary citizens inhabit a multiplicity of cultural spaces. The resulting cultural mix allows them to better negotiate their way through the power dynamics

---

50. Thompson, *Ngoni, Xhosa*, 25–26.

51. Sseppuya, "Brothers of Destiny," published in Relate, a local Ugandan newpaper; also personal correspondence with the office of Rt. Revd. John Sentamu, January 7, 2009.

they face. African evangelists of the 19th and 20th centuries also traveled in and engaged different cultures, settling among new peoples, learning their languages, and negotiating with the powerful in order to gain power themselves. It is this that has enabled African peoples to be the initiators of Christian growth on the continent and to develop distinct expressions of Christianity. The case study of Apolo Kivebulaya has indicated some ways in which early evangelists participated in God's mission in their varied contexts. Apolo helped shape new trans-local identities that were literate, Protestant, and Hema or Nandi; and as a Ganda Protestant Christian working in Toro and Ituri, he negotiated boundaries between communities that shaped his own hybrid identity.

Accounts of those who effected religious change in the early days of the Christian movement in central east Africa can inculcate a cross-cultural understanding of the church that enriches Christians from other parts of the world. As the Christian church grows in new areas of the globe, this acquaintance remains important.[52] A familiarity with early African evangelists can also aid the continued growth of a confident African church and sustain Christian communities in their life and their mission of service to the wider society. Negotiations for empowerment taken by the evangelists need first to be assessed in their own historical context before their value for the contemporary context can be analyzed. For, just as Apolo cannot be a template for all past evangelists, so their approaches cannot be replicated—or ignored—in any direct and unthinking way in the present. As Africans continue to evangelize on the continent, as they migrate from Africa to become foreign missionaries across the globe, and as many use the language of spiritual power as they do so, they can be encouraged and challenged by those who have gone before them.

BIBLIOGRAPHY

Anderson, Allan. *African Reformation: African Initiated Christianity in the 20th Century*. Trenton, NJ: Africa World Press, 2001.

Anderson, Gerald H. *Biographical Dictionary of Christian Mission*. Grand Rapids: Eerdmans, 1998.

Balisky, E. Paul. *Wolaitta Evangelists: A Study of Religious Innovation in Southern Ethiopia, 1937–1975*. Eugene, OR: Pickwick, 2009.

Brock, Peggy, editor. *Indigenous Peoples and Religious Change*. Studies in Christian Mission 31. Leiden: Brill, 2005.

---

52. Noll and Nystrom, *Clouds of Witnesses*, provide short stories of "noteworthy Christian believers" in Africa and Asia with the intention of introducing a new generation of readers in the West to the dynamism and diversity of Christianity elsewhere in the world.

Byaruhanga, Christopher. "Alfred Robert Tucker." *Dictionary of African Christian Biography*. Online: http://www.dacb.org/stories/uganda/tucker_alfred.html.

Comaroff, Jean, and John Comaroff. *Of Revelation and Revolution: Christianity, Colonialism and Consciousness in South Africa*. Chicago: University of Chicago Press, 1991.

Farrant, Jean. *Mashonaland Martyr: Bernard Mizeki and the Pioneer Church*. Cape Town: Oxford University Press, 1966.

Hastings, Adrian. *Church in Africa 1450–1950*. Oxford: Clarendon, 1994.

Kagwa, Apolo. *Customs of the Baganda*. Translated and edited by May Mandelbaum Edel. New York: Columbia University Press, 1934.

Kalu, Ogbu U. *African Pentecostalism: An Introduction*. New York: Oxford University Press, 2008.

Lloyd, A. B. *Apolo of the Pygmy Forest*. London: CMS, 1936.

Luck, Anne. *African Saint: The Story of Apolo Kivebulaya*. London: SCM, 1963.

Mukasa, Ham. *Sir Apolo Kagwa Visits Britain*. Translated and edited by Taban lo Liyong. London: Heinemann, 1976.

Noll, Mark, and Carolyn Nystrom. *Clouds of Witnesses: Christian Voices from Africa and Asia*. Downers Grove, IL: InterVarsity, 2011.

Oosthuizen, G. C. *Post-Christianity in Africa: A Theological and Anthropological Study*. Grand Rapids: Eerdmans, 1968

Peterson, Derek, and Giacomo Macola. *Recasting the Past: History Writing and Political Work in Modern Africa*. Athens, OH: Ohio University Press, 2009.

Pirouet, M. Louise. *Black Evangelists: The Spread of Christianity in Uganda 1891–1914*. London: Rex Collings, 1978.

Reed, Colin. *Pastors, Partners and Paternalists: African Church Leaders and Western Missionaries in the Anglican Church in Kenya, 1850–1900*. Leiden: Brill, 1997.

Robbins, Joel. "Continuity Thinking and Christian Culture: Belief, Time and the Anthropology of Christianity." *Current Anthropology* 48 (2007) 5–38.

Robert, Dana L. "Cross-Cultural Friendship in the Creation of Twentieth-Century World Christianity." *International Bulletin of Missionary Research* 35 (2011) 100–107.

Roome, W. J. W. *Apolo, the Apostle to the Pygmies*. London: CMS, 1934.

Sanneh, Lamin. *Translating the Message: The Missionary Impact on Culture*. Maryknoll, NY: Orbis, 1991.

———. *West African Christianity: The Religious Impact*. London: Hurst, 1983.

———. *Whose Religion Is Christianity? The Gospel beyond the West*. Grand Rapids: Eerdmans, 2003.

Sinker, Margaret. *Into the Great Forest: The Story of Apolo of Central Africa*. London: Highway, 1950.

Smith, Edwin. "The Language of the Pygmies of the Ituri." *Journal of the Royal African Society* 37 (1938) 464–70.

Stanley, Brian. *World Missionary Conference*. Grand Rapids: Eerdmans, 2009.

Sundkler, Bengt. *Bantu Prophets in South Africa*. 2nd ed. Oxford University Press, 1961.

Thompson, T. Jack. *Ngoni, Xhosa and Scot*. Zomba, Malawi: Kachere, 2007.

———. *Touching the Heart: Xhosa Missionaries to Malawi, 1876–1888*. Pretoria: University of South Africa, 2000.

Ustorf, Werner. "Kimbangu, Simon." In *Dictionary of African Christian Biography*. No pages. Online: htt://www.dacb.org/stories/demrepcongo/kimbangu3_simon.html.

Walls, Andrew F. *The Missionary Movement in Christian History: Studies in the Transmission of Faith*. Maryknoll, NY: Orbis, 1996.

Ward, Kevin. "Alfred Robert Tucker." In *Biographical Dictionary of Christian Missions*, edited by Gerald H. Anderson, 682. Grand Rapids: Eerdmans, 1998.

———. "The East African Revival in the Study of African Christianity." In *The East African Revival: History and Legacies*, edited by Kevin Ward and Emma Wild-Wood, 201–11. Farnham, UK: Ashgate, 2011.

Wild-Wood, Emma. "The Making of an African Missionary Hero in the English Biographies of Apolo Kivebulaya (1923–1936)." *Journal of Religion in Africa* 40 (2010) 273–306.

———. *Migration and Christian Identity in Congo (DRC)*. Studies of Religion in Africa 35. Leiden: Brill, 2008.

———. "Powerful Words: Reading the Diary of a Ganda Priest." *Studies in World Christianity* 18 (2012) 134–53.

———. "Saint Apolo from Europe, or 'What's in a Luganda Name?'" *Church History* 77 (2008) 105–27.

Williams, C. Peter. *The Ideal of the Self-Governing Church: A Study in Victorian Missionary Strategy*. Studies in Christian Mission 1. Leiden: Brill, 1990.

Yates, Pat. *Apolo in Pygmyland*. London: Highway, 1940.

Zorn, Jean-François. *The Transforming Gospel: The Mission of François Coillard and Basuto Evangelists in Barotseland*. Translated by Dora Atger. Geneva: WCC, 2004.

PART 2

Other Selected Essays

15

The Medium and the Message

Miriam Adeney

"A word aptly spoken is like apples of gold in settings of silver."

—Proverbs 25:11

In the beginning was the word: God said, "Let there be light." And there was light. Words were not necessary. God could have vibrated radio waves. Or thunder storms. But in his wisdom, God boomed out words as tools of power. Eons later, the Person who is the foundation of the universe would shock humans by appearing among them as a baby:

> *That glorious form, that light insufferable,*
> *And that far-beaming blaze of majesty . . .*
> *He laid aside; and here with us to be,*
> *Forsook the courts of everlasting day*
> *And chose with us a darksome house of mortal clay.*[1]

---

1. Milton, "On the Morning," 456.

How did he label himself when this happened? He chose to use the metaphor of the word. "The Word became flesh and lived among us" (John 1:14).

Thirty years onward, Jesus would empower his followers to focus on words. They were to make disciples and teach all that he had commanded. This is the culminating peroration to which all the Gospel of Matthew points: "All authority . . . has been given to me. Therefore go and makes disciples of all nations, baptizing them . . . and teaching them to obey everything I have commanded you. And surely I am with you always, to the very end of the age" (Matt 28:18–20).

Long before Jesus walked the dusty roads, God had been shaping his servants as wordsmiths. Word work is hard work, and many felt inadequate. "Oh Lord, I am not eloquent . . . I am slow of speech and of tongue," Moses groaned. "I am a man of unclean lips," Isaiah confessed. "I am just a child," Jeremiah protested. "I am no prophet. I'm a farmer," Amos demurred but then described what happened to him: "And the Lord took me as I followed the flock, and the Lord said to me, 'Go, prophesy to my people.'" And the sheepherder proceeded to make words fly. (Exod 3:11—4:13; Isa 6:5; Jer 1:6; Amos 7:14–15.)

Words matter. Today evangelists, disciplers, teachers, trainers of leaders, and those who do holistic ministry through relief, development, or advocacy need skill with words. In this essay we will explore three families of media through which to channel words. Yet we must warn against over-preoccupation with media. The message is not an afterthought. It is not just entertaining content that we pour into our chosen medium. Nor is it a numbingly familiar Gospel. Making disciples, teaching them all things, honoring the source of the words we articulate, will require full attention to medium *and* message. Tite Tiénou has modeled that dual focus, speaking with authority, and choosing his words carefully. For that we honor him in this volume.

ELECTRONIC MEDIA

Anybody want to talk about Jesus?

Hanif is in charge of TV programming for youth on a Christian station beamed into Iran via satellite seven days a week, twenty-four hours a day. Questions ferment among the youth. What about a job? Romance? Family quarrels? Islamic rigidity? Iran's place among the nations? Drugs entice many.

Hanif never demeans Islam. He talks reverently about God and shows the beauty of Jesus. Some Muslim parents, desperate for positive influences on their children, require their teens to watch Hanif's programs. Then the teens get interested and continue on their own.

What do they see? In a studio that looks like a stylish living room, Hanif answers calls. If it is a repeat caller, Hanif refers to their earlier conversation and asks, "Did God make any difference in that problem we discussed last time?" Then Hanif prays on behalf of the caller. Music, discussions of current issues, and chat rooms are supplemented by email follow-up. And the youth of Iran are ushered into the presence of Jesus.

When I visited Hanif in his office, I saw his first two Persian Christian rap videos. One opens with a man lying on train tracks. Every couple of seconds the camera shifts to a different angle. Poetry pounds and throbs. Is there a meaning to life? The viewer ponders the train tracks. Then a lovely woman emerges out of a mist, singing beautifully and simply about Jesus.

The second video opens with a man in the throes of withdrawal from a drug. Jesus comes to him in a vision. Just a few minutes long, the videos are compelling. Hanif's earlier training as a mosque poet has prepared him to introduce thousands—maybe millions—of Iranians to Jesus through compelling rhythms and words.[2]

Making disciples through the internet is the concern of the Internet Evangelism Alliance, which networks over 1,350 evangelistic sites in 850 languages. To start a conversation, an evangelist may enter a native-language chat room and ask, "Anybody want to talk about Jesus?"

In major Arabic internet outreaches, 70 to 80 percent of the responses are called in on cell phones. Whatever medium people use when they respond—email, cell phone, letter, or visit—it has been found that it is essential to stay with that medium as long as possible. Switching the medium causes respondents to drop away. And there is no way to hold them. On the internet, no one knows who they are. Ties are ephemeral. They can evaporate instantly. So communicators must stick with the respondent's medium of choice until eventually the seeker himself or herself suggests moving to a medium where more complete interaction can occur.

Cell phones have somersaulted to significance on the world scene. Popular Japanese novelists upload chapters daily onto websites accessible by phone. For example, a senior in high school named Rin wrote *If You*. She typed out episodes en route to her part-time job over a six-month period. Cell phone readers voted her novel no. 1. Subsequently it was published as a hardcover book, sold 400,000 copies, and became the fifth best-selling novel

---

2. Adeney, *Kingdom without Borders*, 139–42.

in Japan in 2007. Another recent novel, *Love Sky*, has been read by 20 million people on cell phones or computers. Ideally each chapter is of a length suitable for reading during one train ride.

In the United States, daily phone messages are sent to teenagers with diabetes, reminding them to take their medicine. The results are encouraging. In some other countries, banking by cell phone is drawing the poor into long-term financial planning.

Internet communication is not a one-way street. Interactivity is the name of the game. Readers comment on Japanese novelists' works while the writings are in progress. Teenagers ask immediate questions of their diabetes counselors. Spiritual seekers can do the same. "Social networking" is a buzz phrase that Christian communicators must heed. More than getting information through the internet, people like being able to respond and know that they are heard. Christian witnesses cannot just post messages. We must enter into two-way interchanges.

What about blogs? Tan Soo Inn of Singapore has found success in this medium. His 10-year-old weekly blog (www.graceworks.com.sg) is read by 30,000 people, mostly in Asia. How does he hold these readers? First, he writes on Fridays, because he has found that his audience prefers to read on the weekend. Second, he maintains consistent quality that is contemporary, sometimes a little shocking, but set in a well-thought-out Christian worldview. When people tap in, they know they will be enriched and stimulated.

Yet in the blogging world many people would rather write than read. Christian witnesses can capitalize on this. Don't beg them to read your blog. Instead, read theirs. Encourage their writing, connect networks of writers with each other, and keep asking questions that stretch them to think more carefully, more deeply, more broadly, more powerfully, more sacrificially.

Other electronic media help make disciples, such as radio, TV, videos, and DVDs. Consider the *Jesus* film. Most of the text is from the Gospel of Luke. This film is in 1,040 languages and has been shown approximately six billion times around the world, with significant impact.

At the local level, consider the work of a communicator in one New Guinea tribe. People here did not want to read the Bible even after it was translated into their language. Although some held advanced degrees, they had gone straight from illiteracy to cell phones and visual and audio media. So the translator has created "Scripture DVDs." He uses video clips and photos of scenes from village life, including special events and cultural practices like women weaving. The audio tracks are the Gospel of John (three DVDs), Romans (two DVDs) and Colossians and 1 John. These have proved popular. For every 100 printed Bibles sold, 500 copies of the DVDs are purchased.

PRINT MEDIA: EXPOSING THE NON SEQUITURS OF SOUND BITES

Indonesia is famous for visual symbols, puppets, and live dramas. Yet when I walked down the street in Jakarta, I saw the peanut seller reading a newspaper. I saw the elevator operator with his nose buried in a novel.

Burmese vendors spread their wares on sheets laid out on the sidewalks. Next to the vegetable hawkers and tool merchants, booksellers lay out their volumes. As the day cools, potential customers stroll by. Some will squat on their haunches and peruse the pages of the books.

In Africa people "hold small print up to their eyes under tiny bulbs while radio sets blare, children yell, societies dance, and drunks fight, all within yards of them. People will read anything, provided it is not frivolous, is related to something significant for them, and that they can make intellectual contact with it."[3] Though Andrew Walls made this observation years ago, it still holds true in many places.

The influence of readers is disproportionate to their numbers. This is because reading encourages reflecting on a wide range of ideas. Both electronic and print media provide information across time and space. Both allow people to create and consult complex records. Print goes further. It encourages people to think sequentially, to connect cause and effect, to compare, to distinguish contradictions. It facilitates the development of systematically framed perspectives on issues, and of integrated, unified worldviews. Of all media consumers, readers are in the best position to expose the non sequiturs of those raised on sound bites.

The effect of books in history is beyond measure. Consider the writings of John Bunyan, or C. S. Lewis, or even *The Purpose-Driven Life* by Rick Warren.

Yet an irony arises. We see it illustrated in the life of Moses. For 40 years, the people of Israel had trudged through the wasteland between Egypt and Canaan, between slavery and *shalom*. Finally they stood poised to enter the land of promise. At this point, Moses paused and reviewed publicly all that God had taught them. Then he wrote it down. This became the book of Deuteronomy.

Imagine Moses's feelings when, very shortly after he had signed off on the last line, God told him, "This book will not have much impact. The people won't pay attention. They're going to carry on without any regard for all your words" (Deut 29:22–28). Then God advised him to switch to an oral

---

3. Chaplin, *Adventure with a Pen*, 18 (quoting Andrew Walls).

medium. "Write the message all over again, but this time put it into a song. They'll remember it longer." So Moses wrote a song (Deuteronomy 32).

Moses, at the end of his life, hands over the leadership to Joshua, teaches the people his song, blesses the community tribe by tribe, and then trudges up Mount Nebo to Pisgah Peak with the entire Promised Land spread out before him in a wide-screen vista. There he dies (Deuteronomy 34).[4]

Why bother writing a book or a song? The subsequent experience of the people of Israel is not encouraging. They drifted away from what Moses had taught, even patronizing prostitutes in the temple and burning their own children as sacrifices to idols. But six centuries after Moses something surprising happened. A young man, Josiah, came to the throne. He determined to follow the God of his predecessor King David. Destroying the pagan shrines and sweeping out the temple, his staff discovered a book. It turned out to be Deuteronomy. For the rest of Josiah's reign, Moses's words would shape Israelite society. Throughout the next 400 years, a faithful remnant held this vision until Jesus came. Indeed, print can have a very long reach.

The word "Scripture" means "writings." From the time of Moses to the present, thousands have spent their lives copying and translating God's Word in the languages of many peoples. Where Christians have gathered to study the Scriptures, mature churches have grown. Where Scripture has not been studied—even when it has been honored in theory—churches have fossilized. Print is the easiest medium for close study of the text.

Ideally, those who write the books should be indigenous people. Imported and translated books may make a splash, but how deep can they penetrate? Writers of the people can capture kingdom stories on the ground. They can preserve the wisdom of mature local saints. They can help unbelievers learn about God and his world in ways that make sense. They can apply the whole counsel of God to their own time and place.

ORAL MEDIA: DO CHRISTIANS NEED TO READ?

Every Christian needs the Bible. But reading is not the only way to access it. Throughout history, most Christians have received Scripture orally. When Moses taught Deuteronomy, the original audience heard it spoken or sung. When Nehemiah rebuilt the wall of Jerusalem and invited Ezra to reacquaint the people with God's Word, the masses gathered like a stadium crowd and listened to the Word read aloud. Then section leaders explained it, translating it into the people's spoken language, Aramaic.

4. Peterson, *Christ Plays*, 266.

When Jesus learned Scripture, he went to the synagogue, heard it read aloud, read it aloud himself, and memorized passages. He never wrote anything, as far as we know, except some scribbles in the sand.

During the Middle Ages, the church taught through dramas, stained glass windows, catechisms, pilgrimages, statues, processions, liturgies and feasts. Visual and kinesthetic elements reinforced oral teaching.

Proto-Protestants taught orally too. At the end of the tenth century the Waldensians spread the Bible in the Provencal language. "Much of the preaching consisted in reciting long passages of Scripture in the vernacular. Many could not afford an expensive handwritten copy of the Bible, and the ecclesiastical authorities could too easily rob them of such a book, but they could not erase the words which were treasured in the heart," because memorized Scripture cannot be taken away.[5] Two centuries later, Wycliffe's "Poor Priests" walked from town to town across England, reading the Bible but also reciting extensively from memory.

In regions where millions of people do not read today, Scripture continues to spread orally. Consider the Santal people in South Asia. Literacy is less than 1 percent. They have no written history. Their documents are the elders' memories. Into this community came some Christians. They shared a flowing stream of Bible stories through dramas, songs, dances, and testimonies. A man named Marandi believed, as did his family. They were baptized and shared the Good News with other relatives, who also believed and were baptized. Marandi formed a team to travel to nearby villages to tell stories and sing and act. More people have believed and in turn formed more teams reaching out to still more villages.[6]

In another South Asian community, more than 600 Muslims have come to Jesus as Lord over a thirty-year period through the ministry of two single women. Memorization of Scripture has been crucial in their work. As soon as a Muslim commits to Jesus, he or she is required to learn thirty-four set verses from the Gospel of John. If the new believer is not literate, they must find someone else who knows the verses who will teach them. This empowers non-literates. They feel they own the message. Some have become superb grassroots witnesses.

Do Christians need to read? Not everybody in the congregation needs to tap into Scripture through reading. Certainly, text readers should be sought out, honored, and listened to. At the same time, nonreaders also should be held to high standards of accountability for knowing Scripture.

---

5. Nida, *God's Word*, 83.
6. International Orality, *Making Disciples*, 43–44.

Is this possible? Consider a case from North Africa. Seventeen believing men learned Bible stories for two years. Their curriculum was ambitious: A sequence of 135 stories. Along with each story they also learned some songs and dramatic action to equip them to teach Scripture throughout the region. After two years a seminary professor gave them a six-hour exam. He wondered, Did they understand theology? Did they grasp the nature of God? Could they explain the Christian life? Could they connect the stories with doctrines?

Indeed they could. Given a theological theme, they quickly referred to multiple stories to demonstrate the theme. They answered a variety of theological questions using the stories as illustrations.[7]

Further south on the continent of Africa, a Nigerian pastor named Timothy has switched from preaching doctrines to telling Bible stories, followed by discussion. After he finishes a story, he invites someone to retell it. Then he asks the others, "Is it correct? Has he got the details right?" Together they go back over the narrative, supplementing and correcting each other, and reinforcing the story in everyone's mind.

Through skillful questioning, Timothy helps his congregation think through the story's meaning and application. In the other direction, as people ask questions, Timothy has seen how little they understood his preaching in the years before he switched to stories. Through dialogue he can clarify many points. But sometimes he leaves people hanging: "As I tell more stories, you'll discover that for yourself." Suspense rises and the listeners are propelled into active inquiry.[8]

STORY: AWESOME ENTERTAINMENT

For oral teaching, stories are central. The Bible is filled with the stories of people who have known God. These people are our reference group, our heritage, our roots. Through the story of Joseph, we learn about handling family rejection. With Elijah, we see depression in long-term perspective. And as the book of Hebrews records, when these great men died, they had not yet received fulfillment of all the promises because they were waiting for us. Without us, the story was not complete. We are called to participate in the ongoing story.

Anthropologists employ at least five approaches when analyzing stories as part of cultural systems: content analysis; psychological analysis;

---

7. Ibid., 48–49.
8. Ibid., 44–46.

metaphor analysis; drama analysis; and ideological analysis.[9] What is considered good form varies from culture to culture. Cliches, though disdained in Western literature, are basic to oral art in many countries. In some Southeast Asian traditional dramas, stock characterizations and stock plot elements carry the narrative. An actor's speeches are spontaneous to the extent that, given a plot outline shortly before curtain time, he will pull out of his standard oral repertoire the units required such as a love speech or a battle charade. Accompanying musical strains also convey meaning. Each musical motif is associated with some particular action. A knowledgeable listener can follow the plot even when out of visual contact. Such use of formulaic expressions and conventional structures makes it possible to expand or contract a performance, adapting to circumstances.

Chronological Bible story telling is popular in missions today. A storyteller begins with the story of creation, and continues through many other stories, including Jesus's death and resurrection. In his classic *Communication of the Gospel to Illiterates,* H. R. Weber observes,

> It is fundamentally wrong to treat illiterates as children, and merely to tell them Bible stories. They are much better equipped than many Western intellectuals to see the whole: the complete redemptive history—creation and eschatology, Christ the centre of redemption, and, linked with this centre, the history of Israel and of mission . . . Every Bible story that is told must be set within the framework of the whole history of redemption. Every Biblical figure must be shown as having a part in the great drama of salvation. This is best done when every story is set within the context of liturgy and sacraments. And the whole redemptive drama must be confronted with the mythological cycle, the mythological frame, thus making apparent to everybody that the Christian faith means revolutionizing all patterns of thought.[10]

Myths in primal religions deal with ultimate realities, supernatural powers and supernatural events, both good and evil. Many of these events take place in primordial, sacred time. Key characters may figure in a whole cycle of stories. Myths function to explain, to teach the next generation, to validate behaviors, to integrate a community, to renew power, to allow artistic expression, to enable spiritual transcendence, and to provide for communal catharsis and emotional purging. Myths are serious. In the same vein, Scripture stories should not be seen as mere entertainment to lure

9. Adeney, *Filipino Narrative.*
10. Weber, *Communication of the Gospel,* 44.

people to consider doctrines. Scripture stories are themselves profoundly serious, and should be presented with a degree of awe and reverence.

SONG: MY OWN FAMILY'S STORY

Like stories, songs are a powerful oral genre. Songs teach, keep memory accurate, help us party, help us cry, and witness. In his thesis, *Toward an Indigenous Hymnody*, Eugene Goudeau suggests practical strategies for creating songs: nurture local composers; facilitate group writing; run contests for hymns on particular subjects; and borrow from near cultures.[11] In his article "Developing an Indigenous Hymnody," Delbert Rice recommends studying each local song genre regarding its appropriateness for Christian communication. Rice distinguishes four song genres among the upland Filipino people where he lives: ceremonial music (*baki*); conversational music (*ba-liw*); recreational music (*dayomi*); and proverbial music (*gomigom*). The local church has chosen to create songs in three of these genres.[12]

Clearly, the task involves more than just finding a good tune. The roles of songs and singers in a given culture must be studied. In some places, singers and actors are assumed to be immoral, given their public, traveling lifestyle. In other cases, certain genres may be sung only by certain genders, ages, or classes. Sometimes songs express ideas which have no other outlet. Among the Bedouin of western Egypt, anthropologist Laila Abu-Lughod listened to her friends burst into simple folksongs marked by vulnerability and longing. Since everyone's situation was well known, the causes of these feelings were clear. Yet the singers never would talk about their feelings. They seemed unable to give voice to their passions except through song. Abu-Lughod came to believe that songs were necessary to provide balance in the Bedouin worldview.[13]

My grandfather was a preacher. One day I asked my dad, "Did you become a Christian because of your father's preaching?" After a quiet moment, he answered, "No, I think it was because of my mother's singing." Songs are central in teaching, whether the listeners are literate or not.

---

11. Goudeau, *Toward an Indigenous Hymnody*.
12. Rice, "Developing an Indigenous Hymnody," 97–113.
13. Abu-Lughod, *Veiled Sentiments*.

COMBINED MEDIA: MAXIMUM POWER

The strongest communication combines two or more media complementarily, employing each in the area of its strength. For example, we can use the internet, radio, or TV to attract interest. If literate people respond, we send them a book. That will provide detailed explanations that inquirers can reread privately at their own pace. Finally, we can follow this up with a personal call or visit.

Multiple media reinforce a message. In an award-winning public health campaign in Mauritania, World Vision used a diverse array of media:

Radio spots

A radio storyteller

Radio talk shows

TV music mini-videos

Traveling drama troupes

Newspaper opinion pieces

School textbook inserts approved by the Department of Education

Telephone calls to radio broadcasts that hosted personal messaging

Billboard murals

Posters and stickers

T-shirts with slogans

Reasoned arguments appeared in newspaper pieces and school textbook inserts. But printed arguments were only the beginning. A wealth of media supplemented and reinforced these.

MESSAGE: DEVELOPING CHRISTIAN MINDS

This paper has explored a range of media useful for Christian communication. Yet a danger looms. Media can preoccupy our attention as we tinker endlessly with improvements. We must resist becoming enslaved to that fascination. We must not be so mesmerized by the media that we skimp on attention to the message. Whatever the medium, communicators must pour energy into content that is biblically-rich, culturally-rich, balanced, and fresh. The goal is to help Christians grow to maturity, and to help non-Christians glimpse a Christian worldview that is winsome, intelligible, and powerful.

Because of a gap between media specialists and message specialists, churches have not taught as powerfully as they might have. Although original dramas and songs and other artistic presentations of the Christian message have been created over many centuries in many cultures, church teachers have tended to use them sparingly: a pre-evangelistic event; a Christmas or Easter program; an entertainment; a variation in the curriculum. Then the teaching has reverted to didactic lessons, Bible studies, and talks.

Why is innovative form marginalized? Artists are not systematic. What they create is not a balanced curriculum. Teachers see this. Therefore they use such imaginative creations in small doses. If, however, artists and curriculum planners were brought together for a sustained period of time, and charged to create communication/teaching programs with balanced content in culturally-appropriate genres, that might happen.

Godly words have power. They can cut to the bone: The word of God is living and active. Sharper than any double-edged sword, it penetrates even to dividing soul and spirit, joints and marrow; it judges the thoughts and attitudes of the heart (Heb 4:12). Godly words also renew and nourish life:

> As the rain and snow
> *come down from heaven,*
> and do not return to it
> *without watering the earth*
> and making it bud and flourish,
> *so that it yields seed for the sower*
> and bread for the eater,
> so is my word that goes out from my mouth
> *It will not return to me empty,*
> but will accomplish what I desire
> *and achieve the purpose for which I sent it.*
> –Isaiah 55:10–11

"All our preaching week in and week out, should gradually unfold the 'whole counsel of God,' and so contribute to the development of Christian minds in the congregation," says John Stott.[14] Every communicator should accept a similar mandate. Over time, we must aim to develop Christian minds in our people.

---

14. Stott, *Between Two Worlds*, 170.

BIBLIOGRAPHY

Abu-Lughod, Laila. *Veiled Sentiments: Honor and Poetry in a Bedouin Society*. Berkeley: University of California Press, 1988.

Adeney, Miriam. *Filipino Narrative: A Model for Ethnic Identity Balancing Pakikisama and Protest*. PhD diss., Washington State University, 1980.

———. *Kingdom without Borders: The Untold Story of Global Christianity*. Downers Grove, IL: InterVarsity, 2009.

Chaplin, Joyce. *Adventure with a Pen*. Kumasi, Ghana: Africa Christian Press, 1968.

Goudeau, Eugene. *Toward an Indigenous Hymnody*. MA thesis, Harding Graduate School of Religion, Memphis, 1980.

International Orality Network and Lausanne Committee for World Evangelization. *Making Disciples through Oral Learners*. Bangalore, India: International Orality Network, 2005.

Milton, John. "On the Morning of Christ's Nativity." In *Masters of British Literature*, edited by Robert A. Pratt et al., 456–60. Boston: Houghton Mifflin, 1958.

Nida, Eugene. *God's Word in Man's Language*. New York: Harper & Row, 1952.

Peterson, Eugene. *Christ Plays in Ten Thousand Places*. Grand Rapids: Eerdmans, 2005.

Rice, Delbert. "Developing an Indigenous Hymnody." *Practical Anthropology* 18 (1971) 97–113.

Stott, John. *Between Two Worlds: The Art of Preaching in the Twentieth Century*. Grand Rapids: Eerdmans, 1982.

Weber, Hans Reudi. *Communication of the Gospel to Illiterates*. London: SCM, 1957.

16

Inculturation and the Church's Mission
Theological and Trinitarian Foundations

STEPHEN B. BEVANS, SVD

Two decades ago, in 1993, Tite Tiénou wrote that mission theologians in Africa needed to develop "a theology that seeks to permanently plant the Church of Christ in Africa and anchor the gospel deeply into current African cultures.... This kind of theology will help reduce the perception that the Christian gospel is foreign to Africa and Africans.... African ownership of the gospel is critical for African participation in mission."[1] Developing an authentic African missiology and theology—while not neglecting classical exegesis and theology and avoiding a compromising syncretism—has been one of Tiénou's chief concerns as a theologian, missiologist, and theological educator.[2] Like the late Paul Hiebert, Tiénou is consistent in calling for a *critical* contextualization, or inculturation.

In recognition of Tiénou's incisive contributions to theology and missiology, I propose to sketch the foundations of a "theology of inculturation." I want to ask, Why is contextualization, or inculturation, so important? Why is it a process that must not be confined to theology done in the "Two Thirds World," but one that is integral to theology as such? Why is it a theological

---

1. Tiénou, "Themes in African," 240–41.
2. Tiénou, "Training of Missiologists," 97.

imperative? Why, finally, is inculturation—to use the term Catholics prefer—an essential part of the church's mission?[3] Although my approach is primarily from a Roman Catholic perspective, I believe it will be basically acceptable to evangelicals like Tiénou.

In part 1, I cite several statements by the Roman Catholic Magisterium and by several theologians on the theological foundations of inculturation/contextualization. Then, in part 2, I address the theological imperative of inculturation and its Trinitarian basis. My thesis is that since inculturation is an integral part of mission, and since mission is always participation first and foremost in God's mission, inculturation has the Trinity as its very foundation. The church must promote the contextualization or inculturation of the Gospel because, ultimately, God promotes it.

THEOLOGICAL FOUNDATIONS

Roman Catholic Magisterium

Roman Catholicism has a strong central authority known as the Magisterium (from the Latin *magister*, teacher). While the entire church is called to participate in Christ's teaching office, one of the duties of the bishop's office is to articulate this in a particular way, and this is coordinated and led by the Bishop of Rome, the pope. In Catholic theology interpreting the Magisterium is a complex task. Statements that carry the most weight are those made by ecumenical councils like the Second Vatican Council (1962–1965), followed by statements of individual popes and conferences of bishops. In what follows I will survey the teaching on inculturation articulated implicitly by Vatican Council II, then the more explicit teaching of Paul VI (1963–1978) and John Paul II (1978–2005), followed by a statement of the Federation of Asian Bishops' Conferences.

Vatican II

The word "inculturation" began to appear in Catholic theological literature with frequency in the years after Vatican II. It found its way into documents of the Magisterium in 1979.[4] Under the guise of "adaptation" or "accommodation," the idea was present in church teaching in the years prior to the Council. It certainly found expression in the Council itself, particularly in

---

3. Bevans, *Models*, 3–15.
4. Shorter, *Towards a Theology*, 10.

the documents on the liturgy,[5] missionary activity,[6] and the church in the modern world.[7] The Council speaks of God's "secret presence" in history and culture, by which God distributes "treasures . . . among the nations of the earth." When a missionary is truly in relationship with God's Spirit, the Spirit will impel the missionary to discover those treasures—"seeds of the Word" in Justin Martyr's phrase—through "sincere and patient dialogue" (*AG* 9, 11). Secondly, there is a strong theology of creation, by which human activity, including the development of a culture, has a genuine value and "earthly affairs" enjoy a "rightful independence" (*GS* 34, 55, 36, 59). Third, a theology of incarnation roots Jesus's own ministry in a particular context (*GS* 22; *AG* 3). The dynamic of incarnation continues on in the church, which "can enter into communion with various cultural modes, to her own enrichment and theirs too" (*GS* 58). A fourth theological foundation points to the universal reality of creation's imperfection and, particularly, to human sinfulness. The dialogue between faith and culture, therefore, "must be purified and perfected by the power of Christ's cross and resurrection" (*GS* 37; *AG* 9, 11).

Evangelii Nuntiandi

Ten years after the Council, in *Evangelii Nuntiandi*, Pope Paul VI expresses another theological foundation for the "evangelization of cultures."[8] It was prompted by the recent emphasis on liberation as a central theological theme and task of the church.[9] Presupposing a theological anthropology that sees humanity as an integral whole, the salvation offered by the Gospel is seen to address every aspect of humanity. Evangelization, says the pope, is a "message touching life as a whole," and so it needs to be a message "adapted to the different situations constantly being realized, about the rights and duties of every human being, about family life . . ., about life in society, about international life, peace, justice and development—a message especially energetic today about liberation" (*EN* 29, 30–31). Because the Gospel has to touch the whole person, then, "every effort must be made to ensure a full evangelization of culture, or more correctly of cultures" (*EN* 20). Regeneration is not

---

5. *Sacrosanctum Concilium*, 37–40. Documents of Vatican II, 136–78.

6. *Ad Gentes* (*AG*), 9, 11. Documents of Vatican II, 584–630.

7. *Gaudium et Spes* (*GS*), 40–45, 53–62. Documents of Vatican II, 199–308.

8. Burrows, *Redemption and Dialogue*, 20, quoting from Paul VI's *Evangelii Nuntiandi* (*EN*).

9. Pernia, "Mission for the Twenty-First Century."

just a spiritual reality, confined to individual human beings. The healing the Gospel brings to a broken world is offered to cultures as a whole.

Redemptoris Missio

The strong Christocentric emphasis of John Paul II's *Redemptoris Missio* finds an echo in his reference to inculturation as the *incarnation* of the Gospel in peoples' cultures. In the same way as humanity was enriched by the Word taking on human flesh, so the Gospel enriches, ennobles and heals humanity by its "insertion into peoples' cultures," and the church is changed by introducing "peoples, together with their cultures, into her own community." But, it is implied, just as the Word assumed human nature "without any commingling or change or division or separation,"[10] the process of inculturation "must in no way compromise the distinctiveness and integrity of the Christian faith." In addition to this Christological foundation for inculturation, the pope articulates the ecclesiological dynamic: inculturation makes the church a sign and instrument of God's saving presence in the world. To be church, in other words, is to be about the communication of the Good News of salvation. Only if the church engages in the "lengthy" and "difficult" task of authentically incarnating the Gospel can it be worthy of its name and of its mission.[11]

John Paul II's reflections on the work of the Holy Spirit in evangelization echoes Vatican II's assertion that culture and history are filled with God's "secret presence" (*AG* 9). It is the Holy Spirit who is the source of every "existential and religious questioning," and so the questions and concerns of all peoples of all times have not only a human foundation, but are grounded in the Spirit's gentle and provocative presence. "The Spirit's presence and activity," says the pope, "affect not only individuals but also society and history, peoples, cultures and religions." Connecting this to his Christocentric vision, the pope speaks of the Spirit as sowing the "seeds of the Word" that are "present in various customs, and cultures, preparing them for full maturity in Christ" (*RM* 28).

Federation of Asian Bishops' Conferences

Although other sources could be cited, I will limit myself here to a reflection on the theological basis of inculturation as set forth in the documents of the

---

10. Denzinger and Schönmetzer, *Enchiridion Symbolorum*, 302.
11. Burrows, *Redemption and Dialogue*, 5–55.

Federation of Asian Bishops' Conferences (FABC). In my opinion the FABC documents express some of the best Catholic theology on inculturation by our episcopal Magisterium.

Perhaps the richest basis for the Asian bishops' emphasis on inculturation is what might be called the "imperative of grace."[12] FABC documents make the point that God's presence has always permeated Asian realities. God has drawn Asian peoples through Asian religions, in which are hidden genuine seeds of the Word.[13] Forms of prayer in these religions can enhance and greatly enrich the prayer life of the Christian church; all Asians are on a common pilgrimage "in restless quest for the Absolute," and are all "attuned to the work of the Spirit in the resounding symphony of Asian communion."[14] God's saving grace is at work in all religions; it is not limited to Christians but is offered to every person. God's grace, says the Bishops' Institute for Interreligious Affairs, "may lead some to accept baptism and enter the Church, but it cannot be presumed that this must always be the case."[15] God's ways are mysterious and unfathomable, and no one can determine the direction of divine grace. Each people, and each culture, says the International Mission Congress of 1979, is called by the Spirit "to its own fresh and creative response to the gospel. In every local church, each people's culture, meanings, values, and traditions are taken up, not diminished or destroyed, but celebrated and renewed, purified if need be, and fulfilled."[16] Asia is the context "of God's creative, incarnational and redemptive action,"[17] in which Asia's salvation is being enacted, "in ever new, ever mysterious ways."[18]

The "basic theological orientation" of the FABC documents is clearly "creation centered."[19] The religions, the cultures, the social movements of Asia are transparent to God's activity and grace. The "natural" in Asia is more than natural; it is "holy ground." The Asian bishops insist that theology and Christian life take place in a "threefold dialogue," with culture, religion, and Asia's poor.[20] This is why inculturation is not simply a "one way" encounter of fulfillment and purification, but a "two way" encounter of

---

12. Bevans, "Inculturation of Theology," 1–23.

13. FABC, "Evangelization in Modern Day Asia," 14–15, and "Prayer—the Life of the Church in Asia," 31.

14. FABC, "Church—Community of Faith," 49–65.

15. FABC, Bishops' Institute for Interreligious Affairs II, 113–17.

16. FABC, "International Mission Congress," 125–63.

17. FABC, "Journeying Together," 273–89.

18. FABC, "Christian Discipleship," 1–12.

19. Bevans, *Models*, 21–22.

20. Bevans, "Inculturation of Theology," 9–10; Tan, "Towards Asian," 26–38.

mutual critique and enrichment. And this is why ultimately, inculturation is not a mere option, or one item on a list of agenda for the Asian church. Inculturation, rather, is demanded by the nature of the Gospel itself, for it is the Gospel of a God who calls women and men to salvation through dialogue with their humanity. The stuff of ordinary everyday Asian experience cannot be regarded as something that the Gospel replaces, or something to be used as a mere vehicle for more relevant evangelization. Rather, such ordinary experience can be seen as a true theological source, to be taken on an equal basis with Christian attempts to express and embody their faith. Because of their universal presence, grace, Scripture, Christian tradition, culture, religiosity, social location, and movements of social change are all partners in a mutually critical conversation of inculturation.

Aylward Shorter

In *Toward a Theology of Inculturation*, British anthropologist and missionary Aylward Shorter devotes an entire section to the theological foundations of the inculturation task.[21] First of all, inculturation has strong *Christological* foundations. Shorter refers to the work of Benin theologian Efoé-Julien Pénouko, who himself builds on Justin Martyr's notion of the *logos spermatikos*, or the presence of "seeds of the Word" sown in all the world's cultures. While the presence of these seeds does not make cultures entirely good and holy, nevertheless there can be posited a continuity between their values and the values offered by the Gospel. In purifying cultures the Gospel fulfills them and calls them to their full potential. For Pénoukou, therefore, inculturation "is not a compromise with paganism. . . . Africa remains African, not in spite of, but because of being evangelized." This is because, "however darkly or obscurely, the dialogue between the eternal Logos of God and human cultures has been going on since the creation of the world."[22] The Incarnation, Shorter continues, "possesses a logic of its own," in that "once the mystery of the Word made flesh is grasped . . . [e]very cultural reality is graced and transformed."[23] Ultimately, the theology of inculturation is found in the entire Paschal Mystery of Jesus's life, death and resurrection. On the one hand, the Paschal Mystery invites every culture to "'die' to all that is not worthy of the humanity in their traditions,"[24] and so find new life with the Risen Christ who is now available to every culture. "It is precisely

21. Shorter, *Toward a Theology*, 73–134.
22. Ibid., 78.
23. Ibid., 81.
24. Ibid., 84.

because of the Resurrection that we can become members of Christ and that Christ, in his members, can become African, Indian, American and so on."[25]

Shorter also devotes a chapter to the soteriological foundations of inculturation. In previous times the Catholic Church's mission was driven by the conviction that not to confess Christ explicitly and be admitted into the church through baptism would end in damnation. In the latter part of the twentieth century, however, Catholic theology was able to articulate a theory of salvation that took into account both God's universal salvific will and the centrality of Christ for the efficacy of that salvation. In this way of thinking, God, through the Spirit, offers to all humanity—members of all religions, of all cultures—"the possibility of being made partners . . . in the paschal mystery."[26] And so, because God is present through the *logos spermatikos* and the Holy Spirit, peoples' cultures and religions are genuine, though imperfect, ways of salvation. The Gospel, when it is preached, can and does use the goodness of culture and religion as it searches for expression. And, conversely, the entire church is enriched in its understanding and expression of the Gospel as it employs these elements.[27] This is central in Catholic teaching and pivotal for its foundation of inculturation.

Finally, Shorter traces the *biblical* foundations for inculturation. In both the Old Testament and the New, we recognize the "essentially intercultural character of God's revelation."[28] The Scriptures themselves are exercises in inculturation. "Whether it responds positively or negatively to the covenant," Israel "does so in harmony with the religious psychology of the contemporary cultural framework."[29] Images in the psalms, for example, reflect Canaanite culture; much of Hosea's prophecy was a challenge to that culture's dominance in Israel's thinking.[30] In later years, when Israel became influenced by the expanding Hellenistic culture, books like Wisdom and Ecclesiastes reflect a critical dialogue with Hellenistic thought forms. Particularly in diaspora, Israel had no choice but to express its faith in terms that both took cognizance of the dominant culture and critiqued it. In the New Testament, although Jesus is thoroughly immersed in his Hebrew culture, he is surprisingly open to others and strongly opposed to narrow interpretations of Judaism.[31] The early Christian community, in its acceptance

25. Ibid., 83.
26. Ibid., 94 (quoting GS 22).
27. Ibid., 99–100.
28. Ibid., 102.
29. Ibid., 108.
30. Ibid., 109–11.
31. Ibid., 119–20.

of Gentile converts, and in particular Paul with his strong sense of the universality of the Gospel and its freedom from restrictive Jewish cultural and religious customs, are witnesses to the fact that Christianity from the start was engaged in a dialogue of faith and culture. The biblical witness, then, points to both the fact and necessity of inculturation. To practice biblical fidelity is to take culture seriously as one lives out and expresses Christian faith.

Peter Schineller

Jesuit Peter Schineller's *Handbook on Inculturation* contains a chapter entitled "Theological Bases."[32] Schineller sees inculturation as rooted in the revelation of God experienced through the "seeds of the Word," sown in all cultures. This means that "the agent of inculturation does not enter into godless contexts, but rather steps onto holy ground, insofar as God is already in contact with a given context even if in imperfect and hidden ways. . . . Revelation does not enter as universal magic, but rather occurs in particular histories to concrete persons and communities in particular contexts and cultures."[33] Revelation, says Schineller, is not a mere collection of propositions, but is an ongoing, contextual, culturally conditioned action of God at all times and all places.

Secondly, inculturation presupposes a theology of God's universal grace, operative at all places and at all times. Since our world is a "world of grace," no person, time or culture remains untouched by God's presence.[34] Though grace always calls for transformation in situations shot through with sin, we deal nevertheless, with values, customs, ideas, thought forms, desires and situations that are good and worthy of incorporation into Christian practice and thought.

Since that grace is always the grace of Christ,[35] inculturation must rest as well on a *Christological* foundation. Inculturation involves our imitation of Jesus, not "to the last detail (how he dressed or ate)," but in what Jesus did for the sake of the Reign of God, siding with "the poor, the weak, the sinners, the needy."[36] Similarly, this imitation leads to the same fate that Jesus underwent, as well as to the same breakthrough to new life. Analogously, inculturation for the followers of Christ means they must die to limited cul-

---

32. Schineller, *Handbook*, 45–60.
33. Ibid., 46.
34. Ibid., 47.
35. Ibid., 48.
36. Ibid.

tural views and be open to "the new, rich directions in which God calls."[37] Above all, insists Schineller, the Christological foundation of inculturation leads us to appreciate the importance of the fully human. As Jesus was not only divine and but also fully human, our faith needs to be deeply rooted in culture, history, humanity, creation.

Inculturation also has an ecclesiological foundation, which calls forth a deeper understanding of the church's catholicity. It is committed to an openness to, and appreciation of, all peoples, all cultures, all historical periods, all points of view.[38] It is this catholic appreciation that provides a strong foundation for some of the risks and adventures that inculturation entails.[39] The communal nature of faith does not leave behind the counsel and wisdom of Magisterium; yet, at the same time, it is rooted in the *sensus fidelium* given to all the baptized.[40] The community of faith works together to read the "signs of the times," knowing that God's dynamic truth is present not only in the words of Scripture or the wisdom of Tradition, but in God's saving presence in the warp and woof of people's lives.[41]

In a section entitled "The Center of Christianity," Schineller draws a theological foundation for inculturation from the doctrine of the "hierarchy of truths."[42] Since the content of the hierarchy is not really defined,[43] Schineller suggests that the content of Christianity be imaged as a "series of concentric circles, with the more important content at the center and the less important at the periphery." What exactly is at the center is not all that clear—perhaps, as Karl Rahner says, not just one thing but a complex of ideas involving Holy Mystery in self-communication in history.[44] In any case, this idea of hierarchy of truths or concentric circles indicates that "Christianity is to be viewed not as a book or series of teachings, but as a way of life, the life of Christ lived in our day and age under the inspiration of the Spirit." If this is clear, then expressing and living Christianity becomes an adventure, full of risks but also full of surprises. It is carried out in a sense of confidence, rejoicing, and marveling in "the myriad ways in which different communities of Christians, old and new communities, African and

---

37. Ibid., 48–49.
38. Ibid., 50.
39. Ibid., 52.
40. Ibid., 50–51.
41. Ibid., 52–56.
42. Vatican II, *Unitatis Redintegratio*, 11.
43. Schineller, *Handbook*, 57.
44. Ibid., 59.

American communities, point to and reflect the unfathomable riches of the mystery of Christ."[45]

Jan H. Pranger

Writing in the context of Tamil and Sinhalese communities of Sri Lanka, Dutch Reformed missiologist Jan H. Pranger observes that where two communities use ethnicity to construct their identities vis-à-vis one another, racial hatred and violence are all but inevitable. Rather than religion serving as a source of reconciliation, it becomes an "uncritical ethno-cultural alliance and a covert form of nationalism," promoted as inculturation. The result is a divided church.[46]

Pranger says it is a mistake to understand culture in a more traditional "integrated" sense.[47] Inculturation in the Sri Lankan context needs to be seen in a wider framework. Real inculturation in Sri Lanka will reflect not only on cultural values and practices but on issues arising from daily life, chief among them being violence, hatred, and racial exploitation.[48]

Pranger concludes, "The theological basis of inculturation is only found in God's incarnation in human reality, that is, God's taking our human situation seriously as the location of God's saving involvement with us."[49] While that "location" is always cultural, the ambiguity of culture means that God's saving involvement is always dialectical, "both affirming and critically transforming, and this includes our cultural or ethnic identities as well."[50] Pranger's approach emphasizes that even inculturation's theological foundations are contextually conditioned. Particular contexts will demand particular encounters between faith and culture if authentic inculturation is to be achieved.

---

45. Ibid., 60.
46. Pranger, "Culture," 158, 156. Pranger quotes A. J. V. Chankdrakanthan, *Catholic Revival in Post-Colonial Sri Lanka: A Critique of Ecclesial Contextualization.*
47. Schreiter, *New Catholicity*; Tanner, *Theories of Culture.*
48. Pranger, "Culture," 170.
49. Ibid.
50. Ibid.

Stephen B. Bevans

My own work, *Models of Contextual Theology*, identifies several theological dimensions of inculturation.[51]

First, there is the incarnational nature of Christianity. Revelation is an authentic communication event: God speaks to humanity concretely and fully in the particular and culturally limited nature of Jesus of Nazareth. If Christianity "is to be faithful to its deepest roots and most basic insight," it "must continue God's incarnation in Jesus by becoming contextual." As expressed by evangelical theologian René Padilla: "God does not shout his message from the heavens," but "becomes present as a man among men."[52]

Second, I focus on the sacramental nature of reality. The concreteness of Jesus is a signal that all of God's creation—including human situations and human cultures—can become transparent and revelatory of God's saving presence. Just as the Bible is the record of Israel and the early Christian community interpreting the ordinary and secular in terms of religious meaning, so the continuing task of theology is "to reveal God's presence in a truly sacramental world."[53]

Third, inculturation is built on relatively recent understandings of the nature of God's Revelation. Contemporary Catholic theology has moved from a *propositional* notion of Revelation to one that recognizes that Revelation is an offering of God's very self in human life and history. This does not exclude propositional expressions; Revelation does offer saving truths. But ultimately, Revelation offers a living theology that people of particular cultures and historical eras can understand.[54]

Fourth, I point to the church's catholicity as a foundation for doing a theology rooted in a particular context.[55] Catholicity is that dimension of the church that on the one hand, enables the Christian community to balance the universal validity of Christian doctrines and the particularity of expressions and preferences of a local church. On the other hand, catholicity witnesses to the fact that only when every particular context has appropriated the Gospel, and enters into dialogue with every other context, do we have the complete fullness of the riches of Christ. In the words of Andrew Walls,

---

51. Bevans, *Models*.
52. Ibid., 12.
53. Ibid., 12–13.
54. Ibid., 13–14.
55. Ibid., 14–15.

"The full-grown humanity of Christ requires all the Christian generations, just as it embodies all the cultural variety that six continents can bring."[56]

Finally, I focus on the Trinity as a theological foundation for inculturation,[57] and it is this that I wish to develop in the second section of this study.

TRINITARIAN FOUNDATIONS

Clearly, inculturation is at the center of the church's mission, and as such it is a theological imperative; it is not optional. In the context of today's globalized world, we need, in Tiénou's words, "a theology that seeks to permanently plant the Church of Christ . . . and anchor the gospel deeply." As Pope John Paul II expressed it, "a faith which does not become culture is a faith which has not been fully received, not thoroughly thought through, not fully lived out."[58]

In this section, I propose that inculturation is an imperative in theology and in the church's life because it is grounded in the central mystery of Christianity: the overflowing communal life of the Triune God. I believe that the trinitarian foundation of inculturation is particularly proper to the task of inculturation. God's trinitarian nature points to the fact that God's identity is inextricably bound up with creation and, in particular, with humanity. The diversity-in-unity within God as such is a model of the rich diversity to which the Christian community is called. The mission of each person of the Trinity reflects a particular way in which God blesses and challenges human life and calls it to fulfillment and transformation.

In addition, a trinitarian foundation of inculturation reveals the intimate link between inculturation and mission itself. Mission is participation in the mission of God. Inculturation shows how that mission is carried out—in a dialogue that illumines and critiques, that struggles and learns, that calls for change and is changed in the process. The triune God invites the world to fullness of life through a "prophetic dialogue" with men and women as they are. As Christians, we are called to participate in that dialogue by involving ourselves in the process of inculturation.

---

56. Walls, *Missionary Movement*, xvii.
57. Walls, *Models*, 15.
58. John Paul II, address to the Italian National Congress.

The Holy Spirit: God "Inside Out"

The God of Christians, the God of Jesus Christ, is a *communion-in-mission*. God cannot fail to be involved in the world, for to be God is to be self-diffusive. Theoretically, of course, God could choose not to create; God could choose not to be always and everywhere present in created reality. But God's centrifugal nature does in fact express itself in self-giving and self-communication, and in saving dialogue.[59] God, as incomprehensible and ineffable Mystery, is always and everywhere in the world through the palpable yet mysterious presence of the Holy Spirit.[60] There has never been a place or time that was not touched by God's hand, or by the "finger of God's right hand," as the ancient hymn "Veni Sancte Spiritus" puts it. All of creation is holy.

God's Spirit points to the "immanent transcendence" of created things.[61] On the one hand, the Spirit is God's "secret presence" in all peoples, cultures and events. Christians who attend closely to human experience will find clues to God's presence and how to respond to it, express it, and celebrate it in the fabric of their concrete lives. On the other hand, Christians realize that no response, expression, or celebration can capture the mysterious reality of God's saving presence. This is humbling and freeing. It is humbling because no language or action can express the miracle of God's involvement; it is freeing because all the rich and diverse resources of the world can be the stuff of religious, ethical, and ritual expression of faith. Because of God's presence through the Spirit, genuine and deep inculturation can take place. At the same time, such expression can remain open to possible enrichment and even correction from other peoples' cultural and historical experience.

Jesus: "Face" of the Spirit

Ultimately God's presence is not limited to the undifferentiated activity of the Spirit. For, "in the fullness of time" (Gal 4:4), God "became flesh" (John 1:14). God's more "anonymous" presence became a "concrete presence."[62] Jesus of Nazareth is the Spirit's "face."[63] Through incarnation, God holds nothing back. The very particularity of Jesus—nationality, language, eye-

---

59. Rahner, *Trinity*. See 282 regarding the "supernatural existential."
60. Bevans, "God Inside Out."
61. Ibid., 103–5.
62. Welker, *God the Spirit*, 183–227.
63. Breck, "Face of the Spirit," 165–78.

color, blood type—points to the length to which God goes to invite humanity into God's own communion. Such completeness is summed up and fully expressed by Jesus's death on the cross. Through that Paschal event, completed in his victory over death in the resurrection, Jesus bequeaths the Spirit in a new and concrete way upon those who acknowledge him as Lord, continue his ministry of divine compassion, and continue to see the ordinariness and concreteness of human life as the place and time of God's salvation.

It is in and through Jesus's scandalous particularity that humanity is assured of God's saving action. Because the Son is fully human, humanity is able to enter into relationship with God: only because God fully assumed our flesh are we fully redeemed. The flesh, the concrete, the particular, the ordinary is the way to God. In an even more radical way, whatever is good in God's creation is material for human response, expression, and celebration. Inculturation is a natural and inevitable response to incarnation.

Incarnation's very particularity, however, also reveals something of the nature of inculturation. Jesus's concreteness points to the fact that the communication and expression of God's saving presence has particular parameters. Not everything holds the "secret presence." Jesus is, as it were, God's standard, against which all other concrete expressions are measured and in relation to which they are validated. The life and death of Jesus point to the "logic" of salvation. The Gospel provides the criterion against which all efforts of inculturation are to be judged. While Christians should not be too swift to think that they have fully understood the Gospel,[64] it is the Gospel nonetheless, in all its concreteness, that inculturation more or less successfully communicates. To do this, human experience has to undergo the transformation of the Paschal Mystery, finding new life through *metanoia*, change, even "death."

The Immanent Trinity: Communal, Relational, and Dialogical

It is through the "secret presence" of the Spirit in the rhythm of creation and human history that God is known. That presence becomes fully revealed in the concrete presence of Jesus of Nazareth. God is revealed as a communion of self-diffusive love, a community of dialogue that—like the church it calls into being—is not centered on itself but overflows in creation and invites creation to mission. As Leonardo Boff insists, "Christianity's most transcendent assertion may well be this: In the beginning is not the solitude of One,

---

64. Newbigin, in review of *Salvation and Humanization*, writes, "The gospel is greater than our grasp of it."

but the communion of Three eternal Persons: Father, Son and Holy Spirit. In the remotest beginning communion prevails.... Communion is the first and last word of the mystery of God and the mystery of the world."[65] It is in this dialogical and relational inner life of God, manifest in God's immanent presence in creation, that we can also discern a rich theological foundation for the practices of inculturation.

Christian monotheism is not about a monolithic "One" who rules the universe; it is a doctrine about the life-giving power of community. Relationality, not individuality, is at the heart of the universe. Revelation does not originate in a monarchical monologue but in a persuasive dialogue. In this dialogue each person receives identity from and bestows it on the others, and all form one dynamic reality of "giving over and receiving back, being obedient and being glorified, witnessing, filling and actively glorifying."[66]

The life of community, relationality, and dialogue overflows into the divine missionary presence and action. Revelation is about God speaking to men and women "as friends," inviting them "into fellowship with Godself."[67] As Pope Paul VI points out, "The whole history of human salvation is one long, varied dialogue, which marvelously begins with God and which God prolongs with men and women in so many different ways."[68]

Mission, therefore, is relational and dialogical. One does not do mission without first cultivating *relationships* with people—learning language, appreciating and adapting to the local culture, forming friendships. As my colleague Claude Marie Barbour has expressed it, missionaries and ministers must first be "evangelized" by the culture and people they have come to evangelize. Barbour is fond of quoting the famous lines of Max Warren to the effect that when one comes to "another people, another culture, another religion," we are to "take off our shoes, for the place we are approaching is holy."[69] This sense of listening, relationship, and appreciation is essential for the process of inculturation and has its roots not in any kind of tactic but in the being and activity of God as such—a community of relationship and love.

Relationship and communion originate and bear fruit in dialogue. As both the Catholic Magisterium and the theologians cited above have noted, dialogue is a process whereby both parties, or all parties, give and receive.

---

65. Boff, "Trinity," 389, 391.
66. Johnson, *She Who Is*, 195.
67. Vatican II, *Dei Verbum* 1, 111.
68. Paul VI, *Ecclesiam Suam* 70.

69. Barbour et al., "Gospel, Culture," 135–50, quoting from page 10 of M. A. C. Warren's introduction to John V. Taylor, *Primal Vision*.

Although it focuses on interreligious dialogue, the 1991 Vatican document *Dialogue and Proclamation* offers a wider definition of dialogue as "reciprocal communication, leading to a common goal or, at a deeper level, to interpersonal communion." It is "an attitude of respect and friendship, which permeates or should permeate all those activities constituting the evangelizing mission of the Church."[70] The Catholic Bishops of Asia speak of mission—and in that context inculturation—in terms of a triple dialogue with the poor, with other religions and with cultures.[71] Such a dialogical understanding of inculturation implies that it is a process of giving and receiving, challenging and being challenged, purifying and being in turn purified. Rooted in the dialogical life of the Trinity, and in the Trinity's dialogical outreach in the history of salvation, the process of inculturation is an exciting process of discovery both for agents of the Gospel and of those who are receiving the good news. If we are serious about grounding inculturation in the doctrine of the Trinity, inculturation will be much more than the application of a "thin veneer" or superficial translation of "supracultural" expressions. While it is certainly true that the Gospel is "not identical" but "independent in regard to all cultures," the communal, relational, and dialogical nature of God calls for a process that takes particular people as the starting point, "always coming back to the relationships of people among themselves and with God."[72]

Unity and Diversity

In his marvelous book *These Three Are One: The Practice of Trinitarian Theology*, David Cunningham takes issue with the notion that trinitarian theology has nothing to do with the numbers "one" and "three."[73] He argues that the core truth "these three are one . . . calls into question our assumption that the categories of oneness and difference are incommensurable, incompatible, or even necessarily in tension with one another."[74] Against the Western fixation on the identity and inviolability of the individual, trinitarian theology underlines the biblical vision of the communal nature of human personality and the interconnectedness of all that exists.

---

70. Burrows, *Redemption and Dialogue*, on *Dialogue and Proclamation* 9.
71. Bevans, "Inculturation of Theology," 9–10.
72. *EN* 20.
73. Cunningham, *These Three*, x.
74. Ibid., 8.

Cunningham asserts that the unity and diversity of the Trinity, rather than making contrasting "claims about God and the world,"[75] are in fact complementary and mutually enriching. Just as in a Byrd motet or a Palestrina Mass we experience beauty and meaning in the interconnecting, interweaving, and yet distinct melodies and lines of text, so unity and diversity reveal the beauty and meaning of God's inner life of relationship. As Hans Urs von Balthasar has written, "Even eternal Truth is symphonic."[76] God's symphonic unity and diversity is reflected in God's missionary activity, as clearly seen at Pentecost, when Parthians, Medes, Elamites, Mesopotamians, Judeans, Cappadocians, people from Pontus, Phrygia, Pamphylia and Rome, Egyptians, Cretans and Arabs heard in their own language the one message "about the marvels God has accomplished" (Acts 2:7–12).

Trinitarian relationality can be understood as a basis for the unity-in-diversity that inculturation strives for in Christian theology. While the Gospel provides an unmistakable salvific message, cultural and historical events call forth variations on the theme, contributing to its complexity, providing it with depth, and taking it in new directions. "Where the *cantus firmus* is clear and plain, the counterpoint can be developed to its limits," wrote Bonhoeffer.[77] In a workshop at an annual convention of the Catholic Theological Society, a Vietnamese-American theologian made the same point: Instead of speaking of the need to correspond to traditional or orthodox expressions, we should ask whether our insights are in *harmony* with them. The harmony found in the Trinity is a model for authentic inculturation.

Vestigia Trinitatis

Once we accept the trinitarian nature of God, says David Cunningham, we become free to find in the fabric of God's creation, historical events, and human culture certain "triune marks"—what the tradition calls *vestigia Trinitatis*—that help us understand what God is like. Trinitarian faith, in other words, allows us to have recourse to our own, always contextual, experience to find ways of expressing God's healing and redeeming presence in the ebb and flow of life.

Cunningham makes it clear that such a search is always a consequence of revealed faith. (A discernment of *vestigia* is not the mere "natural

---

75. Ibid., 129.

76. Ibid., 132, quoting Balthasar, *Truth Is Symphonic*, 7–8.

77. Cunningham, *These Three*, quoting Bonhoeffer, *Letters and Papers from Prison*, 303.

theology" to which Karl Barth was so opposed.[78]) The search for traces of God in creation always looks back "to the missions of incarnation and inspiration as touchstones of theological adequacy."[79] But once the truth of revelation is acknowledged, "we should construe the created order as bearing triune marks."[80] What this means concretely for inculturation is that every culture and moment in history may contain elements that can be taken up in an understanding of who God is and what God's work is in the world.

CONCLUSION

At the beginning of these reflections, I expressed hope that what I had to say would be acceptable to our Festschrift honoree, Tite Tiénou. I express that hope again, knowing that Tiénou's acceptance may include a friendly but serious challenge to enter into dialogue and even debate. It is this acceptance-with-challenge that has made Tiénou such an engaging friend through the years, to me and no doubt to many others. But it is this *engagement* more than any simple acceptance or agreement that is important. It is, I would venture to say, a model of authentic contextualizing or inculturating—and that is because it is a model of who our God is and who our God calls us to be.

BIBLIOGRAPHY

Barbour, Claude Marie, et al. "Gospel, Culture, Healing and Reconciliation: A Shalom Conversation." *Mission Studies* 16 (1999) 135–50.
Bevans, Stephen. "God Inside Out: Toward a Missionary Theology of the Holy Spirit." *International Bulletin of Missionary Research* 22 (1998) 102–5.
———. "Inculturation of Theology in Asia. The Federation of Asian Bishops' Conferences, 1970–1995." *Studia Missionalia* 45 (1996) 1–23.
———. *Models of Contextual Theology*. Rev. ed. Faith and Cultures Series. Maryknoll, NY: Orbis, 2002.
Boff, Leonardo. "Trinity." In *Mysterium Liberationis: Fundamental Concepts of Liberation Theology*, edited by Ignacio Ellacuría and Jon Sobrino, 389–404. Maryknoll, NY: Orbis, 1993.
Breck, John. "The Face of the Spirit." *Pro Ecclesia* 3 (1954) 165–78.
Burrows, William R., editor. *Redemption and Dialogue: Reading Redemptoris Missio and Dialogue and Proclamation*. Maryknoll, NY: Orbis, 1993.
Cunningham, David S. *These Three Are One: The Practice of Trinitarian Theology*. Oxford: Blackwell, 1998.

78. Ibid., 106.
79. Ibid., 107.
80. Ibid.

Denzinger, Heinrich, and Adolf Schönmetzer, editors. *Enchiridion Symbolorum*. 34th ed. New York: Herder, 1997.

FABC, Bishops' Institute for Interreligious Affairs II (1979). In *For All the Peoples of Asia*. Vol. 1, *Federation of Asian Bishops' Conferences: Documents from 1970 to 1991*, edited by G. B. Rosales and C. G. Arévalo. Maryknoll, NY: Orbis, 1992.

———. "Christian Discipleship in Asia Today: Service to Life" (1995). In *For All the Peoples of Asia*, vol. 2, *Federation of Asian Bishops' Conferences: Documents from 1992 to 1996*, edited by Franz-Josef Eilers, 1–12. Manila: Claretian, 1997.

———. "The Church—Community of Faith in Asia" (1982). In *For All the Peoples of Asia*, vol. 1, *Federation of Asian Bishops' Conferences: Documents from 1970 to 1991*, edited by G. B. Rosales and C. G. Arévalo, 49–65. Maryknoll, NY: Orbis, 1992.

———. "Evangelization in Modern Day Asia" (1974). In *For All the Peoples of Asia*, vol. 1, *Federation of Asian Bishops' Conferences: Documents from 1970 to 1991*, edited by G. B. Rosales and C. G. Arévalo, 11–25. Maryknoll, NY: Orbis, 1992.

———. "International Mission Congress" (1979). In *For All the Peoples of Asia*, vol. 1, *Federation of Asian Bishops' Conferences: Documents from 1970 to 1991*, edited by G. B. Rosales and C. G. Arévalo, 125–63. Maryknoll, NY: Orbis, 1992.

———. "Journeying Together toward the Third Millennium" (1990) 1.5. In *For All the Peoples of Asia*, vol. 1, *Federation of Asian Bishops' Conferences: Documents from 1970 to 1991*, edited by G. B. Rosales and C. G. Arévalo, 273–89. Maryknoll, NY: Orbis, 1992.

———. "Prayer—the Life of the Church in Asia" (1978). In *For All the Peoples of Asia*, vol. 1, *Federation of Asian Bishops' Conferences: Documents from 1970 to 1991*, edited by G. B. Rosales and C. G. Arévalo, 27–48. Maryknoll, NY: Orbis, 1992.

John Paul II. Address to the Italian National Congress of the Ecclesial Movement for Cultural Commitment. *L'Osservatore Romano*, English ed., June 28, 1982.

Johnson, Elizabeth A. *She Who Is: The Mystery of God in Feminist Discourse*. New York: Crossroad, 1992.

Newbigin, Lesslie. Review of *Salvation and Humanization*, by M. M. Thomas. *Religion and Society* 18 (1971) 71–80.

Paul VI. *Ecclesiam Suam* 70. Encyclical on the Church, August 6, 1964. Online: http://www.vatican.va/holy_father/paul_vi/encyclicals/documents/hf_p-vi_enc_06081964_ecclesiam_en.html.

Pernia, Antonio M. "Mission for the Twenty-First Century: An SVD Perspective." In *Mission for the 21st Century*, edited by Stephen Bevans and Roger Schroeder, 8–20. Chicago: CCGM, 2001.

Pranger, Jan H. "Culture, Ethnicity, and Inculturation: Critical and Constructive Comments in Relation to Sri Lankan Contextual Theology." *Mission Studies* 18 (2001) 154–80.

Rahner, Karl. *The Trinity*. New York: Herder & Herder, 1976.

Schineller, Peter. *Handbook on Inculturation*. Maryknoll, NY: Orbis, 1990.

Schreiter, Robert J. *Constructing Local Theologies*. New York: Orbis, 1985.

———. *The New Catholicity: Theology between the Global and the Local*. Maryknoll, NY: Orbis, 1997.

Shorter, Aylward. *Toward a Theology of Inculturation*. Maryknoll, NY: Orbis, 1988.

Inculturation and the Church's Mission 233

Tan, Jonathan Y. "Towards Asian Liturgical Inculturation: Investigating the Resources in the Documents of the Federation of Asian Bishops' Conferences for Developing an Asian Theology of Liturgical Inculturation." *FABC Papers* 89 (1999).

Tanner, Kathryn. *Theories of Culture: A New Agenda for Theology*. Guides to Theological Inquiry. Minneapolis: Fortress, 1997.

Tiénou, Tite. "Themes in African Theology of Mission." In *The Good News of the Kingdom: Mission Theology for the Third Millennium*, edited by Charles van Engen et al., 239–43. Maryknoll, NY: Orbis, 1993.

———. "The Training of Missiologists for an African Context." In *Missiological Education for the Twenty-First Century: The Book, the Circle, and the Sandals; Essays in Honor of Paul E. Pierson*, edited by J. Dudley Woodbury et al., 93–101. American Society of Missiology Series 23. Maryknoll, NY: Orbis, 1996.

Vatican Council II. "Constitution on the Sacred Liturgy [*Sacrosanctum Concilium*]." In *The Documents of Vatican II*, edited by Walter M. Abbott, 133–82. New York: Herder & Herder, 1966.

———. "Decree on Ecumenism [*Unitatis Redintegratio*]." In *The Documents of Vatican II*, edited by Walter M. Abbott, 336–70. New York: Herder & Herder, 1966.

———. "Decree on the Mission Activity of the Church [*Ad Gentes*]." In *The Documents of Vatican II*, edited by Walter M. Abbott, 111–28. New York: Herder & Herder, 1966.

———. "Dogmatic Constitution on Divine Revelation [*Dei Verbum*]." In *The Documents of Vatican II*, edited by Walter M. Abbott, 107–32. New York: Herder & Herder, 1966.

———. "Pastoral Constitution on the Church in the Modern World [*Gaudium et Spes*]." In *The Documents of Vatican II*, edited by Walter M. Abbott, 183–316. New York: Herder & Herder, 1966.

Walls, Andrew F. *The Missionary Movement in Christian History: Studies in the Transmission of Faith*. Maryknoll, NY: Orbis, 1996.

Warren, M. A. C. "Introduction." In *Primal Vision: Christian Presence amid African Religion*, by John V. Taylor. London: SCM, 1963.

Welker, Michael. *God the Spirit*. Translated by John F. Hoffmeyer. Minneapolis: Fortress, 1994.

17

Pre-Christendom Faith in a Post-Christendom World

Jonathan Bonk

I AM HONORED TO contribute to this Festschrift for my friend Tite Tiénou.[1] Known for his attention to the social, political, and theological dynamics of ethnicity, Tiénou has helped us recognize the ambiguities that must be confronted as we relate to the racial, ethnic, social, and religious "other." This essay offers a similar focus.

Writing from a Mennonite perspective, I wish to give priority to the teaching and example of Jesus as recorded in the Gospels. I argue that ethical practices shared by people across time and religions reflect a God-implanted awareness that we live in a moral universe, a universe in which everyday behavior matters—*really* matters. In the case of those who are followers of Jesus, this means giving diligent, life-long attention not only to who Jesus was and what he did—doctrine and creedal confession—but to

---

1. This essay evolved from a paper prepared for the Theology Working Group International Consultation on "The Whole Gospel" in Chiang Mai, Thailand, February 11–15, 2008. A version appeared as "The Gospel and Ethics" in *Evangelical Review of Theology* 33.1 (January 2009). It was also presented at Luther Seminary, St. Paul, Minnesota, on November 5, 2008, and at the Evangelical Missiological Society annual conference, September 17–19, 2009. The text has been edited to meet the page requirements of the present publication.

what he said about how we are to live in community, how we are to relate to families, neighbors, strangers, and enemies.

In what follows, "Christendom" is viewed as a synonym for "The West."[2] It includes old Christendom, that is, Europe; and neo-Christendom, the countries emerging from a millennium of European migration: United States, Canada, Australia, New Zealand, and South Africa. This widens the discussion from specifically religious categories to the entire range of social, political, and economic impulses within societies that have long defined themselves as Christian.

A faith prescribed by Western culture, history, concepts, categories, and self-interests is a religion tied to the West's fortunes. This implies that expressions of Christian faith found outside the West will at times be unrecognizable from a Western perspective. And therefore, proof of family affinity across the centuries and around the world will ultimately be seen more on the basis of behavior than doctrine.

There has always been an awareness that the mere assembling of the doctrinal bits and pieces of the God-puzzle—a multidimensional mental Rubik's Cube—is not the same thing as being a Christian. At the same time, Western Christendom has supposed that there could be only one correct solution to the puzzle. Every face of the Rubik's Cube must find its rightful place. Those who assemble its pieces in unconventional patterns face ostracism by the West.

But the West no longer has a monopoly on Christian theology, Christian forms, or ecclesiastical emphases. Christianity is now predominantly a non-Western religion. Take the continent of Africa, for example. The religious scene is bewildering for most Westerners. Although a majority of Africans—an estimated 470 million men and women—regard themselves as Christian, standard definitions are hard-pressed to accommodate

---

2. Herrin, *Formation of Christendom*, 8, 47. Also see Abramsky, "Defining the Indefinable West," and Walls, *Missionary Movement*, 3–15. Exploring the term "the West," Abramsky concludes that it is a "vague and spectacularly imprecise intellectual organizing tool." In her words, "[It] means a state of mind more than a distinct plot of land." She concludes, "Perhaps the only three constants in Western history are the totemic power of the phrase 'the West'; the flexibility of the definition and boundaries as it morphs to meet changing intellectual and geopolitical realities; and an assertive self-confidence, a haughty sense of its own infallibility and righteousness. In truth, because we think there is a West, as a result there is a West; and it does somehow encompass both the Inquisition and the Enlightenment; it does have room for both Marx and Dante; it does, in the information age, even have room to expand into lands formerly considered the heart of the East." The Walls essay, "Gospel as Prisoner and Liberator of Culture," which first appeared in 1982, is probably one of the most influential and frequently cited articles in mission studies over the past twenty-five years. It has done as much to renovate and enlarge our understanding of what it means to be a Christian as anything else published.

on-the-ground realities. Comfortably established old Christendom formulations and practices have been displaced by much that is unfamiliar and disorienting.

Take, for example, the phenomenon variously referred to as African Independent Churches, African Initiated Churches, or African Instituted Churches. Commonly known as AICs, these unique expressions of Christian faith and life can be disconcertingly pre-enlightenment in their worldviews and pre-Christendom in their theologies. While churches elsewhere tend to stress Christology and individual salvation, the emphasis in AICs tends to be on the Holy Spirit and community. And the Holy Spirit is not simply some kind of ethereal sanctifier, but the power of God who heals, delivers, and persuades.

AIC names hint at religious epistemologies and worldviews more reminiscent of first-century Pentecost than of twenty-first-century Geneva: "Prophesying and Evangelizing Daughters of God," "Celestial Church of Christ," "Redeemed Christian Church of God," "Church of the Lord Aladura," "Sweet Heart Church of the Clouds," "Musama Disco Christo Church," "Spiritual Healing Church," "Church of Christ on Earth by the Prophet Simon Kimbangu," "Church of the Cherubim and Seraphim," and so on. David Barrett first drew attention to the explosive profusion of AICs in *Schism and Renewal in Africa: An Analysis of Six Thousand Contemporary Religious Movements* (Oxford University Press, 1968). Matthew Ajuoga—an Anglican clergymen excommunicated in 1957 because of his affiliation with such fellowships—is today chairman of the Organization of African Instituted Churches, an Africa-wide confession linking 92 national councils of independent churches, by some estimates now 85 million strong.

CASE STUDY FROM BANGLADESH

Any of the AICs could serve as a case study of contemporary expressions of faith that are chronologically post-Christendom but ecclesiastically pre-Christendom. But to help us reflect on the theological implications of such movements, I have chosen to focus on a movement in Bangladesh known as *Isā al-Masih* (Jesus the Messiah).

Isā al-Masih is a movement of Bengali-speaking Muslims, tens of thousands strong, who view themselves as *Isā imandars* ("those faithful to Jesus").[3] The movement is found throughout Bangladesh, with organized fellowships (*jama'at*) in 41 of the 64 districts of the country, each village

---

3. *Isā imandars* is the term used by Jørgensen, "Jesus Imandars," 171–76.

jama'at having a minimum of twenty believing families.[4] The movement has spread to India, with followers in West Bengal on the western border of Bangladesh and Assam to the north; groups are also found among Bengali-speaking Muslims in Mumbai and Delhi. *Isā imandars* have sent missionaries to Singapore and other countries to work among Bengali Muslim guest workers. With the assistance of the United Bible Society, the movement produced its own translation of the Gospels, which avoids cultural issues and terminology offensive to Muslim sensibilities.

Many *Isā imandars* continue to attend their mosques and participate in their communities while acknowledging and following Jesus as Lord.[5] In this regard they are like the earliest followers of Jesus, who continued worshiping in their synagogues. In their *jama'ats*, *Isā al-Masih* members engage in Bible study, hear the Gospel preached, and study and memorize the Scriptures.

Participants have faced resistance not only from Muslims but also from local Christians who are identified with churches rooted in the West. Books, newspaper advertisements, and flyers emanating from these Christians have been widely circulated, inciting Muslims to persecute and Christians to shun those identified as *Isā imandars*.

A leading source of such material is a rural church planter by the name of Rev. Edward Ayub, himself a convert from Islam.[6] His publications have identified *Isā imandar* leaders, congregations, and organizations by name and place. As a result, followers of Jesus in Bangladesh have suffered persecution, including several assassinations. One of Ayub's books opposed the *Isā Imandar* as a Muslim friendly translation of the *Injil* (the Gospels).

In response, Abdullah Mannan, a representative of *Isā al-Masih*, visited Ayub in his home and raised the subject while they were drinking tea.[7]

> I [said to Rev. Ayub], "Brother, I came to talk with you following the Lord's advice [in] Matthew 18:15. . . . Because of your book,

---

4. Abdullah Mannan, a leader of the movement for more than three decades, in a letter written in March 2007, adds, "The country is divided into 16 areas with supervisors, each responsible for four districts."

5. See online: http://isaalmasih.net.

6. This information came to me in December 2007 from a member of the board of the American Bible Society, who had just returned from a visit to Bangladesh. In his report to the ABS, he noted that Ayub had threatened Isā al-Masih members with civil and criminal charges unless they withdrew their translation. My friend assured the ABS board that the translation "is not flawed, either exegetically or linguistically, and that the Movement is not heretical."

7. I quote from a letter the ABS board member sent to the Asia director of a well-known, conservative denominational mission agency.

our people have been attacked in many places. Our people were beaten in the villages; our children facing rejection in schools; our people facing persecution in the businesses, in their homes and their market, in their families." I requested him to withdraw his book . . . He replied, . . . "I am very happy that my book is working. People are reading my book and acting on it . . ." He also said, "Matthew 18:15 does not apply to you. You are not one of us. You are outside our community . . ."

After a few days I sent four of our supervisors to meet Rev. Ayub . . . They requested him to withdraw his book from the market, because his books were bringing persecutions. They told him that our leader "came to you secretly, but you did not listen to him . . . Now we came, and we request you to withdraw your books and stop attacking us or any believers." He told them the same way . . . "Matthew 18:15 doesn't apply to you or your group. You are not one of us."

Abdullah Mannan received his theological training in England and was ordained as elder and pastor by the largest Presbyterian synod in India (now within Bangladesh), and at one time served as general secretary of the synod. He also had a role in the development of the Theological Education by Extension program for Presbyterian pastors. Mannan cannot imagine someone saying that Matthew 18:15 doesn't apply, or "I cannot pray for you."

As this ongoing episode illustrates, the harshest critics of movements of the Spirit are sometimes found within the religious establishment.

CHRISTIAN BELIEF VERSUS CHRISTIAN PRACTICE[8]

How can it be that in liturgical communions the ancient creeds are recited regularly while the Sermon on the Mount is scarcely mentioned? How could it have come about that men and women were burned at the stake, tortured on the rack, and otherwise subjected to agonizing executions in the name of Jesus for holding doctrinal opinions at variance with the prevailing view? How did it come about that those who identified themselves as Christian paid so much attention to who Jesus was in the Godhead, reverencing him in the Eucharist, and yet gave scarce heed to what he said? Today, are there those who say "Lord, Lord" even as they threaten his followers? I offer Ayub as a case in point; likewise the evangelical mission agency working in Bangladesh.

---

8. The following account includes material adapted from my article "Following Jesus," 342–57.

During its Jewish and Gentile genesis, the church engaged in joyful proclamation with a view to inviting men and women to belief in the risen Lord, and to a new way of life as Kingdom citizens, described in Acts 2:42–47. In its earliest days as a Jerusalem-based Jewish sect, the church offered converts teaching, fellowship, prayer, miracles, and a common life. The Good News was much more than a set of new theories about God, although it was certainly that. Belief in Jesus produced ethical transformation—what Jesus had once referred to as "fruit in keeping with repentance." Converts believed that Jesus was the Son of God, who offered the gift of eternal life to all who believed in him. But more than that, they believed he provided the only sure guide for the everyday life of his people in relation to neighbors, strangers, and enemies. The early church grew at an estimated 40 percent per decade. By the time of Constantine's public concurrence with Christianity in AD 312, Christians constituted a significant portion of the imperial population, perhaps as much as 10 percent.[9] This growth occurred in the face of formidable disincentives. Alan Kreider—mindful of the sporadic, sometimes lethal persecution that awaited converts—observes, "If one wanted a soft life, or to get ahead in respectable circles, one did not become a Christian."[10] Conversion to Christianity was the sure road to marginality.[11]

FROM CHRISTIANITY TO CHRISTENDOM

Between the Edict of Milan in AD 313 and Justinian's edict of AD 529, Christianity's status in the empire evolved from being one among several religious options to being the only legal public cult. While Jesus successfully resisted the temptation to yield allegiance to earthly powers (Matthew 4), his namesakes embraced political and military power as legitimate and even essential for the Christianizing of peoples. Having moved from the margins of society to its center, the Christian community became the only option.[12]

---

9. Stark, *Rise of Christianity*, 8. MacMullen provides much higher growth estimates in *Christianizing the Roman Empire*, 86, 109–10.

10. Kreider, *Worship and Evangelism*, 6.

11. Hoornaert, *Memory of the Christian People*, 81.

12. Kreider, *Origins of Christendom*, 22–24. See also Wilkin, *Spirit of Early Christian Thought*. Wilkin observes that the early Church Fathers lived in a pagan world in which they represented a marginalized minority of the population around the Mediterranean. After Constantine, however, they made their pronouncements as secure spokesmen for a state-supported religion. How this process contributed to our contemporary notions of orthodoxy and inspired canon is the subject of Dungan's *Constantine's Bible*. As Brown points out in *Augustine of Hippo*, fierce debates characterized Christianity in the eras preceding and following the sack of Rome. These debates were won, not by argument alone but by legal compulsion and force of arms. Each of the protagonists—Augustine,

With the conversion of increasing numbers of powerful political leaders—for whom Constantine serves as a convenient symbol marking the beginning of a prolonged, complex, and extraordinarily violent process—Christianity evolved into Christendom, the great-grandsire of what is today known as "The West." Christendom was a civilization in which Christian religious dominance was achieved not only through voluntary association but by social, legal, and violent compulsion.[13]

The Church's absorption of powerful political and military figures necessitated a hermeneutic that would give central place to sacraments, canon, and doctrine rather than to compliance with Jesus's teaching. While there continued to be a strong emphasis on his salvific work, Jesus's distinctive ethical teaching was marginalized, if not contradicted, throughout most of Christendom. Much of his teaching was relegated to the world to come. The powerless were given promises of heaven, while the powerful identified with the church only insofar as their position was not contravened or undermined.

Since what Jesus advocated and modeled for his followers seemed utterly impractical for the maintenance, protection, and expansion of civil society, the category "Christian" came to serve primarily as an indicator of assent to those doctrinal formulations approved by the politically powerful.

In the prolonged, highly politicized, and often violent conversion of Europe to the Christian religion, much was lost to the Church. Swept away were biblical emphases on the fruit of the Spirit, the purity of Christ's Bride the Church, and the idea of a sojourning community of pilgrims following the Lord through alien territory. Lost was the idea that Christians should make growth in Christ-likeness the goal of life. Personal, voluntary faith in God through Jesus Christ was displaced by a coercive system that obliged everyone to be a member of the Church. Admission standards were minimal. Ethics meant little more than compliance with the laws of the dominant state. With Charlemagne's ascent to power several centuries later, Christendom emerged full-blown, infusing the West's self-perception in its rise to global economic and military hegemony.[14]

This does not diminish the accomplishment of our forefathers in distilling from the Scriptures a core body of doctrine on which a majority could agree. They—like all of us—were products of their time and its cultural milieu. For any would-be synthesizer, the Bible is a notoriously untidy

---

Donatus, Pelagius, and Julian—was able to muster strong biblical arguments for their particular views. But in the end, it was imperial power rather than theology that assured an outcome favorable to Augustine.

13. Holland, *Forge of Christendom*.
14. Barbero, *Charlemagne*; Wilson, *Charlemagne*.

book. Since the fine points of Trinitarian formulae are not easily extracted from the pages of Scripture, achieving doctrinal consensus was a formidable task. But it seems to have been a good deal easier to formulate what Jesus did for us than what he said we should be doing in everyday life.

Ramsay MacMullen analyzes the ecumenical councils from AD 325 to 553, in the course of which doctrinal orthodoxy was decided by majority vote.[15] It was by means of an estimated 15,000 councils convened during this two-century period—most significantly the one convened at Nicaea in AD 325 and another convened at Chalcedon in AD 451—that church leaders came to agree on an acceptable theological formulation of the Trinity.[16]

These councils were often raucous and riotous, occasionally to the point of bloodshed. Not surprisingly, emperors played a significant, often decisive role, in both staging the major councils and influencing their outcomes.[17] It does not appear that the bishops were unduly troubled by the deep involvement of Constantine—dubbed *koinos episkopos* (universal bishop) by Eusebius—in the internal affairs of the Church.[18] Whatever else might be said of these councils, they were certainly not marked by the fruit of the Spirit. As MacMullen, an unbeliever, aptly observes, "How different the course and outcome of church history might have been . . . had the church's intellectual heroes been a little less heroic, had they more often deferred to those of their colleagues who were a little less intellectual!"[19]

Despite such prodigious efforts, it was never possible to achieve absolute consensus, and Christendom's posterity remains deeply divided: Roman Catholic and Arian in the West, Syrian or Assyrian (Nestorian) in the East, and Coptic Orthodox with Greek or Melkite, and Syrian Orthodox or Antiochene or Jacobite or Monophysite.[20]

"By Their Fruits"

In the course of Christendom, a goodly portion of what we have come to associate with the category "Christian" was derived from the use of the

---

15. MacMullen, *Voting about God*. Also see Pelikan, *Credo*.

16. MacMullen, *Voting about God*, 7. Cf. n. 10.

17. MacMullen provides a list of some 250 Synods between Carthage in AD 253 and Constantinople in AD 553.

18. In chapter 6 of *Constantine's Bible*, Dungan provides an overview of interventions made by Constantine that profoundly shaped Church polity, practice, status, and self-perception.

19. Ibid., 118.

20. The terminologies themselves are the invention of Western European church historians. See Brock, "'Nestorian' Church," 279–85.

Scriptures to legitimate, facilitate, and sustain political and military power, and to ensure the Church's privileges issuing from its accommodation to this power. It is within the cocoon of Christendom that the doctrinal assumptions and theological formulations of the missionary movement from the West were gestated. Even today the various Christian doctrines explaining what triggers God's salvific grace rely far more on the cogitations of our Christendom forebears than on what Jesus himself taught. As a result, it is not uncommon to hear "the Gospel" presented as though it were one thing, while "life in Christ" were quite another.[21] It is within the various currents and eddies of Christendom's powerful river that Western followers of Jesus have tried to keep from drowning spiritually.

Our Lord's own criteria for determining those who are his almost inevitably has to do with behavior rather than doctrine and prescribed religiosity. It is of no little significance that in all of his pronouncements on the final judgment, doctrinal correctness seems to play little, if any, role. Instead, judgment is rendered on the basis of personal qualities and relational behavior. God's people are those who do the will of the Father. Jesus even suggests that those welcomed into the kingdom of heaven may not be aware of the good they have done (Matt 25:31–46). This must surely be taken into account in our consideration of individuals or groups who do not self-identify as Christian but who behave like the men and women our Lord would find commendable.

What characterizes his followers, according to Jesus? Consider this partial list, based on his recorded teaching in the Gospel of Matthew: Restraint from murder; refusal to hate; fidelity in marriage; trustworthiness; compassion for enemies; openhanded generosity toward the destitute; genuine attention to the spiritual disciplines; simplicity of material wants; restraint from the idolatrous accumulation of possessions; simple and grateful trust in God as the supplier of all that is good and necessary to sustain life; generosity of spirit in our dealing with our protagonists; and persistence in prayer. In short, those who follow Jesus are expected to yield what Jesus calls "good fruit," building their lives upon the foundation modeled by him.

Given the extent to which the so-called Christian nations of the West have failed to yield good fruit, might not one legitimately conclude—as many Muslims and other observers frequently do—that Christendom itself is a rotten tree, a false prophet, or a house built upon the sand? If the behavioral standards outlined in St. Paul's famous fruit-of-the-Spirit passage (Gal 5:16–26) are normative for followers of Jesus, and if our Lord's own

---

21. Dallas Willard observes that many professed Christians practice "vampire Christianity." In effect, they say to Jesus, "I'd like a little of your blood, but I don't care to be your student" (*Great Omission*, 14).

frequently reiterated teaching is to be taken seriously, then old Christendom, and neo-Christendom cannot credibly claim to set the boundaries for what it means to be Christian. A tree is known by its fruit.[22]

Identifying Believers

For the greater part of human history, those whose faith has been credited to them as righteousness (Rom 4:3–8) have presented no uniform pattern of religious belief or practice, let alone knowledge of Jesus the Christ. Jesus was well aware that "many prophets and righteous men longed to see what you see but did not see it, and to hear what you hear but did not hear it" (Matt 13:17). But for those many, lack of direct knowledge of Christ did not diminish their standing before God. (Those who subsequently saw and heard Jesus were simply more privileged.)

To suggest today that there are people of saving faith who fall outside Western Christian boundaries can be very unsettling. Such ideas are "intellectually threatening, requiring the abandonment of too many certainties, the acquisition of too many new ideas and skills, the modification of too many maxims, the sudden irrelevance of too many accepted authorities. It [is] easier to . . . carry on with the old [theological] maps."[23]

God's grace has always been extended to his creation on the basis of pure mercy. There is nothing in the Hebrew and Christian Scriptures to suggest that this mercy is triggered solely by mental appropriation of insider theological information. Whether the beneficiaries of God's mercy are followers of Jesus, or simply righteous persons who would rejoice to see Jesus, the mercy they receive is the result of God's action, not ours. The Father sees the lives of "righteous men" through the cross of Christ, where the Lamb of God gave his life for "the sins of the whole world" (1 John 2:2).

The question is, How can we get behind the accepted wisdom of our traditions? How might our understanding of the mercy of God be affected

---

22. Many in the United States argue that religion is an essential component of societal health. Social surveys have found that the United States has the highest percentage of citizens "absolutely believing in God" (63 percent), regularly participating in religious services (39 percent), and engaging in prayer (60 percent). Yet in a survey conducted by the International Social Survey Programme, in a range of 1 to 10, the United States scored "0" (!). The clearly secular nations of Sweden, Denmark, and Germany achieved scores of 9.7, 9.1, and 10, respectively. See Paul, "Chronic Dependence," 398–441, online: http://www.epjournal.net/wp-content/uploads/EP07398441_c.pdf. (One is put in mind of James 2:14: "What good is it, my brothers, if a man claims to have faith but has no deeds?")

23. Walls, "Structural Problems," 150.

in connection with those who do not self-define as Christians? What is to be learned from some of the significant movements to Christ in the Muslim world and across the continent of Africa, movements that have eschewed the religion of Christendom? How might our missiological understanding and practice be rethought?

A key to this question may lie in the *direction* people are moving in relation to the revelation God has provided in particular times and places. Paul Hiebert illustrates the relevance of direction by posing a hypothetical case of a non-literate Hindu peasant who responds positively to the Gospel the first and only time he hears it:

> Imagine . . . Papayya, an Indian peasant, returning to his village after a hard day's work in the fields. His wife is preparing the evening meal, so to pass the time he wanders over to the village square. There he notices a stranger surrounded by a few curiosity-seekers. Tired and hungry, he sits down to hear what the man is saying. For an hour he listens to a message of a new God, and something he hears moves him deeply. Later he asks the stranger about the new way, and then, almost as if by impulse, he bows his head and prays to this God who is said to have appeared to humans in the form of Jesus. He doesn't quite understand it all. As a Hindu he worships Vishnu, who incarnated himself many times as a human, animal, or fish to save humankind. Papayya also knows many of the 330 million Hindu gods. But the stranger says there is only one God, and this God has appeared among humans only once. Moreover, the stranger says that this Jesus is the Son of God, but he says nothing about God's wife. It is all confusing to Papayya.
>
> The man turns to go home, and a new set of questions flood his mind. Can he still go to the Hindu temple to pray? Should he tell his family about his new faith? And how can he learn more about Jesus—he cannot read the few papers the stranger gave him, and there are no Christians in a day's walk. Who knows when the stranger will come again?[24]

The key question is this: "Can Papayya become a Christian after hearing the Gospel only once?" The answer must be yes, for as Hiebert puts it, "If a person must be educated, have an extensive knowledge of the Bible, or live a good life, the Good News is only for a few."

But one must take into account the *direction* of life.

Hiebert observes that human language typically maps the internal and external worlds by means of bounded-set and centered-set categories. A

---

24. Hiebert, *Anthropological Reflections*, 107–36.

bounded set is marked by characteristics that an object or event must display in order to be within the set. Thus, traditionally in the West Christians are recognized as they share a recognizable set of beliefs and standard of behavior; they fall within a familiar boundary.

A centered set, on the other hand, "is created by defining a center or a reference point, and the relationship of objects to that center."[25] Hiebert asks, Just what is it that incorporates Papayya into the Christian category? How comprehensive must the list of essential characteristics be? Which beliefs are essential? In what ways will Papayya be visibly different from his Hindu neighbors? What are the cognitive and behavioral boundaries that place him inside the set? As Papayya is drawn to Jesus, he is included in a centered set, participating with others who are focused on Jesus, however limited their current understanding.

In Jesus's own time, this was illustrated as publicans and sinners were drawn to him. Those who were preoccupied with the details of theology and its application to their lives were not. They were within a bounded set, effectively putting them on a course away from Christ. Finally, they arranged for his extermination. The faith of the former—expressed by their movement toward Christ—was credited to them as righteousness (Rom 4:3, 5). The self-righteousness of the latter took them in the opposite direction, to damnation.

IMPLICATIONS FOR MISSION

We come at last to the core question implicit in the title of this essay: What is the relationship between the Gospel and ethics?[26] To push this question to the limit, can the ethics of someone who is not self-defined as a Christian be "credited to him [or her] as righteousness"? Can someone who has never heard of Jesus—or who has heard such garbled, conflicted, and ethically compromised message as to make Christianity either incomprehensible or morally reprehensible—be saved? Is it possible for such a person to be on a life trajectory that aims at Christ the center without even being aware of it?

---

25. Ibid., 123.

26. Discrepancy between words and deeds gave rise to the Reformation, to which evangelicalism traces its roots. The title of a book by William Wilberforce, the most prominent Evangelical of his day, reflects awareness that the established churches of England were far from "Christian": *A Practical View of the Prevailing Religious System of Professed Christians, in the Higher and Middle Classes, Contrasted with Real Christianity*. For an account of evangelical social action in North America, see Magnuson, *Salvation in the Slums*; for Great Britain see Heasman, *Evangelicals in Action*. Also see Bradley, *Call to Seriousness*.

In light of the Scriptures discussed above, I am persuaded that there is abundant evidence for this understanding of God's mercy.

What might a more biblical understanding of the Gospel and ethics mean for evangelical theology and for the ways in which we proclaim the Good News?

What if the church synods had been as concerned about Christ-like behavior as with coherent, internally consistent doctrine? What if post-Constantinian Christianity had been as preoccupied with what Jesus taught as with what people should be permitted to think about him? What if instead of, or in addition to, a creed that distilled the doctrinal essence of Christianity, the council of Nicaea had formulated a manifesto or charter of Kingdom Citizenship—the identifying behavior of a follower of Jesus, based on what Jesus himself said? What if those charged with administering, defending, and expanding Christian territory had been as concerned about Christ-like behavior as they appeared to be about doctrinal beliefs and sacraments? What if the Church Fathers had wrestled as long and hard with the implications of our Lord's Sermon on the Mount as they did in puzzling out normative theories about the nature and work of the triune God?

Our answers to such questions profoundly influence our understanding of a sinner's standing before God, and the way that we proclaim the Good News of reconciliation with God through our Lord Jesus Christ. These answers also directly affect those of us who—because we are professionally religious people who make a living from maintaining and promoting our several versions of orthodoxy—easily slip into the error of the Pharisees, reifying our self-justifying pieties to such an extent that sometimes there is no room for God himself. When he comes among us, we get rid of him, because he is too unlike the god over whom we imagine ourselves to have achieved a theological monopoly.

Anyone familiar with powerfully hegemonic Western cultural forces and with the history of Western migrations, can appreciate how difficult it would be for a morally upright person in a Muslim culture to associate himself or herself with the category "Christian." All too often the term is associated with behavior that is inconsistent with Jesus's teachings. Who would want to identify himself or herself with a movement historically associated with violence, imperialism, slavery, economic and military hegemony, unjust treaties, pornographic arts, dysfunctional families, and greed?

The various unfamiliar Christian movements in the non-Western world may one day prove to have been God's way of preserving the true Church. Christians in the West have no monopoly on mercy, purity of heart, or peacemaking. Of course, those of us who call ourselves Christians should be at once recognizable by these identity tests of our Lord, but we have no exclusive monopoly on them. And when we see these qualities in persons whose geographical and social circumstances have not provided them with the luxury or opportunity to meet Jesus personally, we should nevertheless recognize them as brothers and sisters, bearing a distinct family resemblance to Jesus our Lord and Savior, whose advent, death, and resurrection they would rejoice to see! Of course, we should introduce them to Jesus, and invite them to be his disciples.

The most fundamental implication for missions is that we are called to *make disciples*; strictly speaking, we are not called to make Christians. (The word "disciple" occurs 269 times in the New Testament, while the word "Christian" occurs only three times. In Acts 11:26 "Christian" is a designation for disciples of Jesus who could no longer be regarded as simply another Jewish sect.) One is either a follower of Jesus, or one is not.

There can be no Christian conversion without ethical repentance and a life of steady transformation, until we are like him when we see him face to face. There is nothing in the teaching of Jesus that suggests the option of enjoying forgiveness at Jesus's expense, and then skipping his ethical demands. There is nothing in Scripture to suggest that the *belief* of faith and the *life* of faith are two different things—the first compulsory and the second optional. On the other hand, there is much evidence in our Scriptures that those who pursue righteousness are God's children, beneficiaries of his grace and mercy through Christ Jesus, whom, like Abraham, they long to see, and through the shedding of whose blood they, like Abraham, have redemption.

Missiologically, this takes us back to Jesus's original commission, not to make converts or save people, but to make disciples who—with us—learn of Jesus and from Jesus. Such an understanding will ensure a whole Gospel, alive with the life-transforming Good News of what Jesus did and what he promises to those who follow him as the way, the truth, and the life. There is a promise for those who follow Jesus in discipleship: *God is not ashamed to be called their God, for he has prepared a city for them*" (Heb 11:16).

CONCLUSION: FIVE QUESTIONS FOR THE TWENTY-FIRST CENTURY

1. Must we assume the timeless and universal legitimacy of the theological categories, emphases, and boundaries that have come to define the orthodoxies and practices of Christendom and neo-Christendom?

2. If so, what are we to make of Christocentric movements in parts of Asia and across Africa that do not qualify for inclusion in category "Christian" as recognized in the West?

3. Are there ways beyond mere shared vocabulary and religious culture of recognizing and acknowledging Christian affinity? In other words, can the "DNA" of God's people manifest itself in distinctive behavior that the Scriptures refer to as "righteous"? Is it possible to recognize and permissible to acknowledge a long-lost relative when we see one?

4. If so, how can churches and communions whose theologies are prescribed and proscribed by the doctrinal formulations of neo-Christendom accommodate and welcome those whose theologies put them outside the boundaries of "Christian" but whose behavior and direction mark them as kindred?

5. What do those of us involved in the documentation of Christian churches and movements do with such phenomenon? And missiologically, what does proclamation of the Good News then mean?

Finding and recognizing biblical answers to such questions requires revisiting the debates and their outcomes of the first five centuries of our Christian faith. This is one of the supreme missiological and theological challenges of the twenty-first century.

BIBLIOGRAPHY

Abramsky, Sasha. "Defining the Indefinable West." *Chronicle of Higher Education*, March 23, 2007.

Barbero, Alessandro. *Charlemagne: Father of a Continent*. Translated by Allan Cameron. Los Angeles: University of California Press, 2004.

Bradley, Ian C. *The Call to Seriousness: The Evangelical Impact on the Victorians*. New York: MacMillan, 1976.

Brock, S. P. "The 'Nestorian' Church: A Lamentable Misnomer." *Bulletin of the John Rylands Library* 78 (1966) 23–35.

Brown, Peter. *Augustine of Hippo: A Biography*. Los Angeles: University of California Press, 2000.

Dungan, David L. *Constantine's Bible: Politics and the Making of the New Testament*. Minneapolis: Fortress, 2006.

Heasman, Kathleen J. *Evangelicals in Action: An Appraisal of Their Social Work in the Victorian Era*. London: Bles, 1962.

Herrin, Judith. *The Formation of Christendom*. Princeton: Princeton University Press, 1987.

Hiebert, Paul G. *Anthropological Insights for Missionaries*. Grand Rapids: Baker Academic, 1985.

Holland, Tom. *The Forge of Christendom: The End of Days and the Epic Rise of the West.* New York: Doubleday, 2008.

Hoornaert, Eduardo. *The Memory of the Christian People.* Translated by R. R. Barr. Maryknoll, NY: Orbis, 1988.

Jørgensen, Jonas Adelin. "Jesus Imandars and Christ Bhaktas: Report from Two Field Studies of Interreligious Hermeneutics and Identity in Globalized Christianity." *International Bulletin of Missionary Research* 33 (2009) 171–76.

Kreider, Alan, editor. *The Origins of Christendom in the West.* Edinburgh: T. & T. Clark, 2001.

———. *Worship and Evangelism in Pre-Christendom.* Cambridge: Grove, 1995.

MacMullen, *Christianizing the Roman Empire.* Yale University Press, 1986.

———. *Voting about God in Early Church Councils.* New Haven: Yale University Press, 2006.

Magnuson, Norris. *Salvation in the Slums: Evangelical Social Work, 1865–1920.* Grand Rapids: Baker, 1990.

Paul, Gregory. "The Chronic Dependence of Popular Religiosity upon Dysfunctional Psychosociological Conditions." *Evolutionary Psychology* 7 (2009) 398–441.

Pelikan, Jaroslav. *Credo: Historical and Theological Guide to Creeds and Confessions of Faith in the Christian Tradition.* New Haven: Yale University Press, 2003.

Stark, Rodney. *The Rise of Christianity.* Princeton: Princeton University Press, 1996.

Walls, Andrew F. *The Missionary Movement in Christian History.* Maryknoll, NY: Orbis, 1996.

———. "Structural Problems in Mission Studies." *International Bulletin of Missionary Research* 15 (1991) 146–55.

Wilkin, Robert Louis. *The Spirit of Early Christian Thought: Seeking the Face of God.* New Haven: Yale University Press, 2003.

Willard, Dallas. *The Great Omission: Reclaiming Jesus' Essential Teachings on Discipleship.* San Francisco: HarperCollins, 2007.

Wilson, Derek. *Charlemagne.* New York: Doubleday, 2007.

18

World Christianity and the New Ecumenical Frontier

WILLIAM R. BURROWS

To PHILIP JENKINS GOES the prize for bringing "world Christianity" to the attention of the Christian and secular academies. Andrew Walls and Lamin Sanneh were the first to note the implications of the shift of balance in Christianity from the European and North American continents to Africa, Asia, Latin America, and Oceania. But Jenkins's *The Next Christendom: The Coming of Global Christianity* (New York: Oxford, 2002) created the splash that got that shift noticed. His book sparked the race of divinity schools, seminaries, colleges, and universities to hire men and women to teach world Christianity in their theology and religious studies departments. In addition, numerous historians and theologians in such schools added courses on the subject.

The present volume salutes the dedication of Tite Tiénou to the integrity of African Christianity and the process of forming workers in the Lord's global vineyard. I hope this brief contribution will shed some light on the relevance of Tiénou's concerns. Ultimately, those concerns involve the questions raised in this essay, and I see them to be of vital importance for world Christianity.

THE THEOLOGICAL ISSUE AT STAKE

World Christian studies is more of a field than a discipline. It entails a variety of approaches by specialists in several disciplines who enter into conversation to gain insight into the area of study. For the subject to serve Christian purposes, the horizon of world Christian studies must be at least implicitly theological. What is at stake in laying out the goals of the field requires response to three critical questions: (1) What does the new demographic shape of the Christian movement mean in regard to the mission of the church? (2) What does *that* say about the need to make the world Christian movement a global communion of churches with felt bonds of communion, churches that give witness to their Lord and are prepared to cooperate in the sharing of that witness and in the alleviation of suffering? (3) What is the role of human judgment in determining whether local churches exhibit the appropriate unity, catholicity, apostolicity, and holiness to merit inclusion in the Great Church?

THE PRIME GOAL: RECONCILIATION OF ALL IN CHRIST

In a 1998 issue of *Mission Studies* I proposed "reconciliation" as a major theme for the Church's mission in coming years.[1] The modern era of mission is finished, that is, finished in the sense that churches planted by foreigners are now to be found virtually everywhere. Therefore the question of mission is, What does God want these churches to be and do to be the sort of churches God calls into mission? Bring people to Christ, to be sure. And yes, there are at least four billion unbaptized people and untold millions of nominal Christians among the baptized. In that sense, the classic goal of mission—explicit conversion of non-believers to conscious acceptance of Jesus as the Christ—is never over and will never be completed.

The "reconciliation" of the world in God is a biblical concept encompassing both the discipling and servant dimensions of membership in the body of Christ. Reconciliation also brings to mind the second-century rabbinic Hebrew concept of *tikkun olam* ("repairing the world"). The present generation—including the Lausanne movement[2]—echoes *tikkun olam* as we embrace the human obligation to repair an earth threatened by environ-

---

1. Burrows, "Reconciling All," 79–98.

2. "All three [persons, society, creation] are broken and suffering because of sin; all three ... must be part of the comprehensive mission of God's people." Lausanne Movement, Capetown Commitment, part 1, section 7, "We Love God's World."

mental degradation. My concern is to see that both Christian proclamation and the Christian vocation of service are included in our concept of mission.

But in a broader sense the reconciling mission of the church in our globalizing world also necessitates reaching beyond the boundaries of the church in what the Pontifical Council for Interreligious Dialogue calls the "dialogue of life," which includes simple neighborliness and where "witness" is by informal example, not explicit.[3] Is there a danger that what I am saying will be interpreted as my being squeamish about the notion that the reconciliation we seek should be confined to being nice? Or that we should focus on earthly problem solving at the expense of working toward reconciliation between an estranged humanity and a loving God? Yes, there is that danger, but this is not what I am talking about. The mission of God is reconciliation, and discipleship is inherently directed to making manifest God's reconciling activity in Christ. I turn now to making that case.

FROM *MISSIO AD GENTES* TO *MISSIO INTER GENTES*

Communities founded in the modern missionary movement when foreigners came from outside in *missio* ad *gentes* ("mission *to* the nations"), are now themselves called to *missio* inter *gentes* ("mission *among* the nations"). That is to say, all are called to mission among families, fellow citizens, tribe members, worker circles and unions, and so forth. In addition, the former sending churches need today to carry on *missio inter gentes* in the midst of once-Christian peoples. We all know this, of course, and the man whom we celebrate in this volume, Tite Tiénou, knew it before most of us, for his work has long centered on the integrity of church life both *ad intra* ("within" the community) and *ad extra* ("outside" the community).

My question revolves around what this vision of mission means in a "world" Christian context. I think it comes into focus when one asks the following question: When we talk with our fellow Christians about our common mission, should we not be devoting efforts to making the world Christian movement resemble more and more a world church?

This is what Jesus was seeking when he spoke the words,

> My prayer is not for them alone. I pray also for those who will believe in me through their message, that all of them may be

---

3. See Pontifical Secretariat for Non-Christians, "Dialogue and Mission," 837–38 (para. 28–35 in original, *Acta Apostolicae Sedis* 84 [1984] 816–28). Pope John Paul II cites "Dialogue and Mission" at a crucial point in his 1991 encyclical on mission, *Redemptoris Missio* (para. 55).

> one, Father, just as you are in me and I am in you. May they also be in us so that the world may believe that you have sent me. I have given them the glory that you gave me, that they may be one as we are one: I in them and you in me. May they be brought to complete unity to let the world know that you sent me and have loved them even as you have loved me. (John 17:20–23)

For Jesus, unity is required if his followers are to give witness in deeply troubled times. At the time the Gospel was composed, the church in Asia Minor was enduring harsh persecution. It was in trouble with Roman authorities in large measure because it was using words like "savior" to refer to the mission and work of Jesus, a word that was supposed to be used only for Caesar. Eventually, of course, Christianity triumphed in Constantine's Edict of Milan in 313, and from that time forward the papacy developed from its then embryonic stage to its modern shape. From about 461 to 1000, an era that Eamon Duffy characterizes as the church "between two Empires,"[4] the papacy's role was understood quite differently in the West and the East. In the West the papacy donned as much imperial vestments and exerted as much power as local churches would tolerate. This is crucial for the non-Catholic members of today's world Christian movement. The pre-Reformation prophets such as John Wycliffe (1330–1384) and John Huss (1372–1414) and the better known Reformers of the sixteenth century demanded a return to an ecclesial shape warranted in the Scriptures. Like much of history, the Constantinian legacy is ambiguous, but Constantine was not the villain he is often portrayed to be.[5] Where Protestants are surely right is in their judgment that the papacy by the end of the middle ages and the beginnings of modernity scarcely resembled the office of the *vicarius Petri* ("vicar of Peter") of early centuries.

But the Reformers failed to reckon with two things. First, as the Reformation shifted into high gear, Protestant rejection of Catholic theological claims for legitimacy provoked Catholics to make those claims all the louder, and the Council of Trent centralized papal power as never before. Second, they could not foresee the fact that both in its Lutheran and Calvinistic forms, and under Henry the Eighth and the left-wing forms of Christianity, the Reformers had loosed currents of individualism that would dissolve the bonds of communion that the papacy sought to nurture and enforce.

---

4. Duffy, *Saints and Sinners*, 37–86.

5. Protestant historiography has generally interpreted the fatal departure of Catholicism from faithful primitive Christianity with the Edict of Milan (313). If a recent study is correct, however, the pre-Constantinian church was not a united, pacifist body of true Christians, and the evolution of medieval Catholicism and the papacy needs to be understood in a far more nuanced manner. See Leithart, *Defending Constantine*.

The dawn of the era of world Christianity brings all this into sharp relief and requires a theological response. What follows is one way of articulating that response.

MOVING BEYOND THE REFORMATION

In the late 1990s when Dale Irvin, Scott Sunquist, and I began planning a two-volume work entitled *The History of the World Christian Movement*, we were pushed toward an ad hoc theological reading of the signs of our times. The life trajectories of the three of us conspired to bring together three of the main strands of Western Christianity: Independency (Anabaptist-evangelical-pentecostal churches) in Dale; ecumenical (Presbyterian and World Council of Churches member churches) in Scott; and Roman Catholicism in Bill.[6] Each of us, moreover, had been profoundly affected by immersion in Asian, Melanesian, Latin American, African, and African-American strands of emergent world Christianity, which made us realize Western Christianity was simply *a* form of Christianity and extremely pluriform in its own right. We agreed that the history we wanted to record should emphasize the Christian movement as a whole, made up of discrete parts that interacted with the various cultures and religious traditions of humankind. We saw that the process of interaction with cultures and becoming embedded in them while attempting to turn them to Christ was basic to Christian life.

Finally, we believed that world Christianity should enter into a deeper self-understanding, namely, that the churches that comprise world Christianity are a kaleidoscopic sign of Christ's presence and action that none of them is singly. This is the leading theological idea that underpins our *History of the World Christian Movement*, a theme that we believe flows from the narrative, not one that is imposed upon it.[7]

Aided by grants from the Luce Foundation, we assembled a group of more than forty experts in various phases of Christian history and thought. At one of our earliest meetings, it became clear that if we were to end volume 1 in 1517, as in the case of most histories of Christianity, we would be beginning volume 2 in Wittenberg, giving the Reformation an importance it did not warrant. We decided that a much more natural division point was 1453, when Constantinople fell to the Muslim Turks and the process

---

6. We were also determined to give Orthodoxy in its ancient Eastern, Coptic-African, Greek-Byzantine, and Russian formations a position in our history that it seldom receives in standard histories of Christianity.

7. Irvin et al., *History of the World Christian Movement*, vol. 1 (*Beginnings to 1453*), was published in 2001; vol. 2 (*1453–1900*), in 2012.

of suppressing Christianity in western Asia and North Africa, begun in the seventh century, reached its apogee. The confrontation with Islam, we wanted to show, had begotten a Western Christendom that aligned itself with the crown and thought of itself as a "Christian civilization," an idea that would have great importance in shaping the modern missionary movement.

Thus, volume 2 begins in 1454 with the beginning of the Portuguese exploration of West Africa. Those voyages began the transatlantic slave trade, the modern missionary movement, the dismantling of the Eurocentrism of Christianity, and the attempt to bring non-European peoples under Western economic and military hegemony. For the first time humanity began to comprehend that the earth is a sphere. Meanwhile, within Europe, the Renaissance was moving into high gear and sparking not just the Reformation but also the introduction of new information technologies like printing, the growth of merchant classes that would spark the bourgeois revolution, and the rise of economies based largely on capitalism, trade, and banking, less so on lands owned by aristocracies. In addition, we determined that much more weight had to be given to reform movements that antedated the classic Reformations, movements that presaged the rise of the Anabaptists and Independents and from which would spring contemporary evangelical and pentecostal movements.

All this raises the question whether these many forms of Christianity comprise a pluriform reality that deserves being called a "world church" participating in a global *missio inter gentes*. The jury has yet to return a verdict. Yet the stubborn facts remain: first, Jesus prays for Christian unity so the world may believe; and, secondly, Christian unity is seriously less vital than it ought to be. The various churches, of course, have ways of explaining that each of them is in compliance with Jesus's teaching and the beneficiary of Jesus's prayer for unity, while deploring the shortcomings of others. I suspect, however, that we do our deploring with consciences nagging. Pope John Paul II seems to have had one of those moments in his encyclical on Christian unity *Ut Unum Sint* ("That They May Be One"). There he said two salient things about his own position. The first is somewhat traditional:

> The Catholic Church is conscious that she has preserved the ministry of the Successor of the Apostle Peter, the Bishop of Rome, whom God established as her "perpetual and visible principle and foundation of unity" and whom the Spirit sustains in order that he may enable all the others to share in this essential good. In the beautiful expression of Pope Saint Gregory the Great, my ministry is that of *servus servorum Dei* ["servant of the servants of God"]. (§88)

The second is little short of startling:

> As I acknowledged on the important occasion of a visit to the World Council of Churches in Geneva on 12 June 1984, the Catholic Church's conviction that in the ministry of the Bishop of Rome she has preserved, in fidelity to the Apostolic Tradition and the faith of the Fathers, the visible sign and guarantor of unity, constitutes a difficulty for most other Christians, whose memory is marked by certain painful recollections. To the extent that we are responsible for these, I join my Predecessor Paul VI in asking forgiveness (§88).

On the Roman Catholic side, everyone who has examined the history seriously realizes that what has been called the papal office has become more powerful in recent centuries. In the process, the authority it gained in early centuries by being acknowledged as the see founded by Peter and Paul, is quite different from the authority exercised by Pius IX in the First Vatican Council (1869–1870).

Evidence of that may be seen just five years after John Paul II wrote *Ut Unum Sint*. In 2000 he signed *Dominus Iesus* ("The Lord Jesus"), subtitled "Declaration on the Unicity and Universality of Jesus Christ and the Church." It was issued by the Congregation for the Doctrine of the Faith (CDF), then headed by Joseph Ratzinger, and the tone with which §16 reiterated Roman claims that the "Church of Christ . . . continues to exist fully only in the Catholic Church" caused heads to snap, making many wonder who was in charge and what were they trying to signal. In fact, the people at CDF were aiming their guns at *Catholics* who seemed to forget this teaching, while they themselves were tone deaf to the real change in tone and substance of inter-ecclesial relations brought about by ecumenical dialogues.

On the other hand, when *some* Evangelicals and Pentecostals declare that Catholics are not Christians, reciprocating attitudes like those in *Dominus Iesus,* it is clear that world Christianity is a long way from being a communion of churches whose members go out of their way to acknowledge their unity in the Spirit.

My next question naturally follows: If an imperial papacy cannot serve as a credible sign and instrument of communion among churches at the dawn of the era of world Christianity, what kind of ministry might bring about an appropriate change in tone? If it goes against the Roman grain to consider a Petrine ministry more like that of the early centuries, it goes just as much against the grain of churches that had to fight long and hard against Rome to even imagine a vicar of Saint Peter exercising leadership and having real authority over them. They imagine a world in which the Bible is the only authority; but at the same time they seem to ignore the incompatibility of the many readings of that book.

At another level altogether lies the fact that the "independent" branches of the Christian movement are today the most vital. But they have bred into their genetic structure an independent, entrepreneurial spirit without the sense of communion that a Martin Luther, a John Calvin, a Pope Paul III, or a Menno Simons had in their bones. Martin Luther sought to reform *the* church, not start a new one. I fear this is not true of independent churches, in whose numbers I include North American non-denominational churches and the self-initiated churches of Africa, Asia, and Latin America. These never had or have long ago cast off ties to the older churches.

Viewed from a sociological and historical perspective, these independent churches are part of an ad hoc networking model of affiliation with like-minded churches. And I am convinced that the older churches have much to learn from that model. Catholicism in particular often seems sclerotic and unable to adapt itself to new situations. For at their best the results of the Independents are shown in the dynamism that leads to huge numbers of house churches in places like China, the vital new churches of Africa, and the grassroots spread of Pentecostalism in Latin America. At its worst, however, some of the founders of these self-initiated independent churches are charlatans preaching a self-aggrandizing gospel of prosperity. This is no less dangerous than the deformations of the Christian message that occurred in Europe when adaptations to Germanic culture from the eighth century onward produced devotions to saints and indulgence practices that almost totally obscured Christ and his Gospel.

If we are to know what is truly authoritative for world Christians, we must learn to separate out the emanations of mere human authoritarianism.

CONCRETE RECOMMENDATIONS

What can be done to promote a sense of our being part of a world communion of churches? I make two recommendations. The first is that we meditate on the following words from St. John's Gospel: "It was not you who chose me, but I who chose you and appointed you to go and bear fruit that will last. Then the Father will give you whatever you ask in my name. This is my command: Love each other" (John 15:15–16).

We in our various churches must give up defining ourselves by our disagreements with one another. Let us replace that with a habit of heart and mind that always remembers we have been chosen and commissioned to bear fruit. The now-foundering Geneva-based ecumenical movement became a prolongation of Christendom concerns just as Christendom was coming to a screeching halt. The executives and leaders in Geneva got far out in front of their membership, advocating goals and programs that men and women of good will can legitimately disagree on. But the line from Geneva, as well as that from Rome, seemed unable to discern that distinction.

In a paragraph that speaks to the Christian reality that is far more complex than that recognized in Rome, Geneva, or Lausanne, the controversial historian Paul Johnson once said of the teaching of Jesus,

> [It is] more a series of glimpses or matrices, a collection of insights, rather than a code of doctrine. It invites comment, interpretation, elaboration, and constructive argument, and it is the starting point for rival, though compatible, lines of inquiry. It is not a summa theologica, or indeed ethica, but the basis from which an endless series of summae can be assembled. It inaugurates a religion of dialogue, exploration, and experiment. Its radical elements are balanced by conservative qualifications, there is a constant mixture of legalism and antinomianism, and the emphasis repeatedly switches from rigor and militancy to acquiescence and the acceptance of suffering. Some of this variety reflects the genuine bewilderment of the disciples, and the confusion of the evangelical editors to whom their memoires descended. But a great deal is essentially part of Jesus's universalist posture: the wonder is that the personality behind the mission is in no way fragmented but is always integrated and true to character. Jesus contrives to be all things to all men while remaining faithful to himself.[8]

Johnson himself may be controversial, but he has said something very true. In the context of a political-religious stew no less complicated than our own, the early church somehow managed to become the most numerous religious movement in the Mediterranean world. Within three centuries it had expanded into Assyria, Persia, India, and Upper Egypt, this despite immense theological plurality. Rodney Stark's work shows that this expansion took place despite these disagreements, in large part because Christians took care of both their fellow Christians and others during times of plague and danger and not because there was complete unity of doctrine.[9]

My second suggestion is this: In all our seminaries, adult education classes in congregations, clergy conferences, and conventions, let us take a new approach in telling the Christian story. The first part of that narrative

---

8. Johnson, *History of Christianity*, 29.
9. Stark, *Rise of Christianity*.

should be straightforward, a presentation of Christian origins and its history according to the best data available. If a pope is a scoundrel, let the story present the evidence. If a Reformer was happy to see an opponent burnt at the stake, present the evidence. If God's love was palpable in a given church, tell that story without respect to whether it is within my church. If missionaries in Congo were up to their ears in the slave trade, say so. But also let us tell the story of miracles both at Lourdes and in a Brazilian Assemblies of God church. Tell the stories of one's own saints and the saints of other people's churches. Let the reader make up his or her own mind. The story of one's particular church needs to be told but requires special care. Here the *theological* cannot be avoided. How, for example, did the papacy, the Anabaptist movement, and Anglicanism begin and why? But another chapter is needed. Can the story be told both from within, say, a Mennonite perspective and from the point of view of the Lutheran or Catholic persecutors? Can Catholics present their self-understanding in ways that their historians can recognize while explaining in accurate, sympathetic terms the splitting off of the Orthodox and the Protestants? Can Baptists do the same? African Methodist Episcopals?

Specialists, of course, know that much in the history of their respective denominations undermines its claims to uniquely genuine status. But presenting the other side's point of view as sympathetically as possible, along with its genuine charisms,[10] does not need to undercut self-understanding and love of one's own community. It would, by contrast, advance a view of Christian pluriformity not as a deformity or as an invitation to ecclesial relativism. No. In the spirit of Johnson's observations, let us be faithful to the dynamic incarnated in Jesus, whose teaching was "the starting point for rival, though compatible lines of inquiry" as well as "dialogue, exploration, and experiment." At the same time, the relative adequacy of developments in particular churches need to be the subject of discussion and the testing of spirits.

It will not always be pleasant. Paul's letter to the Romans shows that even at the start there were tensions. The Roman church was, in fact, a congeries of communities. He writes to communities that, despite being baptized in Christ, are not living up to their vocation. To them he gives both

10. In Catholic parlance, a charism is a special gift of the Spirit that inspires a movement such as a religious community or underlies a saint's particular gifts. It is given not to benefit the individual or his or her followers but for the church as a whole as a revelation of God's power and wisdom incarnated here and now in this concrete situation. The genius of Catholicism, when respect for charisms is not squashed, results in creativity and initiative being furthered, self-aggrandizing "enthusiasm" being curbed, and splitting away from the larger church being avoided. See Sullivan, *Charisms and Charismatic Renewal*, and Azevedo, *Consecrated Life*, esp. ch. 1 on vocation in biblical perspective, 1–12.

straightforward moral exhortation and a reminder that their righteousness comes from being rooted in Christ, not from their own works.

The whole is summed up in a peroration from chapter 12 to the end, urging the communities to become a church presenting their members' entire being to God in spiritual worship, not conformed to the world but renewed in their minds, "so that [they] may discern what is the will of God—what is good and acceptable and perfect" (12:1–2). He is telling the communities of Rome that no one should think more highly of themselves than of others. Once one realizes that the many communities of Rome were being called to be one church, I think my second practical suggestion takes on new importance in the context of world Christianity. We might then rejoice that the charisms of every genuine church are given to make Christ alive. Let our common mission be responded to by the many communities. Let us nurture global bonds of solidarity, recognizing that the test of authenticity for any local church is that of Galatians 5:13–22, Paul's meditation on the fruits of the Spirit: love, joy, peace, patience, kindness, generosity, faithfulness, gentleness, self-control. This is the key to bringing about the reconciliation of the world to God as God makes his appeal to the world through us (2 Cor 5:19–21).

And the question that brings it into focus is simple, even if hard to implement: Do the efforts of *my* church in its educational and Bible study programs promote a Galatians 5 mindset in regard to other churches? If we manage to promote this sort of attitude—without giving in to a mindless "let-one-thousand-flowers-bloom" mushiness—a world church dedicated to mission has a much better chance to emerge from world Christianity.

BIBLIOGRAPHY

Azevedo, Marcello. *The Consecrated Life: Crossroads and Directions*. Translated by Guillermo Cook. Maryknoll, NY: Orbis, 1995.

Burrows, William R. "Reconciling All in Christ: The Oldest New Paradigm for Mission." *Mission Studies* 15 (1998) 79–98.

Duffy, Eamon. *Saints and Sinners: A History of the Popes*. New Haven: Yale University Press, 1997.

Irvin, Dale T., et al., editors. *History of the World Christian Movement*. Vol. 1, *Beginnings to 1453*. Vol. 2, *1453–1900*. Maryknoll, NY: Orbis, 2001 & 2012.

Johnson, Paul. *A History of Christianity*. New York: Atheneum, 1980.

Leithart, Peter J. *Defending Constantine: The Twilight of an Empire and the Dawn of Christendom*. Downers Grove, IL: InterVarsity, 2010.

Stark, Rodney. *The Rise of Christianity: A Sociologist Reconsiders History*. Princeton: Princeton University Press, 1996.

Sullivan, Francis A. *Charisms and Charismatic Renewal*. Ann Arbor, MI: Servant, 1982.

19

Funerary Rites and Ancestral Roles in Japan

Reassessing Their (Non-)Religious Character

How Chuang Chua

IN THE EARLY 1980s a Japanese medical encyclopedia suggested that one reason people suffer from an unsound mind is that they or their parents have not fulfilled their obligations to their ancestors.[1] The press had a field day when a high ranking bureaucrat from the prime minister's office donated a copy of the book to a hospice. Whatever motive the author might have had in making what was viewed by many as a preposterous statement, the incident shows that even among educated Japanese, ancestral veneration is viewed not as a relic of a superstitious past but as an important tradition that deserves continuing observance.

Indeed, caring for the dead and revering the ancestors are still very much a constitutive part of the modern Japanese psyche. However, with the rapid modernization of postwar Japan, there appears to be a gradual decline in the *religious* significance of ancestral practices.[2] At the same time, the psychological and socio-cultural aspects of ancestral veneration, which

---

1. Horikoshi, *Nihonjin no kokoro to kirisutokyō*, 81–82.
2. Morioka, "Ancestor Worship," 207–12.

have for too long been hiding in the shadows of its religious meanings, are beginning to surface.

This essay seeks to show the state of current research and clarify the key issues involved in the study of funerary and ancestral practices in Japan, and posits the thesis that the non-religious functions of the ancestral tradition are a key reason that these practices have such an enduring character even in modern Japanese society.

THE PLACE OF THE DEPARTED DEAD IN JAPANESE CONSCIOUSNESS

One of the most frequently cited sources of data on Japanese religious practices is the NHK National Survey on Modern Japanese Consciousness.[3] The 2008 survey shows that 68% of the respondents visit their family grave at least once a year. What is interesting is that this figure has not changed much from that of the previous seven surveys: 62% in 1973; 65% in 1978; 68% in 1983; 65% in 1988; 70% in 1993; 68% in 1998; and 68% in 2003.[4]

According to figures from various other sources, approximately 60% of Japanese households have a *butsudan* (Buddhist family altar), where deceased family members are memorialized.[5] An equal number have a *kamidana* (Shinto god shelf), that enshrines household Shinto deities. Only 25% have neither, and about 45% have both. In addition, Mark Mullins cites these findings from the 1983 NHK survey: 60% of the respondents affirmed feeling "a deep spiritual connection with the ancestors," and 28% said they performed rites for the ancestors before the family altar every day.[6] These statistics are indeed consistent with the results from all the NHK national surveys conducted from 1973 to 2008. It can be concluded that visiting the family grave is the most widely practiced "religious" (*shūkyōteki*) activity in Japanese society today, being observed by about two-thirds of the population. It is clear that even among modern Japanese, there is still a rather strong consciousness of continuing family ties beyond death.

The spirits of the dead venerated in Japan include more than just the ancestors. In a key article on how Japanese traditionally understand the role

---

3. NHK stands for Nihon Hōsō Kyoku, the government-owned Japan Broadcasting Corporation. The national survey, first launched in 1973, is conducted every five years by the NHK Cultural Studies Institute.

4. NHK Cultural Studies Institute, *Gendai Nihonjin no ishiki kōzō*, 133.

5. See Swyngedouw, "Religion in Contemporary," 4–5; Yanagawa, *Seminā shūkyōgaku Kōgi*, 12; and Mullins, *Christianity Made in Japan*, 131.

6. Mullins, *Christianity Made in Japan*, 131.

of the dead in the family, anthropologist David Plath distinguishes three categories of spirits who could become objects of veneration: the recently departed, ancestors proper, and outsiders.[7]

The Recently Departed

The first category includes spirits of household members who died in recent memory, and secondarily, souls of recently deceased non-members whom the living choose to honor. The spirits of the recently departed (*shirei* or *shiryō*) are customarily venerated through an elaborate set of Buddhist rituals so that they can, over time, attain the status of ancestral spirit (*sorei*). Mourning takes place over the course of forty-nine days, at the end of which a Buddhist ceremony is performed to confer on the deceased a posthumous Buddhist name. The name is written on a memorial tablet which is then placed on the family altar. The spirit of the deceased is believed to reside in the tablet, and family members can afterwards venerate or pray to the spirit at the altar.

What is also commonly practiced is the observance of the third death anniversary. And then there is, of course, the annual visit to the family grave around the summer solstice in August, the two equinoxes, and usually around New Year's Day. Notwithstanding the great variation in practice, traditionally, the thirty-third or fiftieth anniversary of death is chosen for the final memorial service, after which the individual spirit is believed to have become an ancestral spirit and joins the pantheon of gods and other ancestors.[8] The individualized memorial tablet is then disposed of, and the spirit fades from living memory.

However, it is doubtful whether individualized memorial observances beyond the third anniversary are widely observed today in view of the fast-paced modernization and secularization of the country. The important point to note is that as long as they are remembered personally by those who venerate them, the departed are *never* referred to as ancestors.[9]

---

7. Plath, "Where the Family of God," 301–4.
8. Takeda, *Sosen sūhai*, 104; Smith, *Ancestor Worship*, 96.
9. Unfortunately, in the literature, the word "ancestors" is often indiscriminately used to refer to the spirits of all dead family members, even if they have just died. Greater caution needs to be exercised here.

Ancestors, the Long Dead

The second category consists of all the regular members of the household who died long ago and who have been expunged from living memory. These are ancestors in the truest sense of the word. This category does not include non-members, who presumably retire to join the ancestors of their own family line or else are relegated to the third category. The key point here is that the category "ancestor" is not a particularizing concept but a generalizing one. Chōshū Takeda puts it well: "Spirits of family members retain their uniqueness for a set interval of death, but in time they are sacralized, shed their individuality and the pollution of death, and are assimilated into the collectivity of ancestors of the *ie* [household]."[10]

In other words, when Japanese people use either *senzo* or *sosen* to refer to their ancestors, they always do so in the collective sense. Even though they are given respect as suprahuman beings, the ancestral spirits do not necessarily have individual names or personalities.

This generalized conception of the ancestors concurs well with the practical reality that, with the exception of members of the Imperial House and some aristocratic families, most Japanese do not know the names and histories of their family members beyond the third or fourth generation preceding them.

The Spirits of Outsiders

The third category of spirits to be venerated, according to Plath, are the spirits of outsiders who are not affiliated with any family line, or whose line has lapsed without any descendants, as well as souls of dead guests. These wandering spirits (*muenbotoke*, literally, "spirits with no ties") are deprived of comfort, hence potentially dangerous.[11] If the person had died under conditions of deep sorrow or suffering, his or her spirit could become vengeful, and therefore needs to be appeased through special rituals.

In sum, although various spirits of the dead could be venerated, ancestors occupy a very specific category in the Japanese mind.

---

10. Takeda, "'Family Religion,'" 136.
11. Plath, "Family of God," 304.

FOUR APPROACHES TO STUDYING JAPANESE ANCESTRAL RITES

For some unexplained reason, serious scholarship on the subject of ancestral veneration in Japan began only after World War II. Western studies on the subject before that are not only sparse but problematic in that they portray Japanese ancestral veneration as little more than an aberration of orthodox Chinese practice.[12] This stereotypical interpretation of Japanese ancestral practices was exposed as erroneous through the work of four important Japanese scholars: Kunio Yanagita,[13] Ichirō Hori,[14] Kizaemon Ariga,[15] and Chōshū Takeda.[16] Two common themes run through the works of these scholars: first, Japanese ancestral practices are rooted in Japanese folk religion that predates the arrival of Buddhism Japan;[17] and second, ancestral practices in Japan cannot be understood without a proper knowledge of the nature and significance of the Japanese family.

Indeed Western scholarship on Japanese ancestral practices today owes a huge debt to these four scholars. Most contemporary studies focus on one of four areas, each of which is discussed below. These four areas are neither discrete nor mutually exclusive, and one would therefore expect to find overlapping relationships between them.

Ancestral Veneration as a Religious Phenomenon

First, much scholarly interest is to be found in the ritualistic aspects of ancestral practices and the religious meanings these rituals signify. This is especially true of most of the work produced in the 1970s. Anthropologist Robert Smith's seminal work, *Ancestor Worship in Contemporary Japan*, is a prime example of this approach. To be fair, Smith, while tracing the historical development of ancestral practices in Japan, did correctly identify the systematic politicization of these practices from the Tokugawa period in the

---

12. See, e.g., Lay, "Japanese Funeral Rites," 507–44; Duyvendak, "Buddhistic Festival," 39–48.
13. Yanagita, *About Our Ancestors*.
14. Hori, *Minkan Shinkō*.
15. Ariga, "Nihon ni okeru senzo no kannen," 1–33.
16. See Takeda, *Sosen sūhai*.
17. The misconception that Japanese ancestral rites are derived wholly from Buddhism persists even today in some circles. One only needs to look at Indian and Chinese Buddhism to realize that Buddhism has indeed little to say about the ancestors.

seventeenth century until the end of the World War II.[18] He also discussed at length the future of ancestral practices in light of the changing structure of the Japanese family.[19] But the assumption underlying Smith's work is unambiguously clear; namely, that ancestral veneration is a *wholly* religious phenomenon. This is most evident in the unqualified way Smith uses the expression "ancestor worship" throughout his book, beginning with its title. In fact, the confidence with which Smith expresses his position is rather unnerving: "I have no doubt that the family's dead are its gods. Like all gods they are worshiped and petitioned."[20]

Smith's description of the funeral rites and memorial ceremonies is undeniably rich and fascinating. However, it is hard to argue that these are not religious in nature. Strictly speaking, they are pre-ancestral rather than ancestral, for these are rites of passage to ensure that the spirits of the departed achieve ancestral status at some future time. The veneration of true ancestors as a collective whole is given scant treatment. Strictly speaking, the term "ancestor worship" as used by Smith, is a misnomer, because its limited reference is generally and uncritically applied to the whole ancestral phenomenon.[21]

Moreover, Smith seems to imply that the religious nature of the rites invariably reflects the religious motives of the person performing them.[22] The relationship between the two, however, is not so clear. Smith insists that "the crux of the matter" is that the Japanese pray *to* the ancestors as well as *for* them, "depending on the category of the deceased and on the ritual context."[23] This, of course, begs the question as to what the act of praying entails.[24] That aside, Smith's distinction between "praying to" and "praying

---

18. Smith, *Ancestor Worship*, 20–38.

19. Ibid., 219–26.

20. Ibid., 146.

21. For our purpose, we will use the terms "ancestral veneration," "ancestral rites," and "ancestral practices" to cover the gamut of funeral and memorial rites, as long as we keep in mind the technical distinction between ancestral spirits and other spirits, including pre-ancestral spirits.

22. Smith, *Ancestor Worship*, 218.

23. Ibid.

24. In the last scene of the Steven Spielberg's 1998 movie *Saving Private Ryan*, James Ryan, an old man, stood before the tombstone of Captain John Miller who, during World War II, sacrificed his life to save Private Ryan in the frontlines of a battle. In that moving scene, the old man Ryan fixed his gaze on the tombstone and made an extended speech: "My family is with me today. They wanted to come with me. To be honest with you, I wasn't sure how I'd feel coming back here. Every day I think about what you said to me the day on the bridge. And I've tried to live my life the best I could. I hope that was enough. I hope that at least in your eyes, I've earned what all of you have done for

for" implies a relationship of interdependence between the living and their ancestors. On the one hand, the ancestral spirits "exercise direct tutelary functions" on behalf of the living; on the other, the spirits depend on the living for comfort and support.[25] The question is: *To what extent do Japanese people today construe the relationship with their ancestors in such religiously motivated terms?* We will return to this question later.

Still, it cannot be denied that the spiritist-religious framework that Smith works with has provided us with an unsurpassed and intricate exposition on Japanese folk beliefs surrounding the dead and on how these beliefs shaped the different ways their spirits are to be approached. For this reason, Smith's work could arguably be considered the most important resource in the English language to date on the subject of ancestral veneration as a religious phenomenon. Indeed, Smith's work has greatly influenced missiological thinking in a particular direction.

Another scholar who takes a prominently religious view of Japanese ancestral practices is Herman Ooms. Although he acknowledges that Japanese ancestral practices do not quite fit into Clifford Geertz's definition of religion as a system of symbols that formulates "conceptions of a general order of existence,"[26] Ooms regards ancestral rites nonetheless as "a religious phenomenon which has more modest ambitions."[27] He rightly locates the center of ancestral practices in the particular concept of the Japanese household (*ie*), whose membership includes both living descendants and departed ancestors.[28] For Ooms, "the *ie* is a spiritual community, and ancestor worship is its religion."[29] Through his interviews with his subjects, Ooms concludes that the religious dimension in ancestral practices is not to be found in the expectation of either blessings or punishments from the ancestors but rather in the experience of an emotion or an encounter.[30]

Three levels of experience are distinguished, depending on the level of intimacy between the worshiper and the ancestors. The first level is

---

me." (Captain Miller's last words to Private Ryan were "Earn this. Earn it," referring to Ryan's life that he had saved.) The scene ended with Ryan saluting the tombstone. Now, some Japanese Christians have expressed difficulty in understanding why missionaries have no problems with Ryan's speech, even finding it stirring, and do not see this as idolatrous prayer or worship, since Japanese people talk to their deceased in a similar way.

25. Smith, *Ancestor Worship*, 145.
26. Geertz, *Interpretation of Cultures*, 98.
27. Ooms, "Structural Analysis," 61–90.
28. Ibid.
29. Ibid., 71.
30. Ibid., 74–77.

brought about by "official contact," and limits the religious experience of the worshiper to only "a feeling of fulfillment of duty."[31] At this level, the person does not feel the ancestors' presence at all, but is still motivated to participate in the religious rites out of a deep sense of obligation and a desire to express thankfulness for benefits received from the ancestors when they were alive. The second level of encounter is the experience of the awareness of the ancestors' presence.[32] And the third, and most intimate, encounter is one of mutual awareness of each other's presence. Here the person is not only aware of the ancestors' presence but is at the same time conscious that they notice and care for him or her.[33]

Ooms predicts that with increasing secularization, people experiencing the second and third levels of encounter will become fewer and fewer over time, but "ancestor worship" will persist, as it still provides a legitimate frame through which people are able to cope with the fundamental human problem of death.[34] Ooms considers this aspect of the ancestor rites "religious" as well, simply because it deals with the existential dilemma of human mortal existence.

> [The ancestor cult] gives order to the inevitable fact of death and by the same token orders life: everyone is destined to become an ancestor. The order is structured as a process where the stages leading to this final purpose of life are clearly outlined (memorial services, steps on the path of ancestorhood). Everyone finds himself in due time on the appropriate stage.[35]

Two comments are in order here. The first relates to the three levels of experience that Ooms posits with regard to the ancestors. While the second and third level of encounter can be legitimately understood as religious, there is doubt as to how at the first level, "a feeling of fulfillment of duty," no matter how strong, could be regarded as religious, especially when "an experience of the ancestors, in whatever form it might be, is absent."[36] Next, to view the ancestral rites as "religious" just because they offer a mechanism to cope with death is highly suspect. All societies have culturally-conditioned ways of coping with death, but can it be assumed that they are all therefore necessarily religious in content? While his analysis of the Japanese ancestral rites on the whole is original and thought provoking, by considering a priori

31. Ibid., 74.
32. Ibid.
33. Ibid.
34. Ibid., 84–85.
35. Ibid., 87.
36. Ibid., 76–77.

ancestor rites as "worship" in the religious sense, Ooms leaves himself with little room to maneuver beyond a strictly religious interpretation.

A Historical Approach to Understanding Ancestral Roles

The second approach to the subject of ancestral practices in Japan is historical, whereby the origins of ancestral beliefs and rites are investigated and their development traced diachronically. Ancestral practices are not understood as a static set of received tradition. Rather, the ancestral cult went through a process of metamorphosis as it encountered socio-political and religious forces at different periods in the history of Japan. The actual origins of Japanese ancestral practices are unclear. Indeed, there are many competing theories, none of which is conclusive.[37] Nonetheless, most scholars agree that Japanese ancestral practices are rooted in folk beliefs. What is indisputable is that the ancestors have always occupied an important place in Japanese primal consciousness.[38]

In a careful study of three ancient Japanese texts, *Kojiki* [Record of Ancient Matters], completed AD 712, *Nihon Shoki* [Chronicles of Japan], completed AD 720, and *Shinsen Shōjiroku* [New compilation of register of families], completed AD 815, Richard Miller shows that in the eighth and early ninth centuries ancestry played an important role in defining the social and political hierarchy of the noble clans, even if many of the lineages on record were shrouded in myth rather than historical fact.[39] On this latter point, there is evidence to suggest that some of the genealogies were manufactured "to fit a certain political and social scheme of things."[40] Miller also notes that the three ancient sources have little to say about the worship of ancestors.[41] This is noteworthy, considering that Confucianism came to Japan from China at the end of the fourth century, a full 300 years before the complete compilation of the *Kojiki*. With its emphasis on filial piety and respect for the ancestors, one would have expected Confucianism to play a key role in shaping Japanese ancestral practices. Yet the silence of the ancient texts with regard to ancestral rites and rituals is revealing. It is

---

37. See, for instance, Ariga, "Nihon ni okeru senzo no kannen"; Hori, "Manyōshū ni arawareta sosei," 49–93; Hall, "Monarch for Modern Japan," 11–64; Enns, "'Making All Things,'" 55–84. See also Smith, *Ancestor Worship*, 6–12, for a helpful overview of some of the theories of how Japanese ancestral veneration came about.
38. Shibata, "Some Problematic Aspects," 39.
39. Miller, "Ancestors and Nobility," 163–75.
40. Ibid., 175.
41. Ibid.

apparent that even in ancient Japan, ancestry was not only a religious matter, but perhaps valued more for its socio-political significance.

The most significant historical development with regard to ancestral practices is the decisive influence of Buddhism. Although Buddhism came to Japan via the Korean Peninsula in AD 538, it remained basically the religion of the elite for the next 500 years or so. It was not until the Kamakura Period (1185–1333) that Buddhism saw itself transformed into a popular religion. The so-called Great Kamakura Buddhist Transformation helped common people find a way to take care of the ritual pollution that was then associated with Japanese burial rites. Until then, people lived in fear of harmful spirits that might attach themselves to the rotting corpse.

The potential harm that the polluted dead could cause the living seems to have been derived from an ancient Shinto myth recorded in the *Kojiki* and *Nihon Shoki*, in which the god Izanagi was stalked by eight ugly females after he looked at the hideous and maggot-eaten corpse of his dead wife Izanami.[42] To neutralize the danger of being haunted by the spirits of the dead, Buddhism provided new structural rituals to care for them. In particular, two new funerary practices were introduced: memorial services to pacify the souls of the departed, and disposal of corpses by the purifying process of cremation.[43] The spirit of the dead became referred to as *hotoke*, literally "Buddha," a development unique to Japanese Buddhism. This appellation was intended to convey the notion that ancestral spirits are worthy of homage, but it seems, unwittingly, to have given the ancestors a new elevated status of enlightened deity.[44] In any case, Japanese mortuary rites were completely transformed, and Buddhist funeral rites, with some variation, continue until this day.[45]

Socio-political factors also contribute to the way Japanese people approach their ancestors. Paul Varley writes, "One of the most conspicuous features of the transition from medieval to early modern (Tokugawa) times in Japan was the precipitous decline in vigor of Buddhism."[46] In its stead was a great revival in Confucianism. Buddhism became relegated to a status of a caretaker religion dealing with funeral and memorial practices. So detrimental were the effects of the neo-Confucian reaction against Buddhism in

---

42. Goodwin, "Shooing the Dead," 65.

43. Ibid.

44. This particular instance of language shaping theology is still very much conjectural. On this point, see Berentsen, "Ancestral Rites," 10–12.

45. See Goodwin, "Shooing the Dead," 63–76, for an excellent and historical account of how the ancestors came to be venerated in medieval Japan as the result of the Great Kamakura Buddhist Transformation.

46. Varley, *Japanese Culture*, 151.

Tokugawa Japan that even today, many so-called Japanese Buddhists know little more than a "funeral Buddhism."[47]

The contribution of Confucianism to Japanese ancestral rites cannot be denied, but as suggested earlier, its influence seems to have come at a rather late stage despite its presence in the country from the end of the fourth century. Nonetheless, its emphasis on filial piety provides yet one more compelling reason why ancestors should be revered.[48] Nobuyuki Kaji further claims that the Japanese attachment to the bones of the deceased is derived from the Confucian thought that the bones constitute the source of *kō* (filial piety), thus symbolizing the regeneration and continuation of the ancestral lineage.[49] This idea, however, is somewhat alien to Chinese and Korean Confucianism. In sum, suffice it to say that while ancestral veneration has its genesis in Japanese folk religion, it was Buddhism that provided its religious structure, Confucianism its ethical basis.

Next, the Meiji period saw the politicization of the ancestral cult when a policy was briefly implemented in 1868 to bind Buddhism to emperor worship through domestic ancestral rites.[50] The government promoted the idea of *kokutai*, "based on the theory that Japan is a patriarchal state, all of whose people are related to one another and to the emperor, who is the supreme father."[51] For a time, the ancestors once again enjoyed not only religious, but also political significance. But it was only a short time. As he grew in power, Emperor Meiji began to invoke the Sun Goddess, the supreme Shinto deity, as the progenitor of the imperial lineage, and the cult of emperor worship was instituted. The corresponding rise of national Shinto in the late nineteenth century greatly marginalized the political influence of Buddhism. In fact, the Meiji government tried to divest Buddhism of its funerary role, intending to transfer it to Shinto, but failed. Such was the stronghold that Buddhism had—and still exerts—on the people in funerary matters.[52]

Another key development in the Meiji period was the Civil Code of 1898, which reinforced ancestral practices at the domestic level by

47. Indeed, most Buddhist temples in Japan are financially dependent on income derived from funerals and memorial rituals. See Enns, "Making All Things New," 57; Smith, *Ancestor Worship*, 214.

48. See Hori, "Appearance of Individual Self-Consciousness," 201–27; Varley, *Japanese Culture*, 152.

49. Kaji, *Jukyō to wa nani ka*, 9–21.

50. Smith, *Ancestor Worship*, 29.

51. Ibid., 26.

52. It is interesting to note that to this day, the Imperial Family is one of the very few Japanese families that observe Shinto funeral rites.

designating the oldest son as the heir and keeper of the family grave and genealogical records. Among the siblings, the eldest son was the only one who was forbidden by law to leave the household by marrying out, or by being adopted by another family. His inheritance included not only property but also the responsibility for the succession of the household and the continuing care of the ancestors.[53] It was only after the end of World War II that the Civil Code of 1947 legalized the equal inheritance of property. However, social expectations that the oldest son and his family will inherit the family altar and perform the ancestral rites remain largely unchanged to this day.

Ancestral Rites as Illuminated by Their Familial Functions

Besides focusing on the religious and historical aspects of the subject, many, especially Japanese scholars, take a third approach of viewing ancestral practices as fulfilling important familial functions. Takeda believes that any study on the subject of Japanese ancestral veneration must begin with the premise that the life of the Japanese family is "based religiously and socially upon ancestor worship."[54] The traditional Japanese family system, the *ie*, constitutes the basic unit of Japanese society, with each family having its own genealogy. The *ie* is to be understood as "a vertical lineage consisting of member families, living and dead, which are all related by blood and collaterally."[55] The rule of descent governing the *ie* is patrilineal, although exceptions are made to ensure its succession without break, either by adoption or by having a son-in-law assume the family name.[56] It is clear that the succession of the *ie* lineage takes priority over the matter of blood connection.

The ancestors are regarded as the root source of the *ie* line, and as such they are the ultimate guarantors of the family's well-being through the generations. Takeda makes the interesting point that in this regard, "'ancestor' is not an existential concept (Being) but a postulate (Having to Be) conception of an entity that cannot not be."[57] This fits well with Takeda's other observation, mentioned earlier, that ancestors, as a collective postulate, do not need individual names and personalities once they pass out of memory.[58] The understanding of the ancestors as the postulated primal source of the *ie*

53. See Hozumi, *Ancestor-Worship*.
54. Takeda, "Family Religion," 119.
55. Ibid.
56. Ibid.
57. Ibid., 137.
58. Ibid.

means that the *ie* in turn is obligated to honor them. Indeed, as the primary domain of relationships in Japanese life, consisting of both the living and the living dead, the *ie* has the crucial function to maintain harmony with the dead through observing various rituals and memorials. Takeda maintains that even in modernized Japan, it is unwise to separate the Japanese family and the "family religion" of ancestral veneration, for they belong together as an intact whole.[59]

Kiyomi Morioka lists four principal functions of ancestral veneration within the traditional context of the *ie*: 1) status authentication of the present head of the household as its legitimate successor; 2) stabilization of intergenerational relations through the ethics of filial piety; 3) unification of kin (in the legal sense); and 4) strengthening motivation for household continuation.[60]

Notwithstanding the endurance of the *ie* system in the more traditional parts of the country, it is important to note the radical legal and social transformation of the *ie* after World War II, especially with the abrogation of primogeniture.[61] Along with urbanization comes the rise of nuclear families and a sharp drop in birth rates. Morioka notes that the focus of the Japanese family today is placed on the husband-wife relationship, with the inevitable consequence that the notion of the *ie* continuing over generations has all but evaporated.[62] But the ancestors are not to be marginalized in any way. Morioka offers the further insight that along with the changing structure of the family, ancestral veneration as supported by the family has also changed, not only in its ceremonial aspects but also in the very concept of the ancestor.[63] On the latter, Morioka describes a conceptual shift as "a change from a unilineal view which includes distant ancestors beyond even indirect experiences, to say nothing of direct personal contact, to a concept which limits ancestors to close kin within the range of direct experience, but extends bilaterally; and as such a change from an obligatory concept which should include all the dead on one's descent line regardless of personal preference, to an optional one which limits ancestors to the deceased close kin whose memories are cherished by the offspring."[64]

---

59. Ibid., 127.
60. Morioka, "Ancestor Worship," 202–3.
61. Ibid., 204.
62. Ibid.
63. Ibid., 203–9.
64. Ibid., 206.

It is evident that with this new understanding of the ancestor comes a change of function in ancestral practices. Morioka believes that the four social functions mentioned above are being replaced, at least in part, by more personal and psychological functions such as the quest for solace and inner peace through "an affectionate reminiscence of the dead."[65] As can be expected, the increasing dominance of personal functions has led to a more informal and privatized way of remembering the ancestors, which may not have anything directly to do with the family per se. Not unexpectedly, the religious aspects of ancestral veneration are also gradually being cast off. There is evidence to suggest that the act of praying to or praying for the deceased is being replaced by a growing emphasis on the memories of the deceased.[66] Even Smith, toward the end of his book, has to admit that the ancestral spirits, who once had been "strong agents of social control within the household," are now more likely to serve as "sources of emotional support" for family members.[67] One could interpret this development as a secularizing effect of modernity.

With the advent of the Internet, the practice of memorial rites has been made a lot more convenient—and private—just with the click of a mouse. A growing number of people have pictures of their family graves posted on the Internet so that they can perform the ancestral rites in the comfort of home. Ancestral veneration as "family religion," using Takeda's words, is becoming more and more a tenuous concept.

Psychological Motives behind Ancestral Practices

This leads us to the fourth approach to the subject; namely, explaining Japanese ancestral practices in psychological and emotional terms. We have seen a little of this already in Morioka's analysis above. Susumu Shimazono, an authority on the New Religions of Japan, observes that in recent years, there has been a visible move away from community and family orientation to individualism among young people.[68] What is startling is that some of the newer religions have actually transformed family principles of ancestral veneration so radically that ancestral spirits have taken on a new role

---

65. Ibid.
66. See Suzuki, "Japanese Death Rituals," 171–88.
67. Smith, *Ancestor Worship*, 225. Smith, however, is confident that "ancestor worship" as a religious phenomenon will continue in modern Japan, but "in an increasingly bilateral mode, and for one or two generations of parents and grandparents."
68. Cited in Reader, "Recent Japanese Publications," 237.

somewhat akin to that of guardian angels of individual persons.[69] Traditional beliefs concerning the ancestors are all but jettisoned. Perhaps this is what Munataka means by the "ambivalent effects" of modernization.[70] On the one hand, there is the individual, the proud product of modernization; on the other, we have a metamorphosis of traditional religion to meet the individual's psychological needs.

The psychological aspect of ancestral veneration, however, is not as new as it seems, even if research in this area is only in its infancy. Masami Katsumoto, for instance, notes that ancient Japanese, who lived close to nature and had to struggle to survive through natural disasters, had always referred to their ancestors as *kokoro no yoridokoro* (the place where one's heart finds refuge and comfort).[71] This sentiment is not lost on modern Japanese.[72] Perhaps in the fast-secularizing society of modern Japan today, both ancestors and descendants need the security of each other even more than before!

Katsumoto also observes correctly that the traditional observance of elaborate memorial rites over months, even years, has functioned as a socially sanctioned means through which grieving family members find emotional and psychological comfort.[73] In their insistence on doctrinal purity, missionaries have not quite appreciated this vital emotional role of the ancestral rites.

Besides providing the means to grieve, ancestral rites are also a channel through which family members express and deal with various emotions toward the dead, such as affection, nostalgia, gratitude, respect, fear, and regret. According to a survey conducted by Clark Offner, a Catholic missionary scholar, 44 percent of his respondents ranked the element of bringing comfort and consolation to the deceased as the most important reason for their engaging in ancestral rites.[74] This was followed by the element of expressing gratitude. Twenty-three percent said they considered gaining a sense of personal satisfaction important when participating in the rites. Offner also notes that in performing these rites, respondents felt "no sense of a humble creatureliness nor a feeling of awe before an all-powerful deity, no sense of divine glory which invites praise nor an idea of holiness that

69. Ibid.
70. Munataka, "Ambivalent Effects," 100.
71. Katsumoto, *Nihonjin no kokoro ni fukuin wo dō tsutaeru ka*, 130.
72. A Japanese lady in her forties, who lives in Chicago because of her husband's job posting, recently told my wife that she has been able to cope with life in a foreign land because of the support of her parents and her ancestors!
73. Katsumoto, *Nihonjin no kokoro ni fukuin wo dō tsutaeru ka*, 58.
74. Offner, "Continuing Concern," 11.

stimulates confession of sin."⁷⁵ In other words, the act of participating in these rites does not constitute "worship" in the biblical sense. The emphasis of the rites, rather, is upon "maintaining human relationships and regularly bringing the dead loved ones to mind."⁷⁶ Offner adds, "To be forgotten is, so to speak, to be condemned to torment. For this reason, it is considered a profound act of mercy to perform rites on behalf of spirits of the dead who have been forgotten or neglected."⁷⁷

We have made a survey of the four main areas in which much research has been conducted in postwar years on the subject of Japanese ancestral veneration. Christian missiologists are also contributing their fair share to the debate, and their focus, as can be expected, is on developing a proper biblical response to what is perceived as the formidable challenge of the ancestral cult.⁷⁸ However, a fundamental missiological obstacle, relating to language and its referent, remains to be surmounted.

THE PROBLEMS OF TERMINOLOGY AND CONCEPTUALIZATION

Norwegian missiologist Jan-Martin Berentsen, in his doctoral dissertation *Grave and Gospel*, applies Robert Smith's core ideas in a missiological context and explores the theological possibilities of a contextualized liturgy and practice with regard to the ancestors. Berentsen observes correctly that the English expression "ancestor worship" is "unfortunate" since there are no less than eight distinct expressions in the Japanese language employed to refer to different aspects of ancestral practices.⁷⁹ However, it is rather baffling that despite his recognition of the "unfortunate" expression, Berentsen goes on to declare, "[I]n *all* these verbal expressions both the idea of religious worship and that of veneration/respect are included."⁸⁰ As a result, he does not favor the expression "ancestral veneration" for fear that it might convey the "wrong impression of Japanese ancestor worship as simple memorialism and nothing more."⁸¹

---

75. Ibid., 12.
76. Ibid., 13.
77. Ibid.
78. See, e.g., Enns, "'Making All Things New'"; Berentsen, *Grave and Gospel*; Fukada, "Remembering the Dead," 1–10; Ronan, "Biblical Conversion"; and Mullins, "What about the Ancestors?" 41–64.
79. Berentsen, "Ancestral Rites," 3.
80. Berentsen, *Grave and Gospel*, 27–28. Emphasis added.
81. Ibid., 28.

Berentsen's claim that all the Japanese expressions pertaining to the ancestral practices carry religious connotations is debatable. Wisdom would dictate the use of the term "ancestral veneration" rather than "ancestor worship." "Veneration" is, semantically, a more comprehensive term that covers all the Japanese expressions for ancestral practices, including worship; on the other hand, "worship" is a narrow defining term that necessarily excludes all non-religious connotations that may otherwise be implied in some of the Japanese expressions. In other words, using the expression "ancestor worship" is designed to convey the thought that everything about the ancestral rites involves religious worship. Admittedly, part of the problem lies in defining what is "religious" and what is not, as well as what "worship" is. But precisely because the final word remains to be said, we cannot use a term that prejudges the *whole* ancestral phenomenon as religious.[82] It is clear that Berentsen, following Smith, sees no possibility that at least for some Japanese, ancestral practices could have a wholly non-religious significance.

Berentsen's assumption highlights a common problem among Christian scholars, especially Protestants; namely, an uncritical tendency to assess ancestral practices in wholly religious terms, in other words, as idol worship. Offner laments that missionaries often too hastily conclude that what Japanese people do before commemorative monuments, whether at home, at the cemetery, or at a shrine or temple, violates in no uncertain terms the First Commandment.[83] Offner points out that contrary to what most missionaries believe, even the English word "worship" does not have a static meaning, "for the precise content of this word . . . varies according to its object and context."[84]

---

82. Of course, the phrase "ancestor worship" could and should be used whenever an explicitly religious part of the ancestral practices is referred to. A less frequently used Japanese expression, *sosen saishi*, for instance, would be rightly rendered as "ancestor worship."

83. Offner, "Continuing Concern," 3.

84. Ibid. Similarly, the Hebrew word translated in the New International Version as "to bow down and worship" in Exod 20:5, 2 Kings 17:35, and Neh 8:6 is simply translated as "to bow down" in Gen 23:7 and 42:6. In the latter, there is no religious connotation whatsoever. Second Kings 5:18 presents an interesting case in which the word appears twice. From the context, it would appear that the first instance refers to a religious act of worship on the part of Naaman's master, and the second instance refers to a simple act of bowing on the part of Naaman (see Harris et al., *Theological Wordbook*). This Hebrew word is translated as *proskuneō* in the Septuagint. In the New Testament, *proskuneō* similarly has two meanings: "to bow down and worship" and "to prostrate oneself," as in Matt 4:9 and 20:20, respectively. I was first alerted to the polysemous nature of these biblical words by Robert Priest.

The most common Japanese expression to describe ancestral practices as a whole is *sosen sūhai*. Offner shows correctly that the word *sūhai*, most often translated "worship" in English as part of the expression "ancestor worship," refers to a profound, reverential feeling toward another person.[85] Whether the person in question is living or dead does not constitute a criterion for its usage. In some contexts, the word is better translated as admiration or adoration. Against Takashi Maeda's point cited in Berentsen that *sūhai* "implies a recognition that the object of *sūhai* is superior to man and is in a position to control the life of the worshipper,"[86] there is an effective counterexample in Offner's *Rōdōsha sūhai ron* (On showing respect to the common worker). Offner notes that the Christian evangelist and social reformer Toyohiko Kagawa exhorted his readers "to *sūhai* the common worker."[87] Obviously Kagawa did not mean for his readers to "worship" the common worker. His message was that we must especially "respect and admire" those engaged in menial tasks. Of course, it cannot be denied that *sūhai* can be used as a religious term to designate an explicit act of worship, for example, even in the expression *sosen sūhai*. The point here is that *sosen sūhai* need not necessarily be understood as ancestor worship.

Offner rightly warns, "Unless the missionary understands the inner motivation and moral character of the act *sosen sūhai*, his judgment should be reserved."[88] His warning, unfortunately, often goes unheeded. It is a pity that the uncompromising attitude of many Western missionaries has often led to a "fundamental clash between their individualistic message and the religious consciousness of and values of most Japanese."[89] Renouncing the ancestors as a necessary condition for receiving the gift of personal salvation constitutes, for most Japanese, "an overwhelming existential crisis."[90] While it is true that ancestral practices often do involve religious elements that contravene scriptural teachings, and these cannot be ignored, it is also necessary for missiologists to acknowledge and examine more deeply the psychological and sociological dimensions of these practices in order to forge a response which is both biblically sound and culturally intelligible.

---

85. Offner, "Continuing Concern," 5.
86. Berentsen, *Grave and Gospel*, 27–28.
87. Offner, "Continuing Concern," 5.
88. Ibid.
89. Mullins, *Christianity Made in Japan*, 129.
90. Ibid., 136.

THE WAY FORWARD

If we look at the whole range of veneration rites and rituals, we find that the most obviously religious ones are located in the funeral, the mourning rites, the memorial service on the forty-ninth day, and the anniversary services. Special ceremonies to appease the wandering spirits of non-family members are also invariably religious in nature, often motivated by the fear of being harmed by a superior supernatural force.

Attending to the family altar and visiting the family grave include *both* religious *and* non-religious elements. These are, admittedly, difficult to separate, but they cannot, in principle, be reduced to either one or the other. When it comes to venerating the ancestors as a collective whole, things become even murkier. Many family activities and community festivals organized to venerate the ancestors have become less explicitly religious, and are increasingly viewed as social events. Certainly more research needs to be done to disentangle the religious from the non-religious elements. It confuses the issue, not to mention that it is bad scholarship, when conclusions drawn from a study done on the obviously religious aspects of the memorial rites are generalized uncritically to define all ancestral practices as acts of worship.

In a fascinating article published in 1998, Suzuki describes the great social changes that Japan has undergone following World War II, resulting in a more distant, more commercialized, and less personal relationship between the Japanese family and the Buddhist temple.[91] There is also the changing meaning of death. Suzuki observes rightly that the longevity of Japanese people today has created a situation whereby family members have to care for the bed-ridden elderly for many years before their death.[92] Death, under such circumstances, is often received more with a sense of relief rather than grief. Increasingly, we hear of funeral ceremonies being marred by the difficult memories of a prolonged process of dying rather than being marked with remembrance of a life well lived. For this reason, more and more elderly people today are holding their own living funerals when they are still healthy as "a way to combat the uncertainty about the meaning of death by reasserting one's own feeling of worth."[93]

More people are also expressing their desire to have a non-religious funeral so that their families can remember them not as household ancestors

---

91. Suzuki, "Japanese Death Rituals."
92. Ibid., 175.
93. Ibid.

but for the way they lived.[94] Another growing trend is the dispersing of ashes after cremation, usually at a favorite place frequented by the deceased, or at a place that the deceased wanted to go but never had a chance.[95] Suzuki calls the dispersing of ashes "the purest form of remembering loved ones," presumably because it is devoid of all the religious trappings of ritualistic memorialism.[96] Meanwhile, ordinary places where the deceased ashes are scattered are transformed into "intimate places where the bereaved could commune with their departed."[97] The apparent move away from the traditional Buddhist funeral to new ways of remembering and celebrating the life of deceased family members is symptomatic of a visible shift from the collective meaning of belonging to a household to a more individual evaluation of one's life, based on one's character, deeds, and relationship with significant others. In the light of this transition, what new meanings will ancestral veneration assume in the future? This is fertile ground for future research.

CONCLUSION

Like any cultural phenomenon, Japanese ancestral tradition is complex. While the motives that people have in participating in ancestral rites are largely the result of socialization, they are also varied and mixed. From the literature, we have seen that besides religious motivations, there are historical, socio-functional, and psychological reasons behind the ancestral practices as well. And it appears that it is precisely the non-religious aspects of the ancestral tradition that have withstood the battering forces of secularization, and in the process helped preserve the tradition, but not without effecting some change first. And the metamorphosis of the tradition continues.

In a lecture series held in 1987 at the Japan Bible Seminary in Tokyo, Paul Matsumoto, an evangelical pastor, argued for a systemic and multidimensional analysis of ancestral practices. For too long, missionaries have been fixated solely on the religious dimension. Matsumoto suggests that death rituals in Japan should be understood as a system with six dimensions: religious, psychological, social, ethical, ceremonial, and worldview.[98] Matsumoto's appeal for missiological research to be done on each of these

---

94. Ibid., 185.
95. See Yasuda, *Haka nanka iranai*.
96. Suzuki, "Japanese Death Rituals," 181.
97. Ibid., 182.
98. Matsumoto, "Bunka jinrui gaku teki shiten."

areas, or on all the areas as a systemic whole, issued more than twenty years ago, continues to be urgently heeded today.

BIBLIOGRAPHY

Ariga, Kizaemon. "Nihon ni okeru senzo no kannen—ie no keifu to ie no hommatsu no keifu to." In *Ie—sono kōzō bunseki* [Ie—Analysis of Its Structure], edited by Seiichi Kitano and Yuzuru Okada, 1–33. Tokyo: Sōbunsha, 1959.

Berentsen, Jan-Martin. "The Ancestral Rites in Missiological Perspective." *Japanese Religions* 13 (1983) 2–27.

———. *Grave and Gospel*. Beihefte der Zeitschrift für Religions- und Geistesgeschichte 30. Leiden: Brill, 1985.

Duyvendak, J. J. L. "The Buddhistic Festival of All-Souls in China and Japan." *Acta Orientalia* 5 (1926) 39–48.

Enns, Robert. "'Making All Things New'? Remembering the Ancestors in a Japanese Protestant Family." *Japanese Religions* 26 (2001) 55–84.

Fukada, Robert. "Remembering the Dead: Practical Issues." *Japanese Religions* 13 (1984) 1–10.

Geertz, Clifford. *The Interpretation of Cultures: Selected Essays by Clifford Geertz*. New York: Basic Books, 1973.

Goodwin, Janet R. "Shooing the Dead to Paradise." *Japanese Journal of Religious Studies* 16 (1989) 63–80.

Hall, John Whitney. "A Monarch for Modern Japan." In *Political Development in Modern Japan*, edited by Robert E. Ward, 11–64. Princeton: Princeton University Press, 1968.

Harris, R. Laird et al., editors. *Theological Wordbook of the Old Testament*. Chicago: Moody, 2003.

Hori, Ichirō. "The Appearance of Individual Self-Consciousness in Japanese Religion and Its Historical Transformations." In *The Japanese Mind: Essentials of Japanese Philosophy and Culture*, edited by Charles A. Moore, 201–27. Honolulu: East-West Center, 1967.

———. "Manyōshū ni arawareta sosei to takai kan reikon kan ni tsuite" [Concerning funeral customs, conceptions of the other world and souls of the dead as found in the *Manyōshū*]. *Nihon shūkyō kenkyū* 2 (1963) 49–93.

———. *Minkan Shinkō* [Folk religion]. Tokyo: Iwanami shoten, 1951.

Horikoshi, Nobuji. *Nihonjin no kokoro to kirisutokyō* [The Japanese Mind and Christianity]. Tokyo: Word of Life, 1986.

Hozumi, Nobushige. *Ancestor-Worship and Japanese Law*. Honolulu: University Press of the Pacific, 2003.

Kaji, Nobuyuki. *Jukyō to wa nani ka* [What Is Confucianism?]. Tokyo: Chūō kōronsha, 1990.

Katsumoto, Masami. *Nihonjin no kokoro ni fukuin wo dō tsutaeru ka* [How to Communicate the Gospel to the Hearts of Japanese People]. Tokyo: Word of Life Press, 1999.

Lay, Arthur Hyde. "Japanese Funeral Rites." *Transactions of the Asiatic Society of Japan* 19 (1891) 507–44.

Matsumoto, Paul. "*Bunka jinrui gaku teki shiten kara mita sosen sūhai*" [Understanding Ancestral Veneration from the Perspective of Anthropology]. Tokyo: Yūhisha, 1991.

Miller, Richard J. "Ancestors and Nobility in Ancient Japan." In *Ancestors*, edited by William H. Newell, 163–76. The Hague: Mouton, 1976.

Morioka, Kiyomi. "Ancestor Worship in Contemporary Japan: Continuity and Change." In *Religion and the Family in East Asia*, edited by George A. De Vos and Takao Sofue, 201–13. Osaka: National Museum of Ethnology, 1984.

Mullins, Mark R. *Christianity Made in Japan: A Study of Indigenous Movements*. Honolulu: University of Hawaii Press, 1998.

———. "What About the Ancestors? Some Japanese Christian Responses to Protestant Individualism." *Studies in World Christianity* 4 (1998) 41–64.

Munataka, Iwao. "Ambivalent Effects of Modernization on Traditional Folk Religion." *Japanese Journal of Religious Studies* 3 (1976) 99–126.

NHK Cultural Studies Institute. *Gendai Nihonjin no ishiki kōzō* [The Structure of Modern Japanese Consciousness]. 7th ed. Tokyo: NHK, 2010.

Offner, Clark B. "Continuing Concern for the Departed." *Japanese Religions* 11 (1979) 1–16.

Ooms, Herman. "A Structural Analysis of Japanese Ancestral Rites and Beliefs." In *Ancestors*, edited by William H. Newell, 61–90. The Hague: Mouton, 1976.

Plath, David W. "Where the Family of God is the Family: The Role of the Dead in Japanese Households." *American Anthropologist* 66 (1964) 300–317.

Reader, Ian. "Recent Japanese Publications on the New Religions: The Work of Shimazono Suzumu." *Japanese Journal of Religious Studies* 20 (1993) 229–48.

Ronan, David W. "Biblical Conversion and Japanese Ancestral Practices: How Japan's Church Leaders Interpret Attitudes, Actions, Direction, and Relationship in Local Churches." PhD diss., Trinity International University, Deerfield, IL, 1989.

Shibata, Chizuo. "Some Problematic Aspects of Japanese Ancestor Worship." *Japanese Religions* 13 (1983) 35–48.

Smith, Robert J. *Ancestor Worship in Contemporary Japan*. Stanford: Stanford University Press, 1974.

Suzuki, Hikaru. "Japanese Death Rituals in Transit: From Household Ancestors to Beloved Antecedents." *Journal of Contemporary Religion* 13 (1998) 171–88.

Swyngedouw, Jan. "Religion in Contemporary Japanese Society." *Japan Foundation Newsletter* 13 (1986) 1–14.

Takeda, Chōshū. "'Family Religion in Japan.' Ie and Its Religious Faith." In *Ancestors*, edited by William H. Newell, 119–38. The Hague: Mouton, 1976.

———. *Sosen sūhai* [Ancestor veneration]. 2nd ed. Kyoto: Heirakuji shoten, 1961.

Varley, Paul H. *Japanese Culture*. 3rd ed. Honolulu: University of Hawaii Press, 1984.

Yanagawa, Keiichi, editor. *Seminā shūkyōgaku Kōgi* [Lectures in Religious Studies]. Tokyo: Hōzō Sensho, 1998.

Yanagita, Kunio. *About Our Ancestors*. Translated by Fanny Hagin Mayer and Yasuyo Ishiwara. Tokyo: Japan Society for the Promotion of Science, 1970. Originally published as *Senso no hanashi* (Tokyo, 1946).

Yasuda, Mutsuhiko. *Haka nanka iranai: Aisureba shizensō* [Who Needs a Grave? Natural Burial for Your Loved Ones]. Tokyo: Yūhisha, 1991.

20

The 2008 Financial Crisis and the Great Commission

J. Nelson Jennings

TITE TIÉNOU HAS OFTEN demonstrated how to create new approaches to familiar subjects. Several years ago he shared one of his unabashed category-rearrangers: "I'm not here at Trinity simply to teach about African theology: I am here to teach Christian theology." Tiénou asserted what was obvious to him but not so obvious to many others: Mainstream Christian theology and those who teach it are not confined to one small (Western) sector of the planet, while other sectors are somehow exotic or worthy of only specialized interest.

MISSIONS AND THE GREAT COMMISSION

In this essay I explore a topic in the spirit of Tiénou's boundary pushing. I wish to demonstrate that in light of the 2008 financial crisis, Christian mission takes on fresh hues and new possibilities. First I will summarize how missions are commonly understood, particularly in relation to the Great Commission of Matthew 28.

Understanding Missions

For many Christians, missions consist of missionaries "going out to the mission field" to serve the cause of the Christian Gospel, particularly among the world's unreached peoples. After all, the thinking goes, Jesus said "Go and make disciples of all nations." Others participate by supporting missionaries through finances and prayer. Short-term missions enable more Christians to get a taste of missions, but the basic go-send-pray framework remains intact.

Given this common understanding of Christian missions, the relationship between the 2008 financial crisis and the Great Commission clearly involves an impact on missions funding. As one missions and financial expert noted, the accelerating economic downturn "put pressure on [donors'] discretionary income" because "so many people today are tied to the stock market, either through their retirement plans, or they are retired and they're getting money off their portfolios, or [people wonder] whether or not their employment is going to continue."[1]

That observation is obvious and important. However, in this essay I want to explore something different: I want to push the boundaries by asking what Jesus meant by his imperative to "make disciples of all nations."[2]

Jesus's words recorded as the conclusion of Matthew's Gospel have come to be called the "Great Commission," but they were not spoken or written as a missions slogan apart from the rest of Jesus's teachings, life, death, and resurrection.[3] Jesus's and Matthew's first audiences were religious minorities who needed assurance of Jesus's power and presence, for they were being asked to undertake a monumental project beyond their strength and abilities. Hence Matthew recorded Jesus's declaration that "All authority in heaven and on earth has been given to me" (Matt 28:18), as well as his assurance "I am with you always, to the end of the age" (Matt 28:20b).

Christian missions of yesteryear sometimes thought that converting a kingdom's ruler would amount to Christianization. More recently, discipleship has focused on individuals. But Jesus did not specify "make disciples of *individuals* within all nations." While Jesus did not prohibit or preclude such individual discipleship, his focus on "all nations" must not be overlooked. There is something corporate, collective, and public about Jesus's focus on "nations."

---

1. Granger, "U.S. Financial Crisis," n.p.

2. I have written more extensively on this subject elsewhere; see Jennings, *God the Real Superpower*, 111–24.

3. Other gospel writers recorded similar sayings, but Matt 28:18–20 has a preeminent place in what Evangelicals call the "Great Commission."

Jesus's Followers and "All Nations"

There are three important notions to address. First is the framework of God's mission and Christian missions. God's mission, the *missio Dei*, is his covenantal commitment to display his glory and goodness throughout the world he has made. Christian missions represent our efforts to participate with God in his mission. It is the "zeal of the Lord of hosts" (Isa 9:7) that carries his mission through to completion; we who are his followers are enlisted to cooperate with God through our missions initiatives.[4]

The second notion concerns a Christian understanding of "nations." Jesus's first disciples no doubt heard him referring particularly to the non-Jewish Gentile peoples of the world, but such categories for defining "nations" have not remained static. We can safely say today that "all nations" are various kinds of groups of people with common or shared traits.

The third notion is the relationship between "all nations" and Christians. For Jesus's first disciples, "nations" were separate and distinct peoples. Jesus's imperative "Go therefore" indicates that the disciples, and those who became followers through their witness, were commanded to go to different peoples, even as they rubbed shoulders with fellow human beings through the natural course of their daily lives.[5] Subsequent generations of Christians, including those of us alive today, have in large part been members of these formerly separate and distinct people. We Christians are part-and-parcel members of "nations" or groups with common characteristics. Nations are not just people "out there" somewhere. Rather, just as first-century Christians in Rome were included among those whom Paul saluted for their "obedience of faith for the sake of his name among all the nations," those of us throughout subsequent generations, "called to belong to Jesus Christ," live among and are members of the nations (Rom 1:5–6).

That obedience of faith that Paul sought is a discipleship, a learning, a belief in and following of Jesus and his words. Hence, to disciple nations means that we Christians are to bring to bear the saving work, teachings, and standards of Christ on the shared traits, assumptions, values, and ways of thinking that our nations embody.[6] Evangelism and church planting certainly are necessary components of this discipleship process. But along with these responsibilities, even though the specific ways our nations are to be taught or discipled may not always be crystal clear, we are expected to address the corporate, collective, and public sense of discipling nations,

---

4. Jennings, *God the Real Superpower*, 16–18, 217–25.

5. Ibid., 116–17.

6. I am particularly indebted to Andrew Walls for this understanding of public, corporate discipleship vis-à-vis Matt 28:19.

teaching them to observe all that Jesus has commanded (Matt 28:20a). That is what Jesus, the one with all authority who is always with us, leads and empowers us to do in our respective communities.

The specific example that this study addresses is the 2008 financial crisis. We will consider how to understand discipleship in relationship to what was a deeply ethical event that had near cataclysmic economic effects. One difficulty we face here is that Christians are by no means agreed as to how to address economic matters. Furthermore, I am not a trained economist and thus will rely heavily on the expertise of others. Even so, insofar as we as Christians are responsible to contribute to the discipling of our nations, and insofar as the 2008 financial crisis needs to be brought into the purview of Christian concern, we will dare to press ahead.

We will examine some economic and financial minutiae that ordinarily are not part of a consideration of Christian mission. If what immediately follows appears familiar, feel free to skim the next section. However, if you are in the position I was in until recently, you have not worked through the following details, especially for the purpose of integrating them with an understanding of Christian mission.

What Was the 2008 Financial Crisis?

> The subprime lending crisis evolved into a full market meltdown in the second half of 2008. In short order, nearly all of Wall Street's major investment firms had either collapsed or suffered staggering losses. Even insurance giant AIG had to secure an emergency loan from the federal government in order to avoid bankruptcy . . . In fact, at the end of 2008, the federal government pledged more money to bail out the financial services industry (as well as other segments of the economy) than it spent on the Louisiana Purchase, the New Deal, the Marshall Plan, the Korean War, the Race to the Moon, the Vietnam War, the Savings and Loan Crisis, Operation Iraqi Freedom, and NASA's lifetime budget *combined* [emphasis original].[7]

Many economists consider what happened in the first decade of this century to be the worst financial crisis since the Great Depression of the 1930s. The liquidity shortfall that developed in the U.S. banking system triggered not only the collapse of financial institutions, massive government bailouts, and the market's precipitous decline, but the U.S. housing market also suffered with countless evictions, foreclosures, and vacancies.

---

7. Coffin, "2008 Financial Crisis," n.p. (italics in original).

Businesses failed, overall economic activity dropped, and trillions of U.S. dollars' worth of consumer wealth is estimated to have evaporated. A global economic recession ensued.

I suspect that most readers were personally affected and knew several others who also felt a major impact. Most anyone with any sort of investments saw a rapid, inexorable, and in many cases devastating drop in portfolio value; investors in or near retirement suffered particularly painful losses. It was a classic case of "Main Street" and "Wall Street" showing deep interconnections—though the folks on Main Street could not figure out why many on Wall Street seemingly showed no ill effects of the crisis they allegedly brought upon the rest of us. Along with the widespread personal financial toll were ethical, political, and legal issues. What actually caused the crisis, and who was responsible, economically, morally, and otherwise?[8]

What Caused the Crisis?

"The crisis was not a natural disaster, but the result of high risk, complex financial products; undisclosed conflicts of interest; and the failure of regulators, the credit rating agencies, and the market itself to rein in the excesses of Wall Street." That is the one-sentence summary given at the beginning of a 639-page report published in 2011 by the U.S. Senate.[9] A much briefer but representative analysis boils the cause down to greed, claiming "The whole thing was one big scheme."[10] Given the fact that most economists failed to anticipate the crisis, Robert Hall and Ricardo Caballero offered a multi-causal explanation and a complex tapestry of events.[11]

All analyses include the U.S. housing mortgage industry as a crucial, causal component of the crisis. On average, home prices more than doubled during the decade leading up to 2006. In the midst of that expanding bubble, both the so-called dotcom crash and post-9/11 adverse economic conditions led the Federal Reserve to keep interest rates low to enable easier credit flow. Investors demanded higher returns than interest-based investments could yield. In response, financial institutions created new products, particularly mortgage-backed securities (MBS) or those indecipherable collateralized debt obligations (CDO) that bundled home mortgages and

---

8. I have relied on a combination of sources in compiling this section. In particular, Wikipedia, s.v. "Financial Crisis of 2007–08," (online: http://en.wikipedia.org/wiki/Financial_crisis_of_2007%E2%80%9308) and Guina, "2008–2009 Financial Crisis."

9. US Senate Permanent Subcommittee on Investigations, "Wall Street."

10. Pinyo, "What Caused the Economic Crisis?," n.p.

11. See Hall, "Why Does the Economy." See also Caballero, "Macroeconomics."

other financial instruments. Investors' demands and expectations pushed financial institutions to keep producing competitively high-yield investment products, which in turn pushed lending to homebuyers even if they could not afford to make the resulting mortgage payments; that is, subprime (high-risk) mortgages increased. When defaults on mortgages accelerated, a downward spiral began of plummeting values both of mortgage-based financial products and of housing prices. Homeowners and investors alike saw their assets plunge.

The excessive leveraging (borrowing) in which financial institutions engaged for the sake of speculative investments, including investments in mortgage-backed securities, was another contributing factor to the collapse that ensued.[12] So was the innovative complexity of financial instruments that were created, including CDOs of various types and off-balance sheet financing. Credit default swaps (CDS), a financial instrument for swapping the risk of debt default,[13] proved to be a particularly damaging contributor to the troubles of insurance giant AIG. One other negative contribution needing mention is the failure of rating agencies to understand and responsibly assign accurate risk ratings to some of the creative, synthetic financial products that were being generated.

Many analysts point to deregulation of the U.S. financial industry as a primary culprit for the 2008 crisis.[14] (Political preference seems closely tied to how such analyses are offered and evaluated.)

Outrageous Elements of the Crisis

Certain components of the 2008 financial crisis have been deeply irksome, not only to the general public but to those who have delved into understanding the event in greater detail.[15] One of those maddening elements is the predatory lending that persuaded non-qualified homebuyers to take on unrealistic mortgage payments, often without their clear understanding

12. Note the helpful clarifications regarding the different senses in which the term "leverage" is used in relation to the 2008 financial crisis; see subsection Leverage and the Financial Crisis of 2007–2009, within the larger article, Wikipedia, s.v. "Leverage (finance)," online: http://en.wikipedia.org/wiki/Financial_leverage#Leverage_and_the_financial_crisis_of_2007-2009.

13. Pettinger, "Credit Default Swaps," n.p.

14. Eg., Charles Ferguson's Oscar-winning 2010 documentary "Inside Job" has as its central theme the role that deregulation, in place since the 1980s, played in enabling the greedy speculation and excesses of Wall Street that resulted in the 2008 financial crisis.

15. This section is my own summary of information culled from the various sources cited in the previous section. Certain specific points are individually cited.

of the terms. Mortgage lenders, the financial institutions that subsequently purchased the mortgages, and investors all stood to gain at the expense of unwitting new homeowners upon whom lenders mercilessly and deceptively preyed.

Another bothersome and related component was the creation of financial products that forecast at least some of the profits based on anticipated mortgage defaults and home repossessions. Assuming a continued rise in housing prices, lenders could turn around and sell repossessed houses at a profit—with brokers and lenders gaining the associated fees to boot—and repackage CDOs for investors. The fact that brokers and lenders, plus others down the investment food chain, would profit by intentionally designing and selling mortgages that they knew would cause substantial loss to new homeowners is outrageous.[16]

Yet another related element is the lack of personal responsibility that particular parties bore—morally, financially (until the crisis caught up with hosts of people), legally, or otherwise. This was the case throughout the complex, multi-step process of selling subprime mortgages to risky borrowers; the selling by lenders of all sorts of mortgages to investment firms; the bundling of mortgages into CDOs and other financial products; and the garnering of profits by investors several steps removed from the homeowners at the front end of the chain. Vast profits were gained by many at the expense of others (as well as through financial wizardry), but few if any profiteers assumed responsibility or blame.

Ratings agencies, such as Moody's and Standard & Poor's, attached inflated credit ratings to unsafe investments. These agencies misled investors who otherwise might not have taken on the high-risk products. Whether due to lack of information from financial institutions, failure to understand complex financial instruments, collusion with financial institutions, or simple dishonesty, the failure of rating agencies to assign accurate ratings betrayed investors' trust.[17]

As outlandish as anything were the deceptive recommendations of investment houses to investors. Financial products were touted that investment firms knew would hurt the investors but bring profit to the investment houses themselves.[18] At Senate hearings investment house representatives back-pedaled and gave obtuse testimonies that served to exacerbate public outrage.

---

16. For a simple explanation of how such profit-making worked so long as housing prices kept on increasing, see the online video by Jarvis, "Crisis of Credit Visualized," particularly starting at approximately the 6:00 mark.

17. See, e.g., U.S. Senate, "Wall Street," 5–7, 243–312.

18. Ibid., 313ff.

Media reports of Wall Street executives' and brokers' lavish, immoral lifestyles—again, at others' expense—added fuel to the public's bitterness. Astronomical bonuses, multiple mansions and yachts, drugs and prostitution, all accompanied by a seemingly callous lack of sympathy toward the very people whose earnings and profits they had reaped, stoked incredulous anger.

Finally, the lack of prosecution against the perpetrators of what some consider immoral and illegal financial activities has sparked attempts to expose the alleged fraud and deception that has left the wealthy beneficiaries of the financial collapse unscathed.[19]

Effects of the Crisis

> In the fall of 2008, America suffered a devastating economic collapse. Once valuable securities lost most or all of their value, debt markets froze, stock markets plunged, and storied financial firms went under. Millions of Americans lost their jobs; millions of families lost their homes; and good businesses shut down. These events cast the United States into an economic recession so deep that the country has yet to fully recover.[20]

The effect on millions of retirement accounts and pension funds was devastating. So was the effect on the U.S. government's mind-boggling and ever-spiraling fiscal deficit: inestimable loss of tax revenue and an emergency $700 billion bailout do not come without a price tag. Indeed, the eventual geopolitical implications of the U.S. deficit may occupy the significant attention of historians for decades or even centuries to come. The overall decline in financial wealth that occurred is estimated at a staggering $14 trillion.[21]

What the crisis did to widen the gap between rich and poor in the U.S. population is also noteworthy.[22] The economic effects outside the United States must of course be included as well. The intertwined nature of production, consumption, currencies, and investments around the world meant that the drastic fluctuations in the single largest national economy would have

---

19. Alongside Ferguson's "Inside Job" have been the efforts of journalists like Danny Schechter. His 2008 book and film, *Plunder, the Crime of Our Time* (online: www.youtube.com/watch?v=tpcTkfmR8Nw) urge prosecution of Wall Street's alleged criminal activities. In late 2013 it appeared that legal action may take place.

20. US Senate, "Wall Street," 1.

21. See subsection Wealth Effects, in Wikipedia, s.v. "Financial Crisis of 2007–08."

22. See subsection Distribution of Wealth, in Wikipedia, s.v. "Financial Crisis of 2007–08."

significant ripple effects elsewhere. (Interestingly, much of the Islamic world was not as severely affected, having entered the crisis in strong positions and often operating by different, i.e., Islamic, financing mechanisms.)[23]

A different sort of international effect has been the relative strengthening, progressing, and emboldening of other modern economies, including those in Turkey, India, and Brazil. Related to this has been an accelerated "de-coupling and re-coupling" of global trade and investment patterns, with other nations' economies becoming more interconnected apart from the United States.[24]

Clearly world-changing geopolitical and economic seismic shifts, to which the 2008 financial crisis was a major contributor, are occurring.

CONNECTING THE DISCIPLING OF NATIONS AND THE FINANCIAL CRISIS

Following Tite Tiénou's example of adjusting categories of discourse, this essay advocates a wider scope of what discipling all the nations entails. In particular, we have considered afresh the public and corporate meaning of Jesus's words recorded in Matthew 28:19, namely that his directive to "make disciples of all nations" points to addressing the shared assumptions, thinking patterns, and practices of the nations or groups among whom we live. Next, and in anticipation of connecting this understanding of Jesus's Great Commission with the 2008 financial crisis, we have analyzed the crisis—its causes, offensive elements, and effects. Now it is time to connect discipling the nations and the recent economic crisis as concretely as possible.

Our approach involves two stages. First, for clarity's sake we need to identify the aspects of the 2008 financial crisis that connect with Christian discipleship (presented below in two steps). Then, we will consider how particular Christians, as well as Christian groups and institutions, have related and can relate to the crisis in specific ways.

Obviously Relevant Areas

In what ways is following Jesus Christ and his teaching relevant to an economic event such as the 2008 financial crisis? Perhaps the most obvious connecting point involves ethics and morality, even though it might take

---

23. See subsections European Contagion and Global Effects, in Wikipedia, s.v. "Financial Crisis of 2007–08."
24. Gardels, "From a Flattening World," 66–74 (quoted phrase from 72).

care and expertise to identify how ethics and morality were in fact involved. The greed, sometimes blatant, sometimes less evident, spread throughout the event, is clearly an area to be addressed. Homebuyers, real estate agents, mortgage lenders, Wall Street financiers, Wall Street brokers and investors, and investment-rating agents—as well as politicians in possible collusion with deceptive financial products—exhibited greedy consumption. At the same time, where the line was crossed from legitimate need to greed may not always be easy to determine. When did homebuyers become greedy for too much house, for example? At the other end of the investment chain, when did investors start demanding too much profit? At stages within that chain, when did agents or brokers charge excessive fees or earn excessive incomes off of managing others' investments? Even with these questions of ambiguity, however, surely the often ravenous greed that helped drive the mortgage and financial industries into crisis was itself a moral crisis that Jesus's followers should address. (Ways to do that are suggested below.)

Another clear moral area to which Christian discipleship relates is the dishonesty and lack of integrity that marked various parts of the overall event. The deception inherent to the predatory lending to homebuyers—particularly vulnerable, high-risk homebuyers—was patently wrong. Reports of escalating mortgages being thrust on unsuspecting non-native-English speakers,[25] for example, substantiate the common ethical concern about opaque financial jargon in "the fine print" of contracts. Then there were the deceptive recommendations to investors by investment brokers to purchase faulty products against which the brokers themselves, along with their company superiors, wagered their own investments.[26] To what extent ratings agents deceived investors, or simply did not understand certain complex high-risk financial instruments, is difficult to determine.

Immorality associated with lifestyles of exorbitant consumption and alleged drug use and involvement with prostitution is a clear connecting point as well. So are moral matters of justice and injustice, for example "the injustice of government piling up public debt and encouraging individuals, businesses, and financial institutions to do the same."[27] And insofar as criminal behavior was involved not only with Wall Street's drug use and prostitution but also in regard to some of Wall Street's financial maneuverings, Christian discipleship enters the picture.

---

25. Such an instance was included in the documentary "Inside Job," for example.

26. Cf. the cases of Deutsche Bank and UBS, e.g., in U.S. Senate, "Wall Street," 10–11, 286, 319–320, 330–333.

27. Skillen, "Is the Economic Crisis a Moral Issue?," n.p.

Areas Difficult to Discern

When we move from moral matters such as greed, dishonesty, lasciviousness, justice, and criminality into the question of responsibility for what happened economically, the discussion becomes a bit grayer as far as Christian discipleship is concerned. To be sure, bearing responsibility before God and others is a clear and basic point of Christian life and teaching. Indeed, the heart of Jesus Christ's substitutionary atonement is his bearing before God our responsibility for our guilt and rebellion. But one of the frustrating aspects of the 2008 financial crisis has been the lack of clear responsibility and guilt that particular parties bear for what went wrong. For starters, few people who participated in the U.S. economy leading up to the crisis—and that would include me and most likely you—have been quick or forthcoming to assume whatever responsibility or blame we might bear. Moreover, the economic and in particular financial nature of the crisis seems to create a gap between the financial crisis itself and Christian discipleship per se.

We need to recall at this point that all authority in heaven and earth (including over economies) has been given to the risen Jesus. Here is also where an understanding of how God's world operates can help us.[28] On one hand, God has designed the world, as well as how human beings view and live in his world, with differentiated aspects or spheres, including economics and religion. These various spheres within the world function according their own standards and principles. For example, the economic principle of supply and demand, the religious standards of divine love and holiness, and grammatical constructions of human languages, operate with their own integrity and, often, in relative isolation from each other. At the same time, because God has made one world as well as integrated human beings who live in that world, we understand events as integrated wholes and live in relation to those events accordingly. We can analyze shifts in the U.S. housing market according to supply and demand. But we can also analyze and discuss that market in regard to whether linguistic grammatical rules are being followed to assure clarity. And we can honor foundational sensibilities as to how divine love and holiness set the standard for human relations within that housing market.

Using that differentiated-integrated approach to the bearing of responsibility within the 2008 financial crisis, we can on one hand understand in strictly financial terms the products (CDOs) that linked home buyers and investors who were several financial steps removed from each

---

28. I am indebted for the systematization of this approach to my former colleague at Tokyo Christian University Hisakazu Inagaki. See Inagaki and Jennings, *Philosophical Theology*.

other. Furthermore, we can analyze in strictly financial terms what went wrong in the individual steps themselves (for example plummeting housing prices due to foreclosures) as well as what went wrong in the relationships between those steps (for example the way that defaulted, high-risk mortgage components of many CDOs forced the CDO values downward). At the same time, we can see how the particular parties involved in that complex, financialized relationship contributed to what went wrong: some homebuyers overstepped their abilities to repay their mortgages; some real estate agents pushed purchases that were beyond homebuyers' means; some lenders quickly and irresponsibly passed along to investment firms the risk and responsibility of high-risk mortgages; some investment firms in turn irresponsibly bundled and passed along the risk and responsibility of high-risk investments to, at least in some cases, excessive-profit-seeking investors; they in turn were in some cases kept unaware of their investments' high risk by irresponsible ratings agents.

Where discipleship comes into play thus involves an intertwined financial-human scenario. Both the analysis of the seemingly impersonal components of the crisis and people's personal actions must be addressed. Agents, lenders, and investment firms who passed along the *financial* responsibility of risk and earnings down the chain all the way to investors were *personally* responsible to God and to others. Christians can point both to Christ's reign over all spheres of life (financial included) and to people's personal responsibility for their actions in all spheres of life. The financialization of economic life can give the illusion of a depersonalized, mathematical system in which participants bear no personal responsibility for how they conduct economic transactions. In reality, however, the financial area of life is laid bare before the reigning Christ, and we are responsible to God and others for how we conduct our financial affairs.

Among the additional areas of financial life that come into view here—in general terms, not just in specific relation to the 2008 financial crisis—is that of the nature and purpose of investing and lending money. Large questions beyond our scope arise here.[29] For example, there are questions concerning the nature and key historical developments of capitalism, including Christianity's relationship to capitalism and its development. The relevant point here is the necessary relationship between legitimate profit-making through investments and the assistance rendered to those to whom that same money is being lent. Investors are lenders; money invested is money received by borrowers. Discipling nations includes addressing the

---

29. In 2006, the Presbyterian Church (USA) published "A Reformed Understanding of Usury for the Twenty-First Century." Available online: http://www.pcusa.org/media/uploads/acswp/pdf/usury.pdf.

issue—perhaps first by pointing the issue out—of how investing for profit relates with lending to others for their needs and purposes. However else we address that issue, we can rest assured that the Jesus who has all authority in heaven and earth is also with us his people as we creatively venture into such basic, important areas of economic life.

Concretely Addressing the Crisis

It is now time to discuss concrete ways Jesus's followers, whether in 2008 or today, can fulfill the Great Commission by addressing what happened during the financial crisis. Space limitations, coupled with the massive scope of possibilities, necessarily make what follows exemplary and representative rather than exhaustive.

First, consider the opportunity and responsibility that Christian leaders—preachers and other spokespeople—have to speak, publish, and otherwise communicate publically about a crisis such as the nation has experienced. Preachers must not try to speak as economic experts, of course; they must respect the integrity of the economic sphere and its particular intricacies. At the same time, the interconnectedness discussed above between economic matters and following Jesus, matters of morality and responsibility in particular, require leaders to spearhead Christian initiatives aimed at discipling their nations.

Offering prophetic critique is something that Christian spokespeople need to pursue. Such critique should not be negative whining but point toward God's standards to be followed instead of a current course. For instance, when Treasury Secretary Henry Paulson suggested in September 2008 that his proposed bailout plan would get to the root of the economic crisis liquidity problem, James Skillen publically pointed out the deeper root problem: "Real responsibility and genuine accountability [must be] reestablished at every point around the circle."[30] Such critique directed the nation past the false assumption that economic matters are strictly economic matters and toward the necessarily interconnected reality of personal responsibility.

That kind of public critique serves to equip other Christians to participate in discipleship with regard to economic-financial life. An example of how Christian commentary on the 2008 crisis offered such equipping was in the published insight that, unnoticed by media reports, renters were a major casualty. "People of faith can and should be articulating the plight of the renting poor who are getting caught in the web of landlord

30. Skillen, "Root of the Problem," n.p.

foreclosures. . . . Our congregations can offer social and spiritual support that helps to mitigate the pain and the costs, both financial and emotional, of the monetary and economic crisis."[31] The roles of Christian leaders in public, corporate discipleship are thus directed toward both the nation and the embedded Christian communities.

Second, Christian specialists in economics and finances were in a uniquely strategic position to engage the crisis. Some experts contributed to the kind of public discourse outlined above, through blogs, online newsletters, special forums, and other avenues. Interactions within companies—on boards, within team planning sessions, even in informal "water cooler" discussions—were needed. Christian academics could interact through specialized journals and conferences. Most of Jesus's followers will never be able to understand, much less disciple others, in the kind of economic and financial intricacies as those that marked the 2008 financial crisis. Hence Christians directly involved in those fields have a special responsibility to point others toward Jesus and his ways.

A third category of how Christians can disciple their nation during and after such a crisis is in their own personal financial practices, especially regarding their investment criteria. Insofar as discipling others involves "teaching them to observe all that I have commanded you" (Matt 28:20a), Jesus's followers must of course live out his teachings in their own lives. That includes standard of living—keeping greed in check, for example—as well as exemplifying biblical emphases in such areas as generosity toward the poor and avoiding excessive debt.

With specific respect to investment criteria, Christian discipleship must include an approach that goes beyond the commonly assumed (and advertised) personal factors of risk and potential profit.[32] As discussed earlier, investments are also loans to other parties. Hence how the other parties will use what has been invested/loaned must be part of the equation for Christians seeking to disciple their nation in shared financial assumptions and values. Thankfully, some Christians have drawn up helpful guidelines for the rest of us.[33] At issue is not just personal financial well-being but fulfilling Jesus's Great Commission.

---

31. Trulear, "Faith in the Face of Foreclosure?" n.p.

32. Some Christian investment services never move much beyond personal "successful investing plans," ignoring wider socio-economic factors. See, e.g., the "Investing Principles" page of *Sound Mind Investing.com*, online: http://www.soundmindinvesting.com/topics/s_investing.htm.

33. See in particular the "Socially Responsible Investment Guidelines" of the United States Conference of Catholic Bishops, available online: http://www.usccb.org/about/financial-reporting/socially-responsible-investment-guidelines.cfm.

CONCLUSION

Insofar as Tite Tiénou exemplifies an eagerness to clear new paths for Gospel progress, I hope that this exploration of Christian responsibility toward economic realities, in particular the 2008 financial crisis, proves to be a similarly Gospel-enhancing study. The study's foundation is the triune God's reign over the whole world. Moreover, as the Apostle John recorded in Revelation 21:5, God intends on "making all things new." Until the consummation of God's remake of his warped creation, Jesus's followers are to "be steadfast, immovable, always abounding in the work of the Lord, knowing that in the Lord your labor is not in vain" (1 Cor 15:58).

A common Christian instinct regarding finances is one of caution. After all, Jesus pointed out that "You cannot serve God and money" (Matt 6:24), and Paul instructed Timothy to teach contentment, since "The love of money is a root of all kinds of evils" (1 Tim 6:10). For the sake of their witness, Christians are to keep up their guard against the temptations of personal affluence.

At the same time, the Bible and Christian history teach a great deal about proactive engagement with things financial. Not only have people of wealth taken part in crucial parts of redemptive history (e.g., Abraham, Joseph of Arimathea, Philemon), but God's people are instructed to use constructively whatever measure of wealth that God supplies. That the nations among whom we live preeminently value money is indisputable. As prophetic sojourners and exiles among our nations, how we communicate godly attitudes, assumptions, and actions regarding finances is as great an opportunity as any for acting on the Great Commission. May the risen Jesus, to whom all authority has been given, encourage and empower us to disciple our nations both in times of economic crisis and in times of flourishing, "to the end of the age."

BIBLIOGRAPHY

Caballero, Ricardo J. "Macroeconomics after the Crisis: Time to Deal with the Pretense-of-Knowledge Syndrome." *Journal of Economic Perspectives* 24 (2010) 85–102.

Coffin, Bill, editor. "The 2008 Financial Crisis: A Wake-Up Call for Enterprise Risk Management." Risk and Insurance Management Society Executive Report, 2009. No pages. Online: http://www.ucop.edu/enterprise-risk-management/_files/2008fincrisis_wakeupcall.pdf.

Gardels, Nathan. "From a Flattening World to an Interdependence of Plural Identities." *New Perspectives Quarterly* 27 (2010) 66–74.

Guina, Ryan. "The 2008–2009 Financial Crisis—Causes and Effects." *CashMoneyLife.com*. No pages. Online: http://cashmoneylife.com/economic-financial-crisis-2008-causes/.

Hall, Robert E. "Why Does the Economy Fall to Pieces after a Financial Crisis?" *Journal of Economic Perspectives* 24 (2010) 3–20.

Hisakazu, Inagaki, and J. Nelson Jennings. *Philosophical Theology and East-West Dialogue*. Amsterdam: Rodopi, 2000.

Jarvis, Jonathan. "The Crisis of Credit Visualized." Youtube video, uploaded March 9, 2009. Online: http://www.youtube.com/watch?v=hs_9yqQQeD4. Also available at: http://crisisofcredit.com/.

Jennings, J. Nelson. *God the Real Superpower: Rethinking Our Role in Missions*. Phillipsburg, NJ: P & R, 2007.

Mission Network News. "U.S. Financial Crisis to Hit Mission Groups." Interview of Paul Granger, October 1, 2008, online: http://mnnonline.org/article/11723.

Pettinger, Tejvan. "Credit Default Swaps Explained." *Economics Help.org*. November 11, 2008. No pages. Online: http://www.economicshelp.org/blog/finance/credit-default-swaps-explained/.

Pinyo Bhulipongsanon. "What Caused the Economic Crisis?" *Moolanomy.com*. September 22, 2008. No pages. Online: http://www.moolanomy.com/866/what-caused-the-financial-crisis-of-2008/.

Skillen, James W. "Is the Economic Crisis a Moral Issue?" *Capital Commentary.com*. Center for Public Justice. April 11, 2008. No pages. Online: http://www.capitalcommentary.org/economy/economic-crisis-moral-issue.

Skillen, James W. "The Root of the Problem." *Capital Commentary.com*. Center for Public Justice. September 26, 2008. No pages. Online: www.cpjustice.org/content/root-problem.

Trulear, Howard Dean. "Faith in the Face of Foreclosure?" *Capital Commentary.com*. Center for Public Justice. March 27, 2009. No pages. Online: www.capitalcommentary.org/economy/faith-face-foreclosure.

United States Senate Permanent Subcommittee on Investigations. "Wall Street and the Financial Crisis: Anatomy of a Financial Collapse." Majority and minority staff report, April 13, 2011. Online: http://www.hsgac.senate.gov//imo/media/doc/Financial_Crisis/FinancialCrisisReport.pdf?attempt=2.

21

Researching Contextualization in Churches Influenced by Missionaries[1]

Robert J. Priest

In the mid-nineteenth century, Rufus Anderson and Henry Venn articulated the "three-self" principles of mission. Churches initiated by missionaries needed, as they matured, to become indigenous, which they defined as self-governing, self-supporting, and self-propagating. In the latter half of the twentieth century, missiologists pointed out that these criteria, by themselves, are not sufficient to identify a mature and healthy church. The three-self criteria addressed only the sociological (i.e., who it is that does the governing, supporting, and propagating), not the cultural factors. It is quite possible to have a church in which local Christians govern, give, and evangelize but the music, church architecture, homiletical style, ethical reflection, sense of identity, theological discourse, and patterns of bodily expression reflect the foreign culture of the missionary rather than local cultural patterns. Christian anthropologists, in the journal *Practical Anthropology* and elsewhere, increasingly called for indigenous cultural forms and symbols. In 1958, for example, William

---

1. I express appreciation to Hartmut Scherer who worked closely with me in the validity and reliability tests for the questionnaire employed in this research. Thanks also to Craig Ott for feedback provided on an earlier version of this paper. Any weaknesses remaining are my own.

Smalley pointed out that three-self churches often exhibited Western leadership styles and cultural patterns. He stated that such churches should not be considered fully indigenous until believers lived "in the patterns of the local society."[2] Charles Kraft also stressed the importance of focusing on indigenous cultural patterns, meanings, and images.[3]

In 1972, Linwood Barney, an anthropologist with the Christian and Missionary Alliance, rather than focusing on cultural dynamics under the rubric of indigeneity, preferred the term inculturation to capture the relationship of church and Gospel to culture. He defined inculturation as "that process or state in which a new principle has been culturally 'clothed' in meaningful forms in a culture."[4] According to Robert Schreiter, the inculturation concept involves a fusion of "the theological principle of incarnation with the social-science concept of acculturation."[5] But while the term "inculturation" was prominent in Roman Catholic thought, evangelical missiological discussion continued to focus on "indigeneity." Increasingly Evangelicals saw cultural dynamics as the core of indigeneity. (Eventually, however, Evangelicals shifted to the term "contextualization," also introduced in 1972, about which more below.)

Alan Tippett provided a definition of indigeneity that clearly went beyond the three-self construct:

> When the indigenous people of a community think of the Lord as their own, not a foreign Christ; when they do things as unto the Lord, meeting the cultural needs around them, worshipping in patterns they understand; when their congregations function in participation in a body which is structurally indigenous; then you have an indigenous church.[6]

In 1973 Tippett articulated six criteria of indigeneity. He accepted self-support and self-propagation, but split self-governing into self-functioning and self-determining. In addition he spoke of self-image and self-service.[7] Ebbie Smith also called for six criteria, but substituted "self-adapting to local culture" in place of Tippett's "self-image."[8] Perhaps the most influential

---

2. Smalley, "Cultural Implications," 51–65.
3. Kraft, "Measuring Indigeneity," 118–52.
4. Barney, "Supracultural," 57.
5. Schreiter, *Constructing Local Theologies*, 5.
6. Tippett, *Introduction to Missiology*, 136.
7. Tippett, *Verdict Theology*, 148–63.
8. Smith, *Manual for Church Growth*, 41–54.

addition to the three selves of Anderson and Venn was "self-theologizing," proposed by Paul Hiebert.[9]

While indigeneity is generally thought of as a unitary construct, Smalley argued in his 1958 article that each aspect of indigeneity is a separate variable that may or may not be closely linked to the others. In this regard, he particularly pointed to self-support.[10] One of the interests of the present essay is to investigate the relationship between self-support and other marks of indigeneity.

In 1974 Hans Kasdorf called for the development of measures of indigeneity.[11] In 1976 Ebbie Smith proposed measures for six elements of indigeneity.[12] In 1979 Kraft developed four scales focused on cultural patterns, meanings, and images.[13] A number of missiologists worked with Kraft's four scales to analyze indigeneity in specific cultural settings.[14] David Price also published an instrument to measure indigeneity.[15]

Each of these efforts had serious limitations. Kraft's instrument did not feature forced-choice questions, and it was not designed in a way that allowed for statistical analysis. Price employed focused, forced-choice questions, but the choices provided were not exhaustive, mutually exclusive, or consistently scale-like. Smith's instrument was designed to produce actual measures, but each question required a paragraph of accompanying explanation. None of the instruments indicated that any validity or reliability tests were conducted. There do not appear to have been any statistical studies that actually employed any of these measures. At the same time, it is worth pointing out that in a discipline known primarily for *qualitative* research, these efforts highlighted the need to develop *quantitative* measures for missiological research.

In 1972, just at the point when quantitative measures were beginning to be considered by missiologists, Taiwanese theologian Shoki Coe called for a change in terminology from "indigenization" to "contextualization." While noting the close connection between the two terms, Coe indicated that "contextualization" was intended "to convey all that is implied in the familiar term indigenization," and he emphasized that contextualization

---

9. Hiebert, *Anthropological Insights*, 193–224.
10. Smalley, "Cultural Implications," 51–65.
11. Kasdorf, "Indigenous Church Principles," 71–86.
12. Smith, *Manual for Church Growth*, 41–54.
13. Kraft, "Measuring Indigeneity," 139–49.
14. Castillo, "Towards Greater Equivalence," 239–52; Guli, "Strategizing Movement," 226–38; Wisley, "Towards a Dynamic Indigenous," 207–25.
15. Price, "Eliciting the Data," 153–82.

was "a more dynamic concept which is open to change and which is future oriented."[16] Hiebert's discussion of a fourth self, self-theologizing, was in fact elaborated under the heading "contextualization" rather than "indigeneity." The fact that he labeled self-theologizing a "fourth self" illustrates the close connections between indigeneity and contextualization. Simon Kwan's analysis of the shift from "indigeneity" to "contextualization" concludes that this was a shift in vocabulary rather than a fundamental change of paradigm.[17] With this Scott Moreau largely agrees.[18]

Missiological discourses on indigenization/contextualization have been informed by theology and sometimes by historical and ethnographic research. But missiology has not developed quantitative measures of its concepts, employed them in research, and tested theory with the results. Qualitative research is suited for answering a variety of questions. But only quantitative research can test hypothesized relations between variables. For example, older discussions of indigeneity stress that outside funding adversely affects the indigenous church. By contrast, newer advocates of external funding stress the positive outcomes of resource sharing with indigenous churches. Proponents of each ideology make empirical claims about the impact of such funding patterns, but the actual research assessing such empirical claims is minimal. The hypothesized relation between self-support and self-governance is an empirical question, not one to be settled by definition or theological debate. I can find no research that demonstrates statistically that the various attributes thought of as constituting indigeneity/contextualization are closely connected with each other, or alternatively, independent of each other.

STATEMENT OF THE RESEARCH PROBLEM

This essay describes an effort to develop quantitative measures of indigenization/contextualization and to explore statistically the relationship between the following variables: (1) self-support, (2) self-governance, (3) self-propagation, (4) self-theologizing, (5) self-initiated service, (6) use of local cultural forms, and (7) social presence. In addition, the essay explores the following variables related to the well-being of local churches historically influenced by missionaries: (8) numerical church growth, (9) spirituality of the church, (10) perceived foreignness of the church, (11) syncretism exhibited by church members, and (12) social conflict in the church. Finally,

16. Coe, "Contextualizing Theology," 21.
17. Kwan, "From Indigenization to Contextualization," 236–50.
18. Moreau, *Mapping Evangelical Contextualization*.

the research focuses on whether it is the *nature* of external funding, rather than simply the fact of external funding, that adversely affects contextualization (if in fact there are adverse effects). This issue involves examining a final variable, (13) the contrast between external funding through informal and person-based connections as compared to external funding through formal channels, accredited procedures, and church-appointed stewards.

Hypotheses to Be Tested

It is hypothesized that the variables commonly thought of as aspects of indigeneity/contextualization—self-support, self-governance, self-propagation, self-theologizing, self-initiated service, use of own cultural forms, and social presence—are closely and positively correlated, supporting the idea that they constitute a unitary construct.

It is hypothesized that historic mission-influenced churches that demonstrate healthy contextualization (by the above criteria) are more likely to grow numerically and to exemplify a vibrant spirituality, and less likely to be perceived as foreign, less likely to exhibit syncretism, and less likely to have conflict in the church.

It is hypothesized that the nature of external funding, and not merely the fact of external funding, is closely related to negative outcomes on the other variables.

Definition of Terms

Self-support: Local church personnel and ministry are supported materially and financially by church members and local Christians rather than depending primarily on support from cultural outsiders.

Self-governance: Decision-making in the church is done by those who are similar socially and culturally to people who make up the church, rather than being done by people who are nationally, socially, culturally, or ethnically "other" than the membership affected by decisions.

Self-propagation: The vision and motivation for evangelism, and the energy and activity in carrying out evangelistic witness, is sustained by the church and its members, rather than falling largely to missionaries and cultural outsiders.

Self-theologizing: In this church Christians who are insiders to the culture address the issues and lived realities of their own people theologically, rather than simply replicating theologizing done elsewhere.[19]

Self-initiated service: Members of this church serve others and help those in need, rather than simply looking to outsiders for help.[20]

Own cultural forms: The culturally contingent forms and aesthetic judgments which underpin church life are closer to church members' own culture than to the culture of foreign missionaries.

Social presence: The church is comprised of members who are actually present socially in the primary social arenas of their society rather than existing in a kind of ghetto with dense patterns of interaction only with Christians and foreign missionaries.[21]

Numerical church growth: The church experiences steady growth in attendance and membership, with regular conversions contributing to this growth.

Spirituality of church members: Church members exemplify genuine and authentic God-focused discourses and practices.

Perceived foreignness of the church: Local people who are not members of the church perceive the church as foreign in its characteristics and in the interests it serves.

Syncretism in the church: Local Christians continue to embrace beliefs and live out practices from their pre-Christian lives that are fundamentally incompatible with the Christian faith.

Social conflict in the church: Social conflict and discord characterize this church.

Personalistic giving: Giving based on informal and person-based connections rather than through formal channels, accredited procedures, and church-appointed stewards.

Measurement Design, Validity, and Reliability Testing

Unlike gender or age, which require only a single question, variables that are abstract or complex are best measured through a set of multiple questions, yielding results that can be added together to arrive at a composite measurement. The validity of the measuring instrument is the degree to which

---

19. As noted earlier, this variable was first articulated by Paul Hiebert.

20. Tippett appears to have been the first to propose this variable, arguing that loving service is as much a part of the Christian mandate as evangelism.

21. Although I've not seen this variable formally proposed in the literature on indigeneity/contextualization, it is not an uncommon theme in broader discussions of Christian relations with the larger society. See, e.g., Hunter, *To Change the World*.

it measures what it purports to measure. For each variable to be measured, literature describing that variable was carefully studied, and a set of fifteen questions was prepared based on the reading of the literature, with each question intended to be a measure of the variable. As a further validity test, fourteen PhD students in missiology, with first-hand knowledge of congregations originally planted by missionaries, examined all items for content validity. They were given a written summary of each variable definition, along with the accompanying set of fifteen items designed to measure each variable. They were asked to identify the five items they felt best measured the variable and to circle all items they felt were not valid measures of the construct or were problematic for other reasons. They were also asked to provide written explanations of their assessments. Between three and ten of the best questions for each measure were selected after first determining that each set of questions gave a satisfactory reliability score.[22] In addition, the fourteen graduate students completed the survey about a church they knew.[23]

Measures of Each Variable

The following variables were operationalized with the specific questions listed under each. Respondents were instructed to answer with reference to a specific church known to them by personal experience, using a five-point Likert Scale from "strongly disagree" to "strongly agree." The number following each variable represents the reliability score (Cronbach's alpha) for each measure.

Self-Support, .827

Most members of this church support the ministry of the church financially.
- The church building was/is paid for primarily through the giving of local believers.
- Local Bible schools or seminaries that train pastors receive most of their financial support from cultural outsiders to this community. (R)[24]

22. This was determined using Cronbach's alpha.

23. Factor analysis was used to assess construct validity. Items which had loadings >0.5 were interpreted as good measures of the variable. Cronbach's alpha was used to test for internal consistency in the items. Frequency distributions were analyzed and all items with low variance were eliminated or reworded. Items assessed by respondents as not being good for measuring a given construct were eliminated, as were items that produced results markedly divergent from the other items for a given measure. Cronbach's alpha is provided for each scale based on the final survey results.

24. Items marked "R" were "reverse scored."

- Indigenous missionaries or evangelists receive support for their ministry from the local churches.
- Individual indigenous seminary or Bible School professors receive large amounts of financial support from people who are culturally outsiders to this community. (R)
- Within the local Christian community, the most influential indigenous Christian leaders receive most of their funding from outside their own cultural community. (R)
- Pastoral salaries are provided exclusively through the giving of the church membership.

Self-Governance, .904

Foreign missionaries play a key role in determining leadership selection in this church. (R)

- Indigenous church leaders normally handle church discipline without missionary involvement.
- Foreign missionaries are involved in determining how church funds are spent. (R)
- Local church leaders are overly deferential to the wishes and expectations of foreign missionaries. (R)
- If there is a sharp difference in opinion between local church leaders and foreign missionaries, the final decision would probably reflect the opinion of the missionaries. (R)
- Local church leaders fear the consequences of not submitting to missionary wishes. (R)
- The local church selects its own leaders without the intervention of missionaries.

Self-Propagation, .823

Members of the church often share their faith with others.

- Most of the recent converts to the Christian faith were converted under the influence of indigenous believers.
- Members of this church have a deep burden for the souls of those who are lost.

Self-Theologizing, .757

Pastors do a good job helping their congregation understand how the Bible relates to everyday ethical challenges they face.
- Sermon illustrations used by indigenous pastors draw from the everyday life of local people.
- There are major ethical problems which local Christians face that are never addressed by Christian leaders. (R)
- Indigenous church leaders see themselves as transmitting, in an unchanged form, truth originally learned from missionaries. (R)
- Indigenous leaders see themselves as reformulating their proclamation of the Christian message to fit the lived realities of the people being addressed.
- Many of the songs sung in church were composed by indigenous believers.
- Most of the songs sung in church were originally learned from foreign missionaries. (R)
- Indigenous church leaders have significant input in the type of leadership training which is provided.
- Indigenous church leaders have significant roles in training of new leaders.
- Leadership training curriculum reflects indigenous church leaders' contribution to the course content.

Self-Initiated Service, .695

Widows who are members of the church receive help from the church when they are in need.
- Widows who are members of the church receive help primarily from foreign missionaries when they are in need. (R)
- If there are situations of social injustice for widows or orphans, indigenous church leaders willingly intervene on their behalf.
- When community members face hunger and poverty, the primary initiative for help comes from outside sources. (R)
- Service projects in the community are initiated primarily by foreign missionaries. (R)

Own Cultural Forms, .709

Indigenous musical instruments are used in the worship service.

- The church employs decorations and art designed by indigenous believers.
- Many church members would think it sinful to use indigenous musical instruments in the service. (R)
- The architecture of the church building stands out as reflecting foreign architectural patterns. (R)
- Sermon illustrations regularly draw from the popular culture of indigenous people (local proverbs, stories, history, etc.).
- Gifted local musicians who convert to Christianity would be allowed to use their prior musical patterns and instruments to sing praise to God in this church.

Social Presence, .678

Church members are involved in as wide a variety of professions as are non-believers.

- The Christian community encourages their children to withdraw from participation in the major institutions of society. (R)
- A young person from church who wanted to be a journalist would receive strong encouragement from church leaders.
- A young person from church who wished to go into politics would receive strong encouragement from church leaders.
- Most church members have good reputations with their neighbors.

Numerical Church Growth, .916

The total membership of this church is currently higher than it was a few years ago.

- Average attendance at worship services has been growing.
- This church regularly adds new members by conversion.

Spirituality of the Church, .841

Most church members regularly spend time reading/studying/or listening to the Bible.
- Most church members seek God's guidance when making important decisions.
- Most church members talk about God and the Bible with their children.
- Most church members regularly pray.
- Most church members clearly indicate gratitude to God.

Perceived Foreignness of the Church, .704

Non-Christians see the church as serving the colonial interests of foreigners.
- Non-Christians from the community see the church as serving the best interests of the local community. (R)
- Non-Christians who visit the church would immediately assess the music as foreign.
- Non-Christians in the community would view conversion to Christianity as something that makes the convert less indigenous, more foreign.

Syncretism by Christians in the Church, .639

Because of the influence of their culture, many church members hold beliefs which fundamentally contradict the core doctrines of the Christian faith.
- Some members of this church continue to read and trust the scriptures of another religion.
- Some members of this church continue to observe religious practices from their prior religion.
- Church leaders would correct and/or discipline any church member who seeks healing from a non-Christian *religious healer* (such as a shaman or witchdoctor). (R)

Social Conflict in the Church, .798

Members of this church consistently show love for each other. (R)
- There is a great deal of envy and jealousy in this church.

- A large amount of gossip has sometimes been present in this church.
- Harmony and peace characterize this church. (R)
- The pastor of this church is often criticized.
- The pastor of this church is able to trust that others in the church consistently have the pastor's best interests at heart. (R)

Personalistic Giving, .819

Requests for foreign funding are usually formulated through designated channels of authority within the indigenous church. (R)
- Requests for foreign funding are usually made by individuals at their own initiative.
- Requests for foreign funding are usually made through explicit and formal procedures. (R)
- Most recipients of external funding are not accountable to anyone in their own church for the way in which funds are administered.
- Decisions by foreign sources to provide funding here are usually given to support particular individuals.

Survey Respondents and Church Descriptions

In the spring of 2003, a questionnaire with 120 questions was mailed to 288 missiology professors in the United States.[25] The cover letter asked if they had extensive first-hand knowledge of a specific congregation historically influenced by the presence of missionaries, and, if so, to answer each question in the survey to the best of their ability about that church and the church's larger context. One hundred forty-two fully completed questionnaires were returned within four months, a response rate of 54 percent. Since survey recipients who lacked requisite knowledge were asked not to fill out the survey, it is assumed that non-response, for many, simply reflected a recognized lack of relevant knowledge. In any case, for a single mailing, this was a high rate of return.

---

25. The survey was distributed to the US-based missiology professors listed in the *Directory of Schools and Professors of Mission and Evangelism in the United States and Canada: 2002–2004*, ed. Dotsey Welliver and Minnette Smith (Wheaton, IL: Evangelism and Missions Information Service).

The responses indicated that the average age of these 142 congregations was 34 years, the median congregational size was 150, and the mean congregational size was 395. The returns represented 66 countries: Africa 42, Asia 30, Europe 17, Latin America and the Caribbean 29, Middle East 6, Oceania 15, and Native American 3. Altogether these congregations used 82 languages in worship.

More than 90 percent of those filling out the questionnaires had spent more than three years as a missionary in the same country as the church they reported on, with 47 percent having spent more than ten years there. Sixty-eight percent claimed to have attended more than 100 worship services in the church they reported on, and only 15 percent reported that they attended fewer than 50 services at this church. Respondents were asked to rate their linguistic competence on a scale of 0 to 10 in the primary language of the worshiping community. With "10" representing perfect fluency, 65 percent of respondents rated themselves at a 7 or above, with only 13 percent scoring their linguistic fluency as less than 5 percent. In short, respondents appear to have been in a strong position to answer the questions about the churches they knew personally.

The survey asked detailed questions about individual attributes in a specific church. The answer to each question gave a number. The numbers were totaled and added to the numbers from the other questions measuring the same construct, giving a total score for each variable. It was by means of statistical analysis of variables as they co-varied across 142 churches that the relationship of variables was established.

RESEARCH RESULTS[26]

The research findings lend support to the view that self-support, self-governance, self-propagation, self-theologizing, self-initiated service, social presence, and use of own cultural forms are closely linked, just as missiological theorists have proposed. In short, the hypothesis that the variables commonly associated with indigeneity/contextualization are closely correlated is supported by the research, and therefore they may be thought of as constituting a unitary construct.

---

26. The accompanying table and two scatterplot figures are designed for specialists. The general reader is given summary accounts in the main text.

Table: Correlations of 7 variables related to healthy contextualization

		Self-supporting	Self-governing	Self-propagating	Self-theologizing	Self-initiated service	Reflect Culture
Self-governing	Pearson correlation Sig. (2-tailed) N	.627 .000 142					
Self-propagating	Pearson correlation Sig. 2-tailed N	.363 .000 142	.348 .000 142				
Self-theologizing	Pearson correlation Sig. 2-tailed N	.409 .000 142	.478 .000 142	.410 .000 142			
Self-initiated service	Pearson correlation Sig. 2-tailed N	.524 .000 142	.540 .000 142	.366 .000 142	.521 .000 142		
Reflects own culture	Pearson correlation Sig. 2-tailed N	.297 .000 142	.360 .000 142	.252 .000 142	.499 .000 142	.349 .000 142	
Social presence	Pearson correlation Sig. 2-tailed N	.362 .000 142	.486 .000 142	.374 .000 142	.510 .000 142	.462 .000 142	.342 .000 142

Each of the scales strongly and positively correlates with the sum of all of the other scales, as follows:

Self-governance and sum of other scales: r = .680**[27]
Self-initiated service and sum of other scales: r = .654**
Self-theologizing and sum of other scales: r = .641**
Self-support and sum of other scales: r = .607**
Social presence and sum of other scales: r = .581**
Own culture and sum of other scales: r = .484**
Self-propagation and sum of other scales: r = .474**

When added together, these seven variables have a combined Cronbach's alpha of .816.

The scale which is most predictive of all the other scales combined is self-governance (r = .680), as seen in Figure 1. The higher a church scored

[27] The symbol ** indicates that correlation is significant at the 0.01 level.

Researching Contextualization in Churches Influenced by Missionaries

on self-governance the more likely it was to score high on a composite of all other dimensions of healthy contextualization. The lower a church scored on self-governance, the lower it was likely to score on the composite of all other measures of healthy contextualization.

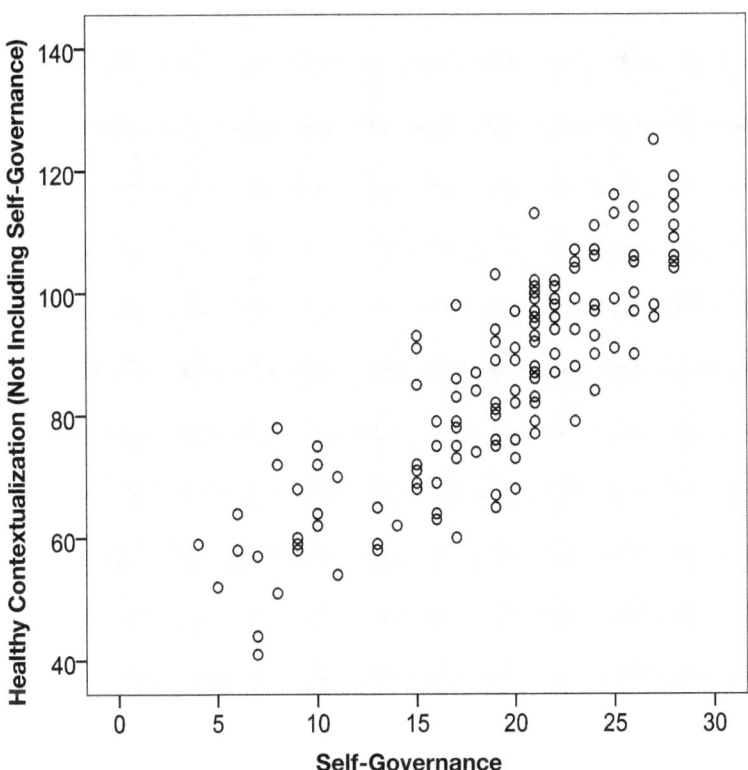

Figure 1: Scatterplot of self-governance and healthy contextualization

The scale which is most predictive of all the other scales combined is self-governance (r = .680), as seen in the Figure 1.

If the seven measures of healthy contextualization are taken as a single composite measure, then the data demonstrate a number of other associations. First, healthy contextualization means that non-Christians are less likely to judge the church as foreign in its characteristics and in the ends which it serves (r = -.588). Second, healthy contextualization is associated with positive numerical church growth (r = .489). Third, healthy contextualization is positively associated with the spirituality of church members, with members of contextualized churches more likely to exemplify genuine and

God-focused discourses and practices in their personal lives than members of non-contextualized churches (r = .573). Fourth, healthy contextualization is negatively associated with social conflict in the church (r = -.342**); and fifth, perhaps most surprisingly, healthy contextualization is negatively associated with syncretism in the church (r = -.445).

Missionaries sometimes frame contextualization as a slippery slope moving a church toward syncretism, asking the question, "How far can we go in contextualizing until it becomes syncretistic?" A key motive on the part of missionaries unwilling to relinquish control is the fear of syncretism. But in fact, the survey results suggest that a mission church with indigenous leadership, making full use of local cultural forms, and doing its own theologizing is likely to create a form of Christian faith that more deeply satisfies and that leaves Christians less likely to feel the need, for example, to go outside the Christian community to shamans or other religious practitioners for help in time of need.

Counterintuitive as it may be, failure to contextualize contributes to syncretism, and church members will be likely to affirm beliefs and continue practices that characterized their pre-Christian lives. The churches with highest levels of syncretism have low levels of contextualization, and churches with higher levels of healthy contextualization have lower levels of syncretism. (See Figure 2.)

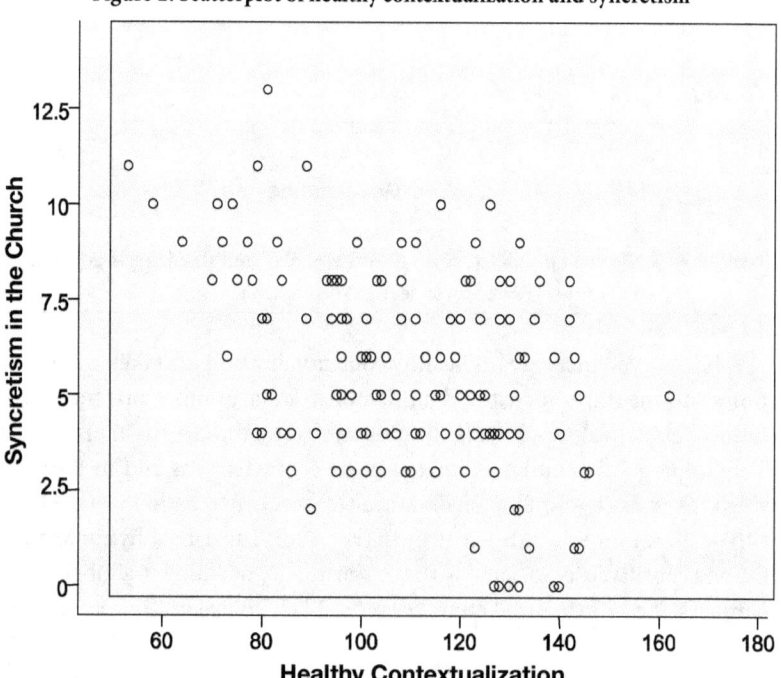

Figure 2: Scatterplot of healthy contextualization and syncretism

Results from the survey indicate that robust levels of self-support are pivotal to the health and well-being of churches. Whether this precludes all outside sources of funding may be another question. Unfortunately, this survey did not differentiate sufficiently self-support from the amount or nature of outside funding that may have been present. One can imagine churches with robust levels of self-support that also accept certain kinds of outside funding.

My own seminary, as with most institutions of higher education in America, is not completely supported through tuition. Rather, our foundation officers seek financial support from around the world, including from Singapore and Korea. While there are always issues of power and control where large amounts of money are concerned, most institutions of higher education believe it is possible to organize structures of philanthropic giving that are not damaging to the integrity of the academic enterprise. Rather than thinking purely in terms of whether or not outside funds are present, we should perhaps think in terms of the manner in which financial resources are given. One can imagine very different outcomes if outside donors to a seminary determined what faculty they would support, as compared to donors giving through accredited procedures.

Results from this survey demonstrate that there is a strong negative association between personalistic patterns of external giving and healthy contextualization ($r = -.526^{**}$). That is, it is the nature of external giving, and not merely the fact of external giving, which may be damaging to contextualization. Unfortunately, new mission structures are sometimes funded by donors who give in "personalistic" ways. Such donors often want a measure of control over how the money is used. Indeed, the more the control over financial matters shifts to donor individuals and churches, the more willing such donors are to give generously. And the more that there is a personal relationship and human face to recipients—duly respectful, appreciative and deferential recipients—the more inclined donors are to give.

Think, for example, of child sponsorship. Donors typically have less contextual knowledge than local leaders or long-term missionaries. Giving based on an outsider's emotional response to the personality of a child or adult may not be contextually wise and balanced. But there are powerful forces pressing towards personalistic patterns of giving, and away from giving which comes through formal channels, accredited procedures, and church-appointed stewards. This research suggests this is harmful to healthy contextualization.

CONCLUSION

Missiology needs to develop stronger foundations in quantitative research. This paper provides a number of validated quantitative measures of missiological constructs that others may wish to utilize in further research, or build on and improve, in order to provide missiology with effective research tools.

The results reported here support the claim that variables related to indigeneity/contextualization co-vary with each other and arguably constitute a single unitary construct. Research results demonstrate that healthy contextualization has positive outcomes in numerical church growth and spirituality, lowers the extent to which churches are perceived by non-believers as foreign and colonial, lowers the extent of social conflict in the church, and lowers the likelihood of church members being syncretistic.

Finally, results highlight the need for further research on funding patterns in global Christianity, and the impact of those funding patterns on healthy church life.

BIBLIOGRAPHY

Barney, Linwood. "The Supracultural and the Cultural: Implications for Frontier Missions." In *The Gospel and Frontier People*, edited by R. Pierce Beaver, 48–57. Pasadena, CA: William Carey Library, 1973.

Bediako, Kwame. *Christianity in Africa: The Renewal of a Non-Western Religion*. Edinburgh: Edinburgh University Press, 1995.

Bevans, Stephen. "Inculturation of Theology in Asia. The Federation of Asian Bishops' Conferences, 1970–1995." *Studia Missionalia* 45 (1996) 1–23.

Castillo, Metosalem. "Towards Greater Equivalence in the CAMACOP." In *Readings in Dynamic Indigeneity*, edited by Charles H. Kraft and Tom N. Wisley, 239–52. Pasadena, CA: William Carey Library, 1979.

Coe, Shoki. "Contextualizing Theology." In *Third World Theologies: Asian, African and Latin American Contributions to a Radical, Theological Realignment in the Church*, edited by Gerald H. Anderson and Thomas F. Stransky, 10–24. Grand Rapids: Eerdmans, 1972.

Crichton, Angus. "Consultation and Cooperation in Disseminating Research on Ugandan Christianity." Paper presented at Yale-Edinburgh, 2010. Published in "Sounding the Ngoma," newsletter of Ngoma Ecumenical Publishing Consortium, Henry Martyn Centre, Cambridge, April 26, 2011. No pages. Online: http://www.martynmission.cam.ac.uk/pages/research-projects.php.

Dallaire, Roméo, and Brent Beardsley. *Shake Hands with the Devil: The Failure of Humanity in Rwanda*. Toronto: Vintage Canada, 2004.

Farhadian, Charles E., editor. *Christian Worship Worldwide: Expanding Horizons, Deepening Practices*. Grand Rapids: Eerdmans, 2007.

Guli, John. "Strategizing Movement Toward Greater Dynamic Equivalence in Lardin Gabas Church." In *Readings in Dynamic Indigeneity*, edited by Charles H. Kraft and Tom N. Wisley, 226–38. Pasadena, CA: William Carey Library, 1979.

Hiebert, Paul G. *Anthropological Insights for Missionaries*. Grand Rapids: Baker Academic, 1985.

Hunter, James Davison. *To Change the World: The Irony, Tragedy, and Possibility of Christianity in the Late Modern World*. New York: Oxford University Press, 2010.

Kasdorf, Hans. "Indigenous Church Principles: A Survey of Origin and Development." In *Readings in Dynamic Indigeneity*, edited by Charles Kraft and Tom Wisely, 71–86. Pasadena, CA: William Carey Library, 1979.

Kraft, Charles H. "Measuring Indigeneity." In *Readings in Dynamic Indigeneity*, edited by Charles H. Kraft and Tom N. Wisley, 118–52. Pasadena, CA: William Carey Library, 1979.

Kwan, Simon Shui-man. *From Indigenization to Contextualization: A Change in Discursive Practice Rather Than a Shift in Paradigm*. Online: http://www.euppublishing.com/doi/abs/10.3366/swc.2005.11.2.236.

Lee, Moonjang. "Reading the Bible in the Non-Western Church: An Asian Dimension." In *Mission in the 21st Century: Exploring the Five Marks of Global Mission*, edited by Andrew Walls and Cathy Ross, 148–56 and 217–18. London: Darton, Longman & Todd, 2008.

Martin, Dale. *The Corinthian Body*. New Haven: Yale University Press, 1995.

Moreau, Scott. *Mapping Evangelical Contextualization*. Grand Rapids: Kregel, 2011.

Nelson, Gary, et al. *Going Global, A Congregation's Introduction to Mission beyond Our Borders*. St. Louis: Chalice, 2011.

Niringiye, D. Z. "The Church in the World: A Historical-Ecclesiological Study of the Church of Uganda with Particular Reference to Post-Independence Uganda, 1962–1992." Unpublished thesis, University of Edinburgh, 1997.

Price, David. "Eliciting the Data for Measuring Indigeneity." In *Readings in Dynamic Indigeneity*, edited by Charles H. Kraft and Tom N. Wisley, 153–82. Pasadena, CA: William Carey Library, 1979.

Rooms, Nigel. *The Faith of the English: Integrating Christ and Culture*. London: SPCK, 2011.

Sacks, Jonathan. *The Dignity of Difference: How to Avoid the Clash of Civilizations*. London: Continuum, 2002.

Sanneh, Lamin. *Whose Religion Is Christianity? The Gospel beyond the West*. Grand Rapids: Eerdmans, 2003.

Schreiter, Robert J. *Constructing Local Theologies*. New York: Orbis, 1985.

Smalley, William. "Cultural Implications of an Indigenous Church." *Practical Anthropology* 5 (1958) 51–65.

Smith, Ebbie C. *A Manual for Church Growth Surveys*. Pasadena, CA: William Carey Library, 1976.

Stone, Bryan. "The Ecclesiality of Mission in the Context of Empire." In *Walk Humbly with the Lord: Church and Mission Engaging Plurality*, edited by Viggo Mortensen and Andreas O. Nielsen, 105–11. Grand Rapids: Eerdmans, 2010.

Thiselton, Anthony C. *The First Epistle to the Corinthians, A Commentary on the Greek Text*. Grand Rapids: Eerdmans, 2000.

Tiénou, Tite. "Christian Theology in an Era of World Christianity." In *Globalizing Theology: Belief and Practice in an Era of World Christianity*, edited by Craig Ott and Harold A. Netland, 37–51. Grand Rapids: Baker Academic, 2006.

Tippett, Alan Richard. *Introduction to Missiology*. Pasadena, CA: William Carey Library, 1988.

———. *Verdict Theology in Missionary Theory*. Pasadena, CA: William Carey Library, 1973.

Vanhoozer, Kevin. "'One Rule to Rule Them All?': Theological Method in an Era of World Christianity." In *Globalizing Theology: Belief and Practice in an Era of World Christianity*, edited by Craig Ott and Harold A. Netland, 85–126. Grand Rapids: Baker Academic, 2007.

Walls, Andrew F. *The Cross-Cultural Process in Christian History: Studies in the Transmission and Appropriation of Faith*. Maryknoll, NY: Orbis, 2002.

———. "The Ephesian Moment." In *The Cross-Cultural Process in Christian History*, 72–81. Maryknoll, NY: Orbis, 2002.

———. "The Gospel as Prisoner and Liberator of Culture." In *The Missionary Movement in Christian History: Studies in the Transmission of Faith*, 3–15. Maryknoll, NY: Orbis, 1996.

———. *The Missionary Movement in Christian History: Studies in the Transmission of Faith*. Maryknoll, NY: Orbis, 1996.

———. "Old Athens and New Jerusalem: Some Signposts for Christian Scholarship in the Early History of Mission Studies." *International Bulletin of Missionary Research* 21 (1997) 146–53.

Wisley, Tom N. "Towards a Dynamic Indigenous Church." In *Readings in Dynamic Indigeneity*, edited by Charles H. Kraft and Tom N. Wisley, 207–25. Pasadena, CA: William Carey Library, 1979.

22

"Please Be Extra Vigilant"
On Being Attentive to World Christianity

CATHY ROSS

"IN LIGHT OF RECENT world events, please be extra vigilant." This announcement at Oxford railway station penetrated my consciousness as I was reading my book, waiting for my train to London. I looked up, speculating how exactly we were to be "extra vigilant." I wondered if my fellow travelers were having the same thoughts. However, everything continued as normal at a railway station—people purchasing tickets and last minute coffees and newspapers, then rushing for trains. This was Tuesday morning, the first day of the Queen's historic visit to Ireland and a little more than two weeks after the royal wedding and the killing of Osama bin Laden.

On further reflection, it struck me that this announcement may be a good metaphor for our Western attitude toward world Christianity. The events of the world do have an impact on our lifestyle, even in a small city such as Oxford on a quiet Tuesday morning. World events, even in far-off places, enter our daily lives whether we like it or not. In the same way, world Christianity is the faith to which we belong and world Christianity does affect our way of being Christian in the world. We belong to a worldwide church, we are inextricably connected to our sisters and brothers in the body of Christ, and so their concerns are our concerns, their joys are ours, their struggles are ours, and their experience of the Christian faith will influence and shape our discipleship.

This opening up of world Christianity, the new vistas and insights that it offers us in our own contexts, has been the most important challenge for me from Tiénou's writings over the years. He has constantly faced us with awareness of the other, of the reality of African Christianity, of the necessity of expressing Christian teaching in language and thought forms understandable in an African context, and of the absolute necessity of doing theology in an "era of World Christianity."[1] In this essay I would like to reflect on the importance of world Christianity for our discipleship, with gratitude to Tiénou for stimulating many of these thoughts.

THEOLOGY IN AN ERA OF WORLD CHRISTIANITY

What does it look like to engage in theology in an era of world Christianity? First, a few thoughts on terminology. Tiénou is careful in his use of language and terminology, as he has pointed out in his use of the term "world Christianity" rather than "global Christianity." This may seem like a pedantic difference to many of us, but in fact it holds an important distinction we would do well to heed. Lamin Sanneh explains this: "World Christianity is not one thing but a variety of indigenous responses through more or less effective local idioms, but in any case without necessarily the European enlightenment frame. 'Global Christianity,' on the other hand, is the faithful replication of Christian forms and patterns developed in Europe."[2]

Immediately we see that this terminology points to important differences—Christianity is a world religion because it is a local religion—flexible and able to adapt and contextualize. Global Christianity alludes to homogenization, sameness, and lack of flexibility to adapt. Tiénou prefers the term world Christianity, as this reminds us that Christianity's center of gravity has shifted and that the Christian faith is at home in any culture and not the prisoner of any.[3] He points to the apologetic value of this understanding, as Christianity can no longer be understood "as a white man's religion."[4] So Christianity can shake off its ambiguous relationship with Empire and begin to flourish in local contexts, by local ways and means.

---

1. Tiénou, "Christian Theology," 37–51.
2. Sanneh, *Whose Religion Is Christianity?*, 22.
3. Walls, "Gospel as Prisoner," 3–15.
4. Tiénou, "Christian Theology," 41.

However, he claims that many around the world still "perceive Christianity as a Western religion."[5] This is surprising, for we have known for many years of the shift in the center of gravity, that representative Christianity is to be found in the Majority World. For example, we are frequently told that the average Anglican is a black, female, Bible-believing teenager. Scottish missiologist and historian Andrew Walls was writing over 20 years ago that "the future of the Christian faith, its shape in the 21st and 22nd centuries, is being decided by events which are now taking place in Africa, Asia and Latin America, or which will do so in the near future."[6] Ten years later he was still reminding us that Christianity is primarily a non-Western religion, that our twenty-first-century faith will require robust scholarship from the soil of Africa, Asia and Latin America, and that the "most urgent reason for the study of the religious traditions of Africa and Asia, of the Amerindian and the Pacific peoples, is their significance for Christian theology; they are the substratum of the Christian faith and life for the greater number of Christians in the world."[7] Fifteen years on from this statement (published in 1997), are we any closer to this reality? Have we in the West really taken on board what it means to be world Christians, or are we still operating under the paradigm of global Christianity? Are we still, as John Mbiti asserted in 1976, kerygmatically universal but theologically provincial?[8] In other words, do we still believe in and proclaim a universal Gospel but allow our theology to remain limited and constrained by our own provincial horizons?

While we certainly want to celebrate the local and allow it to flourish—that is what contextualization is all about—we also need to engage in a conversation that takes us beyond the exotic and occasional short-term mission trip to a place where our discipleship is shaped and refined by worldwide encounter. Why is this so important? It is important because we are all part of one body. Paul's body analogy in 1 Corinthians 12 is crucial to understanding what it means to be a world Christian. "For we were all baptized by one Spirit into one body—whether Jews or Greeks, slave or free—and we were all given the one Spirit to drink" (1 Cor 12:12). By using this body rhetoric Paul explicitly states that we need one another. Paul defines self-sufficiency as having no need of another and believes that this is alien to the body of Christ. Moreover, as Anthony Thistleton elaborates in his superb commentary on 1 Corinthians, this body imagery "explicitly rebukes those who think that they and their 'superior' gifts are self-sufficient for the whole

---

5. Ibid., 42.
6. Ibid., 44 (quoting Walls).
7. Walls, "Old Athens and New Jerusalem," 153.
8. Tiénou, "Christian Theology," 45 (quoting John Mbiti).

body, or that others are scarcely authentic parts of the body, as they themselves are."[9] Paul's rhetoric pushes for a reversal of a worldly understanding of honor and status. "The lower is made higher, and the higher lower."[10] Let us not think of ourselves more highly than we ought. This should give us pause for thought when we are still in a world captivated by honor and status, where the church in the West still commands unimaginable resources, prime real estate, honorific titles, and is sometimes co-opted by or at least colludes with secular powers.

I wonder if the world of theological education in the West suffers from a similar attitude of "superior gifts." Let me give you one small example of the inequities that exist in terms of theological research. Nearly 70 percent of doctoral research into Ugandan Christianity has been conducted by Ugandan researchers, but on analyzing doctoral research on Ugandan Christianity, one discovers that Western authors are twice as likely to publish their research in comparison to their African counterparts. And when published in the West, only half this doctoral research finds its way to libraries in Uganda.

There are complex reasons for this, including economic and cultural ones. African researchers face such heavy personal and professional demands on their time that research and writing are forced down their list of priorities. Yet we know that the church in Uganda has experienced explosive church growth, and as they have grown in their faith they have faced questions peculiar to their situation and context—on the nature of evil, the role of the ancestors, healing, and intergenerational conversion, for example. Theology from the West may be neither directly helpful nor applicable, as we may not be asking the same questions. However, Ugandan researchers have begun to research these issues and have formulated answers. Sadly, this research is not available to the wider church, as it remains unpublished; so we are all the more impoverished. Therefore it is not only the Ugandan church which misses out on the riches and fruit of her own theological reflection, but also the world church suffers from the absence of published reflection.[11]

Furthermore, we rejoice together and we suffer together. As Lionel Thornton observed, "It follows that in the body of Christ there are, strictly speaking, no private sufferings. All are shared because there is one life of the

---

9. Thiselton, *First Epistle to the Corinthians*, 1005.

10. Martin, *Corinthian Body*, 96.

11. Crichton, "Consultation and Cooperation." Crichton's paper utilized the respective strengths of the Centre for African Christian Studies, Kampala, the Department of Religious Studies, Makerere University, St. Mary's National Seminary, and Uganda Christian University.

whole. Accordingly, wrong done to one member is wrong done to the whole Church, and therefore to Christ himself."[12] When our sisters and brothers in the Ugandan church suffer, we too suffer.

Tiénou is blunt about this. He maintains that the West lives with a self-perception that it is the center of scholarship and that the rest, Africa, Asia, and Latin America, fit around the margins. He claims that the "rule of the palefaces" remains untroubled, so that our theology remains not only theologically provincial but also homogenous. This sounds alarmingly resonant of Empire. One of the characteristics of Empire is that it devalues the particularity of peoples and places. "Empires expand and maintain their power by the homogenization of place through the imposition of a unified and totalizing 'order' that erases difference so that one place is the same as another."[13] Majority world theologians believe that this totalizing happens regularly in theology. Choan-Seng Song from Taiwan "complains of Western theology's enslavement to an either-or rationalist logic and of its concomitant lack of imagination."[14] His "third-eye" theology begins with the heart rather than the head. Vanhoozer claims that we have entered into a new era in theology: "The reign of the sovereign knowing subject and of universal method, is coming to an end."[15] Steven Bevans has done us all a service by reminding us that there is no such thing as theology—there is only contextual theology.[16] If theology is genuinely faith seeking understanding, then there can be no such thing as a generic theology, a one size fits all, a universalizing theology; there can only be contextual theologies that are worked out and lived in particular contexts. Theologians construct their theology in their own language from the specificities of their own time, place, social location—their context. Vanhoozer claims that this attention to context "has resulted in a more vital and practical interpretation of Scripture in which understanding is a matter of loving as well as knowing God with all one's heart, mind and strength."[17] We are all the poorer if we do not appropriate this shift. I think Tiénou is fair when he claims that standard texts of systematic theology "either lack any reference to theologians of non-European descent or contain only passing references to some without significant interaction with their ideas."[18]

12. Thiselton, *First Epistle to the Corinthians*, 1012 (quoting Lionel Thornton).
13. Stone, "Ecclesiality of Mission," 109.
14. Vanhoozer, "One Rule," 90.
15. Ibid., 91.
16. Bevans, *Introduction to Theology*, ch. 8ff.
17. Vanhoozer, "One Rule," 93.
18. Tiénou, "Christian Theology," 50.

Today the Christian world is experiencing greater diversity than it has ever known before, and this offers us a new era in theology and in worship. Materials for theology are culturally conditioned. The first believers were Jews who saw Jesus in terms of Jewish history, tradition, and belief. But talking of Jesus as Messiah was meaningless for Greek-speaking Gentiles. They had to "translate," or find a term that meant something to a Greek pagan—so they chose *kyrios*, "lord," a title used for their cult divinities (Acts 11:19–21). Jewish believers had long seen "Messiah" as a rich title, full of biblical allusions and history, so using *kyrios* must have seemed an impoverishment to them, perhaps even dangerous. But this transposition has proved to be enriching and has given rise to different questions. When Stephen claimed that he saw Jesus at the right hand of God (Acts 7:56), does the transcendent God then have a right hand? What is the relationship of Christ to the Father? Were they the same *ousia*? And so Greek traditions, thought patterns, and intellectual methods of discourse were brought into play to explore what Christians believed.

This enriched Christian understanding and theology in a way that could not have happened if it had stayed within Jewish categories of thought and language. The use of new language and thought led to new discoveries about Christ. And we might say the same for later developments in theology such as the classical doctrines of the atonement, even the emergence of systematic theology itself as an exercise. Now the majority of Christians live in the Majority World and they will have to make Christian choices about their issues with their local materials for constructing theology. New questions will be asked about Jesus. "And the materials for constructing theology will be African and Asian as surely as earlier generations used the materials of Platonism and Roman and customary law."[19]

DISCIPLESHIP IN AN ERA OF WORLD CHRISTIANITY

As Paul understood, this interconnectedness, this global awareness, is vital to our well-being and growth as Christians, as members of the body of Christ. Why? Why should I care about the role of ancestors in the African church or what is happening to persecuted Christians? How can their experience—possibly so foreign and alien—have anything to do with my writing this in comfortable and wealthy Oxford? I must care because of the ontological reality that we are all connected, we are part of the body and we all have our humanity in common. Let me tell a story to further illustrate this. It is a story from the troubled Luwero region of Uganda in the 1980s.

19. Walls, *Cross-Cultural Process*, 81.

The bishop asked Serubidde to return to Luwero. He told him: "I have had a vision that we cannot keep away from the Luwero people anymore. With immediate effect, Serubidde, you have to serve the people. The Luwero people are your people. In peace and in trouble, they are your people. Serubidde, you must go to your people. Serubidde, that is what it means to be a people's pastor. I hope Jesus will protect you. In any eventuality, you must stand beside your people. If you cannot stand beside your people at their difficult time, how will you claim to be their pastor when they settle down? And one day they will. Whatever is going on in Luwero, and whatever will come next, God says, Serubidde, go to your people. Go to your people!"

After further prayer together, they made arrangements for him to leave for Luwero the next day. When he told Damallie, his wife, his encounter with Bishop Nsubuga, and the plan to return to Luwero, it was clear to her as well that the only way to be of service to the people of God was to be with them. Serubidde recalled his wife's words: "If that is what God says, we cannot do otherwise. Let us have all our trust in God. God will protect you. Let us serve our flock."[20]

And so for the next three years, Archdeacon Serubidde spent half of each week in the midst of his people in Luwero, visiting each of the camps where the rural population had fled because of insecurity. On every visit, he prayed with his people, preached to them, and handed out what relief items he had brought from the diocesan center. This story is in Bishop David Zac Niringiye's unpublished PhD thesis. It is an extraordinary story of Christian ministry by an archdeacon who chose to remain with his people at great personal cost. This may be a story far from our own personal experience. But I am connected to this story because it is a human story, because Serubidde Daudi and his wife Damallie are my brother and sister in Christ, because they covet our loving prayers and support, and because I need to learn how to identify with suffering not only in the world, but also in my context. This story encourages and challenges me to be a more faithful disciple in my own context.

Perhaps reflecting on the role of the ancestors for African theology is more remote to my experience. Or is it? The role of the ancestors is linked to old religious ways, many of which missionaries in the past demanded be repudiated and rejected. I do not have the space to elaborate a theology of the ancestors here, but allow me to quote Kwame Bediako who has done much work on this. "A theology of the ancestors is about the interpretation of the

---

20. Niringiye, "Church in the World," 252.

past in a way which shows that the present experience and knowledge of the grace of God in the Gospel of Jesus Christ have been truly anticipated and prefigured in the quests and the responses to the Transcendent in former times, as these have been reflected in the lives of African people."[21]

How one deals with this question of the ancestors invokes basic issues of identity, community, belonging, pluralism, our past, and our future. These are questions we all have in common as part of the body of Christ. While these may be worked out in a specific way in the African context, they may challenge us and enlarge our understanding of our own contexts. Indeed a book published in 2011 in Britain, *The Faith of the English*, by Nigel Rooms, draws on Bediako's work where the author makes a plea that the English should not "denigrate [their] own primal religion."[22] And so what may have started off as being far away soon connects with our own story.

When I asked a friend how world Christianity affected and shaped his own Christian faith and discipleship, he told me that Tiénou was the first person he had ever heard lecturing in a serious way on African Christianity. This can be a powerful way for students in the West to engage with world Christianity—at least to hear the voices of those from the Majority World—as long as they are free to articulate their own voice and not a derived discourse. Ten years later, after his first encounter with Tiénou, and having lived in East Africa and interacted with theological reflection from the Majority World, my friend sees the world through very different eyes.

He has realized that his appropriation of the faith is but one appropriation of the faith, shaped by his own cultural context. As Andrew Walls has reminded us, the Gospel is at home in any culture because the Gospel can be incarnated and take root in any culture (the indigenizing principle), but the Gospel is also larger than any culture because it challenges aspects in all cultures (the pilgrim principle.) We also belong to a wider human family, with all the privileges and responsibilities that that entails—the interconnectedness that comes with belonging to the worldwide body of Christ. By living in other cultures, my friend realized that his way of living out and understanding the Christian faith was but one way, a way deeply shaped by the boundaries of his own cultural values and beliefs. But the Gospel can liberate us from our particular cultural vistas by exposing us to other understandings of our faith.[23] I need not be imprisoned in my own individualism and isolation, because I belong to a wider family, a body who will care for me. I need not be afraid that the witchdoctor will strike me dead

---

21. Bediako, *Christianity in Africa*, 224–25.
22. Rooms, *Faith of the English*, 37.
23. Here, I use Andrew Walls's metaphor. See Walls, *Missionary Movement*, 3–15.

with lightning because God is the Creator and all-powerful God and has me in the palm of his hand.

My friend was forced to think in completely new theological directions and categories—the nature of systemic evil, principalities and powers, healings and exorcisms, ancestors, pre-Christian past, the nature of conversion, living with other faiths, the content of worship, attitudes to wealth and possessions, and much more. All this radically expanded his faith, stretched his understanding of Jesus, and challenged his discipleship. This would not have happened if he had stayed at home. There is a proverb from the Akamba of Kenya which expresses this well: "He who has not travelled thinks that his mother is the best cook in the world."[24] This was a painful experience, producing what he describes as a period of epistemic shock. If what he had lived and experienced so far was only part of the truth, then what and where is truth? When teaching contextual theologies in Western contexts, I am constantly asked by worried students, "What is the core of the Gospel?" They probe: Surely the Gospel does not change but only the context? God is unchanging, so surely there are some universal, unchanging, core beliefs to Christianity!

Replying that the core of the Gospel is "Jesus is Lord" is not enough to satisfy some students. The idea that the Gospel may look different in different contexts is deeply suspicious to some. Reflexivity does not seem to sit easily with the Western mindset and the idea that the Gospel and context may interact on each other seems to be outrageous, if not heretical. And yet this is what world Christianity does for you. It opens up different sets of questions, different methodologies, different starting points, and differing languages and grammar with which to worship and understand God.

Of course, this is not new. Andrew Walls has captured this in yet another metaphor, "The Ephesian moment." This is most powerfully expressed in Ephesians 2:22: "In union with him [Christ] *you too are being built together with all others* to a place where God lives though his Spirit." There is to be only one Christian community—we have already seen this expressed in the body metaphor. But diversity was built into the church from the beginning as borders were crossed in the early church in order to allow in the Gentiles as full members. The church is diverse because humanity is diverse, but it must also be one because Christ is one. "Christ is human, and open to humanity in all its diversity; the fullness of his humanity takes in all its diverse cultural forms. . . . Believers from the different communities

---

24. See Mbiti, "Role of Women in African Traditional Religion."

are different bricks being used for the construction of a single building—a temple where the One God would live (Eph. 2:19–22)."[25]

The decision taken at the Jerusalem Council in Acts 15 built cultural diversity, or perhaps we could say world Christianity, into the church forever. At that time it established two different ways of being Christian. There was the old way based on circumcision, observing the Sabbath, ritual and food laws, and festivals. In the new way circumcision was laid aside, and apart from some limits concerning dietary and sexual conduct, the question of lifestyle and worship was left open. Until then there had been only one way of being a follower of Christ—the life of an observant Jew. But now the Hellenist believers are left to the guidance of the Holy Spirit to find a new way, appropriate to them, of being Christian—a way of life that expressed being Christian under the conditions of Hellenist society. This was necessary because they were to represent Jesus in that society. This meant developing a whole new Christian lifestyle for new conditions that no previous believer had ever had to cope with. What to do at a pagan friend's table with meat fresh from the Temple? How to deal with the Sabbath? Many of the guideposts for Christian living were now gone; but they had to develop a lifestyle that could function in Hellenist pagan society and yet display Jesus for who he is. This was biculturalism, and large parts of the New Testament show us this process going on.

Each Christian lifestyle, showing a culture converted to Christ, expressed something that the whole body needed. The full stature of Christ is only reached when we all come together; one community or culture or context on its own is defective and deficient. The Apostle knew that there was only one church but that it depended on the union of both cultures. Today there are many cultures but the same principle still applies, each converted entity or culture is necessary for the proper functioning of the body of Christ in the world. "Like the old Jerusalem Christians, Western Christians have long grown used to the idea that they were guardians of a 'standard' Christianity; also like them, they find themselves in the presence of new expressions of Christianity, and new Christian lifestyles. . . [that] display Christ under the conditions of African, Indian, Chinese, Korean and Latin American life."[26] We can react by wanting to protect our own version of Christianity and declare it as the normative one, the default setting. Or we can declare that each expression is indeed valid and then proceed to enjoy our own in isolation from the others. Neither of these options is the Ephesian way. "The Ephesian metaphors of the temple and of the body show each

---

25. Walls, "Ephesian Moment," 77.
26. Ibid., 78.

of the culture-specific segments as necessary to the body but incomplete in itself."[27] We need one another to enlarge, correct, challenge and refocus our own understanding of Christ. This is exactly what my friend was experiencing in his journey towards world Christianity—the richness of the diversity of the worldwide church and the struggle that these new questions and new insights opened up for him.

And so our discipleship will be challenged and changed. Our worship may be different. Being disciples in an era of world Christianity may help us to see not only how culturally relative some of our forms of worship are but also what a worldwide vision might do for our worship. We might consider the politics of worship and consider who is attending; is it risky for them, and do the worshipers reflect the wider community economically, racially, ethnically? Is our worship a place for everyone, or are there constraints that exclude some? Who leads our worship and why? Are they educated, lay, men, women, children? What is the focus of our worship service? How might social, cultural, and economic conditions of an area impact the worship? What are the economics of worship—in other words, how much of the church's resources are invested in it and what does this communicate about our own culture and understanding of God? We may see that vitality and formality can go together, and be reminded of the importance of intercession for the world.[28] Our prayer life may be invigorated by new insights and approaches. Our reading of the Scriptures will certainly be challenged and changed.

Korean scholar Moonjang Lee reports that when he asks Western seminary students why they read and study the Bible, the goal of their biblical studies is not clearly defined. He asserts that our ultimate objective in Bible reading is to become like our Master, Jesus. "First comes perception of spiritual insights through awakening and enlightenment. There follows the embodiment of those insights through meditation, personal application, and practice to achieve personal transformation—to become like Jesus Christ in our thought, word, and deed."[29]

Finally, our awareness of the other may grow and become more acute as we are exposed to the stories of the worldwide church. Hopefully we will become increasingly aware of global injustice, and of what General Roméo Dallaire, Commander of the UN troops in Rwanda during the 1994 genocide, described as the rage that exists in many countries by those who feel

---

27. Ibid., 79.
28. See Farhadian, *Christian Worship*.
29. Lee, "Reading the Bible," 151.

betrayed and in despair as they have no rights, no security, no food, no future. He wrote,

> The global village is deteriorating at a rapid pace, and in the children of the world the result is rage. It is the rage I saw in the eyes of the teenage Interahamwe militiamen in Rwanda, it is the rage I sensed in the hearts of the children in Sierra Leone, it is the rage I felt in crowds of ordinary civilians in Rwanda, and it is the rage that resulted in September 11.[30]

Three Canadian pastors identify what they call "six rage factors" in our world: lostness and alienation, poverty and hunger, environment, human rights violations, civil violence, corruption and failure of leadership.[31] They suggest this is the context for the mission of the worldwide church. As world Christians, we have a responsibility to understand these contexts, to empathize with the rage, and to move beyond simply knowing.

THEOLOGICAL HOMELESSNESS IN AN ERA OF WORLD CHRISTIANITY

Moving beyond simply knowing can lead to painful self-reflection and to what my friend described as a kind of theological homelessness. It has led him to think in directions that leave him disconnected with his home culture. It means that home and the theology with which we were nurtured is never quite the same. Theological homelessness can be painful. It may leave us stranded between two or more worlds. It forces us to look at our theological upbringing with new eyes.

Perhaps a certain amount of theological discomfort is a good thing. Certainly the themes of exile, pilgrimage, and even homelessness are biblical themes. Our ancestor Abraham was uprooted from his home by Yahweh to discover new things about God; the people of Israel were forced to adapt to new cultures and strange ways while in exile; and Jesus knew pilgrimage and homelessness while in his mother's womb. And so our identity as world Christians can leave us in an uncomfortable place—unable to return home and as T. S. Eliot so eloquently expressed it in his poem "Journey of the Magi," "no longer at ease here, in the old dispensation, with an alien people clutching their gods." But the new place is hard also, just as for the Magi: "This Birth was hard and bitter agony for us, like Death, our death."

---

30. Dallaire and Beardsley, *Shake Hands with the Devil*, 521.
31. Nelson et al., *Going Global*, 60.

To be confronted with new issues, to be faced with strange ways of understanding and worshiping God, is hard work. It requires effort from us as well as empathy. It may mean learning a new language, either literally or figuratively. Our worship will be changed. Our prayer life will be challenged. Our understanding of the world will be transformed as we consider the impact of our lifestyle on others. Our reading of the Bible will be confronted with different interpretations from ours. Our appreciation of church history will be enlarged as we are introduced to new heroes and heroines of the faith and learn about our heroes from a different perspective. Most Africans have heard the Gospel from Africans and nearly all the great movements towards Christianity in Africa have been led by Africans. This is obvious when you stop and think, but it is not the story, or the history, most of us have grown up with.[32]

Our theological homelessness may be not only exacerbated but also confronted daily by remembering that world Christianity is no longer over there but has come among us. One in five Europeans migrated between 1800 and 1925, the largest migration movement in history. This period also coincided with the high tide of both the Western missionary movement and Empire. These movements unleashed powerful forces of change that have been reacting on Europe and England, in particular, ever since. For example, at the height of British colonial rule, the Queen of England had more Muslim subjects than any other ruler. This meant that England was open to Muslim immigration and settlement from the late nineteenth century.

The sharp rise in non-white immigration is a good example of one of these powerful forces at work. Former colonies or countries with which England had political or trade links were finding their way back, what has become known in colloquial parlance as "the Empire bites back." The religious implications and complexities of this are huge, as we are all beginning to realize. The migrants from the Majority World are generally religiously devout. They challenge our secularized outlook and our understanding of liberal democracy. This influx of migrants also means that the face of Christianity in England is becoming increasingly non-white; for example, the largest church in England is a Nigerian-led congregation in London.

These new migrants engage in mission around them very differently from the days of Empire. They do not have the complicated and ambiguous relationship with colonial authorities, the territorial and one-directional approach to mission, the support of parachurch structures, the perceived attitudes of cultural superiority. However, they do seem to have a focus

---

32. *Dictionary of African Christian Biography* (http://www.dacb.org/) records the untold stories of African Christians who have transformed the history of the African church.

on spiritual power, a strong belief in the supernatural, a moral and ethical conservatism, a clear belief in the authority of the Scriptures, a sensibility towards injustice, and a communal apprehension and realization of the Christian faith. Perhaps they may offer us fresh insights and help us to re-imagine not only our faith but also our place within world Christianity. So now we find ourselves in the situation that our theological homelessness may begin at home. What better place to start as we are faced with the reality of world Christianity on our doorstep and in our neighborhood.

CONCLUSION

Extra vigilance is required. It does take an effort to be a world Christian. Our interconnectedness within the body, our need of one another to shape and mold our discipleship, the explosive growth of Majority World Christianity—all point to our need to be world Christians. It can be painful and may leave us feeling dislocated and ill at ease at home. We may feel out of step with our own culture and context. The realization that our theology may be only one way of understanding God, the Bible, and the world can be profoundly unsettling and disorienting. The dawning awareness that we may be part of a kind of theological dictatorship is shocking. Our exposure to global injustice and our (sometimes) unwitting collusion can be deeply distressing. The shallowness of our discipleship may alarm us. Our expanded understanding of the Gospel may be astonishing as we begin to understand what is required of us.

However, world Christianity also enables us to celebrate difference and diversity as we learn how to live together. Jonathan Sacks, Chief Rabbi of Britain and the Commonwealth, posed this pertinent question in his superb book, *The Dignity of Difference*: "Can we live together? Can we make space for one another? Can we overcome long histories of estrangement and bitterness? . . . Can we find, in the human 'thou,' a fragment of the Divine 'Thou'?"[33] This is exactly what world Christianity enables us to be and do. It helps us celebrate the local as well as the global, because completion in Christ can only come from all the fullness of humanity—we cannot get there on our own, in isolation from one another. We are indeed part of a worldwide body stretching into history and beyond, stretching around the world, founded on Christ: "From him the whole body, joined and held together by every supporting ligament, grows and builds itself up in love, as each part does its work" (Eph 4:16). Extra vigilance may be required, but the joys and the rewards are immeasurable.

33. Sacks, *Dignity of Difference*, 17.

BIBLIOGRAPHY

Bediako, Kwame. *Christianity in Africa: The Renewal of a Non-Western Religion*. Edinburgh: Edinburgh University Press, 1995.

Bevans, Stephen B. *An Introduction to Theology in Global Perspective*. Theology in Global Perspective. Maryknoll, NY: Orbis, 2009.

Crichton, Angus. "Consultation and Cooperation in Disseminating Research on Ugandan Christianity." Paper presented at Yale-Edinburgh, 2010. Published in "Sounding the Ngoma," newsletter of Ngoma Ecumenical Publishing Consortium, Henry Martyn Centre, Cambridge, April 26, 2011. No pages. Online: http://www.martynmission.cam.ac.uk/pages/research-projects.php.

Dallaire, Roméo, and Brent Beardsley. *Shake Hands with the Devil: The Failure of Humanity in Rwanda*. Toronto: Vintage Canada, 2004.

Farhadian, Charles E., editor. *Christian Worship Worldwide: Expanding Horizons, Deepening Practices*. Grand Rapids: Eerdmans, 2007.

Lee, Moonjang. "Reading the Bible in the Non-Western Church: An Asian Dimension." In *Mission in the 21st Century: Exploring the Five Marks of Global Mission*, edited by Andrew Walls and Cathy Ross, 148–56. London: Darton, Longman & Todd, 2008.

Martin, Dale. *The Corinthian Body*. New Haven: Yale University Press, 1995.

Mbiti, John. "Role of Women in African Traditional Religion." *AfrikaWorld.net*, n.p. Online: http://afrikaworld.net/afrel/atr-women.htm.

Nelson, Gary V., et al. *Going Global: A Congregation's Introduction to Mission beyond Our Borders*. Columbia Partnership Leadership Series. St. Louis, MO: Chalice, 2011.

Niringiye, D. Z. "The Church in the World: A Historical-Ecclesiological Study of the Church of Uganda with Particular Reference to Post-independence Uganda, 1962–1992." PhD diss., University of Edinburgh, 1997.

Rooms, Nigel. *The Faith of the English: Integrating Christ and Culture*. London: SPCK, 2011.

Sacks, Jonathan. *The Dignity of Difference: How to Avoid the Clash of Civilizations*. London: Continuum, 2002.

Sanneh, Lamin. *Whose Religion Is Christianity? The Gospel beyond the West*. Grand Rapids: Eerdmans, 2003.

Stone, Bryan. "The Ecclesiality of Mission in the Context of Empire." In *Walk Humbly with the Lord: Church and Mission Engaging Plurality*, edited by Viggo Mortensen and Andreas O. Nielsen, 105–12. Grand Rapids: Eerdmans, 2010.

Thiselton, Anthony C. *The First Epistle to the Corinthians: A Commentary on the Greek Text*. New International Greek Testament Commentary. Grand Rapids: Eedmans, 2000.

Tiénou, Tite. "Christian Theology in an Era of World Christianity." In *Globalizing Theology: Belief and Practice in an Era of World Christianity*, edited by Craig Ott and Harold A. Netland, 37–51. Grand Rapids: Baker Academic, 2006.

Vanhoozer, Kevin. "'One Rule to Rule Them All?': Theological Method in an Era of World Christianity." In *Globalizing Theology: Belief and Practice in an Era of World Christianity*, edited by Craig Ott and Harold A. Netland, 85–126. Grand Rapids: Baker Academic, 2007.

Walls, Andrew F. *The Cross-Cultural Process in Christian History: Studies in the Transmission and Appropriation of Faith*. Maryknoll, NY: Orbis, 2002.

———. "The Ephesian Moment." In *The Cross-Cultural Process in Christian History*, 72–81. Maryknoll, NY: Orbis, 2002.

———. "The Gospel as Prisoner and Liberator of Culture." In *The Missionary Movement in Christian History*, 3–15. Maryknoll, NY: Orbis, 1996.

———. *The Missionary Movement in Christian History: Studies in the Transmission of Faith*. Maryknoll, NY: Orbis, 1996.

———. "Old Athens and New Jerusalem: Some Signposts for Christian Scholarship in the Early History of Mission Studies." *International Bulletin of Missionary Research* 21 (1997) 146–53.

23

Global Evangelical Theology
"Luke Theology" and the Dialogue of the Deaf

MARK SHAW

IN 1984 WALTER ELWELL's the *Evangelical Dictionary of Theology* was published to great acclaim.[1] Many rejoiced to see the fresh articulation of evangelical doctrine and the updating of evangelical perspectives on a range of important issues. Numerous articles reviewed familiar reformation and enlightenment theologies and theologians. Topics relevant to the North Atlantic Christian community were in rich supply.

When it came to the Majority World, however, the story was different. No articles appeared on the work of African or Latin American theologians. No entry could be found on African or Latin American theology. An article on Asian theology and a critique of liberation theology were almost the only testimonies to contextual theology. The article on contextualization of theology contained more warnings than examples.

Much has changed since 1984. From near invisibility in the seventies and eighties, global evangelical theology has matured, and the contribution of Majority World theologians in the last decade or more has at last been recognized. *Christian Theology in Asia*, a standout volume on Asian theology, edited by Sebastian Kim, was published by Cambridge University

---

1. Elwell, *Evangelical Dictionary of Theology*.

Press in 2008.[2] The theological spectrum in this survey is wide but decidedly evangelical overall. As Hwa Yung writes in his chapter, "Mission and Evangelism: Evangelical and Pentecostal Theologies in Asia," the search for a contextual theology that is deeply rooted in both culture and Scripture has begun.

Confirmation of this is found in Amos Yong's *The Spirit Poured Out on All Flesh*.[3] Yong surveys how pentecostal themes have affected the whole spectrum of theology. His chapter on Spirit Christology, which emphasizes the saving action of Jesus in contrast to Logos Christology focused on ontological questions of "being," is changing the way the Majority World talks about Jesus. Yong's work has been hailed as a truly global pentecostal theology.

Of primary significance is *The Global Dictionary of Theology*, edited by William Dyrness and Veli-Matti Kärkkäinen and published by InterVarsity Press in 2008.[4] This is a feast of Majority World theology, covering persons and issues of truly global significance and representation. Among those contributing to this volume are members of the African Society of Evangelical Theology, including Dr. James Nkansah, my colleague at Africa International University, Kenya.

I can only mention a few outside of Africa who have written extensively on evangelical theology in this decade. Authors include former Palmer Seminary (Philadelphia) professor, Samuel Escobar, and his colleague in the Latin American Theological Fraternity, Rene Padilla.[5] Padilla's daughter, Ruth, is becoming an important female voice in global evangelical theology. Timothy Tennent's latest monograph, *Theology in the Context of World Christianity*, highlights the contribution made by Majority World theologians to many of the traditional topics of theology.[6] He offers creative and critical interaction with these global voices even as he promotes their work.

A most meaningful event for global evangelical theology occurred at Cape Town, South Africa, in October, 2010. We have yet to absorb the theological impact of the Third Lausanne Congress on World Evangelization, but it will no doubt be profound. Its theological vigor and global representation may well make it the crowning evangelical theological event of the first decade of the twenty-first century.

2. Kim, *Christian Theology*.
3. Yong, *Spirit Poured Out*.
4. Dyrness and Karkanian, *Global Dictionary of Theology*.
5. Escobar and Smith, *New Global Mission*.
6. Tennent, *Theology in the Context of World Christianity*.

While recognizing the critical contribution made by the individuals and events mentioned above, I would like to focus on an issue raised in one of the better volumes on theology in the context of world Christianity, Netland and Ott's *Globalizing Theology: Belief and Practice in an Era of World Christianity*.[7] Included in this volume are many compelling essays, including contributions by Majority World theologians such as Tite Tiénou and Vinoth Ramachandra.

Tiénou's chapter joins in the celebration of global evangelical theology's growth. But Tiénou offers a significant qualifier, what he refers to as the "hegemony postulate," the assumption of the West that its theology is and must be dominant.[8] Tiénou notes that developing a truly global evangelical theology requires more than just Majority World productivity. It also requires Western attentiveness and mutuality.

Here is where the breakdown begins. Majority World evangelical theology hardly matters to the Western evangelical mainstream. This is a studied indifference, Tiénou suggests, tied as it is to issues of power and influence. Western Evangelicals exert strong resistance to Majority World theology and hold on dearly to Western dominance. Tiénou mentions the West's perception of itself as the center and the non-West as the periphery. There is also the "dialogue of the deaf," in which the West seems halfhearted in its commitment to listen to the voices of non-Western theology. Per Frostin describes his experience in discussing Majority World theology with a group of Scandinavian theologians. They insisted that the only critique of Western theology they would receive would be one that met their criteria as "scientific." Frostin interprets this attitude as exemplifying the hegemony postulate whereby "the prerequisite of a dialogue is that the other party accepts 'our' rules, since only these rules are genuinely scientific."[9] For Tiénou this assumption means that universal theology is done in the West and local theology is done elsewhere. He looks forward to that day when "the whole people of God have a say in theological decision making."[10]

Is there a hope that the dialogue will continue and that evangelical theologians from the West will begin to embrace their Majority World counterparts with equality and mutuality? Tiénou believes that central to undermining the hegemony postulate is a new theological methodology that will not only enable Majority World contributions to stand out but enable Western World contributions to be more self-critical. Tiénou calls for

---

7. Ott and Netland, *Globalizing Theology*.
8. Ibid., 47.
9. Ibid.
10. Ibid., 51 (quoting Hollenweger).

an international and interdisciplinary scholarship made up of a trialogue called for by Harvey Conn back in 1984 between anthropology, mission, and theology. Theology and these other disciplines have existed in their own silos for too long. Only a multi-disciplinary theology will move us forward in tackling the challenges of the new century. Such is Tiénou's strategy for undermining the hegemony postulate.

The dream of a global theological methodology that combines the above disciplines is an important one, but I suggest that a crucial element is missing in the new theological method Tiénou calls for. I want to propose that the surest way to overcome the dialogue of the deaf as well as to speak to the concerns of Majority World churches is to *rediscover Luke's theological method*. As model and methodology, "Luke Theology," as I call it, involves a marriage between history and theology. This is just what we need in the Majority World to challenge the hegemony postulate. I believe this is so because Luke's theological method is (1) biblically rooted, (2) historically persistent, and (3) contextually relevant.

BIBLICAL ROOTS OF HISTORICALLY GROUNDED THEOLOGY

It was Howard Marshall's *Luke: Historian and Theologian* (1998) that initially drew my attention to historically grounded theology.[11] Though some have followed Marshall's lead, evangelical theology has not gone far in exploring the implications of Luke's dual identity. I do not need to rehearse the reasons Marshall gave in that volume for calling Luke a theologian. It is easy enough to point to but a few passages in Luke-Acts to show how much of a theologian the historian Luke truly was.

Does anyone need convincing that Acts 2 and the story of Pentecost has had as much theological impact as almost any other biblical text? Vast numbers of pentecostal and charismatic Christians who have had their vision of God, Christ, the Spirit, and salvation shaped by this chapter in Acts would lend credence to such a statement. How many of us have turned for our own ecclesiology to the dynamic picture of the new church of Jerusalem presented in the closing verses of that same chapter?

What of Acts 4:10 and Peter's bold proclamation while standing trial for heresy, namely that there is "no other name under heaven [than Jesus] whereby we must be saved." This is not simply an anecdote from an ancient court case. This statement and this verse have defined evangelical Christology and soteriology for centuries. (Thus, it is not surprising that the

---

11. Marshall, *Luke: Historian and Theologian*.

Evangelical Theological Society's 2011 meeting on Christology chose as its theme "No other Name.") For Luke, history is the womb of theology.

Time does not permit us to discuss Acts 17 and its profound theology of God, or Luke's birth narratives and the Christology it presents, or how justification by faith is as powerfully presented in the parable of the two men in the temple (Luke 18) as anywhere in Scripture. I trust enough has been said to support Marshall's portrait of Luke as a master theologian-historian.[12]

I would like to zoom in on one particular passage, however. I refer to the prologue to Luke's Gospel. It is there that one finds the case for the theological use of history carefully made. You may recall the famous statements with which Luke begins his Gospel:

> Many have undertaken to draw up an account of the things that have been fulfilled among us, just as they were handed down to us by those who from the first were eyewitnesses and servants of the word. Therefore, since I myself have carefully investigated everything from the beginning, it seemed good also to me to write an orderly account for you, most excellent Theophilus, so that you may know the certainty of the things you have been taught.

This introduction highlights Luke's commitment to careful history. There is a long tradition in Greek historiography, beginning 400 years earlier with Herodotus and Thucydides, of separating fact from fiction in the reconstruction of the past. Luke carries on in this critical tradition. He leaves no stone unturned in both investigating and crafting the narrative of Jesus Christ and his fulfillment of the messianic promises of the Old Testament.

A second point drawn from Luke's introduction is decisive: Good things happen to people like Theophilus when they are presented with Luke's kind of careful history, history that is evidence based, and that is written with a concern for chronology and theology. Certainty will happen. Assurance occurs. Doubts and unbelief are replaced by vital faith and the new life that flows from such grounded faith.

How is theological certainty produced by mere history? Is it not theology rather than history that produces certainty and keeps one from being blown about by every wind of doctrine? Yes, but for Luke history is the proper vessel of theology. Theology must be built upon a story, the great story of Jesus, firmly established by fact and then theologically interpreted by the Spirit. This is the "Luke Theology" that we need in the Majority World.

---

12. To the objection that one should not extract doctrine from narrative, see Frei, *Eclipse of Biblical Narrative*.

As Evangelicals, it deserves our attention because it is a theological method that is biblically rooted.

HISTORICAL PERSISTENCE OF LUKE THEOLOGY

A second argument for a return to a Luke-type theology has to do with catholicity. Catholicity's original meaning had less to do with an ecclesiastical organization centered in Rome than with a general sense of the "church around the world." "*Kata holos*" simply means "that which is general, universal, or concerned with everyone." I cannot claim this catholicity argument for Luke Theology in a comprehensive sense, that it was the main or most frequently used methodology for Christian theology. What I can claim is that Luke's theology, along with other methodologies, has been there since the beginning and has persisted down through the long march of the Christian movement through time. This is the catholicity argument, that such history-based theology and the method it implies has been used by the church around the world from biblical times to the present.

A few examples will make the point. Is not our Apostle's Creed a short theological history of Christianity? The God we believe in is tied to creation and to the saving events in the life of Christ. Jesus is clearly identified as born of the Virgin Mary and the one who suffered under Pontius Pilate. His death, burial, resurrection, and ascension are all rooted in history. The close relation of articles three and four of the Creed, belief in the Spirit and belief in the church, surely take us back to Acts 2 and the history of Pentecost where both were given to us in rich measure.

Inspired by biblical precedent and creedal example, the early church relied upon history to do theology. The Gnostic heresy of the second and third centuries has been called the greatest challenge ever faced by the Christian church.[13] Standing as we are at the tail end of the Enlightenment with its atheism, its global capitalism, and mania for materialism, we may want to question if that ancient challenge should now take second place. But the fact remains that the theological victory over Gnosticism was won by theologians such as Irenaeus, who grounded their theology in history, the very thing that Gnostics hated most.

Bad theology has always tried to escape time. Not just *kairos* time with its wonderful peaks and magic moments but also *chronos* time. Time in both its forms means change and decay for the Gnostic. Time becomes an enemy that must be slain by leaping to the world of timeless truths or eternal existence. Gnosticism is an escape from a time-bound creation that has lost

---

13. Chadwick, *Early Church*.

its meaning and has become a burden on life and a sentence of death. The second-century theologian, Irenaeus, in *Against Heresies*, saw time not as an enemy but rather as a gift of grace.[14] All time, whether *chronos* or *kairos*, was sacred and the very womb of our salvation. Christ is the second Adam that opens up the new age. He is the new Adam who recapitulates or undoes and redoes the negative history of a fallen world and makes history flow backward to the Garden and to the Paradise that awaits those who live by faith in the historical Jesus who is both lord and savior. Luke Theology in the hands of the church fathers like Irenaeus won the day.

It persisted. Augustine casts the longest shadow on contemporary evangelical theology, both for those who praise him as well as those who reject him. He was the most prolific of all the church fathers; his collected works fill many volumes. His two most famous works, however, are not systematic treatises but rather are experiments in Luke Theology, theological works that base themselves on historical narrative. The first is his *Confessions* in which his reflections on God, man, sin, and salvation emerge from the chronology of his personal life. The second Luke-type work is *The City of God*. In this, his greatest work, Augustine moves from personal history to the grand narrative of world history to produce a theology of the two cities and the love that separates them; *The City of God* remains one of the towering theological achievements of Christian theology in any generation. Whereas Irenaeus stayed within the bounds of biblical history for the most part, it was Augustine who took Luke's theological method to the next level, using both personal history and contemporary history (the fall of Rome to barbarians) as the historical ground for his theological system.

The Middle Ages saw the flowering of Western systematic theology in Thomas Aquinas's magnum opus, the *Summa Theologica*. Yet the narrative-based theology of Joachim of Fiore had arguably more impact on the Christian church then and now then did Aquinas's careful reasoning.[15] Joachim placed Christian truth within the framework of three ages: the age of the Father (Old Testament); the age of the Son (New Testament and the history of the church up to the twelfth century) and the final age the age of the Spirit (to begin in the thirteenth century). Joachim's use of history helped propel his radical vision of the future deep into the imagination of the Western mind. Though condemned by the Roman Catholic Church as a heretic, Joachim's true impact is reflected by Dante in his *Divine Comedy*, when the great Italian poet refused to place the theologian in hell (where the church leadership would have placed him) but rather in paradise.

14. Cf. the discussion in Wingren, *Man and the Incarnation*.
15. See the analysis in Reeves, *Joachim of Fiore*.

Jumping ahead to eighteenth-century America, we come to Jonathan Edwards. Edwards is often called America's greatest theologian, largely on the basis of a series of closely reasoned theological monographs that covered the doctrines of free will, original sin, and true spirituality. Yet Edwards was not completely satisfied with his method for doing theology. At the end of his life he conceived of a new way to do theology that would use history and theology together.[16] He died before he could finish his *History of the Work of Redemption*, but from the notes and fragments left behind there is little doubt that he believed this would have been his most influential work. For Edwards the marriage of history and theology was indeed a marriage made in heaven.

In our own time Kwame Bediako has employed the methods of Luke Theology. His groundbreaking study *Theology and Identity* used comparative history and historical theology to produce an incisive dialogue between contemporary African theology and the pioneer theologians of early Africa.[17] Context was crucial for Bediako, but context is more than simply a place. Context is also a *chronos*, a stage in time. To unleash the meaning of both historic and contemporary theology, the power of *chronos*, the power of history, needed to be tapped. This comment leads us to our last point about theology and history.

CONTEMPORARY RELEVANCE OF HISTORICALLY GROUNDED THEOLOGY

There is a final reason for Luke Theology. The marriage of solid history and reflective biblical theology strikes at the proud tower of Western theology where it is weakest, even while Western theology contributes to Majority World theology where it could be strongest.

The problem of history in Western theology is an enormous one. As rationalism began to dominate Western thinking in the seventeenth and eighteenth centuries, a great crack occurred between history and theology. The basic crack was defined by the German philosopher-theologian Gotthold Lessing. In dealing with the connection between theological truth and historical fact, particularly in the Bible, Lessing declared that a "great ugly ditch" separated the two, a ditch so wide that no rational person could jump across. This crack eventually became the canyon between history and theology that Lessing described in his famous dictum: "Accidental truths of

---

16. Edwards, *Works of Jonathan Edwards*, vol. 9.
17. Bediako, *Theology and Identity*.

history can never become the proof of necessary truths of reason."[18] For Luke it is history alone that is the basis of certainty about the ultimate truths of God and the Gospel. For Lessing history is a dead-end and theology simply an exercise in human speculation.

Much Western theology has accepted the notion of Lessing's ugly ditch. It doesn't know what to do with history. Consequently, Western theology encourages the production of abstract theology divorced from context and *chronos*. Such theology becomes increasingly detached from the church and real life. Bishop Lesslie Newbigin exposed the high cost that Western philosophy, science, and theology has paid for its divorce from history.[19] The price tag, Newbigin argued, was teleology—knowledge of the end purpose of things. Meaning and value come only from knowing what something is for, what its ultimate purpose is. If history is marginalized and truth is abstracted either by the biologist, the mathematician, or the theologian, then description of reality replaces the discussion of what reality means and for what purposes it was created. Only the recovery of history in our theologizing will restore teleology. Such a theology will challenge the hegemonic postulate and shake it to its foundations.

Evangelicals have not completely escaped Lessing's ugly ditch. We need to return to Luke's methodology perhaps as much as non-evangelical theologians do. To that end Kevin Vanhoozer has written widely about theology as "theodrama."[20] Theology is less a scientific construct than it is a story of God and people in conflict through time. Such a model is a fresh statement of Luke Theology. It stands both as a creative rebuke to the a-historical abstract theology of the West as well as a constructive call to the global church to do theology as a multi-act play.

The Majority World is strong where the Western World is weak. Though I cannot explore this point, it is important to at least state it. Just as history is a blind spot in Western theology, it is a strength in many cultures of the Majority World. Throughout the global South there is a respect for the past, a belief that there is no ugly ditch that separates event and meaning, miracle and faith, history and truth. While we have yet to exploit this strength, let us at least recognize that this treasure is there to be found and used. It speaks to us yet again of the contemporary relevance of Luke Theology.

---

18. Cf. Lessing, *Lessing: Philosophical and Theological Writings*.
19. Newbigin, *Gospel in a Pluralist Society*.
20. Ott and Netland, *Globalizing Theology*, 109.

WHAT IS THE WAY FORWARD?

How can Tite Tiénou's challenge, the challenge to the hegemony postulate, be met? As stated earlier, my proposal is that the surest way to overcome the dialogue of the deaf is to rediscover Luke's theological method in our modern context. Can such a theological method flourish once again in the global church? What practical models do we have?

At our school's Centre for World Christianity we are experimenting with Luke Theology, endeavoring to marry history and theology without doing violence to either. Our two research degree programs, the MTh in world Christianity and the upcoming PhD in Intercultural Studies (our center has a world Christianity track), are joint projects of the theology department and the historical studies department of the university. We have looked at a research methodology called the pastoral circle, developed by Catholic missiologists.[21] This research model calls for a careful construction of contextual case studies (recent history), combined with serious theological analysis of the case. The cycle ends with a strategy for action. Whether such a model can stand the weight of serious research on doctoral levels remains to be seen, but the literature on this methodology is encouraging.

We have a long way to go to catch up to the past, to harness the power of Luke Theology the way it was done in the first century and beyond, but we have begun the journey.

What kind of model of theology do we end up with if we harness the resources of contemporary Christian history in producing our Majority World theologies? What might Luke Theology look like in the twenty-first century?

Luke Theology will be about people, all kinds of people: marginalized people whether by gender or age, whether spiritually, socially, economically, or politically. We will write about the poor who are far from the corridors of power and about the rich who are far from the gates of the kingdom of God.

Luke theologians will do contextual theology that takes culture seriously as the arena of God's mission. We shall write about culture and its protean transformation through time. Luke's theological history and contemporary historical theology in Luke-Acts is concerned with the gospel to the nations. It is concerned with the translation of the gospel of Jesus Christ from Palestinian Judaism to Hellenistic Judaism; from Jew to Greek; from Greek to Roman; from Rome to Africa (Acts 8).

Finally, I see a future in which Luke theologians will write about Jesus Christ. Though history is about time and change; though contextual

---

21. Wijsen et al., *Pastoral Circle Revisited*.

theologies are ever moving targets; though all our insights and studies are but candles in the wind, Jesus Christ and his supremacy over the powers is our fixed center. Luke theologians regard all things as relative and all truth as plural except for one absolute and exclusive truth: Jesus is lord of all. Descartes' methodological starting point was "I think, therefore I am." Africa's intellectual starting point has been "we are, therefore I am." There is truth in both. But the hegemonic postulate will not fall simply by the yin and yang of communalism versus individualism. We need a third way to do theology if Evangelicals east and west and north and south are to hear and appreciate one another.

What is that third way? Hear Luke's starting point: "Because he came in the days of Herod, suffered under Pontius Pilate, died and rose again in the spring of AD 33, I am and we are, now and forever more, world without end, amen."[22]

BIBLIOGRAPHY

Bediako, Kwame. *Theology and Identity: The Impact of Culture upon Christian Thought in the Second Century and in Modern Africa*. Carlisle, UK: Regnum, 1992.

Chadwick, Henry. *The Early Church*. London: Penguin, 1993.

Dyrness, William, and Veli-Matti Karkanian, editors. *Global Dictionary of Theology*. Downers Grove, IL: InterVarsity, 2007.

Edwards, Jonathan. *The Works of Jonathan Edwards*. Vol. 9, *A History of the Work of Redemption*. Edited by John F. Wilson. New Haven: Yale University Press, 1989.

Elwell, Walter, editor. *The Evangelical Dictionary of Theology*. Grand Rapids: Baker, 1984.

Escobar, Samuel, and David Smith. *The New Global Mission*. Downers Grove, IL: InterVarsity, 2003.

Frei, Hans. *The Eclipse of Biblical Narrative: A Study in Eighteenth and Nineteenth Century Hermeneutics*. New Haven: Yale University Press, 1980.

Kim, Sebastian C. H. *Christian Theology in Asia*. Cambridge: Cambridge University Press, 2008.

Lessing, Gotthold Ephraim. *Lessing: Philosophical and Theological Writings*. Cambridge Texts in the History of Philosophy. Cambridge: Cambridge University Press, 2005.

Marshall, I. Howard. *Luke: Historian and Theologian*. 3rd ed. Downers Grove, IL: InterVarsity Academic, 1998.

Newbigin, Lesslie. *The Gospel in a Pluralist Society*. London: SPCK, 1989.

———. *A Word in Season: Perspectives on Christian World Mission*. Grand Rapids: Eerdmans, 1994.

Ott, Craig, and Harold A. Netland, editors. *Globalizing Theology: Belief and Practice in an Era of World Christianity*. Grand Rapids: Baker, 2006.

---

22. Recommended in the works of N. T. Wright. Also note that Wright's work on the resurrection combines history and theology in an instructive way for Majority World theologians.

Reeves, Margaret. *Joachim of Fiore and the Prophetic Future*. Oxford: Sutton, 1999.
Tennent, Timothy. *Theology in the Context of World Christianity: How the Global Church Is Influencing the Way We Think about and Discuss Theology*. Grand Rapids: Zondervan, 2007.
Wijsen, F. J. S. et al., editors. *The Pastoral Circle Revisited: A Critical Quest for Truth and Transformation*. Maryknoll, NY: Orbis, 2005.
Wingren, Gustaf. *Man and the Incarnation: A Study in the Biblical Theology of Irenaeus*. Translated by Ross Mackenzie. 1959. Reprinted, Eugene, OR: Wipf & Stock, 2004.
Wright, N. T. *Luke for Everyone*. Louisville: Westminster John Knox, 2004.
Yong, Amos. *The Spirit Poured Out on All Flesh: Pentecostalism and the Possibility of Global Theology*. Grand Rapids: Baker Academic, 2005.

24

The 1860 Liverpool Conference on Missions

ANDREW F. WALLS

THE YEAR 2010 SAW the centenary of the 1910 World Missionary Conference in Edinburgh. That event was widely noticed and rightly celebrated as highly significant.[1] Called in order to mobilize the collective energies and resources of the Protestant churches with a view to bringing the Christian Gospel to the whole world, it was the high-water mark of the missionary movement from the West. It marked not only the climax but the internationalization of the missionary movement, and it inspired the development of resources for study and research in mission, as well as encouraging reflection and self-criticism. Still more importantly, it was at Edinburgh that Protestant Christians got their first glimpse of what a world church might look like. Despite the fact that the benches in the Free Church Assembly Hall were filled by missionaries and mission executives from Britain and the European continent and North America, with only a handful of Asians and a solitary African, the critique of contemporary missions by the Indian priest V. S. Azariah ("Give us friends!")[2] and the eloquent call from Cheng Ching-Yi of China for a church without

---

1. See Stanley, *World Missionary Conference*.
2. Ibid., 126–30.

denominational divisions[3] are among the best remembered conference contributions. Impulses from Edinburgh led to both the Faith and Order movement (since reflection on the mission of the church raised the desire to tackle the issues that hindered the unity of the church), and the Life and Work Movement (since action on mission raises questions about Christian action in society). Along with the International Missionary Council,[4] these movements, and the institutions that embodied them, are products of Edinburgh. It is safe to say that the modern shape of the ecumenical movement derives from Edinburgh 1910.

The World Missionary Conference of 1910 was the culmination of processes long active within the missionary movement from the West. The most immediate of these was the extraordinarily influential Student Volunteer Movement that began in the United States and by the 1880s had spread to Britain and continental Europe, rejuvenating missionary interest as it did so.[5] The student movement held conferences on missions, including the ground-breaking meeting in Liverpool in 1896 under the title *Make Jesus King!* and *Students and the Missionary Problem,* held in London in 1900. There had been major missionary conferences before the days of the student movement: one in London in 1878, another, the largest of all such events, the so-called Centenary Conference on Missions, in London in 1888, and the Ecumenical Missionary Conference in New York in 1900. These large conferences, while they set the stage for Edinburgh, and were not without consultative features, were most notable as missionary exhibitions, presenting missions to the wider Christian public.

LIVERPOOL 1860

Yet the real ancestor of Edinburgh 1910—as a working assembly designed to grapple with the issues arising from missions by bringing those with responsibility for them together for frank and honest discussion—took place in Liverpool in March 1860. While the centenary of Edinburgh 1910 was celebrated round the world, the 150th anniversary of the Liverpool Conference on Missions seems to have been little noticed.[6] Yet the event, it can be

---

3. Ibid., 107ff.
4. See Hogg, *Ecumenical Foundations*.
5. For a recent perspective, see Robert, *Occupy Until I Come*.
6. The event was celebrated at a conference on mission and unity at the Centre for the Study of African and Asian Christianity, Liverpool Hope University, in June 2010.

argued, is a significant landmark in the developing story of mission and unity.

It was not the first missionary conference. The idea goes back a long way; perhaps the first and most crucial missionary conference of all met in Jerusalem when, as described in Acts 15, an assembly of disciples of Jesus, all observant Jews, concluded that Gentile believers in Israel's Messiah did not require Torah or circumcision in order to join the covenant people of Israel, and in doing so built cultural diversity into the church.[7] There is a hint of another important early conference in Paul's apparent reference to a meeting where the Jerusalem apostles recognized his special ministry to Gentiles while affirming their own to Jews[8]—perhaps the first comity arrangement. Many centuries later, William Carey had what a colleague dismissively called a "pleasing dream" of a worldwide conference of missionaries to discuss missionary work, to be held on the mission field (he suggested South Africa as a suitably central location).[9] And indeed on the mission field local conferences developed among missionaries of different societies and churches; first in India, then in China and elsewhere.[10] Meetings in Europe brought together representatives of several continental missionary societies.[11] The year 1854 saw two conferences on missions: one in New York, built round the visit to America of the well-known Scottish missionary and mission theorist Alexander Duff, and one in London, called by the Evangelical Alliance, which made provision for another conference the following year.[12] All these were small in scale; Liverpool 1860 was of a different order.

In some respects, the Liverpool Conference was a child of the revival movement of 1858–1860.[13] This movement, at one time called the Second Evangelical Awakening,[14] may be seen as the last wave of the evangelical revival that began in the eighteenth century. The movement had notable effect in different localities in different regions, without becoming nationwide

---

7. Acts 15:6–29.

8. Gal 2:6–10.

9. The gently dismissive phrase "pleasing dream" was the judgment of Andrew Fuller, who would no doubt have had to cope with many of the logistical issues if the proposal had gone further. On Carey's proposal see Rouse, "William Carey's 'Pleasing Dream,'" 181–92; Meiring, "William Carey's 'Pleasing Dream,'" 219–61.

10. Hogg, *Ecumenical Foundations*, 16–35.

11. Ibid., 38.

12. Ibid., 39.

13. Ibid.

14. So Orr, *Second Evangelical Awakening*. The title can give a misleading impression of the movement; see Bebbington, *Evangelicalism in Modern Britain*, 116ff.

in any.[15] Beginning in North America, it spread to Ireland, where it deeply influenced Protestants, without noticeably moving Catholics. It spread to Scotland, where its effect varied in different parts of the country. In England the revival influences were similarly localized. Revival influences linked the Moray Coast of northeast Scotland, and the coast of East Anglia—the two ends of the North Sea herring fishery. The movement led to quickened interest in missions, and to numbers of offers for missionary service, and such concern evidently provoked the suggestion of a missionary conference.

The idea was taken up by the ad hoc body that was the only existing machinery in Britain for cooperation in mission, the informal meeting of the secretaries of the major mission societies that had their headquarters in London.[16] It is perhaps a sign of the effect of the revival movement, proportionately more significant in Scotland than in England, that the secretaries consulted their counterparts in Edinburgh on the matter. As a result, an English conference organizer and a Scottish assistant were appointed to lay the foundations for a conference on missions. The organizer was a former official of the East India Company government, now of the newly formed Bengal Civil Service, Henry Carré Tucker, who under the company had been commissioner at Banaras. His assistant was an Edinburgh minister, George Cullen.

Tucker and Cullen got to work, and the conference was convened for Monday, March 19, 1860, at Hope Hall, Liverpool, for a preliminary agenda-agreeing evening meeting. The conference proper began the next day, with four days of sessions: three-and-a-half hours each morning and three-and-a-half hours on each of the first three afternoons. These sessions were strictly for the invited members of the conference; but they were set amid early morning prayer meetings and evening soirees that were open to all "friends of missions." The proceedings closed with a mammoth public meeting in the Philharmonic Hall, presided over by the Earl of Shaftesbury, perpetual president of every good cause, and the inevitable choice to preside at any major event.[17] As secretaries of the conference, Tucker and Cullen were joined by Joseph Mullens, missionary of the London Missionary Society in Calcutta and soon to be secretary of that society, and Edward Steane, the distinguished Baptist secretary of the Evangelical Alliance.

15. See Bebbington, *Evangelicalism in Modern Britain*; Jeffrey, *When the Lord Walked*; Gibson, *Year of Grace*.

16. *Conference on Missions Held in 1860 at Liverpool: Including the Papers Read, the Deliberations, and the Conclusions Reached; With a Comprehensive Index Shewing the Various Matters Brought Under Review*, ed. Secretaries of the Conference (London: James Nisbet, 1860), 2. (Henceforth *Conference*).

17. See Finlayson, *Seventh Earl*.

The plan was to bring together "brethren . . . who had reflected on the duty and the lukewarmness of the churches in respect of Our Grand Commission; or could contribute actual experiences; in order that, by their mutual consultations, all Christians of the United Kingdom might be stirred up to greater zeal and to a more complete consecration of time, of effort and of substance, in this work of the Lord."[18] The people to be convened were the "Directors, Secretaries and Missionaries of all Societies and Churches to examine in detail the working of their various missionary agencies, to compare the different plans and to throw into a common stock the results of that valuable experience they have earned hardly upon the very fields of heathenism."[19]

The secretaries say "means were adopted" (they do not say what means) to achieve as complete an attendance as possible of those who could contribute to the discussions while keeping the size of the meeting manageable, to allow free and "almost conversational" discussion.

The final figure was 126 participants, of whom 37 were serving missionaries, and 52 were executives or committee members of missionary societies. Many of this second group had been missionaries themselves. The mission executives included eminent names: Arthur Tidman of the London Missionary Society, George Osborn of the Wesleyan Methodist Mission Society, Frederick Trestrail of the Baptist Missionary Society, W. K. Tweedie, Duff's successor as convener of the missions committee of the Free Church of Scotland, were all present—but not the most eminent of all the current missionary executives, Henry Venn, clerical secretary of the Church Missionary Society. The CMS was, however, well represented by Colonel Dawes, the lay secretary, Thomas Green, principal of the Missionary College at Islington, and a cohort of missionaries, ex-missionaries, and officers of CMS local auxiliaries. Other, smaller mission societies were represented: the Moravians, the General Baptists, the Welsh Calvinistic Methodists. So were colonial church societies and societies for evangelization of the Jews, and specialist interests such as the Religious Tract Society, the Edinburgh Medical Missionary Society, the Turkish Mission Aid Society, and the Society for Female Education of the East. The last named body (though represented by a man) was known to be a potent source of women workers, "missionaries" in all but name. The Strangers' Home for Asiatics, which served stranded Indian and Chinese sailors in London, was also in evidence.

The notable absentees were the old Anglican societies, the Society for the Propagation of the Gospel and the Society for Promoting Christian

18. *Conference*, 1.
19. Ibid.

Knowledge, in which High Church influences predominated; and since at least the former of these could claim official status as an arm of the Church of England, the omission was significant. Part of the achievement of Edinburgh 1910 was to bring the whole range of Anglican missionary activity, not only the evangelical Anglican missionary societies, into the wider missionary movement.[20] But in 1860, some ecclesial divisions remained impossible to bridge.

Of the thirty-seven attendees not to be found among the directors, secretaries and missionaries, some were notable Liverpool churchmen who could not be kept out, with a few local grandees, including the mayor of Liverpool (who was also treasurer of the Liverpool and West Lancashire Church Missionary Association). A significant grouping consisted of army officers and civilian administrators from India. Their presence, by far the chief source of lay involvement, was noticeable throughout the proceedings; it was the chief source of lay involvement in the conference. As we have seen, one of the India administrators, Henry Carre Tucker, C.B, was the factotum for the conference and one of its secretaries; the most senior of the officers present, Major General Alexander of the Indian Army, was elected its chairman. It is noticeable, too, that while the local clergy and grandees played little obvious part in the conference apart from organizing its hospitality, the officers and civilians from India had plenty to say in the discussion sessions; and while some of the interventions of the military chairman had echoes of the parade ground, others would not disgrace any pulpit.

CENTRALITY OF INDIA

This lay presence points to some striking aspects of the conference. One is *the centrality of India in missionary thinking*. At the conference this was assured by weight of numbers: besides the substantial body of officers and civilians, missionaries with experience of India outnumbered those of any other part of the world. West Africa had only one representative, the redoubtable Hope Waddell of Calabar. Southern Africa, the Pacific, China, the Ottoman Empire, Ceylon, Patagonia, Greenland, and "the Red Indians on [sic] Lake Huron," all had representatives but not in numbers to rival the Indian phalanx. So, despite the fact that the conference documents describe India as the "most difficult" field of missions, India often shaped the discussions. The conference met in the shadow of the cataclysmic events in India of 1857–58, and the restructuring of government that followed: the winding up of the East India Company and the formal establishment of the

20. See Stanley, *World Missionary Conference*, 49–72.

British Raj. There is plenty of reference to those recent developments. Here is a reminder that India received the highest investment of the missionary movement, even though it yielded far from the highest return.

The presence of so many representatives of the British Raj also recalls *the ambiguous nature of the relationship between missionaries and other Europeans*. All, or almost all Europeans, were to be described as Christians, but the lifestyle that many adopted was no advertisement for Christianity. This was regarded as a major obstacle to mission work, and the issue occurred again and again in the conference addresses. On the one hand, there were many references to the welcome assistance and healthy influence that godly officers, soldiers, and administrators were giving to missions. On the other hand, still more attention was given to the baleful influences infiltrating India from Europe, or embodied in India by ungodly Europeans. Nor was it only India that suffered: the expatriate presence was often viewed as injurious, above all to missions to Native Americans: some of the "Red Indians on Lake Huron" had returned from Britain sadly disillusioned.[21]

The Liverpool Conference was not set up as an international meeting; its stated aim, as we have seen, was to reach the churches and mission societies of the United Kingdom. Nevertheless, it had a small but significant international presence. Herman Gundert of the Basel Mission in South India represented one of the largest and most important of these continental mission societies; he was a foremost Malayalam scholar and was later to be known also as a historian of the Basel Mission.[22] He seems to have spoken only once at the conference, and that was to propose the publication of books in Chinese written in Romanized script.[23] There were other missionaries there from the continent. The CMS often drew from continental sources, and C. B. Leupolt of Banaras and C. T. Hoernle of Agra, both Basel products but in Anglican orders and CMS service, were active participants. There was also an American present, D. J. MacGowan, a Baptist medical missionary who had worked both in China and Japan.

And there was one representative of the churches on the mission field: Behari Lal Singh, licensed preacher of the Free Church of Scotland

---

21. *Conference*, 49–50.

22. Notably *Die evangelische Mission: Ihre Länder, Völker und Arbeiten* (Calw: Vereinsbuchhandlung, 1891). His biography of his colleague Hermann Moegling (*Hermann Moegling: Ein siersleben in der Mitte des Jahrhunderts*), was translated into English in India a century later: *Herrmann Moegling: A Biography*, ed. Albert Frenz (Kerala: DC Books, 1997). Gundert had originally been a companion of the radical Brethren missionary Anthony Norris Groves. The novelist Hermann Hesse was his grandson.

23. *Conference*, 148.

in Calcutta. Singh's vigorous independence is manifest in the conference record. No shrinking violet, he intervened time and again in discussion. He was one of the first to respond to the first paper, arguing that the highly respected fathers and brethren who had spoken so far on native agency had not yet understood its value. In particular, translation work had suffered from the assumption that only expatriate missionaries could be competent translators. Friends of the Bible Society in India had serious doubts as to whether the present vernacular translations were sufficiently faithful, intelligible, or acceptable in the Indian church ever to become the standard versions; the best employment of a missionary would be "raising an effective native agency to translate the Bible with far greater purity and precision than had ever been done before."

The same applied to preaching.[24] And in a conference context where many speakers were criticizing the Scottish missions for overconcentration on higher education instead of leaving the proud Brahmin to his own devices and bringing good news to the poor, Behari Lal Singh argued that educational standards in Scottish missions were not nearly high enough. He himself, for instance, had found it necessary to study Hebrew with a rabbi and Greek with another scholar, as the Free Church Institution did not provide enough of either, or of Arabic, for that matter. Christians had to be able to meet both Hindu and Muslim scholars on their own ground.[25]

Behari Lal Singh also entered on the sensitive subject of the salaries of indigenous workers, undermining the simplicities of earlier speakers on the subject by outlining the complexity of the issues.[26] He weighed in on the subject of denominationalism, arguing its irrelevance to India; in India, Christians moved readily from Baptist service to Presbyterian to Anglican to Congregational, because none of these "peculiarities," as he calls them, has any interest; the consideration in governing such moves will not be "is this a better form of theology or church government?" but "will I be more useful in this position than in my present one?"[27] Raising the plight of oppressed Christian *ryots* (cultivators of the soil), he pointed out that few European *zamindars* (collectors of land rents)—he knew, in fact, only of one—protect such people on their own estates.[28] Altogether Behari Lal Singh served very effectively as the voice of the indigenous church in a gathering dominated by missionaries and missionary policy makers.

24. Ibid., 26ff.
25. Ibid., 216ff.
26. Ibid., 217ff.
27. Ibid., 292ff.
28. Ibid., 293ff.

AN ALL-MALE AFFAIR, AND YET...

One feature of the conference will have already been evident by implication: it was an all-male affair. There were, of course, already hundreds of women on the mission field, mostly wives of missionaries, with a few sisters accompanying unmarried brothers; and many of these women not only supported their men folk but themselves undertook some specific aspect of the work, frequently a school for girls. Some such stayed on after the death of their husbands to continue that work; and, occasionally, the work had been seen as so valuable that in the event of the death or departure of the one who had initiated it, the missionary society found it necessary to recruit another woman to take it on. Women missionaries of this sort thus occurred quite early in the Protestant missionary movement, certainly as early as the 1820s; but they were rarely called missionaries until much later in the century.

The reason is revealed in the opening paper and discussion at the Liverpool Conference, on the place of European missionaries abroad, where it is made clear that the missionary is essentially a minister of the Gospel, "a teacher, guide and ruler in the household of faith,"[29] with a special additional representative status. By this date there had been, of course, many lay missionaries, usually teachers and occasionally artisans, and by 1860 the anomaly of the unordained medical missionary was becoming more frequent. But lay missionaries, like women missionaries, had not yet forced the re-designation of the category "missionary."

Things were about to change, however, and this is one of many reasons why 1860 marks a kind of watershed in missions. We have noted the presence at the conference of a male representative of the Society for Female Education in the East, one of several agencies by this time addressing the limitations imposed on male missionaries by Indian, Chinese, and Muslim culture, leading to the dawning recognition of the need for single women who would be missionaries in every sense of the word to half the population of several empires. By early in the following century, women recruits to missionary service would be outnumbering men; even the Student Movement recruiters were complaining that the attitude of many male students had become "Lord, here am I; send my sister."

Missions were being decentralized in other ways, too. The main agent of change was medical missions, which had been breaking the assumption that the head of an institution must always be an ordained minister. That assumption was already getting difficult to maintain for schools, as teaching became more and more a profession; furthermore, it simply did not work

---

29. Ibid., 17ff.

for hospitals. As women doctors began to come to the mission field, the old hierarchical order of Liverpool in the 1860s was increasingly in tatters.[30] In passing, we may note that the soirees and the grand public meeting at the end of the Liverpool Conference were attended by "large numbers of ladies and gentlemen."[31] No one seems to have counted the women, but it would be surprising if their number were not very significant. It is clear that women made a huge proportion of the support base of missions; one can call such witnesses as Charlotte Bronte for that.[32]

The structure of the main meetings at Liverpool, the seven periods of extended discussion, was simple. A paper by a well-known mission speaker was presented in ten minutes. (The length of some of the papers in the printed record of the conference suggests that some speakers took advantage of the opportunity given to revise their texts after the conference.) There was then discussion, again very disciplined as to the length of time any participant might speak. There were thus many contributors to any one session. Two shorthand writers took it all down.

The seven subjects that form the skeleton of the book begin with *European Missionaries Abroad*, with Mullens as the speaker. One of the topics raised was language proficiency, generally rated of the highest importance, especially in India, with speakers suggesting immersion training in rural areas for all missionary recruits, with English forbidden for the first eighteen months of service. A few missionary speakers sheepishly admitted their use of interpreters; only Hope Waddell went on the offensive to declare that the people in Calabar wanted to learn English, not to hear him speak Efik.[33]

The subject of missionary recruitment inevitably cropped up. According to some, new missionaries should not be over 25, or they would be too old to learn a language properly. There was substantial agreement that the missionary should resist temptation to become a pastor, though the reasons given for this differ. Some argued that the prestige, position, and in some cases the innate superiority of the missionary disqualified him from the pastoral office. Behari Lal Singh, on the other hand, argued that missionary pastors induce a cringing attitude in their flocks that is not healthy for the church. But Mullens, a Congregationalist, argued that missionaries, since they are not to be pastors, become in effect bishops, exercising a wider

30. Compare Walls, "Heavy Artillery of the Missionary Army," 211-20.

31. *Conference*, 99.

32. Note in Brontë's novel *Shirley* the inescapable basket of items made and purveyed by the devout women of the parish to the less than devout gentlemen in support of missions or Jewish evangelism.

33. *Conference*, 40.

oversight, and that whatever the form of church government in a given denomination, all achieve similar structures on the mission field.[34]

The second topic was the best means of *exciting and maintaining a missionary spirit at home*, opened by a CMS auxiliary secretary who was engaged in this work, and the third, on *missionary education*. The fourth on *the best means of calling forth home liberality* produced some surprising suggestions. Some of them seem to belong more to the era of Edinburgh, fifty years later. Thus, a substantial journal is suggested, on the lines of the *Saturday Review*, as well as missionary maps and atlases and even a university chair of missions. While waiting for the establishment of the chair, a missionary lectureship, moving each year to a different center of population or center of learning, should be set up. This last idea caused so much excitement that the conference appointed a committee to oversee it, with the absent Henry Venn among its members.

The fifth session was devoted to *native agency* and the seventh to *native churches*. The conference saw these two topics as central. Indigenous churches, notes the conference minutes, are "the germs of those Christianised communities which, according to the same word of prophecy, will at length occupy every country of the world."[35]

R. Spence Hardy, formerly Wesleyan missionary in Ceylon, offered the paper on native agency: "When we speak of Native Agency we include the entire Church of the future; as it is evident that, if Christianity is permanently to live in the lands that are now the object of missionary care, it must be by means of Native Agency alone."[36]

There would never be enough missionaries, or enough funds to support them if there were, and even if both of these resources were provided, it would be very ineffectual: "The truth must be naturalized; it must cease to be regarded as an exotic, before it can thoroughly permeate and permanently regenerate any given nation. Its power can only be universally diffused by that which is alike native in its fount and its flowing: look, tone, word, imagery, idiom, all must be native."[37]

The intermediate session, the sixth, dealt with the candidates for missionary work and the best means of acquiring those who were to be the "founders, instructors and advisors" but not the pastors of those indigenous congregations.[38]

34. Ibid., 17–24.
35. Ibid., 309.
36. Ibid., 194.
37. Ibid., 195.
38. For the minute, see ibid., 264ff.

And so the conference concluded. At the end of the public meeting that followed the sessions, the veteran Anglican Evangelical Hugh Stowell, who had been at the conference throughout, testified, "I convey away a refreshing influence in my spirit, such as I scarcely remember to have carried away from any other assembly." He put this down to the "spirit of apostolic brotherhood, devotion and simplicity of purpose that is needed more than anything besides in order to unite the disunited members of the church of Christ." He went on, "There is no way of uniting the servants of the cross so effectually as uniting them in common action in a common cause."[39] In the final session, Cullen had said, "I suppose there has never been such a gathering of brethren from all parts of the world, or from so many different countries and Societies, enjoying such a free interchange of thought and opinion, without any jarring word or painful feeling of regret."

To many of those who attended, therefore, the Liverpool Conference on Missions was a unique experience of unity in missions, the more striking since at its opening some stress had been laid on the variety of standpoints represented in the conference.

CONCLUSION

With hindsight, how significant was the conference?

Here we must make a double answer. First, the missionary movement that it represented was the most powerful influence working toward unity in the Western church, coping with historical legacies that enforced separation within Western Christianity. Second, the particular effect of the influence from Liverpool was limited by the ecclesiastical conditions obtaining in Britain at that time.

It was in the era of the Reformations, Protestant and Catholic, that the long isolation of Europe from Africa and Asia, and still longer ignorance of America, came to an end. This happened at a time when Europe was more Christian than ever before, both in terms of geographical extent and in cultural immersion, and when Christianity was more European than ever before because of the eclipse of so many of the older Asian and African Christian communities. The prerequisites of the missionary movement included a body of people of the highest spiritual commitment in order to face its demands, with the intellectual and cultural preparation to carry them out. It required a movement of intense spiritual renewal to produce such people, and an infrastructure to support them. Catholic southern Europe first met these conditions, and the Catholic mission story begins almost two

---

39. Ibid., 355.

centuries before the Protestant. Catholics and Protestants alike saw spiritual renewal in the era of the sixteenth-century Reformations, and both produced many radical Christians. But Catholics, by maintaining, reforming, renewing, and extending their religious orders, had an infrastructure to support the communities of radical Christians from which the first missions came.

The Protestant Reformers, on the other hand, killed the goose that laid golden eggs. They did so both by abolishing the monasteries and orders and then by suppressing the Anabaptists, who had produced a Protestant version of the holy community based on families, rather than on celibacy. It is no accident that the Moravians, who developed a new form of radical Christian community, were so prominent in the early Protestant missionary movement. Most of the later Protestant missions wanted to emulate them, but could not without adopting the community structure that gave them their focus. Eventually, Protestants found their own vehicle in the voluntary society. The antecedents of the voluntary society were basically secular and commercial, but they adapted readily to religious purposes. The Liverpool Conference is the heir of that arrangement; it was in essence a meeting of members of societies. The voluntary society did not fit into any of the existing Protestant forms of church government—Episcopal, Presbyterian or Independent. At the same time, none of those forms of church government had in themselves the capacity to establish missions in the world beyond the West.

The fundamental Christian experience of Europe since the fall of the Western Roman Empire was Christendom, created as the barbarian tribes of the North and West adopted Christianity as or into their customary law. Customary law is binding on the whole community; it does not allow for opting out. So the logic of Christendom is a single church. The Protestant Reformation retained that logic, but asserted it on a national basis, a single reformed church in a single political entity. In the event, the logic had to be in part abandoned; religious tolerance is less the fruit of Christian charity than of political realism. The legacy of the Reformation was thus to make, first the nation, and then the denomination, the ecclesial unit.

But the missionary movement simply did not fit either the national or the denominational ecclesiastical structures. It began from the acceptance of plurality but opened ways to new forms of unity.

The Liverpool Conference stands at an early point in the process but also at a time of transition within it. When it took place, Protestant missions had recovered from their shaky start—many missions were not just failures but disasters—and had made substantial progress. They were no longer the preserve of Evangelicals who had driven them on, though they were still the sphere of radical Christians. Indeed they were about to undergo a midlife crisis as new ideas of prophecy, and of holiness, and new types of devotion appeared, and as the voluntary society further subverted denominational structures. The great missionary explosion of the 1880s was yet to come, bringing a missionary invasion of the upper classes and the universities. The influences from across the Atlantic had yet to take hold in Britain. But we are on the edge of the story of the Student Movement; and that story takes us to the edge of the story of Edinburgh 1910. The modest meeting that took place in Liverpool 50 years before is the true parent of the 1910 World Missionary Conference.

BIBLIOGRAPHY

Bebbington, D. W. *Evangelicalism in Modern Britain: A History from the 1730s to the 1980s*. London: Unwin Hyman, 1989.

Finlayson, Geoffey B. A. M. *The Seventh Earl of Shaftesbury, 1801–1885*. London: Eyre Methuen, 1981.

Gibson, William. *The Year of Grace: A History of the Ulster Revival of 1859*. Belfast: Ambassador Emerald, 1998.

Hogg, W. Richey. *Ecumenical Foundations: A History of the International Missionary Council and Its Nineteenth Century Background*. New York: Harper, 1952.

Jeffrey, Kenneth C. *When the Lord Walked the Earth: The 1858-62 Revival in the North East of Scotland*. Studies in Evangelical History and Thought. 2002. Reprinted, Eugene, OR: Wipf & Stock, 2007.

Meiring, Piet G. J. "William Carey's 'Pleasing Dream.'" *Missionalia* 21 (1993) 219–28.

Orr, J. Edwin. *The Second Evangelical Awakening in Britain*. London: Marshall, Morgan & Scott, 1953.

Robert, Dana. *Occupy until I Come: A. T. Pierson and the Evangelization of the World*. Grand Rapids: Eerdmans, 2003.

Rouse, Ruth. "William Carey's 'Pleasing Dream.'" *International Review of Mission* 38, 150 (1949) 181–92.

Stanley, Brian. *The World Missionary Conference, Edinburgh 1910*. Grand Rapids: Eerdmans, 2009.

Walls, Andrew F. "The Heavy Artillery of the Missionary Army: The Domestic Importance of the Medical Missionary." In *The Missionary Movement in Christian History: Studies in Transmission of Faith*, 211–20. Maryknoll, NY: Orbis, 1996.

25

Asia and Latin America
Taking the Gospel to the "Ends of the Earth"

ALLEN YEH

THIS COLLECTION OF ESSAYS is in honor of an African, Tite Tiénou. But without a doubt it is a tribute to call Tiénou not just a visionary of *African* but of *World* Christianity.[1] This chapter focuses on two continents, Asia and Latin America; together, with Africa, they constitute the "Majority World."[2] They tell the remarkable story of the shift of the center of gravity of Christianity to the Two-Thirds World in the last half-century. It is not often that Asia and Latin America are spoken of in the same breath, but there are remarkable points of contact that can be drawn out in a side-by-side comparison.

---

1. My doctoral dissertation dealt with the life and thought of Orlando Costas, a Latino missiologist who could not be limited to only one continent but had a heart for the world's Christians.

2. There is a lot of controversy over what terms to employ in describing the continents outside of North America and Europe. "Non-Western world" is derogatory because it defines someone by what they are not. "Third World" is a passé term that was used during the Cold War but is no longer relevant with the fall of Communism. "Southern continents" is inaccurate because it seems to exclude Asia which is not South but East. "Two-Thirds World" and "Majority World" are usually preferred these days because they simply refer to population size.

To be sure, it is clear that Asia and Latin America are vastly different continents. For one, Latin America is rather homogeneous in its language and religion, whereas Asia is about as pluralistic as a continent can be. Of course Latin America has languages other than Spanish, for example Portuguese spoken in Brazil; English spoken in nations such as Guyana, Belize, Jamaica; French spoken in places like Haiti; and indigenous languages like Aymara and Mayan in Bolivia and Guatemala, respectively. However, Spanish is the predominant language and permeates the continent like no other.

In contrast, Asia is the largest continent in the world. But the language most present there, Mandarin Chinese,[3] is dwarfed by the diverse combination of other languages: Arabic, Hindi, Japanese, Thai, various Chinese dialects, and so forth. There is no *lingua franca* of Asia.

Asia itself is the most religiously diverse continent on earth. Every major world religion, including Christianity, Judaism, Islam, Hinduism, Buddhism, Sikhism, Jainism, Baha'I, is found in Asia. There are no European, African, or Latin American indigenous religions that dominate the world scene like those that originated in Asia.[4] Latin America, in contrast, is largely Christian, and indeed mostly Roman Catholic. Today, of course, evangelical Protestantism and especially Pentecostalism have made great inroads in Latin America (particularly in countries like Guatemala and Brazil). In any case, Latin America is a majority-Christian continent. Most Asian Christians daily rub shoulders with people of other faiths, whereas most Latin Americans do not encounter many people who practice other religions. India alone proves the point. It is a sub-continent composed of hundreds of different languages, dialects, religions, and cultures, and alone has perhaps more diversity than the whole of Latin America.[5]

Despite the above differences, there are similarities that warrant several areas of comparison: race, geography and culture, politics and economics, and Christianity.

---

3. Mandarin is the second-most widely spoken language in the world after English, with a greater number of native-born speakers than any other language in the world.

4. The closest would be something like Mormonism, which is widespread because of its missionary zeal, but it is limited in scope compared with other world religions.

5. In the United States, Asians and Latinos account for the majority of immigrants. But there is a difference in mindset: Asians are usually here to stay, whereas it is not uncommon for Latin Americans to come to the United States to work, but still hope ultimately to return home.

RACE

"Race" is a term that does not have categorical meaning scientifically. All human beings are of one race, given the fact that all can interbreed. However, race is a pseudo-scientific social construct, particularly in the United States, related to sociology, anthropology, and inter-class dynamics. The concept is employed even in government surveys, for the purposes of affirmative action, census figures, and politics. It may seem at face value that race is one area in which Latin Americans and Asians do *not* have much in common. After all, Asians seem to be generally defined in terms of their national and ethnic boundaries, whereas Latin Americans are extremely intermixed genetically. The interactions of Spaniards, African slaves, and the indigenous Amerindians[6] have contributed to a cultural and racial mix that remains to this day, denoted by the words *mestizaje* and *mulataje* (literally, "people of mixed race").[7] There are even words for Latin American "miscegenation," which covers every permutation: the offspring of Spaniards and Indians are *mestizos*; of Spaniards and Africans slaves, *mulatos*; and of Indian and black parentage, *zambos*. In the Portuguese territory of Brazil, likewise there are *pardos* (white and black), *mamelucos* or *caboclos* (white and Indian), and *cafusos* (Indian and black).[8]

Many people, however, forget about the Asian presence in Latin America. Alberto Fujimori, of Japanese descent, was President of Peru from 1990–2000. In beating out Nobel Prize-winning author Mario Vargas Llosa for the presidency, Fujimori became the world's first national leader to be drawn from a minority race.[9] Brazil has the largest Japanese population in the world outside of Japan. Peru has one of the largest Chinese populations (and the oldest Chinatown in Latin America), with Peruvian-Chinese restaurants called *chifas*.

It can be argued that the Asian contribution to the Latin American continent is greater than the European, African, and Amerindian influences. Whether one is a Darwinian evolutionary biologist or a biblical literalist/creationist, one thing all can agree on is that humankind comes from a

---

6. The word "Indian" is obviously a misnomer, stemming from Christopher Columbus's mistake in thinking he had discovered India. "Native Americans" is the term used in the United States and "First Nations" is the term used in Canada. "Amerindians" is preferable to distinguish North American Indians from "Indians" in India. Sometimes the word "Iberoamericans" is used, but that mainly connotes the post-Columbian populations of the New World.

7. Rodríguez, "Adiós, Borinquen Querida," 8.

8. Williamson, *Penguin History of Latin America*, 145, 173.

9. Barack Obama is the second national leader in world history to be drawn from a minority race.

single origin, either from Africa or Mesopotamia. (Again, the fact that can all interbreed reflects this). However, this begs the question: How did people first settle in the Americas? The best theory appears to be that they crossed the Bering Strait from the easternmost tip of Siberia to Alaska, across what was once a land bridge at a time when sea levels were low enough to expose terrain. This Land Bridge Theory (also called the "Beringia" theory) has proponents who estimate various dates of crossing, but the theory still posits that the Amerindians were Asian in origin.[10] Physiologically, the indigenous Native Americans, Maya, Zapotecs, Quechuas, and others, have definite Asiatic features. Even some of the cultural preferences have been retained, for example almost all cultures in the world value gold, but only two cultures value jade: the Chinese and the Maya. And the Maya hieroglyphs are pictograms like Chinese characters.[11] That may be coincidence, or it may not be. Whatever the case, there are likely genetic links between the two continents.

Nonetheless, the racial contributions of Latin Americans and Asians are important for social and pragmatic reasons, both in the international sphere and in the domestic realm. Socially and geographically, a Western view of history has always put Europe (and Africa because of its proximity to Europe) at the center of attention. Latin America and Asia have often been relegated to the margins because of the Western perception that they are far-flung. (The very phrases "Middle East" and "Far East" reflect the Eurocentric worldview, though unfortunately there are not alternative terms to be employed.) In the United States, the same can be said of the racial conversation: it is often just between blacks and whites. However, Hispanics[12] are the largest ethnic minority group in the United States and together with Asians/Asian Americans account for the two fastest-growing groups,

---

10. Hoffecker and Elias, *Human Ecology of Beringia*.

11. Logagraphic, as opposed to alphabetic or syllabaric in nature. There are only five original languages that developed independently of any previous influence: Mesopotamian cuneiform, Egyptian hieroglyphs, Chinese pictograms, Indus River Valley script, and Mayan. All forms of writing today derive from one or a combination of these five. Interestingly, none are European. See Montgomery, *How to Read Maya Hieroglyphs*, 1.

12. There is much confusion about the difference between the terms "Hispanic," "Latino," and "Chicano." "Hispanic" connotes someone with a Spanish-speaking origin. Thus, Puerto Ricans, and people with ancestry from Argentina or Spain, are Hispanic and can be of any racial background. Brazilians speak Portuguese so they are not considered Hispanic. Latino is anybody with roots from Latin America; thus Brazilians and even English-speaking Guyanese are considered Latino, but not Spaniards. "Chicano" is a contraction of the word "Mexicano" and basically refers to anybody of Mexican origin living in the United States, but not, for example, people of Honduran or Venezuelan national origin. Clearly there are areas of overlap between these three words but they are not synonymous.

and neither ought to be overlooked.[13] Both groups are sometimes seen as marginal because they are relatively recent immigrants, but the nature of the United States as historically a nation of immigrants should allow for Asians and Latinos to be a natural part of the racial conversation, and the discussion should shift from being bilateral to being multilateral.

GEOGRAPHY AND CULTURE

Israel was the crossroads of the world in Jesus's time. It was the meeting place of Asia, Africa, and Europe and was strategically located to spread the Gospel in all three directions: to Asia (e.g., India), to Africa (e.g., Ethiopia), and to Europe (e.g., Greece). In the first century, "World Christianity" was a tautology, for its intercontinental scope was part of the initial nature of Christianity. Only after AD 1000 did Christianity come to be associated with the West.[14] At the start of European imperial expansion in the fifteenth century, the crossroads of the world had shifted to the Iberian Peninsula. From Iberia, the Gospel (via the imperial engine) spread to the four corners of the globe. The Treaty of Tordesillas was established between the Portuguese King John II and the Spanish monarchs Ferdinand and Isabella in 1494 to divide the world between Spanish and Portuguese territories. The Spanish were given the authority to sail west, thus having jurisdiction over all the territories of the New World, and the Portuguese went south and east to Africa and Asia. These were inherently different categories, as the Americas were unexplored by Europeans up to that point, thus giving Spain unchallenged free reign in these lands, whereas Portugal had competition with other European powers in Africa and Asia. Upon protest by the Portuguese king, who disapproved of the agreement as it stood, the Treaty of Tordesillas was revised to give Portugal an opportunity in the New World; thereby the Portuguese were allowed to colonize what is today Brazil. Just as the Portuguese had one western colony, the Spanish had only one southern and one eastern colony: Equatorial Guinea (in Africa) and the Philippines (in Asia).[15]

The Treaty of Tordesillas profoundly affected the cultural mix of today's world. The most obvious example is the prevalence of Spanish in the Americas—making it, today, the third-most widely spoken language in the world (after English and Mandarin Chinese). If not for Ferdinand and

13. Dougherty, "U.S. Sees Surge in Asian, Hispanic Populations."

14. Jenkins, *Lost History of Christianity*.

15. The Treaty of Zaragoza (the continuation of the Tordesillas line on the opposite side of the world) allowed the Spanish to possess the Philippines.

Isabella's commissioning of Columbus's journeys westward, this certainly would not be a fact today. The Portuguese, because of the competition with other European powers, did not have such a widespread influence of their language as the Spanish did. The largest Portuguese-speaking nation in the world is actually in the Americas, where little resistance to their colonial efforts was encountered. Portugal's linguistic influence on Africa can be seen in pockets on that continent, such as Angola, Mozambique, and São Tomé and Príncipe, and to a much lesser extent in Asia, in places like India, Macau, Taiwan, and Japan.[16]

Among Europeans, the Portuguese Jesuits were often the ones to make first contact with Asians, whereas it was the *conquistadores* from Spain who encountered the Americas first.[17] This difference, religious versus military, created a different culture in these respective continents. Whereas Asia has its own identity apart from Europe (as does Africa), Latin America does not. Because of the military nature of the takeover, "The very idea of America cannot be separated from coloniality: the entire continent emerged as such in the European consciousness as a massive extent of land to be appropriated and of people to be converted to Christianity, and whose labor could be exploited."[18] This accounts for the different nature of the two continents with relation to Europe. Yet, these two continents on the extreme western and eastern ends of the world were both influenced by the Iberian powers, giving them a geographical kinship, linked by the sister cultures of Spain and Portugal. Even apart from the European influence, there are similarities between these two cultures, characterized by strong family-oriented patriarchal social structures.

It is striking that in both Latin America and Asia great ancient empires had existed which rivaled anything in the West. When the conquistadores arrived on the scene in the Aztec capital of Tenochtitlan (now modern-day Mexico City), they were astounded by the majesty of the city, overshadowing anything in Europe at the time in terms of grandeur and size.[19] The

---

16. Though Portuguese is not spoken in India today, the language is still retained in surnames such as "de Souza" and "Fernandes." Likewise in the Philippines, Spanish surnames such as "Velasco" and "de la Cruz" are common.

17. Hernan Cortes in Mexico conquered the Aztecs, and Francisco Pizarro in Peru conquered the Incas; the story of both invasions is remarkably similar in that small bands of European explorers were able to defeat a massive indigenous empire in a short amount of time. The third major society, the Maya, had no centralized authority or emperor, and were already in decline by the time the Europeans arrived. For a good fictional account of the Portuguese contact with Japan, see Shusaku Endo, *Silence*.

18. Mignolo, *Idea of Latin America*, 7.

19. The two greatest pyramids in the world are both in Latin America—they actually are larger than the Great Pyramid of Cheops in Egypt. They are La Danta pyramid

Maya were more sophisticated in astronomy, mathematics, and the calendar, than any Europeans of that time.[20] The Chinese built the Great Wall and the Forbidden City and, at its height, the empire rivaled the Roman Empire in terms of extent of territory and power. Genghis Khan's armies conquered westward more effectively than Alexander the Great's armies conquered eastward. The archaeological ruins at Machu Picchu (in Peru) and Angkor Wat (in Cambodia) are perhaps the greatest religious ruins in the world. Inca gold work[21] and Japanese silks were more exquisite than anything Europe could offer. Yet, for whatever reason, when the West encountered Latin America and Asia, the latter two fell before the former.[22] For all intents and purposes, it could have gone either way, but both Latin America and Asia have had their continents irrevocably changed by their encounters with the West.[23]

POLITICS AND ECONOMICS

Before Christopher Columbus, there was the great Chinese mariner Zheng He, who explored the world between 1405 and 1433.[24] Nicholas Kristof draws some lines here between Asia and Latin America:

---

in El Mirador, Guatemala, and the Great Pyramid of Cholula in Puebla, Mexico.

20. The Maya calculated a year as being 365.242036 days, which is slightly more accurate than the 365.2425 days of the Western Gregorian calendar. The astronomy and mathematics of the Maya were so advanced that they understood the concept of "zero" long before Europeans did, and they could predict the alignment of the Winter solstice sun with the center of the Milky Way once every 26,000 years!

21. See Mann, *1491: New Revelations*, 91: "But just as guns did not determine the outcome of conflict in New England, steel was not the decisive factor in Peru. True, anthropologists have long marveled that Andean societies did not make steel. Iron is plentiful in the mountains, yet the Inka used metal for almost nothing useful. . . . Inka metallurgy was, in fact, as refined as European metallurgy, but . . . it had such different goals that academic experts had not even recognized it."

22. According to Diamond, *Guns, Germs, and Steel*, geography and proximity to domesticated animals played an important part in determining the "haves" from the "have-nots" in providing labor, food, technology, diseases, and immunities to the same. Europeans had all these in spades, which meant they had a tactical advantage when encountering islanders or people from continents that lacked such natural resources.

23. See Kristof and WuDunn, *Thunder from the East*, 29: "For the great majority of the last few thousand years, Asia has been far wealthier and more advanced and cosmopolitan than any place in Europe. . . . So ancient Asia was the longtime champion of commerce and technology, and one of the central questions for the coming decades is whether it is now ready to recover a part of what it lost."

24. For more details, see Menzies, *1421: The Year China Discovered the World*.

Zheng He's expeditions were not flukes, for Asia had been adventurous about travel since ancient times. American Indians came principally from Asia, of course, and some historians believe that there were repeated infusions of East Asian blood and influence into the Americas by sea over the millennia. For example, historians have found evidence that when China's Shang Dynasty was overthrown in about 1045 BC, Chinese refuges may have sailed to the Americas and settled among the Olmec people of Mexico and the Chavin tribesmen of Peru. An ancient Chinese chronicle recounts that in the fifth century, a Chinese monk named Hui Shen traveled with five Afghan monks to a place called the Far East Country, which sounds a great deal like Mayan Mexico... There is some evidence that Indonesians may have landed in Mexico. Scholars have noted similarities between the Sulawesi people of Indonesia and the Otomi tribes of central Mexico, such as in the methods and tools they use to make bark cloth.[25]

Such historical and geographical observations further strengthen the ties between these two continents.

Economically, Latin American nations in modern times have tried to emulate and follow East Asia, especially the four "Little Tigers" of South Korea, Taiwan, Singapore, and Hong Kong.[26] The first two, especially, are a great source of comparison since they are nations rather than city-states like the latter two. Latin American nations likewise can be divided between the larger, more economically autonomous nations such as Mexico and Brazil,[27] and the smaller nations of the Caribbean basin which are more economically dependent on other countries.[28] However, this Latin American emulation of Asian economies has been relatively unsuccessful due to the fact that the former "for historical reasons [has] societies [that] are more cohesive, homogeneous, and egalitarian, and where strong, purposeful governments have been better able to implement coherent development strategies."[29] A prime example of Asia's ability to succeed where Latin America has failed is in China's overtaking of Mexico as the world's number 2 manufactur-

---

25. Ibid., 30–31.

26. They are sometimes known as the "Gang of Four," after Mao Zedong's infamous cohort.

27. Ward, *Latin America*, 19. In a 1994 survey, Mexico and Brazil accounted for over 50 percent of Latin America's population and economic output.

28. Hong Kong is a Special Economic Zone of the People's Republic of China, and El Salvador uses the U.S. dollar as its national currency.

29. Ward, *Latin America*, 16.

ing power after the United States. In 2003, it became cheaper to outsource Mexican labor to China; thus statues of the Virgin of Guadalupe were produced in China and shipped to Mexico, instead of being produced in Mexico itself.[30] Yet there are signs that some Latin American countries are resilient and on the rise: countries like Chile[31] and Brazil are emulating Asian economies and have seen similar growth.[32]

Politically, Asia has had a spate of left-wing dictators such as Mao Zedong in China and Pol Pot in Cambodia. This may seem different from Latin America, which has suffered from right-wing fascist dictatorships such as Juan and Eva Perón in Argentina and Augusto Pinochet in Chile, but those rightist leaders provoked leftist responses by revolutionaries like Che Guevara and Pablo Neruda, rendering the political climates of the two continents similar during the latter twentieth century. Modern Christianity in Latin America and in China has been heavily influenced by Marxism as a result[33] but in different ways: liberation theology gave an initial push to Christianity in Latin America (despite the marked decline today),[34] while the huge current surge of Christianity in Asia is largely a response to the crackdown on religious expression.[35]

A Christianity without context is an impossibility, and though modern Asian and Latin American Christianity may have been beholden to Marxism as an ideology, they have developed very differently from Western

---

30. Friedman, *World Is Flat*, 403.

31. Kristof and WuDunn, *Thunder from the East*, 346.

32. In 2001, the acronym BRIC (standing for Brazil, Russia, India, China) was coined by Goldman Sachs chief economist Jim O'Neill. These four countries may well become future leaders of the world's economy. In 2009, Robert Ward, director of the Global Forecasting team for the Economist Intelligence Unit, coined the term CIVETS (Colombia, Indonesia, Vietnam, Egypt, Turkey, South Africa), highlighting six nations in the developing world that have become increasingly important to the world economic engine. Asia is obviously heavily represented in the BRIC and CIVETS nations, Latin America and Africa to a lesser extent but important nonetheless.

33. The irony of adopting Marxism (a Western ideology) to eradicate other Western ideologies is not lost on Lamin Sanneh (*Disciples of All Nations*, 244): "It remains a puzzle, however, why prominent Western observers—including religious scholars—thought that China's adoption of Marxist revolution was authentically Chinese while Christianity should be repudiated for not being genuinely Chinese."

34. There is an oft-repeated adage: "Liberation theologians chose the poor, but the poor chose Pentecostalism."

35. It is estimated that the number of Christians in China is 5 to 10 percent of the population. (Underground house churches make this estimation difficult.) Given a nationwide population of 1.3 billion, the number of Christians can range anywhere from 65 million to 130 million. This makes China the second-largest Christian nation on earth in terms of absolute numbers.

Christianity, which is beholden to capitalism as an ideology. It may be argued that the former is more similar to the early church found in Acts than the latter. For example, this similar political climate in Latin America and Asia has caused indigenous expressions of Christianity to arise, such as the Base Ecclesial Communities in the 1970s and 80s[36] and the Chinese house churches today.[37] This flattening of society and politics has led to egalitarian expressions of the faith (e.g., the priesthood of all believers) that have caused movements like Pentecostalism and Evangelicalism to make great strides against other more established forms of Christianity[38] (which in Latin America and China would be traditional Catholicism and the Three-Self Church, respectively[39]).

The urbanization of the world is a further phenomenon that is extremely significant in the ascendancy on the global scene of the Two-Thirds World. In 2008 a significant population shift was observed when, for the first time in human history, more people lived in cities than in non-cities.[40] If one looks at the list of the top twenty cities in the world (by population), it is striking that the largest two are in Asia and Latin America (Tokyo and Mexico City, respectively), only two are located in the West (New York and Los Angeles), and the rest, with the exception of Lagos and Cairo, are Asian or Latin American.[41] Cities are not only where major businesses are located, but they are hubs for communication and travel, they are artistic and political centers, and they are at the forefront of trends and culture. However, despite the great potential of cities, the reality of poverty and other problems is not lost on people from the Two-Thirds World and makes for a sobering analysis: "Globalisation and urbanisation have contributed to worsening economic conditions in Latin America. Political instability, social unrest and environmental issues are particularly pertinent to churches seeking to demonstrate biblical ethics and social responsibility in urban regions."[42] Latin America and Asia will have a great role to play in the present century

---

36. For a good study of the Base Ecclesial Communities, see Cook, *Expectation of the Poor*.

37. For an example of a Chinese house church leader, see Yun, *Heavenly Man*.

38. Dodson, "Pentecostals, Politics, and Public Space," 25.

39. The official name is the Protestant Three-Self Patriotic Movement. The "three-selfs" are self-governing, self-supporting, and self-propagating. "Self-governing" is a misnomer inasmuch as the churches are government-sanctioned.

40. United Nations Population Fund. Online: http://www.unfpa.org/swp/2007/english/introduction.html.

41. Mumbai (Bombay), São Paulo, Delhi, Shanghai, Kolkata (Calcutta), Dhaka, Jakarta, Karachi, Buenos Aires, Manila, Rio de Janeiro, Beijing, Osaka, Istanbul.

42. Heaney, *Contextual Theology*, 233.

in shaping globalization so that it is not merely the West influencing the Majority World but perhaps also the reverse.

MISSIONS

Geologically, if one considers Pangaea—the great land mass that existed before the shifting of the continents apart from one another—Asia and the Americas existed on the opposite sides of the world from each other, as the furthest East and furthest West, respectively. In light of Jesus's great commission in Acts 1:8, "But you will receive power when the Holy Spirit comes on you, and you will be my witnesses in Jerusalem, Judea, Samaria, and to the ends of the earth," Asia and Latin America could literally be considered the "ends of the earth."

Again, however, it can be argued that there are more differences than similarities. Asia (in its Western part) was the first continent to receive the Gospel; the Americas were the last (Mormon beliefs of Jesus visiting America notwithstanding!). But the irony is that the Americas are arguably the most Christian continents today, whereas Asia is the only continent without a majority-Christian population.

At the great World Missionary Conference in Edinburgh 1910 (often considered the "birthplace of the modern ecumenical movement"), Latin America was famously left off the map, whereas of the Majority World continents, Asia was the most represented (with 17 Asians in attendance—not a large number compared to the 1,200 present, but certainly more than Africa which had not a single black African represented, and Latin America which had no acknowledgment whatsoever).[43] The result was a very different perspective by Europeans of Asia as a mission field versus Latin America as a mission field.[44]

Nevertheless, today the two continents have a significant role in shaping world missions. As the second-largest Christian nation on earth by absolute numbers, China is becoming a major missionary force. The Back-to-Jerusalem movement is a vision of Chinese Christians to bring the Gospel to every city, town, and region between China and Jerusalem, along the old Silk Road.[45] The Chinese house church leaders who have this vision

---

43. Stanley, *World Missionary Conference*.

44. One of the results of ecumenism is that Latin America was considered sufficiently Christianized since it is majority Catholic. Any attempt by non-Catholics to evangelize the continent was regarded as "sheep-stealing" and ecumenical unity would thus be broken.

45. Hattaway, *Back to Jerusalem*, xii.

observed that "generally speaking, we can see that the flame of the gospel has burned in a westward direction . . . to circle the entire globe and come all the way back to where it started—Jerusalem!"[46] Latin America, with Brazil at the forefront, is poised to become a significant missionary influence on the Arabic-speaking world.[47] Not only are there physiological similarities between Latin Americans and Middle Easterners,[48] but the linguistic ties are strong as well.[49] Unlike white North Americans, Latin Americans do not have a negative political history with the Middle East and therefore are not shunned as readily. And as uncomfortably as this may sit with Western Evangelicals,

> a revived cult of Mary would have an appeal far beyond the Americas . . . (the Virgin Mary is a prominent and beloved figure in the Quran). A Catholic Church dominated by Latin Americans and Africans would prove highly receptive to new concepts of Marian devotion, which might serve as a bridge to other ancient Christian communities, and even to other faiths. A Black or Brown Mary would be a powerfully appropriate symbol for the emerging Southern Christendom.[50]

Though Catholics today would not have the same kind of missionary impulse as Evangelicals, by their sheer size they are "witnesses" of the faith worldwide and are often the representative Christians as far as non-Christians (atheists or those of other faiths) are concerned.

The irony is that this area of the world is the cradle of the Christian faith, if one considers where the Garden of Eden, Abraham's Ur of the Chaldeans, and Israel are located; but it is precisely this area of the world that is most under the sway of Islam, perhaps the world's toughest mission field today. It is quite possible that in the next century Asian and Latin American missionaries will make significant headway in a region of the globe in which Western Christians have had so little success—this despite the fact that, as previously stated, Latin American Christians rarely have contact with

---

46. Ibid., 20.

47. Brazil has the largest Protestant population in Latin America (20 million out of 150 million people), according to Cleary and Stewart-Gambino, *Power, Politics, and Pentecostals*, 123.

48. In fact many people in Latin America are of Middle Eastern descent by blood, and even if they are not, many Latinos can still easily blend in with Arabs and other Semitic peoples.

49. Due to the Moorish occupation of Spain between AD 711 and 1492, more than 2,000 words in Spanish are of Arabic origin, particularly words that begin with "al" (the definite article in Arabic) such as alcohol, algebra, and Alhambra.

50. Jenkins, *Next Christendom*, 119.

people of other faiths, and the Chinese have long been in a communist state that has banned religion, traditional or foreign. But these are the new missionaries who are taking up the mantle of Acts 1:8. As Chinese house church leader Zhang Rongliang said in 2001, "The Chinese church is getting ready to go to the 10/40 window. Chinese people are more suitable than Americans to go to the Muslim world. Muslims prefer Chinese to Americans."[51] Indeed, this is the advent of World Christianity, of contextualized incarnational ministry, and the shifting of the center of gravity of Christianity as the Holy Spirit moves in new and varied ways.

ECCLESIOLOGY

The face of the Church is changing, as Philip Jenkins offers in *The Next Christendom*: Christianity will be comprised mostly of believers from the Two-Thirds World. Soong-Chan Rah posits the same in *The Next Evangelicalism*, but on a domestic level: immigrants and ethnic minorities are becoming the mainstay of U.S. Christianity and will keep the United States as the only Western nation still majority-Christian.[52]

As Hispanics and Asians continue to be the primary source of immigration to the United States,[53] there is fresh vitality and renewed vigor within the churches that stems from their world perspective and prevents the United States from isolationism. Other than whites, Koreans are the primary students who enroll at evangelical seminaries across the country. On the undergraduate level, Hispanics are being heavily recruited by Christian colleges as their numbers increase, and they have the potential to become the largest constituency of the American church.[54]

However, though the constituency of U.S. Christianity is sustained by ethnic minorities and immigrants, the leadership continues to be white. Rah points out,

> The consistently poor record of minority faculty hires at Christian colleges and seminaries is not only disappointing, it is irresponsible. Among evangelical seminaries, the percentage of nonwhite student enrollment has increased from approximately

51. Aikman, *Jesus in Beijing*, 202.
52. Rah, *Next Evangelicalism*, 14.
53. Sanneh, *Disciples*, 276: "Pentecostalism is also riding the wave of Latin American demographic movements, including currents of immigration into the United States. Of about thirty-seven million Latino immigrants in the United States, the vast majority is Pentecostal, with a strong Catholic overlay."
54. Sells, "Hispanic Students."

15 percent in 1977 to 31 percent in 2005. However the percentage of faculty of color in 2005 stood at 12 percent, which is disproportionally and significantly lower than the 31 percent minority student enrollment.[55]

This incongruity between constituency and leadership is unsustainable, and a sea-change seems inevitable in the future, both in theological education and in the church at large.

THEOLOGY

Latin America and Asia have much to offer the global Christian scene theologically. Contextualization remains of primary importance in incarnating the Gospel in parts of the world where it has made few if any inroads. Initially, much of the contextualization was done for the benefit of Asians and Latin Americans, as Don Richardson argues by his Principle of Redemptive Analogy. It is the idea of the Apostle Paul on the Areopagus, enlightening the men of Athens about the "unknown god" they worshiped (Acts 17). Paul contends that they were actually worshiping the Christian God unwittingly. Richardson points out that such general revelation is found in all cultures throughout human history, for example the striking resemblance of the Inca creator god Viracocha and the Chinese supreme god Shang Ti to the Judeo-Christian God Yahweh.[56] However, now in this age of so-called "reverse mission," contextualization goes the other way as well.

Sharon Heaney contends that "the primary significance of the Latin American contribution is in its identification and application of contextual method."[57] In addition to contextualization, Latinos are no longer just Catholic but are increasingly Pentecostal. Edward Cleary writes,

> Pentecostalism's greatest theological achievement in Latin America is freedom of expression and the affirmation of the individual's worth within the community. These are fundamental Protestant emphases. To them may be added a call to sanctity for all members and a missionary zeal for sharing spiritual gifts with others. . . . All this is deeply rooted in Protestant traditions such as interpretation of Scriptures by ordinary Christians, the

---

55. Rah, *Next Evangelicalism*, 19.
56. Richardson, *Eternity in Their Hearts*, 33–71.
57. Heaney, *Contextual Theology*, 1.

priesthood of all believers, and the priority of practice over dogma."[58]

Latin Americans also look at the world through the lens of class and poverty. For some, this gave rise to expressions of liberation theology. For others (particularly Evangelicals) this led to *misión integral*, often translated as "holistic mission." This is "an awareness of the serious nature of the relationship between faith, Christian mission and social responsibility."[59]

Asia brings another lens, namely, religious diversity. This pluralism (which has overlap with, but is not synonymous with relativism) lends itself to a Christian pluralism as well; in other words, a diversity of expressions of the faith. When encountering various religions, especially in India, "the historian is faced with the fact that Christianity in India is anything but a single whole or a monolithic entity . . . This is really a history about many separate Christianities, rather than about one. . . . Christianity within India is 'Indian.'"[60] This is often a frightening concept to conservative Western Evangelicals who fear relative truth but cannot see the difference between that and its close cousin, diversity. Of course the former is wrong because God is Truth, but the latter should be welcome because the diversity of the world displays God's glory. There should be unity in the essentials but diversity in the non-essentials. This is the gift of World Christianity to the church: each culture brings different ways to worship and serve God in keeping with their cultural understanding. The poor understand God's heart for social justice. The orphans appreciate the Fatherhood of God. Rural people can more readily comprehend the Bible's agrarian metaphors. Those Christians who daily encounter other religions know what persecution and suffering really mean. People's cultures matter in how they see God, and a good kind of pluralism (the kind that comes from World Christianity) is necessary for understanding God in all his facets. As John Piper rightly proclaims, "The beauty and power of praise that will come to the Lord from the diversity of the nations are greater than the beauty and power that would come to him if the chorus of the redeemed were culturally uniform."[61]

Both Asia and Latin America have important and necessary contributions to make to the cause of Christ today. Philip Jenkins observes that,

---

58. Cleary and Stewart-Gambino, *Power, Politics, and Pentecostals*, 1: "Pentecostalism has quietly become the largest Christian movement of the twentieth century. . . . Pentecostalism is especially prominent in Latin America, where it challenges Catholic, historical Protestant, and Mormon churches, vodoun, macumba, and indigenous religions."

59. Heaney, *Contextual Theology*, 211, 213.

60. Frykenberg, *Christianity in India*, vii.

61. Piper, *Let the Nations Be Glad*, 216.

contrary to the belief that Two-Thirds World Christians would become "liberal" in the vein of liberation theology, "At present, the most immediately apparent difference between the older and newer churches is that Southern Christians are far more conservative in terms of both beliefs and moral teaching. . . . Southern Christians retain a very strong supernatural orientation, and are by and large far more interested in personal salvation than in radical politics."[62] Both Asians and Latin Americans are very family-oriented, which fits well with the more conservative values of Western evangelical Christianity, and homosexuality is far less socially acceptable in the Majority World than it is in the West.[63] Immigrants to the United States have much more of the so-called "Protestant work ethic" than more "established" Americans. Jenkins further describes the typical Two-Thirds World Christian today:

> These newer churches preach deep personal faith and communal orthodoxy, mysticism and Puritanism, all founded on clear scriptural authority. They preach messages that, to a Westerner, appear simplistically charismatic, visionary, and apocalyptic. In this thought-world, prophecy is an everyday reality, while faith-healing, exorcism, and dream-visions are all basic components of religious sensibility. For better or worse, the dominant churches of the future could have much in common with those of medieval or early modern European times. On present evidence, a Southernized Christian future should be distinctly conservative . . . In the context of global Christianity, [Western] liberalism [eschewing morality and the supernatural] looks distinctly dated.[64]

In other words, while the Western world is debating the merits and demerits of modernism versus postmodernism, Christians from the Two-Thirds World may be more pre-modern than anything else! This is not to suggest that they are primitive in their way of life, as many of the most advanced megacities are to be found in Asia and Latin America, but their worldview is more accepting of the supernatural than the dichotomist thinking of the West. With such a compartmentalized Enlightenment mindset, it is no wonder that Christianity is failing in the Western world—science leaves no room for God. There is no such problem in the Majority World mindset—India is perhaps the most striking example of how widespread

---

62. Jenkins, *Next Christendom*, 7.
63. Ibid., 201.
64. Ibid., 8–9.

technology and fervent religious devotion can coexist with no apparent contradiction whatsoever.

This highlights the problem of the Western church: it is not addressing the issues relevant to the Two-Thirds World. The Western church is often locked in narrow theological debates that the Majority World has no interest in. The former cares about mode of baptism, Calvinism versus Arminianism, debates over cessationism/dispensationalism, and the status of the papacy; the latter is concerned with the fate of dead ancestors, spiritual warfare, the relationship between poverty and faith, and conversion to Christ in a religiously pluralistic world.

Soong-Chan Rah cites the "emerging church" movement:

> Most of the emerging church conversation has focused on postmodernity's impact and role on middle-class, suburban, white churches, resulting in a continuing Western, white captivity of the American church. Evangelical approaches to postmodernity, therefore, are just as captured by culture as ministry to a generation that was raised in the framework of modernity. Because the evangelical perspective on postmodernity is spun from a white, suburban cultural perspective, there is a significant degree of irrelevance to the most significant growth edge in American Christianity—the immigrant of non-European descent, their American-raised children, urban churches and multiethnic churches (i.e., the next evangelicalism).[65]

In order to effectively theologize in this globalized Christian world, we need to be able to speak of the Gospel not only in the language of guilt (Western) but in terms of shame (Eastern).[66] This can be an Asian contribution. We need to not just be Christological (evangelical) but more pneumatological (Pentecostal)[67]—the two are certainly not mutually exclusive as the desire of all Christians is to be more fully Trinitarian! This can be a Latin American contribution. But overall, Asia and Latin America are just two pieces of the puzzle of this phenomenon we now know as World Christianity, a momentous time in Earth's history.

---

65. Rah, *Next Evangelicalism*, 110.
66. Tennent, *Theology in the Context of World Christianity*, 77–101.
67. Ibid., 163–89.

CONCLUSION

Comparisons such as offered in this essay are fraught with difficulties. Ultimately these two continents do not run parallel to each other. But the striking points of contact *in spite of* no intentional parallel are worthy of note. Perhaps this can point to the unique roles that both Latin America and Asia may have on the world scene.

In the midst of all this, let us not forget Africa. This was a comparison chapter between Latin America and Asia, but Africa perhaps more than the other two can today be called the heartland of Christianity in the world.[68] Together these three continents comprise what is termed "World Christianity." This is a theology of the periphery, of Hebrews 13 where Christ died "outside the city gate" (v. 12) for our sins and identified himself with the marginalized and outcast. But the "ends of the earth" is where Christianity has gone, and perhaps it is time for the West to do as the author of Hebrews suggests: "Let us, then, go to him outside the camp, bearing the disgrace he bore" (v. 13). Jesus went to the margins and thereby made that the new center because that's where he is. We live in an exciting time because God is doing something new in the world which is making Christianity what it was intended to be since the first century: a global faith.

BIBLIOGRAPHY

Aikman, David. *Jesus in Beijing: How Christianity Is Transforming China and Changing the Global Balance of Power*. Washington, DC: Regnery, 2003.

Cleary, Edward L., and Hannah W. Stewart-Gambino, editors. *Power, Politics, and Pentecostals in Latin America*. Boulder, CO: Westview, 1998.

Cook, Guillermo. *The Expectation of the Poor: Latin America Basic Ecclesial Communities in Protestant Perspective*. American Society of Missiology 9. Maryknoll, NY: Orbis, 1985.

Diamond, Jared. *Guns, Germs, and Steel: The Fates of Human Societies*. New York: Norton, 1997.

Dodson, Michael. "Pentecostals, Politics, and Public Space in Latin America." In *Power, Politics, and Pentecostals in Latin America*, edited by Edward L. Cleary and Hannah W. Stewart-Gambino, 25–40. Boulder CO: Westview, 1998.

Dougherty, Conor. "U.S. Sees Surge in Asian, Hispanic Populations." *Wall Street Journal*, May 28, 2011.

Friedman, Thomas L. *The World Is Flat: A Brief History of the Twenty-First Century*. New York: Farrar, Straus & Giroux, 2005.

Frykenberg, Robert Eric. *Christianity in India: From Beginnings to the Present*. Oxford: Oxford University Press, 2008.

---

68. Sanneh, *Disciples of All Nations*, 276, projects Africa's Christian numbers in 2025 to be 600 million, making it the "new center of gravity."

Hattaway, Paul. *Back to Jerusalem: Three Chinese House Church Leaders Share Their Vision to Complete the Great Commission*. Atlanta: Piquant, 2003.

Heaney, Sharon E. *Contextual Theology for Latin America: Liberation Themes in Evangelical Perspective*. Paternoster Theological Monographs. Eugene, OR: Wipf & Stock, 2008.

Hoffecker, John F., and Scott A. Elias. *Human Ecology of Beringia*. New York: Columbia University Press, 2007.

Jenkins, Philip. *The Lost History of Christianity: The Thousand-Year Golden Age of the Church in the Middle East, Africa, and Asia—and How It Died*. New York: Harper Collins, 2008.

———. *The Next Christendom: The Coming of Global Christianity*. New York: Oxford University Press, 2002.

Kristof, Nicholas D., and Sheryl WuDunn. *Thunder from the East: Portrait of a Rising Asia*. New York: Knopf, 2000.

Mann, Charles C. *1491: New Revelations of the Americas Before Columbus*. New York: Vintage, 2005.

Menzies, Gavin. *1421: The Year China Discovered the World*. New York: Harper Collins, 2002.

Mignolo, Walter D. *The Idea of Latin America*. Oxford: Blackwell, 2005.

Montgomery, John. *How to Read Maya Hieroglyphs*. New York: Hippocrene, 2002.

Piper, John. *Let the Nations Be Glad! The Supremacy of God in Missions*. Grand Rapids: Baker, 1993.

Rah, Soong-Chan. *The Next Evangelicalism: Freeing the Church from Western Cultural Captivity*. Downers Grove, IL: InterVarsity, 2009.

Richardson, Don. *Eternity in Their Hearts: Startling Evidence of the Belief in the One True God in Hundreds of Cultures throughout the World*. Ventura, CA: Regal, 1981.

Rodríguez, Clara E., et al. *"Adiós, Borinquen Querida": The Puerto Rican Diaspora, Its History, and Contributions*. Albany, NY: Center for Latino, Latin American, and Caribbean Studies, 2000.

Sanneh, Lamin. *Disciples of All Nations: Pillars of World Christianity*. Oxford: Oxford University Press, 2008.

Sells, Heather. "Hispanic Students: The Future of Christian Colleges?" *Christian Broadcasting Network*, December 31, 2010. No pages. Online: http://www.cbn.com/cbnnews/us/2010/November/Hispanic-Students-The-Future-of-Christian-Colleges/.

Stanley, Brian. *The World Missionary Conference, Edinburgh 1910*. Grand Rapids: Eerdmans, 2009.

Tennent, Timothy. *Theology in the Context of World Christianity: How the Global Church Is Influencing the Way We Think about and Discuss Theology*. Grand Rapids: Zondervan, 2007.

Ward, John. *Latin America: Development and Conflict since 1945*. London: Routledge, 1997.

Williamson, Edwin. *The Penguin History of Latin America*. London: Penguin, 1992.

Yun, Brother. *The Heavenly Man*. London: Monarch, 2002.

A Bibliography of the Works of Tite Tiénou

BOOKS

1999 *Understanding Folk Religion: A Christian Response to Popular Religious Beliefs and Practices* (with Paul G. Hiebert and R. Daniel Shaw). Grand Rapids: Baker Academic.

1998 *Issues in African Christian Theology* (co-editor with Samuel Ngewa and Mark Shaw). Nairobi: East African Educational Pub.

1990 *The Theological Task of the Church in Africa.* 2nd rev. ed. Achimota, Ghana: Africa Christian Press.

1982 *The Theological Task of the Church in Africa.* Achimota, Ghana: Africa Christian Press.

1980 *Tâche théologique de l'Eglise en Afrique.* Abidjan: Centre de Publications Evangéliques.

BOOK CHAPTERS AND JOURNAL ARTICLES

2011 "Entering Unfamiliar Territory: Budget Basics for the Dean of a University Theological School." In *C(H)AOS Theory: A Handbook for Chief Academic Officers: Contexts, Commitments, Competencies, and Choices*, edited by Kathleen D. Billman and Bruce Birch, 293–301. Grand Rapids: Eerdmans.

2008 "The Great Commission in Africa." In *The Great Commission: Evangelicals and the History of World Missions*, edited by Martin I. Klauber and Scott M. Manetsch, 164–75. Nashville: B & H.

2007 "Evangelical Theology in African Contexts." In *The Cambridge Companion to Evangelical Theology*, edited by Timothy Larsen and Daniel J. Treier, 213–24. Cambridge: Cambridge University Press.

2007 "The Samaritans: A Biblical-Theological Mirror for Understanding Racial, Ethnic, and Religious Identity?" In *This Side of Heaven: Race, Ethnicity, and Christian Faith*, edited by Robert J. Priest and Alvaro L. Nieves, 211–22. Oxford: Oxford University Press.

2006 "Christian Theology in an Era of World Christianity." In *Globalizing Theology: Belief and Practice in an Era of World Christianity*, edited by Craig Ott and Harold A. Netland, 37–51. Grand Rapids: Baker Academic.

2006 "Missional Theology" (with Paul G. Hiebert). *Missiology* 34: 219–38.
2005 "Evangelicals and Muslims: Interfaith Issues." *Covenant Quarterly* 63: 3–11.
2004 "Biblical Faith and Traditional Folk Religion." In *Biblical Faith and Other Religions: An Evangelical Assessment*, edited by David W. Baker, 138–47. Grand Rapids: Kregel.
2004 "The Christian Response to African Traditional Religion(s)." In *Christian Witness in Pluralistic Contexts in the Twenty-first Century*, edited by Enoch Wan, 209–17. Pasadena, CA: William Carey Library.
2003 "Christian Scholarship and the Changing Center of World Christianity." In *Christian Scholarship . . . for What?*, edited by Susan M. Felch, 87–97. Grand Rapids: Calvin College.
2002 "Missions and the Doing of Theology" (with Paul G. Hiebert). In *The Urban Face of Mission: Ministering the Gospel in a Diverse and Changing World*, edited by Manuel Ortiz and Susan S. Baker, 85–96. Phillipsburg, NJ: P & R.
2001 "The State of the Gospel in Africa." *Evangelical Missions Quarterly* 37: 154–62.
2000 "Does the World Really Need to Hear the Gospel of Jesus Christ?" In *This We Believe*, edited by John N. Akers et al., 175–85. Grand Rapids: Zondervan.
2000 *Understanding Folk Religion*, edited by Paul G. Hiebert et al. Grand Rapids: Baker Academic, 2000.
1999/2000 "Responding to Split-Level Christianity and Folk Religion" (with Paul G. Hiebert and R. Daniel Shaw). *International Journal of Frontier Missions* 16: 173–82.
1999 "The Church in the Pluralistic African Experience." In *Practicing Truth: Confident Witness in Our Pluralistic World*, edited by David W. Shenk and Linford Stuzman, 148–55. Scottdale, PA: Herald.
1999 "Le rôle de la prédication dans l'Eglise." *Diathèkè* 2: 5–11.
1998 "Blyden, Edward Wilmot (1832–1912)." In *Biographical Dictionary of Christian Missions*, edited by Gerald H. Anderson, 70–71. New York: Simon & Shuster Macmillan.
1998 "The Theological Task of the Church in Africa." In *Issues in African Christian Theology*, edited by Samuel Ngewa et al., 58–70. Nairobi: East African Educational Publishers.
1997 "Authentic African Christianity." In *A Reader in African Christian Theology*, edited by John Parratt, 91–98. London: SPCK.
1997 "Religion, Revelation or Christ?" *Trinity World Forum* 23: 1–3.
1996 "De l'actualité de Tertullien, l'Africain." *Diathèkè* 1: 4–14.
1996 "The Training of Missiologists for an African Context." In *Missiological Education for the Twenty-first Century: The Book, the Circle, and the Sandals: Essays in Honor of Paul E. Pierson*, edited by J. Dudley Woodberry et al., 93–100. American Society of Missiology Series 23. Maryknoll, NY: Orbis.
1994 "The Word and the New Arrogance." In *Text and Context in Theological Education*, edited by Roger Kemp, 53–61. Springwood, Australia: ICAA/WEF.
1994 "Why I Believe: Consumer or Ambassador? Why Should We Spread the Good News of Jesus Christ?" *Decision* 35: 13–14.
1994 "Have We Created a Religion of Spectators?" *Alliance Life* 129: 6–7, 10.
1993 "Themes in African Theology of Mission." In *The Good News of the Kingdom: Mission Theology for the Third Millennium*, edited by Charles Van Engen et al., 127–36. Maryknoll, NY: Orbis.

1993 "Forming Indigenous Theologies." In *Towards the Twenty-First Century in Christian Mission*, edited by James M. Phillips and Robert T. Coote, 245–52. Grand Rapids: Eerdmans.
1992 "Which Way for African Christianity?" *Evangelical Missions Quarterly* 28: 256–63.
1991 "Which Way for African Christianity: Westernization or Indigenous Authenticity?" *Africa Journal of Evangelical Theology* 10: 3–12.
1991 "The Invention of the 'Primitive' and Stereotypes in Mission." *Missiology* 19: 295–303.
1991 "The Future of ACTEA." *ACTEA Tools and Studies* 10: 1–8.
1991 "Eternity in Their Hearts?" In *Through No Fault of Their Own?*, edited by William V. Crockett and James G. Sigountos, 209–15. Grand Rapids: Baker.
1990 "Lessons from the Prayer Habits of the Church in Africa." In *Teach Us to Pray*, edited by D. A. Carson, 231–71. Exeter, U.K.: Paternoster.
1990 "The Right to Difference: The Common Roots of African Theology and African Philosophy." *Africa Journal of Evangelical Theology* 9: 24–34.
1990 "The Future of ICAA." *Evangelical Review of Theology* 14: 86–91.
1990 "Indigenous African Theologies: The Uphill Road." *International Bulletin of Missionary Research* 14: 73–77.
1989 "Christianity in Africa." *AIM International* 83: 3.
1987 "Evangelism and Social Transformation." In *The Church in Response to Human Need*, edited by Vinay Samuel and Christopher Sugden, 175–79. Oxford: Regnum.
1987 "The Theological Task of the Church in Africa: Where Are We Now and Where Should We Be Going?" *East Africa Journal of Evangelical Theology* 6: 3–11.
1987 "Christianity in Africa: There's Frost on the Lion." *Pulse* 22: 8.
1987 "Recapturing the Initiative in Theology in Africa." *Evangelical Review of Theology* 11: 152–56.
1986 "Missions Are Caught in the Complexities of Today's Africa." *Pulse* 21: 2–4.
1986 "History and African Theology." *His Dominion* 12: 25–30.
1985 "The Problem of Methodology in African Christian Theologies." *Evangelical Missions Quarterly* 21: 293–95.
1985 "Christians in Africa." In *Christianity: A World Faith*, edited by R. Keeley. Tring Herts, U.K.: Lion. (Served as consulting editor for this volume.)
1984 "The Church in African Theology: Description and Analysis of Hermeneutical Presuppositions." In *Biblical Interpretation and the Church*, edited by D. A. Carson, 151–65. Exeter, U.K.: Paternoster.
1984 "The Problem of Methodology in African Christian Theologies." PhD thesis, Fuller Theological Seminary, School of World Mission.
1983 "Evangelism and Social Transformation." In *The Church in Response to Human Need*, edited by Tom Sine, 273–92. Monrovia, CA: MARC.
1983 "The Church and Its Theology." *Evangelical Review of Theology* 7: 243–46.
1983 "Biblical Foudations: An African Theiology." *Evangelical Review of Theology* 7: 89–101.
1982 "Biblical Foundations for African Theology." *Missiology* 10: 435–48.
1982 "Contextualization of Theology for Theological Education." In *Evangelical Theological Education Today*, edited by Paul Bowers, 42–52. Nairobi: World Evangelical Fellowship.
1982 "The Church and Its Theology." *Perception* 20: 1–4.

1982 "The Church and Its Theology." *Africa Pulse* 15: 2–4.
1982 "Issues in the Theological Task in Africa Today." *East Africa Journal of Evangelical Theology* 1: 3–10.
1981 "Threats and Dangers in the Theological Task in Africa." *Evangelical Review of Theology* 5: 40–44.
1980 "Vrai Dieu et homme vrai: Le mystère de l'incarnation." *Découvertes* 2: 6–10.
1979 "Christianity and African Culture: A Review Article." *Evangelical Review of Theology* 3: 198–205.
1978 "Problems and Issues among the Rural Population of Africa." In *Facing the New Challenges*, edited by Michael Cassidy and Luc Verlinden. Kisumu, Kenya: Evangel.
"Ethnicity as Gift and Barrier: Human Identity and Christian Mission." Annual Seminar offered at the Overseas Ministries Study Center, New Haven, Connecticut.

www.ingramcontent.com/pod-product-compliance
Lightning Source LLC
Chambersburg PA
CBHW071230290426
44108CB00013B/1359